THE HABITATS DIRECTIVE

Biodiversity within the European Union is under threat. In June 2011 the UK said it would '... arrest the decline in habitats and species and the degradation of landscapes'. Yet six months later the Chancellor of the Exchequer, George Osborne MP complained that 'gold plating of EU rules on things like habitats' was putting 'ridiculous costs' on firms. The Habitats Directive imposes a strict regime for environmental protection. The English courts have said that it should not become a property developer's obstacle course. But are we really taking habitats protection seriously enough or on the other hand are we stifling much needed sustainable development? Edited by Gregory Jones QC, *The Habitats Directive: A Developer's Obstacle Course?* brings together a unique combination of leading academics and practitioners in the field of European environmental and planning law to address and debate controversial issues arising from the Habitats Directive in an authoritative and expert manner. A must for anyone engaged in property development and environmental law.

The Habitats Directive

A Developer's Obstacle Course?

Edited by

Gregory Jones QC

·HART·
PUBLISHING

OXFORD AND PORTLAND, OREGON
2012

Published in the United Kingdom by Hart Publishing Ltd
16C Worcester Place, Oxford, OX1 2JW
Telephone: +44 (0)1865 517530
Fax: +44 (0)1865 510710
E-mail: mail@hartpub.co.uk
Website: http://www.hartpub.co.uk

Published in North America (US and Canada) by
Hart Publishing
c/o International Specialized Book Services
920 NE 58th Avenue, Suite 300
Portland, OR 97213-3786
USA
Tel: +1 503 287 3093 or toll-free: (1) 800 944 6190
Fax: +1 503 280 8832
E-mail: orders@isbs.com
Website: http://www.isbs.com

British Library Cataloguing in Publication Data
Data Available

ISBN: 978-1-84946-293-8

Typeset by Compuscript Ltd, Shannon
Printed and bound in Great Britain by
TJ International Ltd, Padstow, Cornwall

This volume is jointly dedicated to my father, Colin F Jones
and to the memory of Lord Kingsland QC.

FOREWORD

The Habitats Directive is a vital tool for the protection of the wildlife and plant species at a European level. It is particularly significant for the town and country planning systems in the United Kingdom because it imposes obligations not only on how the decision-making process must be carried out but also on the decision-making outcome. The issue is topical, not least in view of the review by the Department for the Environment, Food and Rural Affairs (Defra) published on 22 March 2012. The Directive has also been subject to consideration by the courts in cases such as *Hart District Council v Secretary of State for Communities and Local Government* and most recently *Cornwall Waste Forum, St Dennis Branch v Secretary of State for Communities and Local Government*. The book is therefore a timely and welcome contribution to the learning on the subject.

It is based on papers produced for the first Kingsland Conference held at King's College, London on 17 March 2011. It has thus drawn on a powerful combination of leading academics and practitioners in the field. I was pleased to be able to chair one session of the Conference. It was an appropriate memorial to the memory of Christopher Kingsland who was a much admired colleague over many years, and who was a strong advocate of the law in this area. A glance at the chapter headings will show the comprehensive and varied nature of the subjects covered. I congratulate both the authors and the editor for bringing together this impressive volume. I commend it to all interested in this important topic, as practitioners, academics or students.

Robert Carnwath

Lord Carnwath CVO
Supreme Court of the United Kingdom
Parliament Square
London
April 2012

PREFACE

With the exception of Chapter 1, the chapters in this book are based on papers produced for the first Kingsland Conference held at King's College, London on 17 March 2011 and organised jointly by Francis Taylor Building and the Centre of European Law at King's College. The papers have been rewritten and revised for publication. We have endeavoured to state the law correctly as at 1 September 2011 but where possible have included later developments. The title of the book is the same as that of the Conference: 'The Habitats Directive: A Developer's Obstacle Course?' Access to the Directive is widely available but a copy of the Habitats Directive is provided as an appendix in order that the reader might have convenient access to cross refer to particular provisions whilst reading the book.

I edited this book over the Christmas period of 2011 in the coastal town of Hermanus. Situated in the western province of South Africa almost 10,000 kilometres away from the Temple and King's College in London this may seem a strange location for a book about the law relating to species and habitats protection in the European Union. But distance can add perspective. Nicholas Montsarrat wrote *The Cruel Sea*, his epic tale of Second World War escort convoys of the North Atlantic, the Mediterranean and Arctic seas, here in Hermanus. Nestled between the Fynbos and the angry waves of the South Atlantic it is part of a 'Biodiversity Hotspot'[1] known as the Cape Floristic Kingdom. This kingdom is the sixth and smallest of the world's plant kingdoms, home to more than 9,000 vascular plant species, of which 69 per cent are endemic. Yet homelessness in this country is rife amongst its people and the majority of those with a home live in substandard accommodation. In 2011 the unemployment rate in South Africa was 25 per cent and the average life expectancy under 50 years. Power and water shortages in Hermanus are not unknown. The pressure for development is acute. It is thus a very appropriate place and time in which to reflect on the difficult interaction between human economic development and nature.

Biodiversity within Europe is under threat. According to the World Conservation Union, some 21 per cent of Europe's vascular plant species are classified as threatened and in a number of European countries more than two-thirds of the existing plant habitat types are endangered. One hundred and fifty-five species of Europe's 1,000 species of native mammals, birds, reptiles and amphibians

---

[1] A 'Biodiversity Hotspot' is a threatened region with a large range of endemic plant species (at least 1,500) but where more than 70% of the original habitat has been lost because of human activities. Typically, the diversity of endemic vertebrates is also high.

are classified as threatened. Extinction threatens 15 per cent, or one in seven, of Europe's 228 species of mammals. Among the 35 threatened European mammals, six are marine species. Europe's five most endangered mammals are classified as 'Critically Endangered'. That status means that populations have declined drastically, or numbers are already precariously low, or the animals currently survive only in a tiny area.

Realisation in Europe about the threat to our living space came about in two stages. First, there was a growing awareness that since the 1950s new factors had been contributing to the decrease in the numbers of certain wild species. People recognised the old causes of environmental harm but they came to be aware that the direct destruction or modification of the habitats which were home to these species were also major causes of environmental destruction. Previously, conservation activities had been largely piecemeal and focused on eradicating, limiting or controlling human activities such as hunting, fishing, collecting and trade which in the past had been the direct cause of the reduction, or complete extinction, of certain species. The next stage was the public appreciation that environmental protection needed to be more than simply preserving endangered species from being injured or killed, important though that is. Habitats had to be preserved in a way which enabled them to sustain the living species which depended upon them. Discussed in Chapter 1, the 1982 Bern Convention was the first international environmental law treaty to seek the preservation of this link between species protection and their habitats on a regional scale. It used mandatory language and put in place permanent institutions tasked with ensuring its implementation among its Contracting States. Indeed, it was more than 12 years before a global treaty of even more comprehensive coverage was to emerge when the Convention on Biological Diversity (CBD) was signed at the Earth Summit in Rio in 1992. But disappointingly, as MacKenzie points out in Chapter 2, the CBD employed a much weaker form of language and enforcement system than that developed by the Bern Convention a decade earlier.

The Bern Convention's 'nudge' culture has its limits. The Convention was the model for the Habitats Directive but the resultant Directive is more robust than the Bern Convention in a number of respects. First, it is more explicit than the Bern Convention about the need for site protection and a coherent European ecological network. Secondly, the Habitats Directive set a precedent for transboundary coordination in habitat protection by establishing Natura 2000 as a key instrument. Thirdly, the Directive set out a clear timeframe for the transposition and implementation of its provisions. Furthermore, unlike the Convention, the Habitats Directive is directly enforceable within the EU setting out a strict system of protection based upon the precautionary approach. Even so, Stookes suggests in Chapter 8 that: 'There is inherent conflict within the Directive between habitat and species conservation and improvement and the pursuit of plans and projects.' This tension is not a new one. Indeed, the Second European Ministerial Conference on the Environment held in Brussels in 1976 which initiated the process leading to the Bern Convention, identified the key issue as: how can economic development be reconciled with protection of the natural environment? There was an assumption which still broadly exists (see for example, the notion of 'sustainable development')[2] that it can be reconciled. So governments tend publicly to laud the aims of the Habitats Directive: but they fret about its application, finding it at times, both difficult and controversial. A good example of this is the recent attempt by the UK coalition government to address nature conservation and economic development. In its White Paper launched on 7 June 2011, entitled 'The Natural Choice: securing the value of nature',[3] the government stated its ambition:

> We want to improve the quality of our natural environment across England, moving to a net gain in the value of nature. We aim to arrest the decline in habitats and species and the degradation of landscapes. We will protect priority habitats and safeguard vulnerable non-renewable resources for future generations. We will support natural systems to function more effectively in town, in the country and at sea. *We will achieve this through joined-up action at local and national levels to create an ecological network which is resilient to changing pressures.* (emphasis added)

However, less than six months later, when introducing his autumn statement of November 2011,[4] the Chancellor of the Exchequer, George Osborne MP, told MPs he wanted to make sure that 'gold plating of EU rules on things like habitats' were not putting 'ridiculous costs' on firms. 'If we burden them with endless social and environmental goals—however worthy in their own right—,' he said 'then not only will we not achieve those goals, but the businesses will fail, jobs will be lost, and our country will be poorer.' The Department for the Environment, Food and Rural Affairs (Defra) then announced it would be reviewing the impact of the EU Habitats and Wild Birds Directives in England 'focusing in particular on those obligations that affect the authorisation process for proposed development, with a view to reducing the burdens on business while maintaining the integrity of the purpose of the directives.'

The government would no doubt claim that both policy statements are entirely compatible with one another. That may literally be correct, but there is a clear difference in emphasis between the two which is important when individual decisions are determined upon the fine balancing of competing factors. The resultant review by Defra was published on 22 March 2012. The report is of interest because it found that the Habitats Directive was not intended to operate as an obstacle to frustrate development, as indeed, the high court of England had already noted in *Hart District Council v Secretary of State for Communities & Local Government*,

---

[2] Eg the 'National Planning Policy Framework' published on 27 March 2012, available at: http://www.communities.gov.uk/documents/planningandbuilding/pdf/2116950.pdf seeks to establish the presumption in favour of sustainable development as the 'golden thread' of planning decision-making but ironically: 'The presumption in favour of sustainable development does not apply where development requiring appropriate assessment under the Birds or Habitats Directives is being considered, planned or determined.'

[3] http://www.official-documents.gov.uk/document/cm80/8082/8082.asp.

[4] http://cdn.hm-treasury.gov.uk/autumn_statement.pdf.

Luckmore Limited & Barratt Homes Limited.[5] The Defra report found that Natural
England had actually objected to less than 0.5 per cent of the 26,500 consultations
on development it received each year on the grounds of habitat protection and
that: 'Most of these objections are successfully dealt with at the planning stage.'
The review did conclude that some cases encountered delays, and that there was
scope to simplify the guidance, legislation and authorisation process for developments, and to improve the way statutory bodies worked with developers. The
Environment Secretary, Caroline Spelman said: 'The action we are taking will
make it clearer for developers to understand how to comply with the directive.'

Given that EU law requires that the Habitats Directive must be enforced in the
UK there is a limit to what the government can do. Is there in reality much 'gold
plating' which Defra could scrape away? It is true, for example, that the UK has
operated a broad approach in applying the protection of the Habitats Directive to
candidate Special Areas of Conservation (SACs) and potential Special Protection
Areas (SPAs) which may indeed go beyond its obligations under the Directive (see
Jones and Westaway in Chapter 4). Furthermore there is, at least, a suspicion that
its application, in particular, with regard to imperative reasons of overriding public interest (IROPI) 'is often applied more rigidly in the UK in relation to the need
for projects, social or economic factors and the range of alternative solutions to
be considered'.[6] As Clutten and Tafur point out in Chapter 10, even the European
Commission's approach to IROPI has been mixed.

The courts in England and Wales have on occasion taken action against
breaches of the Habitats Directive such as occurred in the case of the introduction of a new class of ferries for the Isle of Wight[7] (see Tromans in Chapter 5) and
more recently, in *R (Cornwall Waste Forum, St Dennis Branch) v Secretary of State
for Communities and Local Government, Sita Cornwall Ltd, Environment Agency
and Cornwall Council*[8] concerning the overlapping competencies in respect of
a decision whether to require an appropriate assessment. But the courts have
generally been cautious in quashing decisions that would actually imperil major
infrastructure developments, such as the decision by the House of Lords to refuse
interim relief in respect of Lappel Bank discussed by Stookes in Chapter 8 and,
most recently, the Supreme Court's judgment on the meaning of 'disturbance' in

---

[5] [2008] EWHC 1204 (Admin); [2008] 2 P & CR 16; [2009] JPL 365.

[6] Duncan Field, 'Finding scope for Habitats Review' Legal Viewpoint *Planning* 13 January 2012 at 29.

[7] *R (Akester) v Department for Environment, Food and Rural Affairs* [2010] EWHC 232 (Admin).

[8] *R (Cornwall Waste Forum, St Dennis Branch) v Secretary of State for Communities and Local
Government, Sita Cornwall Ltd, Environment Agency and Cornwall Council* [2011] EWHC 2761. The
case is wrongly described in the heading of the official transcript as a judicial review claim under CPR
54. As an application made under s 288 of the Town and Country Planning Act 1990 (as amended),
it should properly read *Cornwall Waste Forum, St Dennis Branch v Secretary of State for Communities
and Local Government, Sita Cornwall Ltd, Environment Agency, Cornwall Council*. Collins J quashed
the grant of planning permission on the basis of a breach of legitimate expectation concerning the
application of the Habitats Directive. However, the Court of Appeal overturned the decision of the
high court, see [2012] EWCA Civ 379.

Morge v Hampshire County Council[9] critically analysed by George and Graham in Chapter 3. Indeed, in Chapter 6 Scott sets out the case in support of his belief that '"appropriate assessment" under the Habitats Directive, as it has been interpreted in case law and applied by public authorities in the UK, is characterised on the one hand by scepticism as to its effectiveness to deliver the outcomes required by the legislation and on the other hand, by a perception that the invocation of the process can have a "nuclear" impact on sustainable development simply because of the impossibility of demonstrating a positive conclusion'.

It was Sullivan J (as he then was) who memorably suggested that the Habitats Directive was not intended to be 'a developer's obstacle course'. In so doing, Sullivan J dismissed a legal challenge to the use of Suitable Alternative Natural Greenspace (SANG) as a means of avoiding the need for 'an appropriate assessment'.[10] Nonetheless, the Habitats Directive is intended to set barriers to development, ones which the precautionary principle demands must be clearly overcome if the development is to go ahead. Ricketts and Bischoff in Chapter 7 examine the creation and use of SANGs in respect of the Thames Basin Heaths SPA as a way of meeting the pressures of housing need whilst ensuring that new residential development causes no 'likely significant effect' on the SPA. For Waite in Chapter 13, the question is one of seeking to secure a balance, or an 'environmental equilibrium' of what is absolutely necessary for environmental protection without strangling economic development; and the use of SANGs may be viewed as an application of that principle.

The Habitats Directive will continue to raise practical legal issues. This is not simply because of the inherent tension between the objectives of environmental protection and economic development. The wording of the Directive is general, so that key concepts are not defined, such as what is 'a plan or project' (see Tromans in Chapter 5) or else, unclear, as in the case of Article 6(3), which I discuss in Chapter 9. This problem is exacerbated when the Habitats Directive is applied offshore to the maritime environment. In Chapter 11 Caddell identifies maritime challenges ranging from 'an historical lack of guidance for marine biodiversity policy to the current practical difficulties experienced in gathering the requisite data to develop SACs'. However, according to Edwards in Chapter 12, the problem is actually of a wider nature. For him, it is the failure by the British courts to articulate a clear standard for the intensity of judicial review of environmental decisions generally, and those involving the application of the precautionary principle in particular, which is the underlying fundamental problem.

The Conference was dedicated to the memory of Lord Kingsland QC: 'An eminent barrister with strong academic credentials who developed expertise in

[9] *Morge v Hampshire County Council* UKSC 2; [2011] 1 WLR 268; [2011] PTSR 337; [2011] 1 All ER 744.
[10] *Hart District Council v Secretary of State for Communities & Local Government, Luckmore Ltd & Barratt Homes Ltd* [2008] EWHC 1204 (Admin); [2008] 2 P & CR 16; [2009] JPL 365.

the field of international economics.'[11] Christopher Kingsland was one of very few people able to maintain high-profile careers both at the modern bar and in politics. Had he not died it was widely expected that he would have played an important part in the current coalition government. Christopher was the MEP for Shropshire and Stafford from 1979 to 1994 during which time he came to lead the British contingent of Conservative MEPs. He was elevated to the House of Lords and became Shadow Lord Chancellor. In 2008 he became the opposition spokesman on legal affairs, a post he held at his death in 2009. Christopher also served as Vice-Chair of Justice, the all-party group set up to promote the rule of law and to assist the fair administration of legal process. As an advocate he appeared before the European Court of Justice (ECJ) in some of the leading cases of the day including acting for the whistleblower, Stanley Adams, against the European Commission in the 1980s and, in the 1990s, in high-profile European competition and free trade cases.

Christopher was an engaging and companionable member of chambers but above all he was universally acknowledged as a man of utmost courtesy and integrity. The contributors to this volume have generously agreed to donate their royalties to the Kingsland Mooting Competition, a student mooting competition set up by Francis Taylor Building in memory of Christopher, details of which can be found at http://www.ftb.eu.com/home/student-moots-and-prizes.asp. The final of the first Kingsland moot was held on 12 March 2012 at the Supreme Court judged by Christopher's very close friend Lord Simon Brown, a Justice of the Supreme Court. Appropriately enough the subject of the moot involved the Habitats Directive.

I knew Christopher when he became a leading member of the environmental law bar. He was, not surprisingly, one of the first practitioners to appreciate the impact of EU law upon this field. His standing is illustrated by the fact that he was invited to contribute the chapter on environmental law in the *Practitioners' Handbook of EC Law* published in 1998 by the Bar Council.[12] The list of contributors to the *Handbook* reads as a roll call of outstanding European lawyers from the bar and bench. Save for two, each of the 32 chapters were the work of teams of collaborators. Christopher was the sole author of the environment chapter; his chapter on environmental law was a succinct and masterly treatment of a wide-ranging area of law. He perceptibly identified that the inclination of national governments to adopt environmental protection measures in the Council of Ministers 'unfortunately … has not been matched by a corresponding propensity to implement them on their own territory'.[13] Christopher's measured but robust criticism of the

---

[11] *The Times*, 14 July 2009.
[12] With the passing of over a decade the time has surely come for a new edition of this excellent work.
[13] Chapter 28 on the Environment in the Bar Council's *Practitioners' Handbook of EC Law* (1998) at 28.1.2. Christopher evidenced this statement by citing, amongst other things, The Twelfth Annual Report on Monitoring the Application of Community Law 1994, COM (95) 500 final, which showed that there had been over 60 judgments by the ECJ in respect of infraction proceedings brought by

failure by the English courts to give proper effect to the Environmental Impact Assessment Directive,[14] is particularly worth re-reading as a model guide to the practitioner considering whether to challenge an established but misguided body of high court case law.[15] His views were, of course, entirely vindicated some 14 years later by the House of Lords decision in *Berkeley v Secretary of State for the Environment*[16] and reinforced then by subsequent judgments of the ECJ. More specifically, as a European polymath, Christopher was able to give this wider and chastening assessment in respect of the Habitats Directive:

> It is easy to exaggerate the importance of the Community's efforts here. Even when the European habitats network is fully in place, it will only cover a minute proportion of the total rural area which has been subject to a massive intensification in farming methods over the last 40 years. The consequent removal of hedges and coppice and the indiscriminate application of pesticides and fertilisers are the real threat to flora and fauna and, in this respect, protected sites represent tiny oases in a growing ecological desert. It must be hoped that increased designations of Environmentally Sensitive Areas[17] or bigger incentives to take part in one or more of the various schemes composed in the Agri-Environment Programme,[18] will lead to the reintroduction of farming practices which are compatible, or are in line with nature conservation.[19]

Since then limited progress has been made. According to the European Commission's own analysis of the organic sector published in June 2010,[20] the organic sector which seeks to minimise the input of pesticides and fertilisers amounted to no more than an estimated 7.6 million hectares in 2008, that is, 4.3 per cent of EU-25[21] utilised agricultural area (UAA). In the period 2000 to 2008, the average annual rate of growth was 6.7 per cent in the EU-15 and 20.0 per cent in the EU-12. The area of Europe under organic agriculture is close to or higher than 9 per cent of the total UAA in five Member States: the Czech Republic, Estonia, Latvia, Austria (15.5 per cent) and Sweden. In 2008, it is estimated that there were about 197,000 holdings involved in organic agriculture in the EU-25, that is 1.4 per cent of all EU-25 holdings (0.6 per cent in the EU-12 and 2.9 per cent in the EU-15). The report noted that: 'Consumer food demand grows at a fast pace in the largest EU markets, yet the organic sector does not represent more than 2 per cent of total food expenses in the EU-15 in 2007.' Overall figures are to some

the European Commission concerning the failure of Member States to respect their environmental obligations.

[14] EIA Directive 85/337 EEC as amended by 97/11/EC and 2003/35/EC available at: http://eur-lex.europa.eu/LexUriServ/LexUriServ.do?uri=CONSLEG:1985L0337:20090625:EN:PDF.

[15] *Practitioners' Handbook of EC Law*, above n 12, 28.7.2.10–28.7.2.14.

[16] [2001] 2 AC 603.

[17] Regulation 797/85, Art 19 [1985 OJ L93/1 and the Agriculture Act, 1986 s 18.

[18] Regulation 2078/92 [1992] OJ L215/85.

[19] *Practitioners' Handbook of EC Law*, above n 12, 28.4.5.7.

[20] http://ec.europa.eu/agriculture/analysis/markets/organic_2010_en.pdf.

[21] EU-10 refers to Member States which joined the EU in May 2004; EU-12 refers to EU-10 together with Romania and Bulgaria; EU-15 refers to Member States which joined the EU before 2004, and EU-25 refers to EU-15 together with EU-10.

extent 'improved' by the inclusion of the newer states of Eastern European whose farming systems were less intensive and 'developed'. In the EU-12 organic food consumption stands at lower levels.

The worry must be that the rate of environmental protection is outpaced by its destruction. Indeed, according to the European Environment Agency's report *Landscape fragmentation in Europe*[22] published in September 2011: 'Roads, motorways, railways, intensive agriculture and urban developments are breaking up Europe's landscapes into ever-smaller pieces, with potentially devastating consequences for flora and fauna across the continent.' The same report found that although the situation is critical, proactive planning policies for more effective protection of remaining unfragmented areas, and wildlife corridors could successfully reverse the trend of growing fragmentation. The report identified, for example, that developers could build more tunnels, passages and bridges to allow animals to move more freely and that town planners should aim to upgrade old roads instead of building new roads, and 'bundle' new infrastructure, for example, by building bypasses close to settlements or constructing road and rail routes next to each other.

Lord Kingsland's conclusions written just over a decade ago remain true of EU environmental law in general, and the Habitats Directive, in particular. They bear repeating.

> Despite these not inconsiderable frailties, the [EU's] role in the environmental field is likely to grow. As pressure on the world's limited natural resources accumulate, international society will be compelled to negotiate and adhere to increasingly strict limitations of the outputs of modern industrial society. Moreover the nature of many domestic problems, most obviously in the field of air pollution, can only be tackled on an international basis.[23]

We are fortunate indeed that the Rt Hon Lord Justice Robert Carnwath CVO, a friend and former colleague of Lord Kingsland, not only chaired the final session at the Kingsland Conference but has also kindly agreed to write the forward to this book. He is now Lord Carnwath, a Justice of the Supreme Court, his appointment having been announced as I toiled away on this book in the December sun of Hermanus. I am delighted now to be able to take this opportunity to congratulate Lord Carnwath upon his richly deserved appointment.

Gregory Jones QC
Francis Taylor Building, Temple
Maundy Thursday 2012

---

[22] www.eea.europa.eu/publications/landscape-fragmentation-in-europe.
[23] *Practitioners' Handbook of EC Law*, above n 12, 28.1.6.

TABLE OF CONTENTS

LIST OF CONTRIBUTORS

Sarah Bischoff LLB, LLM is a solicitor and associate in Wragg & Co LLP's Planning and Environment Group.

Dr Richard Cadell LLB, LLM, PhD (Cardiff), ACI Arb is a lecturer at Swansea University and member of the Institute of International Shipping and Trade at Swansea University. Richard is the Regional Seas correspondent for the *Yearbook on International Environmental Law*.

Rebecca Clutten LLB (Cantab) is a barrister practising from FTB, Francis Taylor Building, Temple.

Denis Edwards LLB, LLM is a barrister practising from FTB, Francis Taylor Building, Temple. He is also Treasurer of the Statute Law Society.

Charles George QC, MA (Oxon) is a barrister and a Recorder of the Crown Court. He is also Dean of the Arches and Auditor of the Chancery Court of York and Master of the Faculties. Charles also sits as a Deputy High Court Judge and practises from FTB, Francis Taylor Building, Temple. He is a Visiting Lecturer at King's College London and Fellow of the Centre of European Law, King's College.

David Graham BA (Hons) (Cantab) is a barrister practising from FTB, Francis Taylor Building, Temple.

Gregory Jones QC, MA (Oxon), LLM (Lond) is a member of the bars of England and Wales, Northern Ireland and the Republic of Ireland. He practises from FTB, Francis Taylor Building, Temple. He is a Visiting Lecturer at King's College London and Fellow of the Centre of European Law, King's College. He was Jean Pierre Warner scholar at the ECJ.

Dr Catherine MacKenzie MA (Oxon), MEd (Sydney), PhD (ANU), Barrister (Inner Temple and High Court of Australia) is a University Lecturer in Law at Selwyn College, Cambridge and an Academic Fellow of Inner Temple. She is also a Research Associate, at the Oxford University Centre for the Environment and a Research Associate, at Green Templeton College, Oxford.

Simon Ricketts LLB (Lond) was called to the bar and re-qualified as a solicitor. He is a partner in and head of SJ Berwin's Planning and Environment Group. Simon is a member of the board of the British Council for Offices and is a member of the British Council for Shopping Centres and the Compulsory Purchase

Association. He is a member of Westminster Property Association's Transport Working Party and is on the editorial board of *PLC Property*.

Peter Scott is a partner in Quality Solicitors Parkinson Wright, Evesham and Worcester. He qualified as a solicitor in 1971 and is a member of United Kingdom Environmental Law Association (UKELA) national water working group and nature conservation working groups.

Dr Paul Stookes is a Solicitor-Advocate and partner in Richard Buxton Solicitors and a part-time lecturer at the School of Law, University of Hertfordshire.

Isabella Tafur BA (Hons) (Oxon) is a barrister practising from FTB, Francis Taylor Building, Temple.

Stephen Tromans QC, MA (Cantab), previously admitted as a solicitor, is a barrister and practises from 39 Essex Street where he is also the joint head of chambers. He is also a Member of the Editorial Board of *Journal of Environmental Law* and *Nuclear Law: The Law Applying to Nuclear Installations and Radioactive Substances in its Historic Context*.

Andrew Waite, MA (Oxon) is a solicitor and partner in the environmental law department of Berwin Leighton Paisner. He is a former Vice Chair for Western Europe of the World Conservation Union (IUCN) Commission on Environmental Law and former President of the European Environmental Law Association.

Ned Westaway BA (Hons) (Lond), LLM (Lond) is a barrister practising from FTB, Francis Taylor Building, Temple.

LIST OF ABBREVIATIONS

AA	Appropriate Assessment
ARO	Additional Reasoned Opinion
BAP	Biodiversity Action Plan
BCT	Bat Conservation Trust
CBD	Convention on Biological Diversity
CFP	Common Fisheries Policy
CITES	Convention on International Trade in Endangered Species of Wild Fauna and Flora
CJEU	Court of Justice of the European Union
COP	Conference of the Parties
cSAC	candidate Special Area of Conservation
DDP	Draft Delivery Plan
Defra	Department for Environment, Food and Rural Affairs
DPD	Development Plan Document
EAP	Environmental Action Programme
ECJ	European Court of Justice
EEC Treaty	Treaty establishing European Economic Community
EEZ	Exclusive Economic Zone
EIA	environmental impact assessment
EIP	Examination in Public
EPA	Environmental Protection Agency
EPS	European Protected Species
EU	European Union
FAO	Food and Agriculture Organization of the United Nations
HCA	Homes and Communities Agency
HGRN	Habitats Regulation Guidance Note
HRA	Human Rights Act 1998
ICJ	International Court of Justice
IROPI	Imperative Reasons of Overriding Public Interest
IUCN	World Conservation Union
IUCN	International Union for the Conservation of Nature
JNCC	Joint Nature Conservation Committee

LDD	Local Development Document
LDF	local development framework
LMO	Living Modified Organism
LPA	Local Planning Authority

MPA	Marine Protected Area
MSFD	Marine Strategy Framework Directive

NBSAP	National Biodiversity Strategies and Action Plans
NGO	non-governmental organisation

ODPM	Office of the Deputy Prime Minister
OLD	Operations Likely to Damage

PINS	Planning Inspectorate
PoP	plan or project
pSPA	potential Special Protection Area

SAC	Special Area of Conservation
SANG	Suitable Alternative Natural Greenspace
SCI	Site of Community Importance
SEA	Single European Act
SEERA	South East England Regional Assembly
SNH	Scottish Natural Heritage
SPA	Special Protection Area
SSSI	Site of Special Scientific Interest

TEC	Treaty Establishing the European Community
TEU	Treaty on European Union
TFEU	Treaty on the Functioning of the European Union

UAA	utilised agricultural area
UK	United Kingdom
UNCED	UN Conference on Environment and Development
UNEP	United Nations Environmental Programme
UNGA	United Nations General Assembly
USA	United States of America

WAG	Welsh Assembly Government
WCED	World Commission on Environment and Development
WFD	Waste Framework Directive

TABLE OF CASES

Hong Kong

India

Ireland

Netherlands

United States of America

International

Conference of the Party decisions

TABLE OF LEGISLATION

TABLE OF INTERNATIONAL TREATIES, CONVENTIONS ETC

1

The Bern Convention and the Origins of the Habitats Directive

GREGORY JONES QC

How can one forget those marathon sessions in the committee drafting the future convention, when a Danish pipe-smoking lawyer did all he could to placate the ardent but pragmatic Irishman—a great otter hunter—aghast at the Swiss representative who was justifying the inclusion of this proud carnivore—already on the CITES list and later to become the symbol of the convention—in Appendix II for species which had to be allocated strict protection? Or the 'naval' battles with an illustrious lawyer from St Malo, a relentless negotiator on the law of the sea, who with his logic and rationality steered a more realistic course amongst the bursts of audacity and unfettered idealism of the naturalists present?

Raymond-Peirre Lebeau, sometime Swiss Representative on the
Standing Committee of the Bern Convention[1]

Introduction

Described by the European Commission as: 'the cornerstone of Europe's nature conservation policy,' the Habitats Directive[2] and the Birds Directive[3] are 'generally regarded as some of the most advanced and effective regional conservation instruments [in existence]'.[4] Upon its adoption, the Habitats Directive was immediately recognised as the 'main vehicle through which the EC [was] endeavouring to safeguard its precious natural heritage'.[5] Both directives have their origins in

---

[1] Raymond-Peirre Lebeau, 'The 25 years of the Bern Convention' Editorial, (2004) 101 *Naturopa The 25 years of the Bern Convention* (henceforward *The 25 years of the Bern Convention*).

[2] http://ec.europa.eu/environment/nature/legislation/habitatsdirective/index_en.htm. See also Simon Lyster, *International Wildlife Law* (Cambridge University Press, 2010) ch 8; M Austin and T Richards, *Basic Legal Documents on International Animal Welfare and Wildlife Conservation* (Kluwer Law International, 2000) 171; MJ Bowman, 'International Treaties and the Global Protection of Birds' (1999) 11 *Journal of Environmental Law* 87, 106–19.

[3] http://ec.europa.eu/environment/nature/legislation/birdsdirective/index_en.htm.

[4] See, eg PF Donald et al, 'International Conservation Policy Delivers Benefits for Birds in Europe' (2007) 307 (5839) *Science* 810.

[5] Jonathan Faulks, 'The EU Habitats Directive' *European Environment*, Spring 1994 12–26.

international law, and whilst other treaties have no doubt played a part in shaping the genesis of the Habitats Directive, the principal influence has been the Convention on the Conservation of European Wildlife and Natural Habitats ('the Bern Convention').[6] As Reid notes 'the convention has played a major role in inspiring and providing the formulation for the European Community Directives on Wild Birds and the Habitats and species'.[7] The Bern Convention is the product of the Council of Europe, a quite separate body from the European Union (EU).[8]

By the late 1960s public awareness of the impact of human activities upon the environment was growing. The launch by the Council of Europe of European Nature Conservation Year in 1970 was an apparent success in raising the profile yet further.[9] Indeed, it is claimed that the many scientific studies published in the *Nature and Environment* series undertaken by the Council of Europe during the course of that year

> highlighted new factors which had been contributing to the diminishing number of certain wild species since the 1950s. The old causes contributing to the disappearance of species sometimes persisted, but suddenly had been joined or replaced by the direct destruction or modification of the habitats which are home to these species throughout their life cycle.[10]

Yet there was still no international convention at regional, much less world, level which addressed to the protection of the world's wild flora and fauna. Prior to the adoption of the Convention, conservation activities had been largely piecemeal and were focused upon eradicating, limiting or controlling human activities such as hunting, fishing, collecting, trade and so on which in the past had been the direct cause of the reduction, or complete extinction of certain species.[11]

> In the field of biodiversity, the Bern Convention was the first international European text to try to cover all aspects of nature conservation, and not just a particular group of species or habitats. This approach was bold and innovative and paved the way for the most influential treaty in this field, the Convention on Biological Diversity of 1992.[12]

---

[6] http://conventions.coe.int/Treaty/Commun/QueVoulezVous.asp?NT=104&CM=8&DF=&CL=ENG.

[7] Colin Reid, *Nature Conservation Law* (2nd edn) (W Green, 2002) 7.5.15.

[8] Founded in 1949, the Council of Europe is an international organisation promoting cooperation between the countries of Europe. It has 47 Member States with some 800 million citizens, and is an entirely separate body from the EU, which has 27 Member States. The Council of Europe is to be distinguished from the Council of the European Union or the European Council, which are both EU bodies.

[9] Lebeau, above n 1. A more impartial confirmation of the success can be found in Martin Jones, 'A Lesson from Europe', a book review of Wayland Kennet, *Preservation* in *New Scientist*, 27 April 1972, 217.

[10] Henri Jaffeux, 'The Emerald Network' *The 25 years of the Bern Convention* above n 1, 20. For the UK's planned response to the year see HC Deb 10 March 1969, vol 779 cols 1127–38.

[11] Ibid, Jaffeux.

[12] Eladio Fernández-Galiano, 'A laboratory of ideas' *The 25 years of the Bern Convention* above n 1 at 6. See MacKenzie, ch 2 in this volume, for a detailed comparison of the Convention on Biological Diversity with the Habitats Directive.

This chapter examines the Bern Convention and its impact on the development of the Habitats Directive. It also reflects upon the manner in which, in more recent years, the Habitats Directive has in return affected the implementation of the Bern Convention.

The Road to Bern

Following the European Ministerial Conference on the Environment held in Vienna in March 1973, a recommendation of the Consultative Assembly of the Council of Europe[13] was made that the Committee of Ministers 'define a coherent policy for the protection of wildlife, with a view to establishing European regulations—if possible by means of convention—and involving severe restrictions on hunting, shooting, capture of animals needing protection, fishing and egg-collection, and the prohibition of bird netting'.[14]

The Second European Ministerial Conference on the Environment was held in Brussels in March 1976.[15] It was attended by ministers and officials from 23 European countries.[16] Switzerland presented to the Conference a report entitled 'The protection of wildlife' which recommended the drafting of a Convention.[17] The Conference set itself the task of examining the complexities of managing the natural environment, and taking into account its interaction with the man-made environment in urban, industrial, agricultural and tourist centres. In so doing it identified the following issues:

— Reconciliation of economic development with the protection of the natural environment, including:
  (a) procedures for assessing the effects of development on Nature,
  (b) leisure pursuits and nature conservation,

---

[13] A useful précis of the process leading to the adoption of the Bern Convention can be found in the non-legally binding Summary produced with the Convention available at: http://conventions.coe.int/treaty/en/treaties/html/104.htm. For some anecdotal, but nonetheless useful, reflections by some of the participants involved in the drawing up of the Convention, see *The 25 years of the Bern Convention* above n 1; and for a more detailed examination, see the Convention on the Conservation of European Wildlife and Natural Habitats and Explanatory Report, in Treaties and Reports, (Council of Europe Publishing, 1996); Maguelonne Déjeant-Pons, *European Biodiversity: The Bern Convention of 19 September 1979 on the Conservation of European Wildlife and Natural Habitats, Essays in the Honour of Wang Tieya* (Martinus Nijhoff Publishers, 1993) 211; Maguelonne Déjeant-Pons *Biodiversité européenne, la Convention de Berne du 19 septembre 1979 relative à la conservation de la vie sauvage et du milieu naturel de l'Europe*, Fasc 6 Anno XII (Rivista Giuridica dell'ambiente, 1997).

[14] Consultative Assembly of the Council of Europe, Recommendation 720 on the results of the European Ministerial Conference on the Environment (Vienna, 28–30 March 1973).

[15] 23–24 March 1976.

[16] The 23 European countries comprised the then 18 Member States of the Council of Europe and Finland, Lichtenstein, Portugal, Spain and Yugoslavia. Canada, the host country for the United Nations 'Habitat Conference on Human Settlements' which took place in Vancouver shortly afterwards, also attended. Twelve international organisations also sent representatives.

[17] Hector Hacourt, 'Second European Ministerial Conference on the Environment, held in Brussels, Belgium, 23–24 March 1976' 3 *Environmental Conservation*, 234.–doi:10.1017/S0376892900018750.

(c)   parks and nature reserves, and
(d)   conservation of the natural and cultural values of the countryside;
—   protection of wildlife; and
—   voluntary participation in nature conservation.

More than three decades later the same issues remain live. This is particularly the case in respect of the first issue identified by the conference, namely, how to reconcile economic development with the protection of the natural environment.[18] Indeed, this issue may be said to overshadow the others, producing an ever-present tension in the drafting and application of both the Convention and the Habitats Directive.[19] Some, such as Stookes, would no doubt say that this is because there is 'an inherent conflict' between habitat and species conservation and their improvement, and the pursuit of economic plans and projects.[20]

The Brussels Conference also gave rise to another issue which is common to international arrangements, that is, the extent to which widening the accessibility to the Convention would weaken the 'depth' of its force. At that time a major part of Europe was not included within the membership of the Council of Europe. Norway suggested that an international legal document should be drafted that was not restricted to the Council of Europe members, so that the non-member

---

[18] A recent good example of this is the attempt by the UK coalition government to address nature conservation and economic development. In its White Paper launched on 7 June 2011, entitled 'The Natural Choice', (http://www.official-documents.gov.uk/document/cm80/8082/8082.asp) the government stated that its ambition is 'to improve the quality of our natural environment across England, moving to a net gain in the value of nature. We aim to arrest the decline in habitats and species and the degradation of landscapes. We will protect priority habitats and safeguard vulnerable non-renewable resources for future generations. We will support natural systems to function more effectively in town, in the country and at sea. *We will achieve this through joined-up action at local and national levels to create an ecological network which is resilient to changing pressures.*' (emphasis added) However, less than six months later, in introducing his autumn statement of November 2011, (http://cdn.hm-treasury.gov.uk/autumn_statement.pdf) the Chancellor of the Exchequer, George Osborne MP, told MPs he wanted to make sure that 'gold plating of EU rules on things like habitats' were not putting 'ridiculous costs' on firms. 'If we burden them with endless social and environmental goals—however worthy in their own right—then not only will we not achieve those goals, but the businesses will fail, jobs will be lost, and our country will be poorer.' Later, the Department for the Environment, Food and Rural Affairs announced it would be reviewing the impact of the EU Habitats and Wild Birds Directives in England 'focusing in particular on those obligations that affect the authorisation process for proposed development, with a view to reducing the burdens on business while maintaining the integrity of the purpose of the directives'. The government would no doubt claim that both statements are entirely compatible with one another. That may literally be correct, but there is a clear difference in emphasis between the two which is important when decisions are determined upon by balancing these competing factors.

[19] The comment made by Stephen Milligan MP during the dispute over the building of the final stretch of the M3 motorway from Bar End to the M27 near Southampton across Twyford Down, that: 'Jobs in Southampton are more important than butterflies on Twyford Down' (HC Deb 7 July 1992, col 172) may put the matter crudely but it does identify the issue as many see it. See Clutten and Tafir, ch 10 in this volume for a discussion as to when imperative reasons of overriding public interest may be used to permit harmful development.

[20] See Stookes, ch 8 in this volume at p 140.

States of the communist bloc could accede to it more easily. Pursuant to this proposal, the Council would provide a secretariat for the contracting parties. In the event, this proposal was not accepted because 'the majority of the countries felt that the Council's accumulated expertise in this field should be exploited to the full and, consequently, that the convention should be firmly part of the Council of Europe's corpus'.[21]

This concern that any resultant legal instrument should be effective was reflected in the outcome of the Second European Ministerial Environment Conference. The Ministers for the Environment requested the Council of Europe to draft 'a legal instrument on the conservation of wildlife, with particular reference to migratory species and natural habitats, *which would obviate the difficulties encountered in the implementation of existing conventions*'. (emphasis added) However, the desire to make the Convention open to non-member States was to resurface in the final draft of the Convention.

The Ministers also recommended the creation of procedures for assessing the effects of development on nature. They expressed the wish to create a permanent exchange of information and experience on: (a) the different aspects of examining and evaluating the ecological effects of public measures; and (b) the procedures and methods required to ensure early and coordinated landscape planning. They also asked the Council of Europe to include within its Work Programme 'the development of general principles for procedural patterns and methods for planning of the natural environment and for the assessment of the ecological impact of alternative courses of action on the natural environment'. This was to be based upon exchange of information between the Member States. The Ministers also requested the governments of the Member States should foster cooperation between official bodies and private nature protection organisations, to facilitate the work by giving them appropriate support, and to take account of their consideration and plans as a contribution to comprehensive environmental planning. They expressly recommended cooperation between the Council of Europe bodies and non-governmental organisations (NGOs), both national and international, that are interested in environmental problems 'especially in connection with the information campaigns organized by the European Information Centre for Nature Conservation of the Council of Europe, which must play a coordinating role'. Involvement of NGOs was very much in line with the tradition of the Council of Europe.[22] Finally, the Ministers recommended that a third Ministerial Conference be held in Switzerland 'probably in 1979'.

---

[21] Jean-Pierre Ribaut, 'How the Bern Convention came into being' *The 25 years of the Bern Convention* above n 1, 4.
[22] Ibid.

The Signing of the Bern Convention

The Bern Convention was adopted in Bern, Switzerland in 1979.[23] It came into force on 1 June, 1982 having opened for signature by Member States at the start of the Third Ministerial Conference on the Environment on 19 September 1979. Eighteen of the 21 countries signed the text that day. The Convention had in fact been drafted over a three-year period by an ad hoc committee. The committee met first in November 1976 and there were four further meetings. In addition, eight meetings of working groups took place.

The majority of the delegates were of the view that the correct approach was to draw up a list, based on set scientific criteria of animal species that required total protection (see the approach of the current Appendix II). However, regardless of specified criteria, the German delegation called for the inclusion of all the various species of sparrow and the Danish delegation specifically wanted the inclusion of the nightingale. There was also debate as to whether certain animals such as the lynx, the otter and the wolf which plainly *were* endangered species in Europe but were being legally hunted in various Member States, should be included for protection. Those discussions were described by one of the participants as 'sometimes bitter'.[24] The compromise was Article 9 and Annex III.

The discussions on the protection of habitats under Article 4 were apparently, and perhaps not surprisingly, 'the most difficult'.[25] The main issues were the extent to which Article 4 should lay down identification criteria and implementing conditions and whether Article 4 should refer explicitly to the networks of protected areas which could serve as its basis.[26] The resulting text of Article 4 was very general. This was because the ad hoc committee 'felt that this article should not be too explicit in order to keep it open for developing co-operation between contracting parties, inter alia in respect of the creation of a network of biogenetic reserves, the protection of wetlands, etc'.[27] However, agreement having been secured to the text of the Convention, the Bern Convention Standing Committee subsequently adopted Resolution No 1[28] which interpreted Article 4 in greater detail.

---

[23] http://conventions.coe.int/Treaty/Commun/QueVoulezVous.asp?NT=104&CM=8&DF=&CL=ENG.

[24] Jean-Pierre Ribaut, above n 21.

[25] Ibid.

[26] For example, the networks of biogenetic reserves and the areas awarded the Council of Europe's diploma, plus the Ramsar networks, the Unesco Natural and Cultural Heritage networks and the anticipated results of the work of the European Commission—the future Natura 2000.

[27] Para 23 of the Explanatory Report, above n 13.

[28] Standing Committee, Resolution No 1 on the provisions relating to the conservation of habitats, 9 June 1989.

The Bern Convention

The main objectives of the Bern Convention are to ensure the conservation and protection of wild plant and animal species and their natural habitats (listed in Appendices I and II of the Convention); to increase cooperation between contracting parties; and to regulate the exploitation of those species (including migratory species) listed in Appendix III. The Convention starts with a general chapter requiring parties to take protective measures and a chapter on the protection of habitats. Chapter III contains specific provisions on species conservation. Measures taken under these provisions must be coordinated where they apply to migratory species. The remaining chapters consist of supplementary and organisational provisions.

All signatories to the Bern Convention are required to take action to promote national policies for the conservation of wild flora and fauna and their natural habitats; have regard to the conservation of wild flora and fauna in their planning and development policies, and in their measures against pollution; promote education and disseminate general information on the need to conserve species of wild flora and fauna and their habitats; and encourage and coordinate research related to the purposes of this Convention. Signatories must also cooperate to enhance the effectiveness of these measures through coordination of efforts to protect migratory species, and the exchange of information and the sharing of experience and expertise.

The appendices to the Bern Convention served as the model for the annexes to the Habitats Directive. The approximately 700 plant species listed in Appendix I may not be taken from the wild or harmed. The habitats of these species are subject to strict protection, with the choice of habitat protection measures left to signatory states. Strict species conservation provisions apply to the 710 animal species listed in Appendix II, which include familiar species such as the otter (*Lutra lutra*), the wolf (*Canis lupus*)[29] and the brown bear (*Ursus arctos*) as well as less well-known species such as the dusky large blue butterfly (*Maculinea nausithous*), the Apollo butterfly (*Parnassius apollo*) and the hermit beetle (*Osmoderma eremita*). Animals of these species may not be disturbed, captured, killed or traded. In this regard, the Bern Convention supplements the Convention on International Trade in Endangered Species of Wild Fauna and Flora (CITES),[30] which governs only

---

[29] The wolf's strict protection status granted since the Convention's adoption in 1979 has remained controversial: 'Reasons include its vastly different situation in eastern and western European countries, from relative abundance to near-total extermination by the mid-20th century; complexities of large carnivore management across the national boundaries; and socio economic and cultural factors linked to the continuing fear and myths around the wolf.' Legal Report on the possible need to amend Appendix II of the Convention for the wolf T-PVS/Inf (2005) 18.

[30] CITES is an international agreement between governments. Its aim is to ensure that international trade in specimens of wild animals and plants does not threaten their survival. CITES was drafted as a result of a resolution adopted in 1963 at a meeting of members of IUCN (The World Conservation Union). The text of the Convention was finally agreed at a meeting of representatives of 80 countries in

international trade. Just like Annex III of the EU Birds Directive, Appendix III contains species that are in need of protection but which may be hunted or otherwise exploited in exceptional instances. Similarly, the prohibitions on certain hunting methods and types of hunting equipment listed in Appendix IV are largely identical to those in Annex IV of the Birds Directive.

It is essential to recognise the context and time in which the Bern Convention came into force. Later in this chapter we will examine the limitations of the Bern Convention, its institutional structure and, in particular, its lack of the type of legally enforceable mechanisms available for the enforcement of the Habitats Directive in particular and EU law in general. However, this should not prevent us from recognising that the Bern Convention broke new ground in making Contracting States take their environmental obligations more seriously. As Lyster correctly identifies:

> There are two aspects of the Berne [*sic*][31] Convention which are particularly noteworthy. The first is that almost every one of the provisions is mandatory as opposed to being couched in the hortatory language used by some wildlife treaties. Rather than simply encouraging Parties to do this and that the Berne Convention almost always requires Parties to do this and that. The second important aspect of the Berne Convention is the system of administration it has created to promote and oversee its implementation. It cannot be over-emphasised how vital it is to the enforcement of a wildlife treaty that there are mechanisms—such as the Secretariat, regular meetings of parties, reporting requirements, etc.—to keep Parties on their toes and to make them feel that they will be publicly castigated if they do not comply with the terms of the treaty. It is in this respect, in particular, that the Berne convention has made major advances from the western Hemisphere and African Conventions.[32]

The style of mandatory language was replicated in the Habitats Directive. Moreover, the scope of the Bern Convention was ambitious compared to other international treaties. It is disappointing to record that following the adoption of the Bern Convention

> It took more than 12 years for a global treaty of even more comprehensive coverage to emerge—when the Convention on Biological Diversity (the Biodiversity Convention) [CBD] was signed at the Earth Summit in Rio in 1992. However, the Biodiversity

---

Washington DC, USA, on 3 March 1973, and on 1 July 1975 CITES entered in force. The original of the Convention was deposited with the Depositary Government in the Chinese, English, French, Russian and Spanish languages, each version being equally authentic. CITES is an international agreement to which States (countries) adhere voluntarily. States that have agreed to be bound by the Convention ('joined' CITES) are known as Parties. 'Although CITES is legally binding on the Parties—in other words they have to implement the Convention—it does not take the place of national laws. Rather it provides a framework to be respected by each Party, which has to adopt its own domestic legislation to ensure that CITES is implemented at the national level.' CITES website at http://www.cites.org/eng/disc/what.php.

[31] The city is known as 'Bern' the German spelling and also as 'Berne' the French spelling. This volume adopts 'Bern' since it is the spelling currently used by the Council of Europe in English versions of documentation relating to the Bern Convention.

[32] Lyster, above n 2, 130.

Convention lacks annexes listing the protected species—which, given its global scope, would indeed be a formidable task—and some of the other mechanisms present in the Bern Convention.[33]

Moreover, as MacKenzie points out in the following chapter of this volume,[34] the CBD simply requires that 'each party is responsible for implementation of CBD obligations only "as far as possible and appropriate"'. This is a much less robust form of language and enforcement system than that developed by the Bern Convention a decade earlier.

The Institutional Framework

The institutional framework of the Bern Convention comprises the Standing Committee and its Bureau, the Groups of Experts and the Secretariat. Consistent with the wishes of the Environment Ministers of the Second Conference held in Brussels, NGOs play an important role in monitoring the application of the Convention.

The Standing Committee

The Standing Committee consists of representatives of the Contracting Parties, each with one vote. National and international NGOs and agencies can also be represented at the Standing Committee in an observer capacity under the conditions specified in Article 13 of the Convention the terms of which are quite generous.[35] The Standing Committee has general responsibility for monitoring the application of the Convention, and specifically it may: keep under review the provisions of the Convention, including its appendices, and examine any modifications necessary;[36] make recommendations to the Contracting Parties concerning measures to be

---

[33] Para 6 to App I of the Explanatory Memorandum of M Lotman, *Rapporteur* of Report No 12459 to the Parliamentary Assembly: 'The Need to Assess the Progress in the Implementation of the Bern Convention' (5 January 2011): http://assembly.coe.int/Documents/WorkingDocs/Doc11/EDOC12459.pdf.

[34] See MacKenzie, ch 2 in this volume, at p 41.

[35] Art 13(3) para 3 of the Bern Convention states that: 'Any body or agency technically qualified in the protection, conservation or management of wild fauna and flora and their habitats, and belonging to one of the following categories:

    a. international agencies or bodies, either governmental or non-governmental, and national governmental agencies or bodies;

    b. national non-governmental agencies or bodies which have been approved for this purpose by the State in which they are located, may inform the Secretary General of the Council of Europe, at least three months before the meeting of the Committee, of its wish to be represented at that meeting by observers. They shall be admitted unless, at least one month before the meeting one third of the Contracting Parties have informed the Secretary General of their objection.'

[36] See, eg the report to the Standing Committee: 'Legal Report on the possible need to amend Appendix II of the Convention for the wolf' T-PVS/Inf (2005) 18.

taken for the purposes of the Convention; recommend the appropriate measures to keep the public informed about the activities undertaken within the framework of the Convention; make recommendations to the Committee of Ministers concerning non-member States of the Council of Europe to be invited to accede to the Convention; make any proposals for improving the effectiveness of the Convention, including proposals for the conclusion of agreements with the States that are not Contracting Parties to the Convention, to enhance the effective conservation of species or groups of species; and arrange expert group meetings.

The authority of the Standing Committee to make Recommendations to the Contracting Parties in respect of the implementation of the Convention along with the power to make proposals for improving the effectiveness of the Convention is important. Under these powers the Committee has adopted numerous recommendations, resolutions and guidelines. These provide interpretations of certain provisions of the Convention and instructions to assist Contracting States to apply them in particular cases. Recommendations are usually adopted in accordance with the current work programme of the Committee, this may be as an outcome of expert groups meetings or seminars, or following the examination of the case files placed on the agenda of the Standing Committee meetings.

There are two types of recommendation: General Recommendations relate to the interpretation and implementation of the Convention, and Specific Recommendations relate to topics such as species protection.[37] All Recommendations are transmitted to the Contracting Parties for further action. Significantly, they are made public. The Recommendations are a very important means of giving substance to the provisions of the Convention, particularly where much of the Convention has been drafted in general terms in order to secure initial agreement. Furthermore, it has been suggested that with sufficient passage of time they may also constitute customary international law,[38] and that '[i]n any case, their definite political impact and high ethical value make them a critical component of the Convention's decision-making process'.[39] In this respect, the public nature of the Recommendations can thus be seen to be vital

---

[37] See Veit Koester, 'Pacta sunt Servanda' (1996) 26 *Environmental Policy & Law* 78, 85.

[38] Customary international law is those aspects of international law that derive from custom. Along with general principles of law and treaties, custom is considered by the International Court of Justice, jurists, the United Nations and its Member States to be among the primary sources of international law. The majority of the world's governments accept the existence of customary international law in principle, although there are many differing opinions as to what rules are contained in it. The Statute of the International Court of Justice acknowledges the existence of customary international law in Art 38(1)(b), incorporated into the United Nations Charter by Art 92: 'The Court, whose function is to decide in accordance with international law such disputes as are submitted to it, shall apply ... international custom, as evidence of a general practice accepted as law."Customary international law" ... consists of rules of law derived from the consistent conduct of States acting out of the belief that the law required them to act that way.' Shabtai Rosenne, *Practice and Methods of International Law* (Oceana, 1984) 55.

[39] Sandra Jen, 'The Convention on the Conservation of European Wildlife and Natural Habitats (Bern, 1979): Procedures of Application in Practice' (1999) 2(2) *Journal of International Wildlife Law & Policy*.

in seeking to secure compliance, for once in the public arena such information places interest groups, NGOs and the media in a stronger position to respond to the measures contained in the Recommendation, as well as to pressurise governments of Contracting States to undertake their effective implementation. This, along with the ability of NGOs to attend meetings of the standing committee and participate in expert groups, means, according to Eladio Fernández-Galiano, Secretary to the Bern Convention for more than 20 years, that: 'NGOs are the salt and often the teeth of the convention ...There are few biodiversity-related treaties in which the NGOs participate so actively and influence so much the agenda and the outcome.'[40]

The Committee has also used its power to make Recommendations in order to overcome some of the issues arising from the drafting of the Convention. There was an absence of agreement on the interpretation of terms and provisions under the Convention and this lack of clarity could have led to considerable differences in the legal interpretation of the Convention. The Committee has used its ability to make Recommendations in order to provide standard definitions and interpretations of some of its provisions in order to make it easier for the Parties to harmonise their approaches in achieving the aims of the Convention. The Standing Committee has also adopted a series of guidelines. These guidelines are more detailed than General Recommendations.

Article 18(1) of the Convention provides that 'the Standing Committee shall use its best endeavours to facilitate a friendly settlement of any difficulty to which the execution of this Convention may give rise'. Its supporters argue that as a regional treaty, 'the Convention benefits from the fact that Member States form a relatively homogeneous group'.[41] The Standing Committee meets at least once a year; this is more frequent than for other comparable biodiversity-related treaties. A number of individual delegates from Contracting States have served on the Standing Committee for a number of years and this has promoted continuity. Eladio Fernández-Galiano says that: 'This has created an inspired and confident working atmosphere in which most delegates know each other personally quite well, enabling friendly negotiation of solutions, which a delegate some years ago called "a club spirit built on a gentlemen's agreement"'.[42] According to Veit Koester, President of the Standing Committee from December 1985 to December 1989:

> The recommendations to the Parties are ... explicitly shown as being an instrument in respect of the Article 14 imposed responsibility for the Committee to follow the application of the Convention. The starting point for the guidelines is the consideration that the Standing Committee is the forum in which the Parties assist each other in solving those problems encountered in the application of the Convention. ... It was also agreed at the same meeting where the Guidelines were adopted that when the Committee is dealing with a concrete case, '*it must not turn itself into a tribunal in which*

---

[40] Fernández-Galiano, above n 12, 6.
[41] Jen, above n 39.
[42] Fernández-Galiano, above n 12, 6.

> *the country concerned was put on trial: it must maintain tranquil or—to use the words of the Chairman of the Interim Committee—a "club" atmosphere.*[43] (emphasis added)

It is said that: 'This facilitates the reaching of consensus when making decisions, adopting recommendations, and monitoring the application of the Convention by the Standing Committee in a constructive way.'[44] This may well be so. However, Veit Koester's comment that the Habitats Directive was inspired in part by the fact that 'the European Commission in the late 1980s was worried about the rather poor implementation of the Convention by a number of EC member states, taking also into consideration that the EC as such was a contracting party to the convention'[45] may be intended primarily as a gentle rebuke of the EC and its Member States, but it also highlights the limitations of the Bern Convention's gentleman's club consensus approach as a means of effective enforcement. Boere also notes the complication caused by the fact that 'there is a need for EU members to decide on a common position before meetings of the Standing Committee of the Bern convention'.[46]

The Secretariat

The Convention does not make any specific reference to the responsibilities of the Secretariat but its practical role is essential for the implementation of the Convention. The Secretariat is provided by the Council of Europe. It monitors the implementation of the Convention in accordance with the programme of activities drawn up by the Standing Committee and facilitates all activities implemented under the Convention such as following up complaints by NGOs or citizens.

The Bureau

In January 1991 the Standing Committee established the Bureau. The Bureau is responsible for making administrative and organisational decisions in the periods between Standing Committee meetings. The Bureau normally meets twice a year and membership is comprised of a Chair, Vice-Chair and the previous Chair, and the Bureau advises the Secretariat in the procedure for the follow-up of case files.

Groups of Experts

Article 14 provides that 'in order to discharge its functions, the Standing Committee may, on its own initiative, arrange for meetings of groups of experts'. Obviously, the particular make-up of a group of experts will depend on the

---

[43] Koester, 'Pacta sunt Servanda' above n 37, 78, 83.
[44] Jen, above n 39.
[45] Koester, 'The Bern Convention and I', *The 25 years of the Bern Convention* above n 1, 5.
[46] Gerald C Boere, 'Political aspects and development' *The 25 years of the Bern Convention* above n 1, 11.

subject matter under discussion. Meetings are called on an ad hoc but regular basis.[47] Interested NGOs are invited to participate in the meetings. This means that the Standing Committee can draw upon the wide technical expertise of the groups of experts, and it is also said that the experts through this relationship can better appreciate the political issues with which the standing committee must grapple. The use of the groups of experts has been particularly important for the regular updating of the appendices of the Convention. The assistance of experts is also used for the preparation of legal or scientific studies on specific subjects and for seminars and workshops organised to bring together nature conservation specialists and policy makers and administrators.

Non-governmental Organisations

As stated above, national and international NGOs attend meetings of the Standing Committee in an observer capacity, under Article 13 of the Convention. The NGOs provide a number of benefits. They are a source of information for the Secretariat and they are often the main movers for specific protection or monitoring operations. They may also be invited to participate in groups of experts. This permanent institutional structure facilitates the establishment of strong relations between different bodies of the Convention and the NGOs, and contributes to continuity in the monitoring of the application of the Convention.

Control Mechanisms

The compliance methods employed by the Bern Convention are of particular interest because they also reflect the developing nature of international environmental law. In short, they include those methods which are expressly mentioned in the Convention and those which have grown up subsequently as a form of practice. In so doing the Bern Convention has achieved a certain measure of support within NGOs. In welcoming 30 years of the Bern Convention, Boris Barov, European Conservation Manager of the NGO Birdlife International, called the Bern Convention 'one of the few illegal instruments for biodiversity conservation at Pan-European level with an enforcement mechanism to bite when necessary'.[48] However, in truth, the Convention actually relies on persuasion rather than legal enforcement.

Reports

Contracting states are obliged to submit regular reports on the way in which they are fulfilling their obligations under the Convention. At the time of the Contracting

---

[47] Of particular interest in respect of habitats protection, is the group of experts for the Emerald Network of areas of special conservation interest set up in 1996. See further below in this chapter.
[48] 21 September 2009 available at: http://www.birdlife.org/news/news/2009/09/bern_convention.html.

State's accession an introductory report must be submitted to the Standing Committee describing the domestic legislation on the protection of nature. This may be compared with the reporting obligation placed upon Member States of the EU who must inform the European Commission of the domestic steps taken to implement a directive. Requiring states to inform the international body of the applicable domestic laws relieves the international organisation of having to work out how the obligations imposed upon the Contracting State are being implemented, a task which is burdensome and for which it is not well equipped. Instead, it can focus on examining whether the legislation notified by the Member States actually fulfils the obligations. Following the submission of the initial report, Contracting States are obliged to submit four-yearly reports. They must also submit two-yearly reports on derogations from the specific obligations with which they are obliged to comply.

Files

The Convention has developed the 'file' process as a control process not expressly mentioned in the Convention.[49] The practice was approved by the Standing Committee at its third meeting in 1984. The procedure for this proposal was agreed upon and adopted provisionally at the thirteenth meeting of the Standing Committee in 1993.[50] When the Standing Committee, its Chair or its Secretariat, receives a letter or complaint from an individual or NGO alleging non-compliance with a provision of the Convention by a Contracting Party, the Secretariat considers the evidence before it whether there are grounds to refer the allegation to the Contracting Party concerned for further information, and then, with the approval of the Bureau, considers whether there are grounds to discuss the matter in the Standing Committee, which may decide to open a file and adopt a Recommendation. A number of shortcomings have recently been identified in the case file system in a report entitled, 'Improving The Case-File System of The Bern Convention'. Produced by the Directorate of Culture and Natural Heritage the report was submitted to the Standing Committee for its 31st meeting on 29 November to 2 December 2011.[51] It raises amongst other things the following issues in respect of the case file system.

First, the file system can only be started by a complaint that presumes that a Contracting Party is failing to comply with one or more provisions of the Convention. Given that failing to honour international obligations under a treaty

---

[49] Secretariat Memorandum, 'Follow-up of the Lucerne Ministerial Conference "Environment for Europe" 28–30 April 1993, Procedures for the follow-up of the implementation of the Bern Convention', Document T-PVS (94) 7.

[50] Secretariat Memorandum, 'Opening and closing of files—and follow-up to recommendations', Document T-PVS (99) 16.

[51] https://wcd.coe.int/com.instranet.InstraServlet?command=com.instranet.CmdBlobGet&InstranetImage=1956319&SecMode=1&DocId=1811880&Usage=2.

is a serious matter, 'most governments if not all—refuse to admit such breach of the Convention and dialogue between NGOs and governments becomes difficult since the parties tend to view the position as quasi-litigation'.[52]

Secondly, the Standing Committee is not to act as a judicial body. Instead it seeks in accordance with Article 18 to 'use its best endeavours to facilitate a friendly settlement of any difficulty to which the execution of the Convention may give rise'. Consequently, over the last 30 years, the Standing Committee has only very rarely concluded that a Contracting Party has not complied with its obligations under the Convention. In most cases, the Standing Committee has instead sought to reach solutions between the complainant and the government of the Contracting State agreeable to all. Furthermore: 'There has also been in the last years a certain reluctance in the Standing Committee to "open" new file cases as the opening of a file case there is a certain presumption of the possibility of non-respect of the Convention, the Committee favouring other methods, like fact-finding "on-the-spot appraisals" which in fact permit to foster dialogue and reach "friendly settlements"—often in the form of recommendations—which make unnecessary the opening of a file case.'[53]

Thirdly, a further limitation of the case file system concerns the treatment of complaints by the Bureau. The Bureau may find that there is no breach of the Convention by a Party. The file is consequently closed without providing an opportunity to improve the situation or to establish a meaningful dialogue between the complainant and the government concerned. This tends to undermine the faith of NGOs in the Convention. The Secretariat has noted that some of the issues that are closed without any negotiation or improvement have a tendency to come back as new complaints by NGOs, this is particularly the case for the setting of appropriate 'population levels' for some species where NGOs claim that the levels of permitted culling is too high, government data is inaccurate or that numbers are fixed arbitrarily or are politically motivated. In these cases the Standing Committee has a history of finding no grounds for opening a case-file for presumed non-compliance, in part because the populations may be actually increasing, and in part because of the limitation in the wording of the Convention which sets no other obligation other than to ensure 'the survival of the population concerned'[54] or 'maintain the population of wild flora and fauna, or to adapt it to, a level which corresponds in particular to ecological, scientific and cultural requirements'.[55]

It has also been authoritatively suggested by a former chair of the Bern Standing Committee that: 'the dominant presence of the EU' has also influenced the successful monitor system of the national implementation of the Bern Convention

---

[52] T-PVS (2011) 14: Report of the Directorate of Culture and Natural Heritage (15 September 2011) to the Standing Committee 31st meeting of 29 November–2 December 2011: Improving The Case-File System of The Bern Convention.

[53] Ibid.

[54] Art 9.

[55] Art 2.

under the file system 'in a way which caused some tension among EU members and between the EU and non-EU members of the Bern Convention concerning the possible role of the European Commission in cases where a file was opened against an EU Member State. It took some time before possible tension could be defused thanks to procedural improvements.'[56]

A final problem that has been identified is where important parts of the recommendations are not implemented. As Recommendations are not legally binding, the Standing Committee is hesitant to open case-files as there is absence of an element of non-compliance of obligations. However, this results in the loss of a chance to persuade Contracting Parties to improve the conservation of some species or habitats through a more careful analysis of the implementation of recommendations.

On the Spot Appraisals

The Rules of Procedure of the Standing Committee provide that

> if during discussions on one or more proposals, any doubts and/or difficulties arise regarding the measure to be taken for the implementation of the Convention with regard to a natural habitat essential to the conservation of species, and if it is necessary to obtain appropriate information, the Committee may, if the gravity of the situation so demands, decide that the natural habitat in question should be inspected by an expert instructed to make an on-the-spot appraisal and report back to the Standing Committee.[57]

However, a weakness in this procedure is that this decision is subject to approval by the affected Party and the Standing Committee must draft and convey precise terms and conditions to the expert. The expert is appointed by the Secretary General of the Council of Europe. But again, the Party must agree to the appointment. The expert cannot be a person who represents or has represented a State on the Standing Committee, nor is a national of the Party in whose territory the visit is to take place. At the request of the Standing Committee or its Chair, the expert is to be accompanied during the visit by a member of the Secretariat and by a representative of the Party concerned. The expert is expected to 'evaluate the situation; flesh out certain aspects of the file; meet all parties involved; draw up recommendations'.[58] The expert may also perform an informal mediating role between the national authorities and all parties concerned. Following the visit[59] the expert submits a report to the Standing Committee. The Standing Committee may then issue conclusions in the form of specific recommendations to the Contracting State. Sometimes a

---

[56] Boere, above n 46.

[57] Maguelonne Déjeant-Pons 'The irreversible threat to biodiversity' *The 25 years of the Berne Convention* above n 1, 9.

[58] Françoise Bauer, 'On-the-spot Appraisals', *The 25 years of the Berne Convention* above n 1, 10.

[59] The travel and subsistence expenses pertaining to the visit and those arising out of the presentation to the Standing Committee are borne by the Council of Europe.

preventive visit may be made before a proposed development has taken place. The expert can then provide advice to the national authorities on matter.

Implementation of the Bern Convention

The preamble of the Convention departs from the traditional type of introduction employed for Council of Europe conventions. This is due to the 'special nature of the Convention'[60] which enables non-member States to become Contracting Parties, something which the Norwegian delegation had sought unsuccessfully at the Brussels Conference. The ad hoc committee subsequently recognised that the species of wildlife found in Europe have in many cases a range that extends well beyond the confines of the membership of the Council of Europe.[61] Many of the conservation problems that are encountered and which call for international cooperation are not capable of solution solely within the membership of the Council of Europe, and the endeavour was accordingly made to draft a text that would encourage other States to become Contracting Parties.[62]

Accordingly, to date, 44 countries have acceded to the Convention, including four in Africa—Burkina Faso, Morocco, Senegal and Tunisia—whose territories host over-wintering sites for European bird species.[63] Ironically two Member States, Russia and St Marino are still not Contracting Parties. The EU is also a party to the Convention. As a consequence, all EU Member States are bound by the Convention's provisions. The UK is also an individual signatory to the Convention.[64]

The Birds Directive 79/409/EEC[65] 1979 and the Habitats Directive 1992 were (and are) the means by which the European Community (as it then was) seeks to fulfil its obligations under the Bern Convention. However, the negotiations on the drafting of the Bern Convention actually took place at the same time as the European Commission in Brussels was drafting the Birds Directive. We are told

---

[60] Para 15 of the Explanatory Report, above n 13.

[61] Boere, above n 46 and see also, eg Nigel Haigh, *Manual of European Environmental Policy* (Institute of European Environmental Policy, 2001).

[62] Para 11 of the Explanatory Report above n 13.

[63] Algeria, Belarus, Cape Verde, the Holy See, San Marino and Russia are among non-signatories that have observer status at meetings of the committee. The continued absence of Russia is a long-standing problem. Writing in 2004, Gerard C Boere, Chair of the Bern Standing Committee 1998–2000, noted that: '50% of Europe's remaining high quality sites are in the Russian Federation and its former republics' and concluded that: 'It is one of the greatest political challenges for the Bern Convention to bring the remaining countries under its umbrella as the regional biodiversity convention for the whole of Europe.' Boere, above n 46.

[64] The UK ratified the Bern Convention in 1982. The UK sought to implement the Convention by the Wildlife and Countryside Act 1981 (and as amended).

[65] Subsequently amended and codified as Directive 2009/147/EC of the European Parliament and of the Council of 30 November 2009 on the conservation of wild birds available at: http://eurlex.europa.eu/LexUriServ/LexUriServ.do?uri=OJ:L:2010:020:0007:0025:EN:PDF.

Gregory Jones QC

by one of the Convention delegates that 'it has to be said that the [Convention] drafting process was made more complicated by [that] fact,' but tantalizingly, he declines to go into details.[66] However, we get some flavour of the tension that sometimes exists between the European bodies from the reflections 25 years later of Veit Koester, Chair of the Standing Committee of the Convention from 1986 to 1989, that although the Convention was probably one of the main reasons for the adoption of the Habitats Directive: 'The convention is not recognised and reflected in the "considerations" of the directive (which by the way is an expression of rather typical European Community behaviour!).'[67]

The Influence of the Bern Convention on the Adoption of the Habitats Directive

When the Convention entered into force in 1982 the Birds Directive was the only EC Directive expressly addressing nature conservation issues. It had been introduced following 'strong pressure' from NGOs.[68] Furthermore, notwithstanding the adoption of the Birds Directive, it was not until the coming into force of the Single European Act (SEA) in 1987 that an environment title was added to the Treaty.[69] The legal basis employed for the Birds Directive had of course been a creative interpretation of what was Article 235 of the EEC Treaty.[70] It is true that the EC had previously adopted a general policy on nature conservation in its early Environmental Action Programmes, and that in particular, the Second Programme[71] sought, amongst other things, to 'maintain a satisfactory ecological balance and ensure the protection of the biosphere,' and indeed, the text of the second action plan also noted that the EC Commission was participating in the preparation of a Council of Europe instrument to protect wildlife and biotopes which, of course, subsequently became the Bern Convention. However, in the absence of a suite of legally binding requirements the effectiveness of the early action plans was extremely limited.

---

[66] Ribaut, above n 21.

[67] Koester, 'The Bern Convention and I' above n 45, 5.

[68] See, eg Report No 12459 'The Need to Assess the Progress in the Implementation of the Bern Convention', above n 33.

[69] The SEA, signed in Luxembourg on 17 February 1986 by the nine Member States and on 28 February 1986 by Denmark, Greece and Italy, was the first major amendment of the EEC Treaty. It entered into force on 1 July 1987.

[70] Peter GG. Davies, *European Union Environmental Law: An Introduction to Key Selected Issues* (Ashgate Publishing, 2004) 121.

[71] Adopted in May 1977 to cover the period 1977–81.

The focus of EC nature conservation policy had hitherto concentrated on bird protection[72] and even then, its record was one of poor implementation.[73] The Bern Convention thus obliged the EC to take steps towards the protection of a wider range of species and their habitats than previously. The ratification of the Convention by the EEC in 1982[74] made the implementation of new legislation almost impossible to avoid.[75] This is important because the prospect of extending habitat and species protection beyond the scope of the Birds Directive was not universally welcome by all EEC Member States. Thus, according to Coffey and Richartz, when in 1988 the European Commission brought forward a proposal for a European Directive, aimed at improving the protection of habitats and species in the Community to ensure better implementation of the Bern Convention[76]

> several Member States expressed their doubts over the effectiveness and practicality of a new EU Directive. Member States were also resistant to the idea of a binding directive covering the same issues as the Convention. Indeed, it has been suggested by some that those Member States opposed to a new directive were actively trying to deflect EU initiatives for a Community instrument on habitat protection, by instead proposing the reinforcement of relevant provisions under the Bern Convention (resulting ultimately in Resolution No 1 and Recommendations No 14, 15 and 16).[77]

As Coffey and Richartz note,[78] the resultant Habitats Directive is more robust than the Bern Convention in a number of respects. First, it is more explicit than the Bern Convention about the need for site protection and a coherent European ecological network.[79] Secondly, the Habitats Directive set a precedent for transboundary coordination in habitat protection by establishing Natura 2000 as a key instrument. Thirdly, the Directive set out a clear timeframe for the transposition and implementation of its provisions.

---

[72] The Directive on the conservation of wild birds (79/409/EEC) provides for the protection of all species of wild birds in Europe by controlling the hunting and killing of birds, and by protecting their eggs, nests and habitats.

[73] See, eg Clare Coffey and Saskia Richartz, *The EU Habitats Directive: Generating Strong Responses*, Project Deliverable No D 17 (March 2003), available at http://ecologic.eu/download/projekte/850-899/890/in-depth/eu_habitats_directive.pdf; see also, Haigh, above n 61.

[74] Council Decision 82/72/EEC of 10 February 1982 concerning conclusion of the Convention on the conservation of European wildlife and natural habitats OJ L38.

[75] There was also mounting political pressure from the European Parliament and the non-governmental community on the European institutions and Member States to adopt a definitive legal instrument for nature conservation, see, eg Coffey and Richartz, above n 73 and Haigh, above n 61.

[76] Haigh, above n 61.

[77] Coffey and Richartz, above n 73.

[78] Ibid.

[79] The protection rules laid down in Art 4 of the Convention are general in nature. By contrast, the rules of the Habitats Directive in Art 6 are more specific. Furthermore, the European Commission has issued guidance on management of Natura 2000 sites, but this deals only with interpretation of Art 6 of the Habitats Directive.

The Habitats Directive does, of course, contain many of the provisions set out by the Convention.[80] This is also reflected in the fact that the Directive adopted relevant definitions used by the Convention.[81] Coffey and Richartz offer as an example the reference made in Recommendation 14 to 'species [and endangered natural habitats] requiring specific habitat conservation measures' which is found reflected in Appendix I and II of the Habitats Directive which list natural habitat types, and animal and plant species of Community interest whose conservation requires the designation of Special Areas of Conservation (SACs). They note too, that the very term 'Special Areas of Conservation' has its origin in the terminology employed by Recommendation 16 on Areas of Special Conservation Interest.[82] Resolution No 1 (1989) and Recommendations No 15 and 25, adopted prior to the Directive in 1989 and 1991 respectively, have also influenced the provisions on habitat protection of the Directive.[83]

The Influence of the Adoption of the Habitats Directive upon the Bern Convention

As Boere explains: 'Although the directive and the convention have similar aims there is an important difference between the two texts: non-observance of the first is punishable by a court of justice: the European Court of Justice.'[84] Indeed, the ability to enforce EU law goes beyond the Court of Justice of the European Union and imposes legal obligations that can be directly enforced through court action at the national and European level. The role of the European Commission is also important. 'As the Community's executive body of the Union the Commission also has powers, resources and indeed duties to supervise, support and enforce legislation, far beyond those available to the Council of Europe.'[85] As Reid observes, that means that since the Habitats Directive has 'legal force within the United Kingdom and impose[s] more detailed obligations, especially in relation

---

[80] For a helpful table setting out the main differences between the Bern Convention, the Birds Directive and the Habitat Directive see 'Comparison of the key provisions of the Bern Convention and the European Union nature conservation directives' App 1 to Report No 12459 'The Need to Assess the Progress in the Implementation of the Bern Convention' above n 33.

[81] In 1989 the Standing Committee reinforced the emphasis given to habitat conservation by Recommendations 14 and 16.

[82] T-PVS (2001) 51.

[83] Ibid. Resolution No 1 (1989) of the Standing Committee on the provisions relating to the conservation of habitats; Recommendation No 15 (1989) of the Standing Committee on the conservation of endangered natural habitat types; Recommendation No 25 (1991) of the Standing Committee on the conservation of natural areas outside protected areas proper.

[84] Boere, above n 46.

[85] Coffey and Richartz, above n 73.

to particular sites and the scrutiny of any exceptions to the protection provided, it is the [Directive] rather than the Convention that will have a practical impact'.[86]

The Standing Committee of the Bern Convention identified the potential benefits of coordinating developments under the Habitats Directive and the Bern Convention. Significantly, in this respect, the coming into force of the Habitats Directive coincided with the breakup of the Communist *bloc* in Eastern Europe. With an eye very much to the east, the Standing Committee took the view that it was best to suspend all further administrative activities relating to the establishment of the Convention's Areas of Special Conservation Interest[87] and await the finalisation of site-conservation mechanisms under the proposed Habitats Directive. When the Standing Committee to the Convention resolved in 1996 to set up the Emerald Network[88] it modelled the new network on the new Habitats Directive. It was the express intention of the Standing Committee that the Emerald Network should not only provide a pan-European scheme that would facilitate preparations for Natura 2000 amongst the EU Candidate Countries, but that it would also provide a comparable ecological network to those countries unable or reluctant to join the EU.

The Convention Secretariat also 'revived' ideas introduced in 1989 by resolving to set up an all-embracing ecological network within the framework of the Bern Convention (the Emerald Network).[89] Thus, the regulatory provisions for the Emerald Network were deliberately drafted in such a way that Natura 2000 would effectively constitute a regional unit within the Emerald Network. The Emerald Network is an ecological network made up of Areas of Special Conservation Interest (ASCIs). It aims to identify and conserve areas of a great ecological value for both the threatened and endemic species listed in the Appendices of the Bern Convention and for the endangered habitat types which have been identified by the Standing Committee as 'requiring specific conservation measures'. It contributes to the setting-up of the Pan-European Ecological Network (PEEN) and facilitates the establishment of national networks of protected areas.[90] This network of sites seeks positively to influence the conditions for the survival of habitats and species in the fragmented natural areas and human dominated landscapes of Europe, through creation of 'core areas' (to provide the environmental conditions to conserve important ecosystems, habitats and species populations); 'corridors' (to interconnect the core areas); and 'buffer zones' (to protect the network from damaging impacts).

It is true that the 'network concept' was already a well-established conservation tool within the Council of Europe but the desire of candidate EU states from the Central and Eastern European States to ensure that they were EU-ready in terms

[86] Reid, above n 7, 7.5.21.
[87] Recommendation 16.
[88] Resolution No 3 (1996) of the Standing Committee concerning the setting up of a Pan-European Ecological Network.
[89] T-PVS (2001) 51.
[90] See T-PVS (1996) 102 and Resolution No 3 on the setting up of the Emerald Network.

of habitats law certainly helped increase the pressure for an increased priority for habitat protection. An important motivation for many Eastern European States in participating in the Bern Convention and the Emerald Network was that it assisted their aspirations to join the EU, membership of which would in due course require compliance with the Habitats Directive and implementation of Natura 2000.

Conclusion

Coffey and Richartz are quite correct in writing that: 'In effect, the Convention provided a model for the development of the Habitats Directive.'[91] Species and their habitats are not limited by the accidents of human political history. The Bern Convention's novel approach in allowing non-member States of the Council of Europe to become Contracting States was an important factor in its success, though the failure to secure Russia as a Contracting State remains a notable and significant omission.[92] The Bern Convention forced the EU to look to protecting species other than birds, and to recognise the indivisible link between species and habitat protection. The Bern Convention also set in place the overall structure and approach upon which the Habitats Directive is modelled.

The Bern Convention works very much upon persuasion. The institutional structure and transparency under which the Standing Committee operates means that Contracting States might be shamed into action by pressure brought by NGOs or the press. That may be contrasted with many other wildlife treaties signed before and after the Bern Convention which do not have the same instruments with which to coax Contracting Parties into compliance. But there are plainly limits to how far persuasion can succeed. There is an inherent tension between the needs of protecting species and their habitats and the economic imperatives driving development. The Bern Convention lacks the legal enforcement teeth necessary to deal with hard cases. The obligations under the Habitats Directive are not only more well defined than those under the Bern Convention but, importantly, are backed up by the legal enforcement mechanism of EU law.

The report of 5 January 2011 produced for the European Parliamentary Assembly of the Council of Europe on 'The Need to Assess the Progress in the Implementation of the Bern Convention'[93] highlighted some of the weaknesses of the Convention. It noted the acknowledgement by the Bern Convention that the

---

[91] Coffey and Richartz, above n 73.

[92] Report No12459 'The Need to Assess the Progress in the Implementation of the Bern Convention', above n 33, concluded on Russia's absence that: 'It is thus most unfortunate that a country of extreme importance for nature conservation has not yet joined the Convention.'

[93] Ibid.

enforcement of the Emerald Network through Natura 2000 within EU Member States should be left to the stricter provisions of the Habitats Directive:

> The rules of site designation specified in Article 4 of the Habitats Directive are actually stronger than the ones in Article 4 of the Bern Convention. The European Union also has stronger mechanisms of reporting and implementation: the European Commission monitors the creation of the Natura 2000 network and can react to non-compliance with the infringement procedure. The creation of the Natura 2000 network is followed by means of the so-called Natura 2000 Barometer, which is available to the public. Hence, it is only natural that the Standing Committee's Resolution No. 5 (1998) leaves implementation of the site protection objectives by the European Union member states to Natura 2000.

The report notes that the progress of non-EU Member States in setting up the Emerald Network has been slower than those of Member States. Even so, the record of the EU and its Member States in ensuring the level of strict protection which the Habitats Directive demands is mixed and the pressure to allow harmful economic development particularly in relation to major infrastructure schemes has at times proved difficult to resist. The progress achieved by EU Member States in respect of Natura 2000 is itself far from perfect. The report records that

> problems still exist in European Union countries. The Natura 2000 network has still not been finalised. According to the last Natura 2000 Barometer, the network can be assessed as largely complete for less than half of the European Union member states (Belgium, Denmark, Germany, Estonia, France, Italy, Luxembourg, the Netherlands and Poland for the Birds Directive, and Belgium, Denmark, Germany, Italy and Netherlands for the Habitats Directive) and incomplete for the rest. However, significant progress has been made recently in several member states and there is now no state for which the network would be assessed as notably insufficient.

Existing long before the term was coined, the Bern Convention could be said to be a good example of libertarian paternalism, the concept endorsed by Sunstein and Thaler in their 'nudge' theory.[94] More specifically, it might even be an application of what Waite calls the principle of equilibrium in environmental law.[95] It made an important start to the work of habitat conservation and was a key influence in creating and shaping the Birds and Habitats Directives. It still makes a valuable contribution. It is now plain that the persuasive approach of the Bern Convention alone is unlikely to secure the protection of endangered species. Yet it remains unclear whether the continued degradation of European species and habitats can be halted even with the added weight of the coercive powers of the Habitats Directive.

---

[94] Richard Thaler and Cass Sunstein, *Nudge: Improving Decisions about Health, Wealth, and Happiness* (Yale University Press, 2008).
[95] See Waite, ch 13 in this volume.

2

A Comparison of the Habitats Directive with the 1992 Convention on Biological Diversity

CATHERINE MACKENZIE

Introduction

The Council Directive on the conservation of natural habitats and of wild flora and fauna[1] (Habitats Directive) and the Convention on Biological Diversity[2] (CBD) have much in common. Both were created in 1992 and both seek to protect biodiversity. The aims of the CBD are, however, much more extensive than those of the Habitats Directive. In fact, some scholars suggest that that the CBD protects the evolutionary process within a framework of economic development and does not protect habitats, flora and fauna per se.

This chapter explores the origins and aims of the CBD, discusses its content and implementation, and concludes that although the CBD and the Habitats Directive have a number of common features, they have evolved in very different ways. This is significant because while the Habitats Directive imposes binding obligations, the CBD appears to mandate extensive obligations but is, in fact, a largely aspirational document with few binding requirements. This has implications for any party which seeks to rely on the CBD.

Origins

Biological diversity (commonly known as biodiversity) may be defined as the variety of forms of life that exist on earth. It includes species diversity, genetic diversity and ecosystem diversity. Ecosystem diversity includes habitats and

---

[1] Council Directive 92/43/EEC of 21 May 1992.
[2] Convention on Biological Diversity, 5 June 1992, 160 UNTS 79.

ecological processes and communities. Measures to protect biological diversity include species protection, habitat protection and protected areas.[3]

The origins of the CBD date back to the early 1980s. In the 1970s, population growth, industrialisation and urbanisation in mega-biodiverse regions, including Central America and East and South East Asia, caused demand for timber (for use in construction) to increase. This led to an increase in deforestation and a corresponding reduction in terrestrial biodiversity (much of which is forest-based). The initial response from the United Nations General Assembly (UNGA) was a 1980 resolution which recognised that the benefits which are obtained from nature depend on the maintenance of natural processes and on the diversity of life forms and that those benefits could be jeopardised by excessive exploitation and destruction of natural habitats.[4]

Throughout the 1980s, environmental issues gained political currency. In 1982, the UNGA adopted the World Charter for Nature,[5] Principle 2 of which states that genetic viability shall not be compromised and that habitats shall be safeguarded. The World Commission on Environment and Development (WCED) was the first body to propose that legal protection be developed for biological diversity. In 1987, the Report of that Commission (the Brundtland Report), *Our Common Future*,[6] made a number of recommendations, one of which was for the establishment of a convention under the terms of which wealthy countries would pay for actions to reduce or prevent the extinction of species and the destruction of habitats. This focus on biological diversity differed from the other proposals of the Report, many of which sought to redefine sustainable development. The UNGA accepted the Report,[7] endorsed its proposal for a conference[8] by resolving to convene the 1992 UN Conference on Environment and Development (UNCED) and brought biodiversity (together with deforestation, land-based pollution and climate change) within UNCED's mandate.[9]

Also in 1987, the US proposed that an umbrella convention be created to synthesise existing international agreements on nature conservation. In the same year, the International Union for the Conservation of Nature (IUCN) produced draft articles for inclusion in a biodiversity convention and in 1989, it revised those articles. These drafts addressed the need for global action to conserve biodiversity at the genetic, species and ecosystem levels and focused on *in situ* conservation within and outside protected areas. They also provided for a funding

---

[3] For legal approaches to biodiversity protection see, eg M Bowman and C Redgwell (eds), *International Law and the Conservation of Biological Diversity* (London, Kluwer Law International, 1996); C de Klemm and C Shine, *Biological Diversity Conservation and the Law: Legal Mechanisms for Conserving Species and Ecosystems* (Gland, IUCN, 1993); N Gunningham and MD Young, 'Towards Optimal Environmental Policy: The Case of Biodiversity Conservation' (1997) 24 *Ecology Law Quarterly* 243.

[4] UNGA Res 35/7 (1980).

[5] UNGA Res 37/7 (1982).

[6] WCED, *Our Common Future* (Oxford, Oxford University Press, 1987).

[7] UNGA Res 42/187 (1987).

[8] UNGA Res 43/196 (1988).

[9] UNGA Res 44/228 (1989).

mechanism to alleviate the inequality of the conservation burden between north and south since it was already recognised that without adequate funding, a new convention would achieve little.

Recognising the need to coordinate international efforts to protect biodiversity, the Governing Council of the UN Environmental Programme (UNEP) established a Working Group (which later became an Intergovernmental Negotiating Committee) in 1987 'to consider the desirability and possible form of an umbrella convention to rationalize current activities'.[10] The first meeting of the Working Group found that existing international agreements addressed specific questions of biodiversity conservation but only on a piecemeal basis. For example, at the global level existing conventions covered internationally important natural sites (1972 World Heritage Convention), trade in endangered species (1973 Convention on International Trade in Endangered Species), a specific ecosystem type (1971 Ramsar Convention on Wetlands of International Importance) and a group of species (1979 Bonn Convention on the Conservation of Migratory Species of Wild Animals). There were also numerous regional agreements with varying degrees of comprehensiveness and effectiveness. These agreements did not, however, provide a framework for protection of biodiversity at a global level and by 1989 it had become clear that a new framework treaty was needed.

In 1989 UNEP authorised the commencement of work on a draft treaty[11] and prepared a first draft using the IUCN draft articles, another draft from the Food and Agriculture Organization (FAO) and a number of studies commissioned by UNEP. The result was a broad draft which incorporated all the elements of the constituent drafts and was not particularly well edited. Between 1989 and 1992 the draft was further enlarged to include access to genetic resources and biotechnology, access to the benefits derived from that technology, safety of activities related to modified living organisms and provision of new financial support.

In 1992, UNCED was held at Rio de Janeiro. It was designed to be a comprehensive response to the conflicting priorities of environmental and economic development. However, its preparatory committees, and subsequently the Conference itself, were characterised by north/south dispute about sovereignty over natural resources, the equitable sharing of the costs of conservation, transfer of biotechnology and economic development.[12] Several of these issues were directly related to biodiversity which, together with deforestation, proved to be UNCED's most controversial issues. In general terms, the north interpreted the environmental crises as a technical issue whereas developing states contextualised it as a consequence of development. Attempts by the north to restrict the use of natural resources, including biodiversity, were interpreted by the south as a threat to sovereignty. Similarly, the south resented the north's reluctance to share the costs of action on

---

[10] UNEP Governing Council Res 14/26 (1987).

[11] UNEP Governing Council Res 15/34 (1989).

[12] For the position taken by developing countries, see the Beijing Ministerial Declaration on Environment and Development, adopted at the Ministerial Conference of Developing Countries on Environment and Development on 19 June 1991: UN Doc A/CONF.151/PC/85 (1991).

biodiversity and deforestation since from the south's point of view, biodiversity loss and deforestation were a direct result of development in the north. As a result of this disagreement, UNCED's capacity to reach a binding agreement on major issues was limited.[13] On 22 May 1992 the final draft of the new biodiversity treaty, with significantly weaker obligations than UNEP had intended, was agreed and on 5 June 1992 at UNCED, 157 states signed the CBD.[14] Approximately 18 months later, on 29 December 1993, the CBD came into force.

Aims

The CBD has three aims:[15] the conservation of biological diversity; the sustainable use of its components; and the fair and equitable sharing of the benefits arising from the utilisation of genetic resources. Implementation of the CBD is governed by a Conference of the Parties (COP) established by Article 23 of the Convention, but the CBD has no monitoring or compliance mechanisms, nor does it provide for the settlement of disputes by a third party process.[16]

In contrast, the Habitats Directive aims to contribute to the maintenance of biodiversity through the conservation of natural habitats and wild flora and fauna. It does so by the maintenance and protection of Special Areas of Conservation (SAC).[17] While both instruments include obligations which have been the subject of disputes, it is fair to say that overall, the Habitats Directive is a much more straightforward instrument than the CBD.[18]

Content

The CBD is the first international instrument to address all aspects of biodiversity. Acknowledging the point made in earlier international documents, including the

[13] UNCED agreed the non-binding Rio Declaration, Agenda 21 and Forest Principles and the binding but limited United Nations Framework Convention on Climate Change. For disagreement on biodiversity issues before and at UNCED see, eg G Palmer, 'The Earth Summit: What Went Wrong at Rio?' (1992) 70 *Washington University Law Quarterly* 1005.

[14] For a description of the negotiating history of the CBD, see F McConnell, *The Biodiversity Convention: A Negotiating History* (London, Kluwer Law International, 1996).

[15] CBD, Art 1.

[16] CBD, Art 27 provides that in the event of a dispute concerning 'the interpretation or application' of the Convention, parties are to negotiate and may refer the dispute to arbitration or to the ICJ but neither procedure is compulsory unless it has been so accepted by a party.

[17] As to the designation process and status afforded to candidate SACs see Jones and Westaway, ch 4 in this volume.

[18] For a legal analysis of the CBD see, eg P Birnie, AE Boyle and C Redgwell, *International Law and the Environment* (3rd edn) (Oxford, Oxford University Press, 2009) chs 11–12; AE Boyle, 'The Rio Convention on Biological Diversity' in M Bowman and C Redgwell (eds), *International Law and the Conservation of Biological Diversity* (London, Kluwer Law International, 1996); L Glowka et al, *A Guide to the Convention on Biological Diversity* (Gland, IUCN, 1994).

World Conservation Strategy,[19] *Caring for the Earth*[20] and the *Global Biodiversity Strategy*,[21] that biodiversity and biological resources should be conserved for reasons of ethics, economic benefit and human survival, the CBD extends beyond the straightforward conservation of biodiversity and includes access to genetic resources, the sharing of benefits derived from those genetic resources and access to, and transfer of technology, including biotechnology. This approach makes the CBD significant for three reasons: it takes a comprehensive rather than sectoral view of the conservation of biodiversity; it was the first time that genetic diversity was specifically addressed in a binding international agreement; and it was also the first time that biodiversity was recognised as a common global concern. Unfortunately, this approach also gives the CBD three major constraints: it narrates intentions not obligations; it is characterised by weak commitments not specific obligations; and the comprehensive approach it adopts to biodiversity causes its relationship with existing treaties to be unclear.

Intention Not Obligation

The CBD is a framework agreement in two senses. First, it sets out overall goals and principles for future law-making rather than creating specific obligations. Those obligations are the responsibility of subsequent Conferences of the Parties, which may (or may not) develop protocols which incorporate specific measures. This framework technique is an increasingly common form of international environmental law-making and it distinguishes the CBD from earlier treaties, such as the 1973 Convention in International Trade in Endangered Species which sets out obligations for the parties and includes appendices in which species are categorised according to the extent to which they are threatened with extinction. Secondly, Article 28 of the CBD requires the parties to cooperate in the formulation and adoption of protocols. This provides for development over time as circumstances change and suggests that although the CBD does not include the term 'framework' in its title, it is a framework agreement in the sense that much specific detail is left to the cooperation of the parties in future negotiations.

Weakness of Obligations

Compared with the Habitats Directive, the CBD lacks both overarching principles and the detail which may be necessary for it to be capable of enforcement. It does not, for example, refer directly to the precautionary principle, nor is there any requirement that ecosystem management be undertaken on a scientific basis.[22]

---

[19] IUCN, UNEP and WWF, *World Conservation Strategy* (Gland, IUCN, 1980).

[20] IUCN, UNEP and WWF, *Caring for the Earth* (Gland, IUCN, 1991).

[21] World Resources Institute, IUCN and WWF, *Global Biodiversity Strategy* (Gland, IUCN, 1992).

[22] See, eg LD Guruswamy, 'The Convention on Biological Diversity, Exposing the Flawed Foundations' (1999) 26 *Environmental Conservation* 79.

The CBD begins by outlining its definitions, objectives and jurisdiction[23] but it does not define 'conservation' and defines 'sustainable use' only in very general terms.[24] In environmental law, the concept of sustainable use is articulated in at least four different ways. In fisheries, sustainable use translates into the setting of quotas. In biotechnology and the use of genetic resources, it translates into ensuring that the release of genetically modified organisms will not cause irreversible damage through species pollution. In natural habitats, it is expressed as the development of systems of integrated management, and in sites of global significance, the emphasis tends to be on the preservation of those sites for future generations. The CBD merges the concepts of biodiversity conservation and sustainable use and uses both in a number of different ways. In some places, the text refers to the 'conservation and sustainable use of biological diversity'[25] while in others, it is 'the conservation of biological diversity, the sustainable use of its components'.[26] Consequently, many of its obligations lack specificity.

The definition of biological diversity in Article 2 creates further potential difficulty since it includes 'diversity within species' as well as diversity 'between species and of ecosystems'. This implies the retention both of the number of species and of a viable population size within each species. This requires the retention of representative samples of all natural habitats, together with the retention of an amount of natural habitat sufficient to support viable populations. Many of the CBD's obligations relate to individual biological resources rather than to diversity per se. Arguably, the conservation of biodiversity requires the implementation of separate obligations on the different elements (ecosystems, species and genetic resources) that together comprise biodiversity. While some scholars suggest that the CBD accurately reflects notions of conservation of the period in which it was negotiated, [27] the result is a confusing text.

From the outset, the obligations of the CBD have been weak. For example, customary international law and many international agreements require cooperation between states, supported by prior consultation based on adequate information, in order to minimise the extraterritorial effects of activities within the jurisdiction or control of each state, while the CBD requires only that parties 'promote on a reciprocal basis' notification, exchange of information and consultation.[28]

Article 6, which requires each party to develop national strategies, plans and programs by which the objectives of the Convention are to be achieved, includes the phrase 'in accordance with its particular conditions and capabilities'. This may

---

[23] CBD, Arts 1–4.

[24] Art 2 of the CBD defines sustainable use as 'the use of components of biological diversity in a way and at a rate that does not lead to the long term decline of biological diversity, thereby maintaining its potential to meet the needs and aspirations of present and future generations'.

[25] CBD Arts 5, 6, 7, 8(g), 10(a), 11, 12, 13, 16, 17, 18, 19, 21, 23, 25.

[26] CBD Arts 1, 8(i).

[27] See, eg Glowka et al, above n 18, 4.

[28] CBD, Art 14.

weaken obligations considerably as it enables states to argue that certain measures, while being desirable, are beyond national capacity.

Articles 7 to 13 set out measures which are to be taken by the parties. These include identification; monitoring; *in situ* and (unlike the Habitats Directive) *ex situ* conservation; research and training; and public education. These obligations would be extensive were they to be absolute, but many of these obligations are prefaced with the words 'each Contracting party shall, as far as possible and appropriate'. This was designed to ensure that the extent of implementation of obligations is proportionate to the capacity of each party to meet each obligation, but by permitting states to determine what is possible and appropriate without regard to overarching principles, the obligations of the CBD are considerably weakened. Furthermore, this focus on decision-making at the national level means that there are no annexes of sites or species, no lists of measures to be taken by the parties and no guidance on whether, for example, quotas for species should be established and, if so, on what basis those quotas would operate. These are matters for national governments.

Article 14 refers to environmental impact assessment (EIA). It requires parties to 'introduce appropriate procedures requiring environmental impact assessment of its proposed projects that are likely to have significant adverse impacts on biological diversity'. This appears to refer both to damage within and beyond one's sovereign territory so its scope is greater than that of earlier treaties which require environmental impact assessments solely in the context of transboundary harm (that is, the purpose of those treaties is to protect other States, or areas beyond national jurisdiction such as the high seas).[29] Unlike the Habitats Directive, however, Article 6(3) of which specifies the type of activity which is to be assessed (any plan or project) and the requirement that 'a plan or project'[30] be approved only where it has been ascertained that there will be no adverse effect on a SAC,[31] the CBD leaves these matters to the discretion of the parties. This enables parties to avoid undertaking EIAs by determining that such assessments are not appropriate. Further, the CBD requires public participation only 'as appropriate' with that appropriateness (or otherwise) being determined by each party. Article 14 of the CBD requires that certain measures be taken for projects that are 'likely to have significant adverse impacts on biological diversity' but in many cases, it will not be known whether adverse impacts are likely until some form of environmental impact assessment has taken place. It is, therefore, clear that there are numerous ways in which the Article 14 requirement to undertake an EIA may be minimised or avoided.

---

[29] See, eg 1983 Convention for the Protection and Development of the Marine Environment of the Wider Caribbean Area, Art 12; 1986 Convention for the Protection of the Natural Resources and Environment of the South Pacific Region, Art 16; 1991 Convention on Environmental Impact Assessment in a Transboundary Context.

[30] For consideration as to the meaning of 'plan or programme' see Tromans, ch 5 in this volume.

[31] For a discussion on the meaning of adverse effect on the integrity of the objectives of the SAC see Jones, ch 9 in this volume.

Article 14(2) introduces the notion of liability for damage and compensation. It states: 'The Conference of the Parties shall examine, on the basis of studies to be carried out, the issue of liability and redress, including restoration and compensation, for damage to biological diversity, except where such liability is a purely internal matter.' Again, this is a weak obligation. First, the issue is delegated to the COP. Secondly, the COP is required only to 'examine', not to take action. Thirdly, the final clause appears to exclude from examination damage that takes place within a state's sovereign territory, notwithstanding that almost any damage to biodiversity may have long-term transboundary effects. Customary international law holds states responsible for ensuring that activities conducted within their boundaries do not cause damage to the environment of other states or to areas beyond national jurisdiction but the CBD does not reflect this and is thus inconsistent with that body of law.

Further ambiguity is found in Articles 15 and 16 which provide for the use of genetic resources. During the 1980s as biotechnology developed its value was recognised and several countries restricted access to, and developed intellectual property legislation to protect, their genetic resources. Generally states were concerned about three types of access: access to genetic resources; access to technology including biotechnology; and access to the benefits derived from the use of genetic resources in the development of biotechnology. Article 15 provides that the removal of genetic resources from a country is subject to the consent of the country of origin and is to be on mutually agreed terms. The precise arrangements for this are to be negotiated by each state. As with any negotiation, much depends on the relative bargaining power of the parties and the skill of their representatives, particularly as identification of the material from which benefit is gained may be difficult: benefits may not emerge for many years and may accrue from genetic material gathered from several sources. Article 16 seeks to uphold intellectual property rights over technology and Article 16(2) requires that access to, and transfer of technology, occurs under 'fair and most favourable terms', but for technology which is subject to patents and other intellectual property rights, access and transfer is to be provided on terms which are consistent with the 'adequate and effective' protection of intellectual property rights.

There are at least three reasons why these provisions may be problematic. First, many governments are reluctant to compel companies and private parties to transfer technologies that may not be available commercially, or they may lack effective power to do so. Secondly, there are likely to be objections to the terms on which such transfers take place, particularly if those terms do not reflect market prices.[32] Thirdly, intellectual property rights may be lost, or at least weakened, if transfer is required. Article 16(4) adds to this complexity since it requires each party to take legislative, administrative or policy measures 'with the aim that the private sector facilitates access to, joint development and transfer of, technology ...

---

[32] See, eg DV Eugui, 'Issues Linked to the Convention on Biological Diversity in the WTO Negotiations: Implementing the Doha Mandates' (2002) Center for International Environmental Law, Geneva.

for the benefit of both government institutions and the private sector of developing countries'. How this is to be ensured is not specified and it appears to be inconsistent with the principles of the free market.

Article 16(5) recognises that intellectual property rights may influence the implementation of the CBD and requires cooperation 'subject to national legislation and international law' to ensure that 'rights are supportive and do not run counter to its [the CBD's] objectives'. This creates four further difficulties. First, it is not clear what type of cooperation is required. Second, any cooperation is subject to legislation which is almost invariably designed to restrict access to intellectual property. Third, the objectives of the CBD are so broad that it would be possible for some intellectual property transactions to be consistent with one of the CBD's objectives but inconsistent with others. Fourth, the provisions on technology transfer and on access to the benefits of biotechnology are limited by the definition of genetic resources in Article 15(3). Excluded from the CBD are genetic resources placed in gene banks and other *ex situ* facilities before the CBD entered into force. Consequently, any party which signed the CBD in June 1992 could protect its resources by placing samples in such facilities before the CBD became effective 18 months later, in December 1993.

The CBD raises (but fails to resolve) many questions about the intellectual property of biodiversity which are beyond the scope of this chapter. For example, it seeks to protect intellectual property rights but genetic resources which have not been scientifically altered are generally not patentable but a new process for isolating and developing genetic material from a species usually is, as is a new use for an existing resource. Such questions rarely, if ever, arise in relation to the Habitats Directive.

Article 20 of the CBD seeks to regulate funding for implementation of the Convention. Funds are to come first from states themselves, then from the provision of 'new and additional' financial resources which are to be transferred from north to south and finally by means of multilateral mechanisms. Article 21 provides that there will be a mechanism for the provision of financial resources to developing countries for the purposes of the Convention, but does not state how much assistance is to be provided, to whom, and on what terms. Agreement, however, was qualified. A joint declaration by 19 developed states, issued at the time the CBD was signed, asserted that nothing in Articles 20 and 21 authorised the COP to make decisions about 'the amount, nature, frequency or size' of contributions. A further difficulty was caused by the fact that the CBD does not identify which states are considered to be 'developed' or 'developing' but required that categorisation to be undertaken by the COP. This was not a simple matter.

Article 20(4) significantly weakens the CBD in its entirety by stating:

> The extent to which developing country Parties will effectively implement their commitments under this Convention will depend on the effective implementation by developed country Parties of their commitments under this Convention related to financial resources and transfer of technology and will take fully into account the fact that

economic and social development and eradication of poverty are the first and overriding priorities of the developing country Parties.

This acknowledges that ultimately, implementation of the CBD will be limited by two factors. First, the extent of implementation in the south will depend on the implementation by the north of its commitment to financial resources and technology transfer. Secondly, economic and social development and the eradication of poverty are the 'overriding priorities' of the south. No guidance is offered by the CBD on the complex task of reconciling the protection of biodiversity with the 'overriding priorities' of economic and social development and eradication of poverty and it appears from Article 20(4) that a state may prioritise such development over all other obligations, including the EIA requirement of Article 14. This suggests that the CBD's EIA requirement is considerably less onerous than that of Article 6(3) of the Habitats Directive.

The CBD, like many modern international environmental treaties, gives the COP a supervisory role but on the spectrum of treaty supervisory bodies, the COP is relatively weak. This is because Article 26 requires states to report to the COP on the effectiveness of the implementation of their obligations but there is no means by which this reporting requirement can be enforced since there is no formal non-compliance mechanism or sanction. Parties may opt out of new or amended annexes by express objection within one year so may exempt themselves from certain aspects of the CBD which do not suit their political or other agendas.

The provision the CBD makes for dispute settlement is also not strong.[33] Article 27 states that in the event of a dispute between parties concerning the 'interpretation or application' of the CBD, the parties 'shall seek solution by negotiation'. If negotiation fails, the parties 'may' request mediation by a third party. There is no obligation to seek mediation and no requirement to proceed to arbitration, or to the International Court of Justice (although both are mentioned) and if they do not do so, the dispute is to be submitted to conciliation 'unless the parties otherwise agree'.[34] The conciliation commission will make proposals for resolution of the dispute, which the parties concerned must consider (not accept) in good faith. This, of course, is very different from the enforcement procedures of EU law, of which the Habitats Directive is a part. In practical terms, the Habitats Directive is enforceable while the CBD is not.

In order to ensure that the CBD was agreed at UNCED, three provisions were deleted from drafts. First, a statement that lack of scientific certainty was not to be used as a reason for inaction was transferred from the main text to the preamble, causing its status to be unclear. Secondly, a statement that those responsible for activities that damaged or threatened biodiversity would be liable for the costs of remedying the damage was deleted. Such direct attribution of liability for

---

[33] For a discussion of dispute settlement in the context of benefit sharing see, eg B Pisupati, *Issues of Compliance: Considerations for the International Regime on Access and Benefit Sharing* (Nairobi, UNEP, 2009).

[34] CBD, Art 27(4).

environmental damage was, however, unusual in international environmental treaties so the deletion was consistent with accepted views at that time. Thirdly, a proposal that lists of protected species and areas be adopted by the COP was also deleted, leaving the selection and management of protected species and areas to each party. The outcome was a treaty which, at best, lacks clarity.

Relationship with Existing Treaties

The relationship between the CBD and existing treaties is complex. Article 22 of the CBD states that the CBD 'shall not affect the rights and obligations of a Contracting Party deriving from any existing international agreement, except where the exercise of those rights and obligations would cause a serious damage or threat to biological diversity'. From this, it appears that the CBD is subsidiary to other treaties, except in situations in which other treaties may damage or threaten biodiversity. However, the 1969 Vienna Convention on the Law of Treaties (the authoritative international law on treaties) includes two provisions which are relevant to the interaction between the CBD and other treaties: Article 59 which provides for the termination or suspension of the operation of a treaty implied by the conclusion of a later treaty; and Article 30 which provides for the application of successive treaties relating to the same subject matter. By Article 59 of the Vienna Convention, an earlier treaty will be terminated if the parties conclude a later treaty which relates to the same subject matter and if it appears from the later treaty that the parties intended that the matter should to be governed by that treaty or if the provisions of the later treaty are so far incompatible with the earlier treaty that the two treaties are not capable of being applied at the same time. An earlier treaty will only be considered to be suspended if it appears from the later treaty, or is otherwise established, that such was the intention of the parties (Article 59(2)). Article 59 confirms that in the case of conflicting treaty obligations, the later treaty shall prevail, but this provision has a narrow application since it applies only in cases where it is clear from the treaty itself, or from the conduct of the parties, that the parties intend that their relationship be governed by the later treaty. The alternative, that the provisions of both treaties be so incompatible that they are incapable of being applied simultaneously, would require conflict so extensive that it is difficult to envisage in the context of the CBD.

Article 30 of the Vienna Convention creates rules for interpreting successive treaties which relate to the same subject matter.[35] First, by Article 30(2), when a treaty specifies that it is subject to, or that it is not to be considered as incompatible with, an earlier or later treaty, the provisions of that other treaty prevail. Secondly, by Article 30(3) when all the parties to the earlier treaty are also parties

---

[35] For more detailed discussion of the interpretation of successive treaties see A Aust, *Modern Treaty Law and Practice* (2nd edn) (Cambridge, Cambridge University Press, 2007).

to the later treaty but the earlier treaty remains operative, the earlier treaty will apply only to the extent that its provisions are compatible with those of the later treaty. Thirdly, by Article 30(4), when the parties to the later treaty do not include all the parties to the earlier treaty, the rule in Article 30(3) applies as between states who are parties to both treaties. Fourthly, also by Article 30(4), when one state is a party to both treaties and the other state is a party to only one of the treaties, the treaty to which both are parties governs their mutual rights and obligations. As other conservation agreements are unlikely to be inconsistent with the CBD, complex rules of treaty interpretation are unlikely to be relevant, but there are fisheries agreements under which excessive exploitation of stocks takes place,[36] so it is certainly possible that parties to the CBD could have conflicting commitments in those areas. This suggests a conflict between the holistic approach of the CBD to the protection of species and habitats and the resource management focus of older agreements.

Implementation

The CBD is one of the most widely-accepted international agreements: by early 2011, 192 States and the EU had become parties. Globally, there is extensive evidence of biodiversity and habitat activity, much of which emanates from the CBD. In its early years, for example, the CBD created a Secretariat,[37] a Subsidiary Body on Scientific, Technical and Technological Advice (SBSTTA),[38] a Clearing House Mechanism,[39] and Working Groups of Experts on Biosafety[40] and on Biodiversity Education and Public Awareness.[41] In 2000, in response to increasing concerns about living modified organisms (LMOs), it developed the Cartagena Protocol on Biosafety, the purpose of which is to contribute to the safe transfer, handling and use of bio-engineered products that cross international borders.[42] In 2002, it adopted the Bonn Guidelines on Access to Genetic Resources and the Fair and Equitable Sharing of Benefits Arising out of their Utilization[43] and in 2010, the Nagoya Protocol on Access to Genetic Resources and the Fair and

---

[36] It is likely that exploitation of this nature breaches Art 22 CBD, which refers to 'serious damage or threat to biological diversity'.

[37] CBD COP Decision I/4 (1994).

[38] CBD COP Decision I/7 (1994).

[39] CBD COP Decision I/3 (1994).

[40] CBD COP Decision II/5 (1995).

[41] CBD COP Decision V/17 (2000).

[42] The Cartagena Protocol on Biosafety establishes an advanced informed agreement procedure for ensuring that countries are provided with the information necessary to make informed decisions before agreeing to the import of LMOs into their territory. It also establishes a BioSafety Clearing House to facilitate the exchange of information on LMOs and to assist countries in the implementation of the protocol. The Protocol is one of the most extensive elaborations of the precautionary principle in international law.

[43] CBD COP Decision VI/24 (2002).

Equitable Sharing of Benefits Arising from their Utilization was agreed. The CBD's COP has held 10 meetings and one extraordinary meeting and its Secretariat has signed Memoranda of Cooperation with many other treaty bodies, international organisations and related entities. To date, 173 parties have developed National Biodiversity Strategies and Action Plans (NBSAPs) and at the most recent reporting date, March 2009, 160 parties provided National Reports.

These institutional and administrative measures do not, however, provide comprehensive information on the effectiveness of the CBD in protecting biodiversity and its habitats. In fact, it is difficult to reach conclusions about effectiveness as the Secretariat relies on voluntary national reporting and even if national reporting were to be complete and correct, there is ample evidence from other treaties which confirms that compliance with, and implementation of, international obligations does not necessarily achieve the intended outcomes. There is extensive literature on the text of the CBD[44] but research on its implementation tends to focus on individual species, geographical areas or the relationship of the CBD to other issues (such as biotechnology).[45] In the 1990s, a small number of scholars

---

[44] See, eg AE Boyle, 'The Rio Convention on Biological Diversity' in M Bowman and C Redgwell (eds), *International Law and the Conservation of Biological Diversity* (London, Kluwer, 1996); DT Jenks, 'Comment, The Convention on Biological Diversity—An Efficient Framework for the Preservation of Life on Earth?' (1995) 15 *Northwestern Journal of International Law & Business* 636; C Shine and PTB Kohana, 'The Convention on Biological Diversity: Bridging the Gap Between Conservation and Development' (1992) 1 *Review of European Community and International Environmental Law* 278; C Tinker, 'Introduction to Biological Diversity: Law, Institutions and Science' (1994) 1 *Buffalo Journal of International Law* 1; C Tinker, 'A "New Breed" of Treaty: The United Nations Convention on Biological Diversity' (1995) 13 *Pace Environmental Law Review* 191; C Tinker, 'Responsibility for Biological Diversity Conservation Under International Law' (1995) 28 *Vanderbilt Journal of Transnational Law* 777.

[45] See, eg JH Bock and K Human, 'NGOs and the Protection of Biodiversity: The Ecologists' View' (2002) 13 *Colorado Journal of International Environmental Law and Policy* 167; S Bhutani and A Kothari, 'The Biodiversity Rights of Developing Nations: A Perspective from India' (2002) 32 *Golden Gate University Law Review* 587; RF Blomquist, 'Protecting Nature "Down Under": An American Professor's View of Australia's Implementation of the Convention on Biological Diversity—Laws, Policies, Programs, Institutions and Plans, 1992–2000' (2000) 9 *Dickinson Journal of Environmental Law and Policy* 227; RF Blomquist, 'Ratification Resisted: Understanding America's Response to the Convention on Biological Diversity' (2002) 32 *Golden Gate University Law Review* 493; KC Cha, 'Can the Convention on Biological Diversity Save the Siberian Tiger?' (2001) 24 *Environs Environmental Law and Policy Journal* 3; J Chen, 'Webs of Life: Biodiversity Conservation as a Species of Information Policy' (2004) 89 *Iowa Law Review* 495; H Doremus, 'Biodiversity and the Challenge of Saving the Ordinary' (2002) 38 *Idaho Law Review* 325; LA Firestone, 'You Say Yes, I Say No; Defining Community Prior Informed Consent Under the Convention on Biological Diversity' (2003) 16 *Georgetown International Environmental Law Review* 171; A Goldman, 'Compensation for Use of Biological Resources Under the Convention on Biological Diversity: Compatibility of Conservation Measures and Competitiveness of the Biotechnology Industry' (1994) 25 *Law and Policy in International Business* 695; JH Goldstein, 'The Prospects of Using Market Incentives to Conserve Biological Diversity' (1991) 21 *Environmental Law* 985; CD Jacoby and C Weiss, 'Recognizing Property Rights in Traditional Biocultural Contribution' (1997) 16 *Stanford Environmental Law Journal* 74; BC Karkkainen, 'Biodiversity and Land' (1997) 83 *Cornell Law Review* 1; JC Kunich, 'Fiddling Around While the Hot Spots Burn Off' (2001) 14 *Georgetown International Environmental Law Review* 179; CR McManis, 'The Interface Between International Intellectual Property and Environmental Protection: Biodiversity and Biotechnology' (1998) 76 *Washington University Law Quarterly* 255.

attempted to review the effectiveness of the CBD on a global scale.[46] Generally, that research suggested that the effectiveness of the CBD varies significantly according to region, and overall, the outlook was not optimistic. More recent scholarly work generally accepts that while there may be a correlation between the implementation of the CBD and biodiversity and habitat protection, it is impossible to state categorically that the CBD has caused a reduction in biodiversity loss. Nonetheless, three early accounts are worth a brief mention.

The first, a 1993 comment by Chandler, Counsel to the US negotiating team, is a damning assessment of the CBD text. It did, however, acknowledge that at the time at which it was written, it was too early to comment on implementation.[47] The second is a 1997 assessment by Fiona McConnell,[48] who led the Foreign and Commonwealth Office team which negotiated the CBD. McConnell stated that after a weak start, by 1995 'clearer progress could be discerned'.[49] The progress to which McConnell referred is administrative (for example, the establishment of a Secretariat, strategies, steering groups and action plans) and did not include developments in the progress of species or habitats. McConnell also suggested that it would be 'a long time' before parties agree to practical measures for the 'fair and equitable sharing of the benefits arising out of the utilisation of genetic resources'.[50] At the time of writing, almost 19 years after the CBD was agreed, the Nagoya Protocol on benefit sharing is open for signature. It will be some time before the Protocol is operative.

The third, a 2002 assessment by Le Prestre,[51] adopted a different approach. Describing the CBD as 'wide-ranging, ambitious, and deeply political',[52] it recognised that limited progress had been made and that funding remained inadequate but argued that since knowledge about the state of biodiversity is scant and indicators poor, assessment of the CBD's effectiveness should be based on its ability to promote several of the preconditions of regime effectiveness, such as capacity-building, networking, transparency and the elaboration and diffusion of new norms. It suggested that the CBD offers a set of principles, priorities

[46] See, eg B Hendriks, 'Transformative Possibilities: Reinventing the Convention on Biological Diversity' in GD Lakshman and JA McNeely (eds), *Protection of Global Biodiversity: Converging Strategies* (Durham, Duke University Press, 1998); A Hubbard, 'Comment, The Convention on Biological Diversity's Fifth Anniversary: A General Overview of the Convention—Where It Has Been, and Where Is It Going ?' (1997) 10 *Tulane Environmental Law Journal* 415; D Vice, 'Implementation of Biodiversity Treaties: Monitoring, Fact-Finding and Dispute Resolution' (1997) 29 *New York University Journal of International Law and Politics* 577; C Wold, 'The Futility, Utility and Future of the Biodiversity Convention' (1998) 9 *Colorado Journal of International Environmental Law & Policy* 1.
[47] M Chandler, 'The Biodiversity Convention: Selected Issues of Interest to the International Lawyer' (1993) 4 *Colorado Journal of International Environmental Law and Policy* 141.
[48] F McConnell, 'The Convention on Biological Diversity' in F Dodds (ed), *The Way Forward: Beyond Agenda 21* (London, Earthscan, 1997).
[49] Ibid, 52.
[50] Ibid, 54.
[51] PG Le Prestre, 'The CBD at Ten: The Long Road to Effectiveness' (2002) 5 *Journal of International Wildlife Law & Policy* 269.
[52] Ibid, 270.

and instruments that have the potential to represent a new world order based on natural and human diversity, equity, respect for life, access to basic resources and harnessing of the natural world for human welfare. This, according to Le Prestre, promotes a new relationship with nature that seeks to reconcile the intrinsic value of biodiversity with dominant utilitarian arguments. It also affirms the primary goal of social and economic development. Le Prestre concluded by suggesting that the effectiveness of the CBD will depend on strengthening the determinants of regime effectiveness. For Le Prestre, the CBD goes beyond the protection of biodiversity and offers the promise of reordering fundamental relations among human communities. This it may do, but Le Prestre did not suggest that the CBD had reduced the rate of biodiversity loss.

As more recent assessments have noted, it is difficult to evaluate the effectiveness of an instrument which sets obligations but which requires the implementation of many of those obligations only 'as far as possible and appropriate'. That may be one of the reasons why international courts and tribunals have been reluctant to give much weight to the CBD, although until recently, such courts have been reluctant to consider scientific and technical data on many other areas of environmental protection.

There is one recent international case in which a party sought to rely on the CBD. That is the International Court of Justice (ICJ) case of Pulp Mills (*Argentina v Uruguay*),[53] judgment in which was handed down in April 2010. That case concerned the construction and operation of a pulp mill in Uruguay, on the banks of the River Uruguay, a river which is shared with, and is part of the border between, Argentina and Uruguay. This was a large construction project, funding for which was obtained from several commercial and other sources, including an investment of US$70m from the International Finance Corporation and a Multilateral Investment Guarantee Agency (MIGA) guarantee of up to US$350m. Argentina asserted that Uruguay's approval of the project breached the 1975 Statue of the River Uruguay, a bilateral agreement between Argentina and Uruguay, under the terms of which Uruguay was required notify and consult with Argentina on use of the river. Argentina further argued that operation of the mill had caused, and was continuing to cause ecological damage and so constituted a breach of Uruguay's international environmental obligations, including its obligations under the CBD.

The ICJ refused applications from both parties for provisional measures and held, in its 2010 judgment, that Uruguay had breached its procedural obligations under the 1975 Statute but had not breached its substantive obligations (including an obligations under Article 41 of that Statute to preserve the aquatic environment). The Court did not require Uruguay to pay compensation to Argentina, nor did it order that the Pulp Mill cease operations, both of which had been sought by Argentina. The Court held that it may now be considered a

---

[53] Case Concerning Pulp Mills on the River Uruguay (*Argentina v Uruguay*), ICJ, (2010), para 204.

requirement under general international law to conduct an EIA where there is a risk that the proposed industrial activity may have a significant adverse impact in a transboundary context, in particular on a shared resource, but expressed its view that the content of the EIA is a matter for each State to determine, having regard to the magnitude of the project and the likely adverse impact on the environment. The Court also stated that measures adopted by the parties under Article 41 (that is, for aquatic protection) should reflect their international undertakings in respect of biodiversity and habitats[54] but it did not make any finding on Uruguay's obligations under the CBD and rejected all other submissions. There does not appear to be any other case in which the ICJ has relied on the CBD so it is difficult to suggest that the CBD has influenced that court. In contrast, the Habitats Directive is cited regularly in EU matters and has informed many of the UK's environmental policies.

Conclusion

With hindsight, it appears that many parties understood the CBD as being only indirectly related to the protection of biodiversity and habitats. The G-77 regarded agreement on the CBD as one aspect of a broader agenda by which UNCED was to be used to restructure global economic relations in order to obtain resources, technology and access to markets necessary for economic development. For much of the south, the key issues appear to have been the establishment of mechanisms by which the south would receive compensation for the north's use of its biotechnology and access to biotechnology and the establishment of intellectual property rights over the products of biotechnology. The north's position was also ambiguous. The US, for example, has extensive domestic legislation on biodiversity and habitat protection but it opposed the CBD because it undermined the US's interpretation of intellectual property rights, because of weaknesses in the CBD's text (including the weak EIA obligation and its unclear relationship with other treaties) and the speed at which it had been negotiated (which had prevented proper consideration of the document as a whole).[55] The EU noted that the CBD was weaker than its own directives but it did not share to the same degree the US's objections to the transfer of technology and access to biotechnology.

In contrast, notwithstanding disputes on points of interpretation, it is accepted throughout the EU that the Habitats Directive requires that measures be taken to conserve natural habitats and protect species.

In conclusion, the regime established by the CBD offered an opportunity for States to cooperate in the protection of biodiversity. Had this been fully effective,

---

[54] Ibid, para 262.
[55] The US signed the CBD on 4 June 1993 but has not yet ratified it on the grounds that the text is inherently flawed.

there might have been no need for the Habitats Directive since the CBD and subsequent initiatives developed under the regime it created would have provided adequate protection. History suggests that it was naive to expect that the animosity which characterised international negotiations on biodiversity in the early 1990s would be transformed into cooperation by little more than a signature on an international document. It is now also clear that that the notion that the north would share its financial and technological resources with the south (and provide 'new and additional resources') was equally naive, although not necessarily any more so than the notion that resources provided to the south would be used for the purpose for which they were intended.

Overall, the CBD is weaker than other international environmental agreements of that era and significantly weaker than the Habitats Directive. It does not refer explicitly to the precautionary principle;[56] it gives parties discretion as to whether to undertake EIAs; it mandates only a limited supervisory role for the COP; it is as much concerned with the reallocation of economic benefits from north to south as it is with the protection of biodiversity, and its central obligations of conservation and sustainable use may, in certain circumstances, be mutually inconsistent. It does not require parties to protect the areas which are most important for the conservation of biodiversity and does not even require parties to identify those areas.[57]

In fact, many of the biodiversity and habitats measures set out in the CBD were already incorporated in other international environmental treaties, including CITES and the Ramsar, Berne and Bonn Conventions. The CBD may present the measures in a more comprehensive format than that of other treaties but each party is responsible for the implementation of CBD obligations only 'as far as possible and appropriate'. The CBD does not require uniformity of implementation, nor does it give parties collective power to mandate measures.[58] Consequently, not only may parties determine priorities and methods of implementation, they may also decide not to implement on the grounds that implementation is neither possible nor appropriate in their particular circumstances. This means that the obligations of an earlier treaty are, in many cases, stronger than those of the CBD. All this suggests that while the CBD appears to require more extensive obligations than those of the Habitats Directive, that Directive is, in practical terms, a great deal stronger and more effective.

---

[56] For a critical examination of the application of the precautionary principle to the Habitats Directive see Edwards, ch 12 in this volume.

[57] Annex 1 to the CBD provides guidance for area selection in the form of an indicative list of components of biodiversity important for its conservation and sustainable development but that list is so broad that parties have experienced difficulty in identifying priorities.

[58] Art 41 of the Vienna Convention permits two or more parties to a treaty to modify that treaty between themselves, subject to certain conditions, but no group of two or more parties has done this in respect of their CBD obligations.

3

After *Morge*, where are we now? The Meaning of 'Disturbance' in the Habitats Directive

CHARLES GEORGE QC* AND DAVID GRAHAM

Environmentalists, churches, politicians and science [sic], all are concerned about the damage to the environment. But their concern is for the good of humankind. So deep is this introspection that even now, few apart from eccentrics really care about other living organisms.[1]

Introduction

The European Union (EU) really *does* care about other living organisms, with the protection of biodiversity being the 'main aim' of the Habitats Directive.[2] However, the EU has missed its Biodiversity Action Plan targets for 2010,[3] and a 2007 report[4] found that 27 per cent of EU mammal populations were declining, and 15 per cent of mammal species were 'threatened'.[5]

Article 12 of the Directive aims to protect animal species, and its interpretation was the subject of *R (Morge) v Hampshire County Council*,[6] which reached the Supreme Court. The *Morge* litigation concerned a challenge by Mrs Morge to the grant of planning permission for the South Hampshire Bus Rapid Transit scheme, on the grounds that there had been a failure to have regard to the requirements of the Directive in relation to protected bat species.

---

* Charles George QC was leading counsel for Mrs Morge in *R (Morge) v Hampshire County Council*.
[1] James Lovelock, quoted in Mary Midgley, *Evolution as a Religion* (Routledge, 2002) 174.
[2] Council Directive 92/43/EEC of 21 May 1992 on the conservation of natural habitats and of wild fauna and flora (OJ L206, 22 July 1992, 7), seventh recital.
[3] Commission, *The 2010 assessment of implementing the EU Biodiversity Action Plan,* 8 October 2010, viii.
[4] HJ Temple and A Terry (compilers), *The Status and Distribution of European Mammals,* (Luxembourg: Office for Official Publications of the European Communities, 2007).
[5] 'Threatened' means species which have a small and declining population or range, or whose populations declined by more than 30% in the previous decade: Temple and Terry, ibid, 23.
[6] *R (Morge) v Hampshire County Council* [2009] EWHC 2940 (Admin); [2010] Env LR 26; [2010] EWCA Civ 608, [2010] PTSR 1882; [2011] UKSC 2; [2011] 1 WLR 268.

This chapter considers Article 12 and the way that it has been transposed in England and Wales, before examining the ruling of the Supreme Court in *Morge* and its implications.

Aims of the Directive

The fifth recital to the Habitats Directive refers to Article 130r of the Treaty establishing the European Economic Community (EEC Treaty), which is now Article 191 of the Treaty on the Functioning of the European Union (TFEU).

Article 191(1) TFEU provides that 'Union policy on the environment shall contribute to the pursuit of the … objectives [of] preserving, protecting and improving the quality of the environment'; and Article 191(2) continues, 'Union policy on the environment shall aim at a high level of protection taking into account the diversity of situations in the various regions of the Union. It shall be based on the precautionary principle and on the principles that preventive action should be taken…'.

The fifth recital to the Directive declares that 'the preservation, protection and improvement of the quality of the environment' includes 'the conservation of natural habitats and of wild fauna and flora', and that these 'are an essential objective of general interest pursued by the Community'. The seventh recital tells us that 'the main aim of this Directive' is 'to promote the maintenance of biodiversity'. Article 2 provides that: 'The aim of this Directive shall be to contribute towards ensuring bio-diversity through the conservation of natural habitats and of wild fauna and flora in the European territory of the Member States'.

'ensuring biodiversity'

There is no definition of 'biodiversity' in the Directive. However, it is expected that the phrase should be interpreted consistently with the subsequent UN Convention on Biological Diversity (CBD)[7] to which the EU is now a party. This is likely to have been the legislators' intention. The Convention was drafted in parallel with the Habitats Directive, and the final text of the former was agreed a day after the Council approved the Habitats Directive.[8] In Annex B to its decision to approve the accession of the European Economic Community to the Convention,[9] the Council of Ministers included the Habitats Directive among a list of the 'most relevant' legal instruments that were 'adopted in relation to the matters covered

---

[7] See MacKenzie, ch 2 in this volume.
[8] On 22 May 1992 at the Nairobi Conference. Secretariat of the Convention on Biological Diversity, 'History of the Convention' available at: http://www.cbd.int/history/.
[9] Council Decision 93/626/EEC of 25 October 1993 (OJ L309, 13 December 1993, 1–20).

by the Convention'. The Commission also considers the Directive to be part of the 'implementation' of the Convention.[10] Biodiversity for the purposes of the Convention is defined by Article 2 CBD as 'the variability among living organisms from all sources ... [T]his includes diversity within species, between species and of ecosystems.' The word 'ecosystem' is defined as 'a dynamic complex of plant, animal and micro-organism communities and their non-living environment interacting as a functional unit'.

'through ... conservation'

'Conservation' is defined by Article 1(a) as 'measures required to maintain or restore ... the populations of species ... at a favourable status'. The phrase 'favourable status' is in turn defined at Article 1(i) of the Directive. It means that the species is 'maintaining itself on a long-term basis as a viable component of its natural habitats', in circumstances where the natural range is neither being reduced nor is likely to be reduced, and in which there will probably continue to be a sufficiently extensive habitat to 'maintain its populations' over the long term. There is no mention of the scale at which the populations or habitats are to be assessed.

The Scheme of Strict Protection

There are two balancing provisions in the section of the Habitats Directive dealing with 'protection of species'. The first is a system of protection prohibiting certain activities under Article 12(1). The second is a 'get-out clause' in Article 16 which provides that, in certain circumstances, Member States may allow the otherwise prohibited activities to lawfully take place.

Article 12(1): An Overview

Annex IV(a) to the Directive lists 'Animal ... species of Community interest in need of strict protection', which are either identified by an asterisk as being 'endangered' species within the meaning of Article 1(g)(i) and (h); or merely 'vulnerable', 'rare', or 'requiring particular attention' as defined by Article 1(g) (ii)–(iv). These are referred to below as European Protected Species (EPS).

---

[10] European Commission, *The Convention on Biodiversity: Implementation in the European Union* (2006) 3, 5, 10.

Article 12(1) of the Habitats Directive requires that

> Member States shall take the requisite measures to establish a system of strict protection for the animal species listed in Annex IV(a) in their natural range, prohibiting:
>
> (a) all forms of deliberate capture or killing of specimens of these species [i.e. EPS] in the wild;
> (b) deliberate disturbance of these species, particularly during the period of breeding, rearing, hibernation and migration;
> (c) deliberate destruction or taking of eggs from the wild; [and]
> (d) deterioration or destruction of breeding sites or resting places.

The 'requisite measures' for a system of strict protection have been held not to be limited to the prohibitions set out at clauses (a) to (d).[11] Accordingly, after discussing the meaning of prohibitions (a) to (d) below we shall go on to consider what other protections are required.

The Specific Prohibitions (a) to (d)

'deliberate'

It will be seen that the first three categories of prohibited activity must be 'deliberate'. The Court of Justice of the European Union (CJEU) has given the word a very broad construction, such that it is not a defence that the capture, killing, disturbance, or destruction was the unintended result of the pursuit of other purposes. For example, the use of noisy explosives in order to construct an underwater gas pipeline was held to amount to the deliberate disturbance of cetaceans in *Commission v Ireland*.[12]

Initially, in a case brought by the Commission in relation to Greece's failure to protect the *Caretta caretta* sea turtles on the island of Zakynthos, the Court appeared to indicate that mere negligence would suffice. It held:

> It is apparent from the documents before the Court that at the time the facts were ascertained by the Commission's officials, the use of mopeds on the breeding beaches was prohibited and notices indicating the presence of turtle nests on the beaches had been erected. As regards the sea area around Gerakas and Dafni, it had been classified as an absolute protection area and special notices had been erected there.
>
> It follows that the use of mopeds on the sand beach to the east of Laganas and the presence of pedalos and small boats in the sea area around Gerakas and Dafni constitute the deliberate disturbance of the species in question during its breeding period for the purposes of Article 12(1)(b) of the Directive.[13]

---

[11] See below in this chapter for a discussion of the authorities.
[12] Case C-183/05 *Commission v Ireland*, Opinion of Léger AG, at paras 60–61 and judgment of the Court at para 36.
[13] Case C-103/00 *Commission v Greece*, paras 35 and 36.

However, that was a case about the failure to take preventive measures and so whether or not the turtles were actually 'disturbed' was not determinative. The point was, however, directly at issue in *Commission v Spain*. The Commission alleged that by permitting the use of snares to trap foxes, Spain had failed to strictly protect endangered otters, since otters that were in the vicinity of the traps might be ensnared. The Court held that the test was whether 'the author of the act intended … or, at the very least, accepted the possibility' of the capture of otters. As there was no evidence that the Spanish authorities had any idea that otters were in the area, the Court ruled that there was no infringement.[14] The position is, therefore, that conscious advertence to the risk of the prohibited result is required, akin to 'recklessness' in English criminal law.[15]

In Mrs Morge's case in the Supreme Court, Lord Brown's judgment, concurred in by the majority, stated:

> No problem arises as to what is meant by 'deliberate' in article 12(1)(b). As stated by the Commission in paragraph 33 of their Guidance:
>
>> "'Deliberate' actions are to be understood as actions by a person who knows, in light of the relevant legislation that applies to the species involved, and the general information delivered to the public, that his action will most likely lead to an offence against the species, but intends this offence or, if not, consciously accepts the foreseeable results of his action."
>
> Put more simply, a deliberate disturbance is an intentional act knowing that it will or may have a particular consequence, namely disturbance of the relevant protected species.[16]

Nardell and Simpson suggest that in approving the Commission's guidance Lord Brown meant to limit liability to cases in which the risk of disturbance has not only been recognised as a possibility, but has also been considered to be the 'most likely' result.[17] It is not clear that this was intended, but if it had been then it would clearly be inconsistent with the ECJ's ruling in *Commission v Spain*.

(a) 'capture or killing of specimens of these species in the wild'

An intriguing question, on which there is no authority, is the point at which EPS cease to be 'in the wild'. Does the habitat, rather than the species, have to be under some form of human control to pass from being 'in the wild'? The co-official Italian translation of 'in the wild' is *nell'ambiente naturale* [in the natural environment]. Many animals live in landscapes such as meadows, chalk downland or heathland that form where the naturally-occurring vegetation is selectively

---

[14] Case C-221/04 *Commission v Spain*, paras 70–74, quotation at para 71.
[15] On which, see *R v G and R* [2003] UKHL 50; [2004] 1 AC 1034.
[16] [2011] UKSC 2 at [14].
[17] Gordon Nardell and Penny Simpson, 'A disturbance in the law? Implications of recent case law on the species protection provisions of the Habitats Directive', [2011] 9 *Journal of Planning and Environmental Law*, 1155–73, 1163.

cleared by human activities such as mowing, grazing livestock, felling or burning. Others inhabit hedgerows, gardens or fields whose constituent plants are actively planted and tended by people, but are not themselves under any direct human husbandry. Still others cohabit with people. Bats frequently take up residence in a church, barn or domestic building. If specimens of protected species living in these environments were excluded it would undermine the Directive's 'main aim' of preserving biodiversity.

It seems probable that the distinction drawn is between 'in the wild' and 'domesticated', so that the protection applies only to species not already under the direct control of humans.

(b) 'disturbance of these species, particularly during the period of breeding, rearing, hibernation and migration'

The exact definition of 'disturbance' has never been expressly considered by the ECJ, or the Court of Justice of the European Union (CJEU) as it is now known, and the definition was the subject of dispute in the *Morge* litigation which is considered in detail in the next section.

For present purposes, the Supreme Court's judgment in *Morge* is notable for endorsing the three principles that disturbance can occur at all stages of the life cycle of the species; it can be indirect; and it need not be 'significant' in relation to the whole species.[18]

The use of the word 'particularly' in Article 12(1)(b) indicates that there can be disturbance even outside 'the period of breeding, rearing, hibernation and migration', although disturbance may be more likely, and more serious, during that period. The breadth of (1)(b) is made clearer still by Article 12(3) which provides, 'The prohibition referred to in paragraph (1)(a) and (b) … shall apply to all stages of life of the animals to which this Article applies.'

As a preliminary stage in infringement proceedings under Article 228, the European Commission issued the UK with an Additional Reasoned Opinion (ARO)[19] directed at what the Commission perceived to be the inadequacies of its implementing regulations.[20] The ARO stated unequivocally:

> The concept of disturbance is not limited merely to the survival and breeding of a species or the rearing and nurturing of their young. This is an unwarranted restriction of the wide protection regime foreseen in the Directive.

Although as late as 2009 the Department for the Environment, Food and Rural Affairs (Defra) in its guidance was still wrongly claiming that 'the result of

---

[18] [2011] UKSC 2 at [19] and [22] *per* Lord Brown, [78] *per* Lord Kerr.

[19] European Commission, 'Reasoned Opinion addressed to the United Kingdom … on account of failure to implement the judgment … in Case C-6/04', 23 September 2008, para 30.

[20] The particular regulation was reg 39(1)(b) of the Conservation (Natural Habitats etc) Regs 1994, as amended by reg 5(13) of the Conservation (Natural Habitats etc) (Amendment) Regs 2007.

disturbance must affect important life cycle processes',[21] the Supreme Court has now confirmed that 'it does not follow that other activity having an adverse impact on the species may not also offend the prohibition'.[22]

It has long been clear that disturbance (and also the 'deterioration or destruction of breeding sites or resting places' under Article 12(1)(d)) need not involve direct physical contact with the animals or their resting-places. In *Commission v Greece*, 'deliberate disturbance' of turtles was said to arise from 'noise pollution' from the use of mopeds on the beach.[23] Léger AG in his Opinion referred to 'erosion of the soil', 'noise and artificial light near or at the breeding sites' and 'the use of sunbeds and umbrellas as well as mopeds on the beach' as being 'deliberate acts such as might disturb the species'.[24] Léger AG also had concerns about indirect disturbance under Article 12(1)(b) in *Commission v Ireland*. He noted that 'noise and lighting as a result of human occupation would have a significant impact on bat species' in relation to the Lough Rynn Estate project; and he considered that the deliberate use of explosives in laying a gas pipeline in Broadhaven Bay was 'prohibited under Article 12(1)(b)' because the sound generated would have an adverse effect on cetaceans.[25]

It is also clear from the drafting history of the Directive that disturbances of protected species need not be 'significant' to be prohibited. In the Bern Convention on the Conservation of European Wildlife and Natural Habitats,[26] which was ratified by the European Community on 3 December 1981, and was the origin of the wording of Article 12 of the Habitats Directive, Article 6(c) prohibits 'the deliberate disturbance of wild fauna particularly during the period of breeding, rearing and hibernation, *in so far as disturbance would be significant in relation to the objectives of this Convention*' (emphasis added).

The italicised words find no place in Article 12(1)(b) of the Habitats Directive. This contrasts with Article 12(4) on research and monitoring ('significant negative impact on the species concerned'); and with Article 6(2), which requires avoiding 'in special areas of conservation ... disturbance of the species for which the areas have been designated, insofar as such disturbance could be significant in relation to the objectives of this Directive'.

In the ARO the Commission considered that 'the prohibition in the Directive not to disturb protected species is not limited to *significant* disturbances of *significant groups* of animals'.[27] The Supreme Court in *Morge* agreed that the effect need not be 'significant', although it contradictorily also ruled that in order to constitute

---

[21] Defra, 'The Conservation (Natural Habitats etc) (Amendment) (England and Wales) Regulations 2009 ... Questions and Answers' (28 January 2009), answer to Question 4.

[22] *R (Morge) v Hampshire CC* [2011] UKSC 2 at [23] *per* Lord Brown.

[23] Case C-103/00, para 34.

[24] Case C-103/00, Opinion of Léger AG delivered on 25 October 2001, paras 46, 56 and 57.

[25] Case C-183/05, Opinion of Léger AG delivered on 21 September 2006, paras 56 and 60.

[26] Opened for signature at Bern, 19 September 1979.

[27] European Commission, 'Reasoned Opinion', para 30, 10. The italics are in the original. The Commission was referring to restrictions contained in the 2007 Regs that no longer feature in the 2010 Regs.

a 'disturbance' an activity must have a 'sufficient negative impact on the species' as a whole, because in contradistinction to Article 12(1)(a), Article 12(1)(b) was drafted so as to refer to 'species' rather than to 'specimens'.[28]

(c) 'deliberate destruction or taking of eggs from the wild'

The meaning of 'deliberate' has been mentioned above, as has the uncertainty as to precisely what is meant by 'the wild'. As the creatures are not under direct human control, we suggest that an adder's eggs left in a back-garden are protected, as are the eggs of protected wild birds laid in a stable-block.

It is unclear whether the plural 'eggs' includes a single egg. If the Supreme Court's interpretation of the word 'species' is correct, then it may be that protection is deliberately only afforded to the destruction or taking of more than one egg. However, where species are critically endangered or lay only one egg per breeding season, adopting a strictly literalist construction would defeat the purpose of the Directive.

(d) 'deterioration or destruction of breeding sites or resting places'

There was a careful analysis of the position by Ward LJ in the Court of Appeal in *Morge*, which is likely to remain authoritative in England and Wales for the foreseeable future. The crucial propositions of law he expounded were as follows:

(a) '[T]he deterioration or destruction does not need to be deliberate'.[29]

(b) '[Unlike] the other prohibitions in Article 12 … [Article 12(1)(d)] does not concern directly the species but protects important parts of their habitats'.[30]

(c) '[I]ndirect deterioration or destruction is sufficient'.[31] Thus, it will be unlawful to inhibit the repair or habitability of the site by, for example, removing nearby sources of food, fumigating it, shining a light at it or blocking access to it.

(d) 'Article 12(1)(d) is aimed at safeguarding the ecological functionality of the breeding sites and resting places'.[32] Ward LJ's reference to 'ecological functionality' is derived from the Commission's guidance. He held that on the facts the interference with flight paths to and from bat roosts had 'no impact on the physical degradation affecting the breeding site itself'.[33] However, in cases where sites require maintenance or will be colonised by other species if left unoccupied (for example burrows or nests), impeding access could well lead to deterioration.

---

[28] *R (Morge) v Hampshire CC* [2011] UKSC 2, at [19] *per* Lord Brown.

[29] [2010] EWCA Civ 608, at [46]. *Cf* Case C-98/03 *Commission v Germany*, para 55; Case C-6/04, *Commission v United Kingdom*, para 79.

[30] [2010] EWCA Civ 608 at [48].

[31] Ibid, at [49]. At paras [49]–[53] Ward LJ went on to apply Kokott AG's Opinion, para 74 in *Commission v United Kingdom*, and *Commission v Greece* (above).

[32] [2010] EWCA Civ 608 at [59].

[33] Ibid.

In *Commission v France*, Case C-383/09, Kokott AG expressed the view that Article 12(1)(d) only protects *existing* resting places and breeding sites, and not potential sites.[34] This was also Ward LJ's interpretation of the provision in *Morge*.[35]

In the context of those cases where the Directive is enforced by criminal prohibitions, this limitation is entirely sensible as it would be too difficult to identify potential nesting sites with any certainty. Furthermore, it would plainly be unnecessary to protect potential resting sites that were too far from existing populations of the species to be used by them. However, the limitation would unduly undermine the protection given to the species if there were no *other* measures to protect potential sites, as species cannot usually grow or maintain themselves in numbers unless there are nearby locations for offspring of the current generation to breed and rest without competing with their forebears. Application of Kokott AG's approach to other 'requisite measures' would enable Member States to deliberately operate development policies which prevent their recolonisation by historic species. That would conflict with one of the Directive's objectives—*restoration* of populations in places from which they may have vanished altogether.

In *Commission v France*, the CJEU did not expressly dissent from Advocate General Kokott's approach, but disagreement was clearly implicit in its reasoning. The Court concluded that French measures 'were not adequate to enable effective avoidance of deterioration or destruction of the breeding sites or resting places of the European Hamster', an EPS. In reaching that conclusion it criticised the adequacy of measures designed to ensure repopulation of the historic range of the hamsters by expanding areas of potential lucerne and winter cereal habitat.[36]

The Need for Other 'Requisite Measures'

Article 12(1) of the Directive is very clear that its desired result is 'a system of strict protection', and under Article 288 TFEU, directives are 'binding as to the result to be achieved'. Furthermore, Article 191(2) TFEU states that EU policy must be based on 'preventive action'.

In *Commission v Ireland*, Case C-183/05, the ECJ ruled that

> the transposition of Article 12(1) of the Directive requires the Member States not only to adopt a comprehensive legislative framework but also to implement concrete and specific protection measures (see, to that effect, Case C-103/00, Commission v Greece…, paragraphs 34 to 39).

> Similarly, the system of strict protection measures presupposes the adoption of coherent and coordinated measures of a preventive nature (Case C-518/04 … paragraph 16).[37]

In that case, it held that the existence of a full-time network of conservation officers did not 'in itself demonstrate effective implementation of the system of

---

[34] Case C-383/09 *Commission v France*, Opinion of Kokott AG, paras 50 and 96.
[35] [2010] EWCA Civ 608 at [58].
[36] Case C-383/09 *Commission v France*, judgment, paras 27–31, 33–34 and 37.
[37] Case C-183/05 *Commission v Ireland*, paras 29–30.

strict protection'.[38] In *Commission v Greece*, the use of pedaloes and mopeds on the beaches had been prohibited, but the fact that it was still going on was held to prove that Greece had failed to establish an 'effective system of strict protection so as to avoid any disturbance'.[39]

The most recently decided Article 12(1) infringement case was brought against France for failing to strictly protect hamster burrows. Kokott AG stated in her Opinion that the fact that French law baldly prohibited the destruction or degradation of resting-places was insufficient as the conservation status of the hamsters was 'very unfavourable', and in order to protect the species there also needed to be laws requiring better agricultural practices.[40] She emphasised that the system of protection should 'effectively prevent any damage' to the breeding sites or resting-places,[41] and that the hamsters must be protected not only by a general prohibition on damaging their burrows, but also by town-planning measures that would 'guarantee that the sites in question are not touched by urbanisation'.[42]

It can be inferred from its judgment that the CJEU applied these principles. It cited the Greek and Irish cases, stating, 'Such a system of strict protection must therefore enable the effective avoidance of deterioration or destruction of breeding sites or resting places'. The French had set up 'priority action areas' in which all development was prohibited, and a 'repopulation area' where all urbanisation projects of more than one hectare in size had to prove their lack of harmful effect on hamsters or be exempted by a minister. The Court found that this package of 'measures … in the field of urbanisation' was 'inadequate' to achieve effective avoidance of deterioration, the number of burrows having fallen from over 1,160 to under 180 between 2001 and 2007. In particular, its criticisms were that priority action areas only covered 2 per cent of the zones favourable to the hamsters; the criteria for granting an exemption in the 'repopulation area' were unclear; there was no requirement for compensatory measures where exemptions were granted; and the impact of projects covering less than one hectare was not scrutinised.[43]

In her Opinion, the learned Advocate-General had suggested that a bald prohibition and surveillance might suffice for species that were already at a favourable

---

[38] Ibid, at para 31.

[39] Case C-103/00, paras 35 to 40; quoted text at para 40.

[40] Case C-383/09 *Commission v France*, Opinion of Kokott AG submitted 20 January 2011, paras 26, 37, 44–47, 62–64 and 77.

[41] Our translation. The Advocate-General's Opinion reads: '*Un tel système doit en principe être de nature à faire efficacement obstacle à toute détérioration ou destruction des sites de reproduction ou des aires de repos qui pourrait être préjudiciable au maintien ou au rétablissement d'un état favorable.*' Ibid, para 53.

[42] Our translation. The Opinion reads: '*Les terriers du Grand Hamster et leur environnement doivent également être protégés par des mesures d'urbanisation … Il est … suffisant de garantir que les surfaces en cause ne sont pas touchées par l'urbanisation*'. Ibid, para 89.

[43] Case C-383/09 *Commission v France*, judgment at paras 18–21, 24, and 33–40.

conservation status, considering that the aim of Article 12(1) was to restore the populations *or* to maintain them at levels which were viable in the long term.[44] However, with respect, this ignores the repeated statements by the ECJ[45] that the fact that a species is not declining in population cannot be used as an excuse for not establishing a strict system of protection.

Derogations under Article 16

Article 16 is a 'get-out' provision. Like all provisions for derogations, the enumerated grounds are exhaustive;[46] they must be construed strictly and so as to impose the burden of proof on the authority permitting the derogation. The ECJ stated in *Commission v Finland* that

> Since [Article 16] provides for exceptional arrangements which must be interpreted strictly and must impose on the authority taking the decision the burden of proving that the necessary conditions are present for each derogation, the Member States are required to ensure that all action affecting the protected species is authorised only on the basis of decisions containing a clear and sufficient statement of reasons which refers to the reasons, conditions and requirements laid down in Article 16(1).[47]

Under that article, no licence can be granted for any disturbance if

(a) there is a 'satisfactory alternative' to undertaking the prohibited activity; or

(b) the activity 'is' (which probably includes 'may be') 'detrimental to the maintenance of the populations of the species concerned at a favourable conservation status in their natural range'.

Take the case of a church where bats roost. If church services can sensibly be held, notwithstanding the presence of bats in the church, then doing nothing is a 'satisfactory alternative', and no-one can licence disturbance of the bats or removal of the roosts. If the bats are of an especially rare species, or a more common species whose habitat is shrinking or whose population declining, then there is no possibility of a licence at all.

Assuming these two pre-conditions can be overcome, there are then two relevant permitted grounds for derogation under Article 16(1).

---

[44] Ibid, paras 37 and 82–84.
[45] See for instance, Case C-103/00 *Commission v Greece* (Zakynthos turtles) para 31; Case C-518/04 *Commission v Greece*, (Milos vipers), para 21.
[46] Case C-183/05 *Commission v Ireland*, para 48.
[47] Case C-342/05 *Commission v Finland*, para 25; Case C-183/05, *Commission v Ireland* para 48.

(b) 'to prevent serious damage, in particular to crops, livestock, forests,
       fisheries and water and other types of property'

The list of protected species includes many types of rodent, insects and carnivores such as wolves, lynx and bears. These have the potential to seriously harm
agricultural activities. Bats or bat roosts inside churches could potentially cause
serious damage, for example by harming furnishings with their droppings. But
this derogation will not apply where the damage is slight, both because in such
circumstances the 'do nothing' alternative is available and also because there is no
'serious damage' (nor a real risk thereof).

(c) 'in the interests of public health and public safety or for other
       imperative reasons of overriding public interest, including those
       of a social or economic nature and beneficial consequences of
       primary importance for the environment'

From the word 'other', it is clear that the public health risk in question must call
for 'imperative' action. Thus, if bats in a church merely startled members of the
congregation that would not justify their removal. On the other hand, if bats
regularly let their droppings fall on the altar so as to threaten to contaminate
the sacraments, then there might be a sufficient 'public health' reason to take
action.

    The wording of Article 16(1)(c) led the Court of Appeal in *R (Newsum) v Welsh
Assembly* to hold that in applying the transposed equivalent regulation it was necessary both to identify an imperative reason of overriding public interest, and to
show that this reason would have beneficial consequences for the environment.[48]
Although such a strict interpretation is in keeping with the general approach of
the CJEU, it would seem unduly restrictive.

    One way to retain flexibility is to treat the expression 'the environment' as
being wider than the interests of biodiversity. On that basis, there would be
no reason why the cultural, social or built environment should be excluded.
Therefore, were it to be shown that the appreciation and experience of a listed
church was being prevented by the presence of bats or bat roosts, it is strongly
arguable that a licence should be obtainable on the grounds that their removal
would bring beneficial consequences of primary importance for the environment. Likewise, if the presence of bats prevented the holding of church services,
including baptisms, marriages and funerals, then there would probably be an
imperative reason of overriding public interest of a social nature if there was
'no satisfactory alternative'. This is a point on which there is, as yet, no legal
authority.

---

[48] *R (Newsum) v Welsh Assembly* [2004] EWCA Civ 1565 at [19] *per* Waller LJ.

Domestic Transposition and the Duty
on 'Competent Authorities'

The Habitats Directive is transposed into domestic law through the Conservation of Habitats and Species Regulations 2010 (the Regulations).[49] Article 12 is primarily transposed by creating new criminal offences. Under Regulation 41(1) of the Regulations, the prohibited activities are made criminal offences, unless they are conducted pursuant to a licence made under Regulation 53(1) and (4). In England, licensing on the grounds which are domestic equivalents of Article 16(1) paragraphs (b) and (c) is by the Secretary of State for the Environment.[50] In many parts of the country, arrangements are in place under section 78 of the Natural Environment and Rural Communities Act 2006 by which the licensing duty has been delegated to Natural England.

However, there is also regulation 9(5), headed 'Exercise of functions in accordance with the Habitats Directive', which stipulates that 'a competent authority, in the exercising of any of their functions, must have regard to the requirements of the Habitats Directive so far as they may be affected by the exercise of those functions'.

The term 'competent authority' is defined in regulation 7(1) to include 'any ... public body of any description or person holding a public office', including, therefore, Natural England and local planning authorities, but also Church of England chancellors when considering whether or not to grant a faculty for works in a church or a churchyard which will affect a protected species such as bats. The word 'they' refers to 'the requirements of the Habitats Directive' rather than the competent authority.[51]

By indirectly incorporating the Habitats Directive into the Regulations in this way, the draftsman has deliberately failed to set out a code of prescriptive rules. The problems with this approach are readily apparent: it does not establish what the 'requirements' of the Directive actually are, or whether they affect any given public authority. With so little to go on, the courts have to fall back on the Directive itself to try to divine an answer.

The *Morge* Litigation

Having sketched the legal context for the *Morge* litigation, we can now turn to consider the case itself. Mrs Morge had applied for judicial review of the defendant

---

[49] SI 2010/490.

[50] Under reg 56(3)(a) of the 2010 Regs, the relevant authority for licensing on the grounds enumerated at reg 53(2)(e) and (g) is the 'appropriate authority', which is defined to be the Secretary of State in relation to England and the Welsh Ministers in relation to Wales by reg 3(1).

[51] *R (Friends of the Earth) v The Environment Agency and others* [2003] EWHC 3193 (Admin) at [57] and [58] *per* Sullivan J (as he then was).

Council's decision to permit the construction and operation of a guided busway through a forested area. It was predicted that the felling of trees would deprive protected bats[52] of foraging habitat; while the operation of the busway would interfere with their flightpaths such as to present a risk of collision and cause noise and light pollution. Moderate adverse effects were predicted over a temporary, nine-year period.[53] The two questions which eventually found their way to the Supreme Court related to first, the meaning of 'disturbance' and, secondly, the correct role of the local planning authority under the identically-worded predecessor provision to Regulation 9(5).[54]

The Rulings in Relation to the Meaning of 'Disturbance'

One question for the courts was whether the felling of trees in the New Forest and the construction and operation of a guided busway amounted to 'disturbance' of the local bat population. At each level of the judicature a different interpretation of 'disturbance' was formulated.

In the High Court His Honour Judge Bidder QC, sitting as a Deputy High Court Judge, endorsed guidance from the European Commission (the Guidance)[55] that 'logically, having regard to the aims of the Directive, for disturbance of a protected species to occur a "certain negative impact likely to be detrimental" must be involved'.

He considered that 'further definition by the Court is both unnecessary and unlikely to be helpful' in the light of the Guidance.[56]

The Court of Appeal disagreed, holding that

> for there to be disturbance within the meaning of article 12(1)(b) that disturbance must have a detrimental impact so as to affect the conservation status of the species at population level ... [ie] the long-term distribution and abundance of the population.[57]

Applying this test, Ward LJ held that 'loss of foraging habitat occasioned by cutting a swathe through the vegetation', such 'that the bats have to travel further and expend more energy in foraging' would not constitute 'disturbance' unless 'their survival would be in jeopardy [so that] the population of the species will

---

[52] Members of the sub-order *Michrochiroptera*, which is listed in Annex IV(a) to the Directive.
[53] See [2011] UKSC 2 at [7] *per* Lord Brown. For a useful guide to the impact of road transport infrasructure on bats and possible mitigation measures see Sétra Information Note 91: 'Bats and road transport infrastructure: Threats and preservation measures' (November 2009, translated into English, May 2011) available at: http://www.setra.equipement.gouv.fr/IMG/pdf/NI_EEC_091_GB.pdf.
[54] Reg 3(4) of the Conservation (Natural Habitats etc) Regs 1994, as amended.
[55] Commission's Guidance document on the strict protection of animal species of Community interest under the Habitats Directive 92/43, Final Version, February 2007.
[56] [2009] EWHC 2940 (Admin) at [183] and [186].
[57] [2010] EWCA Civ 608 at [37] and [39] *per* Ward LJ.

not maintain itself on a long-term basis'.[58] Likewise, he held that 'the occasional death of a bat' as a result of collisions with buses 'will be a trivial disturbance not having a negative impact on the species as a whole so as to have any ecological importance'.[59]

Before the Supreme Court neither party contended that the disturbance had to be 'significant'. Mrs Morge submitted that all that was required was some appreciable interference with a protected species (that is, a certain impact likely to be detrimental which is more than *de minimis*, but including disturbance which is less than significant). This reflected the Commission's interpretation in its Guidance, and also its observation in the ARO that 'the prohibition in Article 12(1)(b) of the Directive ... covers all disturbance of protected species'.[60] Hampshire County Council proposed that 'the proper approach is to ask whether the activity in question produces "a certain negative impact likely to be detrimental to the species having regard to its effect on the conservation status of the species"'.[61]

The Justices of the Supreme Court concurred that the Court of Appeal had applied too strict a test. It was accepted that disturbance need neither be 'significant', nor affect the long-term conservation status of the species.[62] Lord Brown accepted that 'obviously, as here, disturbance of habitats can also indirectly impact on species',[63] and that while 'activity during the period[s particularly specified] ... is more likely to have a sufficient negative impact on the species to constitute "disturbance" than activity at other times ... it does not follow that other activity having an adverse impact on the species may not also offend the prohibition'.[64]

Lord Brown's leading judgment concurred with the Court of Appeal in that 'the prohibition ... in contrast to that in article 12(1)(a), relates to the protection of "species", not the protection of "specimens of these species"'.[65] This interpretation of the text is reasonable, but by no means self-evident. Since article 12(1)(a) is concerned with 'capture or killing', it is quite logical to refer in that sub-article to 'specimens' of the species rather than to whole species—which would usually be quite impractical to capture or kill in one go.[66] Article 15 of the Directive refers to 'killing of species' and it would be absurd to interpret this as failing to protect individuals as well as the collective species.

---

[58] Ibid, [74].
[59] Ibid, [45].
[60] ARO, para 32 (and *cf* paras 34 and 36). In his Opinion in Case C-183/05 *Commission v Ireland*, Léger AG seems to have favoured a similar approach in asking whether 'there was an appreciable risk of disturbing', para 61, though this passage was in the context of Art 12(1)(d).
[61] [2011] UKSC 2, [18].
[62] Ibid, *per* Lord Brown at [19] and [22]; *per* Lord Kerr at [78].
[63] Ibid, at [19].
[64] Ibid, at [19] and [23].
[65] Ibid, at [19]. Ward LJ had made the same point in [2010] EWCA Civ 608 at [28].
[66] In para 53 of her Opinion in Case C-221/04 *Commission v Spain*, Kokott AG said that 'the prohibitions in Article 12(1) ... relate to individual specimens', but the comparison she was drawing was with Art 5 of Directive 2004/35 on Environmental Liability, and since that case related to trapping she may have had in mind primarily, or only, Article 12(1)(a) on killing and capture.

Their Lordships rejected the idea of a *de minimis* threshold[67] but declined to further define 'disturbance',[68] leaving unanswered what activity *would* have 'a sufficient negative impact'. Lord Brown stated that what was needed was an assessment of the nature and extent of the negative impact of the activity in question upon the species and, ultimately, a judgment as to whether that is sufficient to constitute a 'disturbance' of the species.[69]

His Lordship commended passages in the Commission Guidance suggesting a 'species-by-species approach' and, within each species,

> [a] case-by-case approach [meaning that] the competent authorities will have to reflect carefully on the level of disturbance to be considered harmful, taking into account the specific characteristics of the species concerned and the situation.[70]

This appears to consider the question to be a matter of fact requiring professional judgment by competent authorities, requiring in-depth knowledge of the characteristics and conservation status of a species.

Lord Brown merely listed some 'considerations' to be 'borne in mind':

> Consideration should … be given to the rarity and conservation status of the species in question and the impact of the disturbance on the local population of a particular protected species. Individuals of a rare species are more important to a local population than individuals of more abundant species. Similarly, disturbance to species that are declining in numbers is likely to be more harmful than disturbance to species that are increasing in numbers.

His Lordship also referred to regulation 41(2) of the 2010 Regulations, which prescribes that activities which are 'likely to impair their ability … to survive, to breed or reproduce, or to rear or nurture their young, or … hibernate or migrate; or affect significantly the local distribution or abundance of the species to which they belong' will all be a 'disturbance'.[71] He left unsaid how the impairment or significance of the effect is to be judged without applying a *de minimis* threshold, such as that which he had rejected.

The Rulings as to the Proper Approach for a Planning Authority under the Regulations

Authorities Entitled to Rely Upon Natural England Advice

Their Lordships all considered that '[w]here … Natural England express themselves satisfied that a proposed development will be compliant with article 12,

---

[67] [2011] UKSC 2 *per* Lord Brown, at [19] and [20]; Lord Kerr, at [79].

[68] Lord Kerr went so far as to say (at [79]) that: 'Trying to refine the test beyond the broad considerations identified by Lord Brown … is not only difficult, it is, in my view, pointless.'

[69] [2011] UKSC 2, at [19].

[70] Ibid, at [21].

[71] Ibid, at [23].

the planning authority are … entitled to presume that that is so', and need not 'go behind that view'.[72]

Duty Limited to Having Regard to the Directive

In the Court of Appeal's judgment in *Morge*, Ward LJ had applied *R (Simon Woolley) v Cheshire East Borough Council*[73] and set out the local planning authority's duty in this way:

> [T]he Planning Committee's duty is prescribed by Regulation 4(3): it must have regard to the requirements of the Habitats Directive so far as they may be affected by the proposed development. The Planning Committee must grant or refuse planning permission in such a way that will "establish a system of strict protection for the animal species listed in Annex IV(a) in their natural range". *If in this case the Committee is satisfied that the development will not offend Article 12(1)(b) or (d) it may grant permission. If satisfied that it will breach any part of Article 12(1) it must then consider whether the appropriate authority, here Natural England, will permit a derogation and grant a licence* … Natural England can only grant that licence if it concludes that (i) despite the breach … there is no satisfactory alternative; (ii) the development will not be detrimental to the maintenance of the population of bats at a favourable conservation status and (iii) the development should be permitted for imperative reasons of overriding public importance. If the Planning Committee conclude that Natural England will not grant a licence it must refuse planning permission. *If on the other hand it is likely that it will grant the licence then the Planning Committee may grant conditional planning permission. If it is uncertain whether or not a licence will be granted, then it must refuse planning permission* (emphasis added).[74]

Before the Supreme Court both parties accepted that this was the correct approach. However, Lord Brown (with the concurrence of all the Justices of the Supreme Court) disagreed. Having set out this passage in full, he said:

> In my judgment this goes too far and puts too great a responsibility on the Planning Committee whose only obligation under regulation 3(4) is … to "have regard to the requirements of the Habitats Directive so far as [those requirements] may be affected by" their decision whether or not to grant a planning permission. … I cannot see why a planning permission (and, indeed, a full planning permission save only as to conditions necessary to secure any required mitigating measures) should not ordinarily be granted *save only in cases where the Planning Committee conclude that the proposed development would both (a) be likely to offend article 12(1) and (b) be unlikely to be licensed pursuant to the derogation powers.* After all, even if development permission is given, the criminal sanction against offending (and unlicensed) activity remains available and it seems to me wrong in principle, when Natural England have the primary responsibility for ensuring compliance with the Directive, also to place a substantial burden on the planning

authority in effect to police the fulfilment of Natural England's own duty.[75] (emphasis added).

The effect of this is to preclude duplication of functions, save only where the italicised exception applies. Much of the reasoning in the *Simon Woolley* case has been swept away. If there is uncertainty whether disturbance will result, the planning authority may grant permission. This is plainly contrary to the precautionary principle and thus contrary to Article 191(2) TFEU. Full planning permission may be granted, without it being conditional upon obtaining a licence. Lord Brown declared:

> I cannot agree with Lord Kerr's view ... that regulation 3(4) required the committee members to consider and decide for themselves whether the development would or would not occasion such disturbance to bats as in fact and in law to constitute a violation of article 12(1)(b) of the Directive.[76]

If his premise is that the planning authority need not reach a view whether the EPS would be disturbed, then it is difficult to see why the italicised exception remains.

Failure to Refer the Question to the CJEU

As the court of final appeal, the Supreme Court was obliged to make a reference to the CJEU under Article 267 TFEU, unless the Directive's interpretation was *acte clair*; that is,

> so obvious as to leave no scope for any reasonable doubt as to the manner in which the question raised is to be resolved ... [and] equally obvious to the courts of the other Member States and to the Court of Justice.[77]

Given that each English court that considered the matter had come to different interpretations, it cannot be said that the answer was 'obvious'. In particular, it is by no means obvious that the Directive was intended to confine prohibited disturbances to those which affect the species as a whole.

Lord Brown refused to refer the matter because 'It seems to me unrealistic to suppose that the Court of Justice would feel able to provide any greater or different assistance than we have here sought to give.'[78] With respect, this reasoning ignored the purpose of the preliminary ruling procedure, which is to ensure that

---

[75] [2011] UKSC 2, [29].
[76] Ibid, [30].
[77] Case C-283/81 *Srl CILFIT and Lanificio di Gavardo SpA v Ministero di Sanità*, para 16.
[78] [2011] UKSC 2, [25].

there is uniform interpretation of law across the EU.[79] Edwards cites this as an example of the more general failure of British public law to produce a consistent and cogent approach to review of public law decisions involving European environmental law.[80]

The Situation after the *Morge* Decision

Unlawful and Problematic Reliance on Administrative Measures

Lord Kerr in his dissenting judgment pithily summarised the court's interpretation of the duty imposed by the Regulations on planning authorities as follows:

> In plain language this means that if you are an authority contemplating a decision that might have an impact on what the Directive requires, you must take its requirements into account before you reach that decision. Of course if you know that another agency has examined the question and has concluded that none of those requirements will be affected, and if you are confident that such agency is qualified to make that judgment, this may be sufficient to meet your obligation under the regulation.[81]

There are, with respect, two problems with this approach. The first and most fundamental is that it begs the question of what the requirements of the Directive actually *are*. No executive agency (or for that matter local authority) can be qualified to decide the nature and applicability of obligations under the Directive. Such matters are eminently matters of law, requiring a scheme of legislation and judicial determinations one way or the other. The ECJ has held that '(t)he provisions of a directive must be implemented with unquestionable binding force and with the specificity, precision and clarity required in order to satisfy the need for legal certainty'; so that mere administrative practice cannot by definition be sufficiently certain.[82]

While it will properly be a matter for naturalists to assess whether a given species will be disturbed, they can only do so if they have a clear legal definition of 'disturbance' to apply. On the facts of *Morge*, there was no evidence that Natural England had applied the definition of 'disturbance' favoured by the Justices as opposed to some other test.

The second, more prosaic problem is that in their desire to avoid a duplication of functions, the Supreme Court increased the risk that neither local planning

---

[79] See, eg Information Note for National Courts issued by the European Court of Justice [now CJEU], [2009[OJ C297/01, 5 December 2009 and further, see in particular, M Broberg and N Fenger, *Preliminary References to the European Court of Justice*, (Oxford University Press, 2010).

[80] See Edwards, ch12 in this volume at pp 229–31.

[81] [2011] UKSC 2, [58].

[82] Case C-427/07 *Commission v Ireland*, paras 55 and 94, and the authorities therein cited.

authorities nor Natural England properly have regard to the requirements of the Directive.

On the facts of *Morge*, the majority considered that the Council had been entitled to grant permission for the development. As Lord Kerr pointed out in his dissenting judgment, Natural England had withdrawn its initial objection to the scheme, but had not expressly stated that it considered that there would be no disturbance. There was no positive evidence that either the Council or Natural England had actively turned their minds to the questions of whether there was a risk of disturbance or whether that disturbance would be licensed under one of the permitted grounds for derogation.[83] Lady Hale and Lord Mance considered that in those circumstances '[t]he planning authority were entitled to draw the conclusion that, having been initially concerned but having withdrawn their objection, Natural England were content that the requirements of the Regulations, and thus the Directive, were being complied with.'[84] However, there is clearly a danger that the local planning authority could mistakenly impute satisfaction to Natural England without requiring clarification of its evaluation of a proposal.

Since the *Morge* ruling Natural England has directed that it does not wish to be consulted in respect of most planning applications which are thought liable to harm protected species; instead, it has published 'standing advice' to provide guidance by which local planning authorities can assess the likelihood of 'disturbance' or derogations being granted themselves.[85]

Natural England's latest guidance also states in relation to the Article 16 derogations

> the planning committee will be required to consider the likelihood of a licence being granted and in doing so, the three tests [i.e. the tests for derogation]. It would be inappropriate for Natural England to tell LPAs [Local Planning Authorities] how to do this as LPAs are the decision-making body and must make the decision themselves and not appear to be fettering their discretion in any way.[86]

Thus in most cases the burden has been shifted back onto local authorities, notwithstanding their Lordships' interpretation of the Regulations as being that Natural England have 'primary responsibility' for enforcing the Directive. There will continue to be some duplication of functions, and planning authorities will have to do the best that they can to second-guess Natural England's approach on the basis of its published advice.

---

[83] Ibid, particularly [75], [76] and [80]–[82] *per* Lord Kerr. Lord Kerr's conclusion on this issue was strongly contested by Lady Hale and Lord Mance.

[84] *Per* Lady Hale, [2011] UKSC 2, [45]; Lord Mance concurring at [48].

[85] Natural England, *Standing Advice for Protected Species* (22 February 2011).

[86] Natural England Guidance Note, *European Protected Species and the Planning Process: Natural England's Application of the 'Three Tests' to Licence Applications* (January 2011), para 14.

Lack of Clarity in the Law of England and Wales

The ECJ has specifically ruled that

in the context of the Habitats Directive, which lays down complex and technical rules in the field of environmental law, the Member States are under a particular duty to ensure that their legislation intended to transpose that directive is clear and precise (see Case C-6/04 Commission v United Kingdom… paragraph 26).[87]

Whatever merit there may be in the Supreme Court's approach to Article 12(1)(b) in *Morge*, it cannot credibly be claimed that its interpretation of disturbance is 'clear and precise'.[88]

There is an urgent need to establish what criteria are to be used to determine whether there is a qualifying disturbance. In particular,

(a) Should the word 'species' include sub-species, or sub-cultures within species with unique behaviours, given that behaviours can reinforce genetic diversity? In a case under the Birds Directive, the ECJ held that the word 'species' included sub-species, and it is submitted that the same should apply to the Habitats Directive bearing in mind the broad definition of 'biodiversity' under the CBD.[89] As the Court recognised in that case, there are significant scientific difficulties in distinguishing sub-species from each other, and it might give rise to further legal argument which criteria—genetic, behavioural or morphological—were to be decisive in defining the subspecies.[90]

(b) To what extent, and in what way, are 'ecological corridors' and contiguous gene pools material? They undermine diversity within species, even as they help to ensure the survival of the species as a whole.

(c) What is meant by 'impact' in the phrase 'negative impact'? Should the focus be on survival of the species and its *numbers* (as their Lordships implied by reference to 'conservation status'), or its condition and quality of life? After all, animals might be agitated, inconvenienced or traumatised by noise, light or vibration without them necessarily becoming infertile. Their behaviour, feeding and sleeping patterns might change in order to cope with anthropogenic disruptions. These would all be considered 'disturbances' in ordinary parlance.

---

[87] Case C-418/04 *Commission v Ireland*, para 219.

[88] One commentator suggests that Article 12(1)(b) disturbance is limited to 'an activity which is likely to impact negatively on the demography (survival or breeding) of the species at the local population level' (Penny Simpson, 'Supreme Court Rules on Habitats Directive', available at: http:// www.cperc.org.uk/assets/news/supreme-court-rules.pdf). But this implies that only harm so defined is significant, when a test of significance was rejected by the Supreme Court. It also begs the question of what is meant by 'negative', 'species' and 'local'. The difficulty that experienced practitioners have in applying the Supreme Court's approach shows how elusive the meaning of 'disturbance' remains.

[89] Case C-202/94 *Godefridus van der Feesten*, para 11; Case C-67/97 *Ditlev Bluhme*, para 34.

[90] See the discussion at Case C-202/94, paras 13–15.

(d) What renders an effect 'negative'? For instance, placing a barrier such as a wind farm, road or canal across a habitat will disrupt the feeding patterns and gene flow of that habitat's species, without necessarily harming any individual creatures or affecting their numbers.[91] Is this a 'negative' impact? It is certainly disturbance in the ordinary meaning of that word, and the CJEU considered it a negative impact when it ruled in a case relating to the Italy's prohibition on the installation of commercial wind turbines in Special Protection Areas for birds. That case concerned Article 6(2) of the Directive, which imposes a duty to 'avoid, in the special areas of conservation … disturbance of the species for which the areas have been designated'. The ECJ ruled that when deciding whether the discrimination between commercial and non-commercial turbines was proportionate, 'the referring court must have regard to the particular features of wind turbines, taking account in particular of the dangers which they may represent for birds, such as the risk of collision, *disturbances and displacement, barrier effects forcing birds to change direction* and habitat loss or degradation'(emphasis added).[92]

(e) How should mitigation measures be taken into account? Natural England's 'standing advice' for assessing whether there is 'disturbance' of species implies that the degree of 'disturbance' must be assessed on the basis of the net effect after 'compensatory measures' have been put in place.[93] This might be thought objectionable if it means that disturbances in the ordinary meaning of that word are permitted without the derogation criteria being met. This might happen, as in *Morge*, where a relatively short-term negative impact was permitted in the hope and expectation that the population would recover later. Alternatively, it might happen where habitat was simultaneously destroyed in one area but compensated for by creation of fresh habitat elsewhere. On one view, the net effect might be neutral, but from another perspective the dislocation of the species and destruction of its habitat would itself be a 'disturbance'.

---

[91] For an illuminating article on the 'barrier effects' of wind turbines on birds, see Allan Drewitt and Rowena Langston, 'Assessing the impacts of wind farms on birds' (2006) 148 *Ibis* 29–42, particularly at 30–34.

[92] Case C-2/10 *Azienda Agro-Zootecnica Franchini Sarl and Eolica di Altamura Srl v Regione Puglia*, para 66. This was in the context of determining whether a national law, which was acknowledged to be stricter than the Directive required, discriminated disproportionately against commercial turbines, as compared with turbines generating less than 20MW of electricity for self-consumption. The Court was not deciding whether these effects constituted 'disturbance' contrary to Directive, but was clearly of the view that displacement and barrier effects were negative. It should be noted that the Italian and English versions of the judgment use the word 'disturbances', which might be read as implying that displacement is a distinct phenomenon, although conversely both are bracketed together in the same clause. The Spanish translation uses the word *perturbaciones* for 'disturbances' in para 66 rather than *alteraciones* which appears in the Spanish-language version of Art 6, but it is doubtful whether any weight can be placed on this.

[93] *Standing Advice Species Sheet: Bats* (February 2011), paras 5.3 and 5.5 and flow chart entitled 'Guidance on how to assess a bat survey and mitigation strategy' after para 7.

(f)   By what test does one ascertain when the negative impact becomes 'sufficient' to engage Article 12(1)(b)? On their Lordships' interpretation, it remains unclear how many individual creatures are needed in any given case before Article 12(1)(b) is engaged. In relation to bats, Natural England formerly gave guidance that hibernation sites 'used on a regular and predictable basis by even 5–10 individuals are significant'.[94] In the absence of legislative or judicial clarification guidance of that type cannot be relied upon.

(g)   Does 'favourable conservation status' have to be judged solely by the numbers of the EPS, or by reference to the effect of increased numbers of the EPS on the ecosystem as a whole? One can think of examples where increased abundance of a rare species then impacts negatively on other species, and vice versa.

(h)   Perhaps most fundamentally, it is unclear at what scale the population of the species should be assessed.[95] Any given species might be increasing in abundance locally but declining across its range as a whole (or vice versa). Some species are rare in Europe but more common globally, or vice versa. As Arie Trouwborst has pointed out in an illuminating article, large carnivores wander over hundreds of square kilometres such that it is not possible to maintain viable long-term populations in any one country. The scale at which populations are to be measured has particular ramifications for small Member States such as the Benelux nations or Malta; as well as for the conservation of transboundary populations like Alpine species.[96]

With no list of relevant and irrelevant factors having been promulgated either by the Regulations or the courts, and no criteria for assigning weight to the various considerations, English law implementing Article 12(1)(b) is too vague to be able to predict with certainty what will or will not be a disturbance.

Since disturbance of protected animals is a criminal offence punishable by a fine and up to six months' imprisonment,[97] in principle it needs to be possible for developers to predict *in advance* what conduct is unlawful.[98] Members of local

---

[94] *Disturbance and protected species: understanding and applying the law in England and Wales* (August 2007), 10. In relation to bats, this advice has been superseded by *Standing Advice Species Sheet: Bats* (February 2011), which provides no figures whatsoever.

[95] Reg 53 of the 2010 Regs requires licensing of 'any disturbance which is likely to affect significantly the local distribution or abundance' of the species, and Natural England considers that the 'rarity of a species in the locality'/'local conservation status' is relevant in deciding whether there is a disturbance, but does not define 'locality' (*Standing Advice Species Sheet: Bats*, 22 February 2011, paras 2.2 and 5.6).

[96] Arie Trouwborst, 'Managing the Carnivore Comeback: International and EU Species Protection Law and the Return of Lynx, Wolf and Bear to Western Europe' (2010) 22:3 *Journal of Environmental Law* 347–72, especially 348–49 and 356.

[97] Reg 41(8) of the 2010 Regs.

[98] See Kokott AG's view that 'The principle of legal certainty ... requires inter alia that legislation be certain and its application foreseeable by those affected by it, *in particular if it entails burdensome consequences*' (emphasis added): Case C-604 *Commission v UK*, Opinion at para 90.

planning authorities who consider the possibility of disturbance but decide to permit development could in theory be liable for aiding, abetting or procuring any eventual disturbance.[99] It is no answer simply to leave the determination of the meaning of 'disturbance' for determination on the basis of experts' evidence in every case.

Ineffective Transposition

In *Morge*, their Lordships decided the second issue as they did because

> the United Kingdom has chosen to implement article 12 of the Directive by creating criminal offences. It is not the function of a planning authority to police those offences ... it is the function of Natural England to enforce the Directive by prosecuting for these criminal offences (or granting licences to derogate from the requirements of the Directive).[100]

Lord Brown in his leading judgment reasoned that since

> even if development permission is given, the criminal sanction against any offending (and unlicensed) activity remains available ... it seems ... wrong in principle, when Natural England have the primary responsibility for ensuring compliance with the Directive, also to place a substantial burden on the planning authority.[101]

In point of fact, their Lordships did not fully appreciate the police role of Natural England. Under a Memorandum of Understanding it is normally the Crown Prosecution Service (CPS) that prosecutes species offences that take place outside protected areas, with the police being responsible for prevention and investigation of the offence, and Natural England being limited to an advisory role.[102] Natural England only prosecute breaches of licences issued by them.[103]

Be that as it may, the problem with relying on criminal sanctions to found a system of strict protection is that they are inherently *reactive* rather than preventive, as they only punish acts after they are carried out. Given that it can be predicted that certain proposed developments will impact upon protected species, it would be more in keeping with the preventive principle to restrict activities at the planning stage rather than wait until the animals are disturbed. This is why the CJEU

---

[99] Accessories and Abettors Act 1861 s 8; Magistrates' Courts Act 1980, s 44. The accessory would be liable for the activity if he foresaw a real risk that it would happen; and either encouraged it, assisted with it, or failed to intervene to prevent it if he was in a position to do so (*R v Rook* [1993] 1 WLR 1005, CA; *R v JF Alford Transport Ltd* [1997] 2 CrAppR 326).

[100] [2011] UKSC 2, [45] *per* Lady Hale.

[101] [2011] UKSC 2, [29].

[102] Memorandum of Understanding on the prevention, investigation and enforcement of Wildlife Crime between Natural England, Countryside Council for Wales, Crown Prosecution Service and the Association of Chief Police Officers of England, Wales and Northern Ireland, dated November 2008, available at: http://www.defra.gov.uk/paw/files/ne-mou-2008.pdf.

[103] Natural England, *Enforcement Policy* (March 2009) para 6, 2.

in *Commission v France* proceeded on the basis that Article 12(1) requires effective protection to be built into the town planning laws.[104]

Furthermore, the approach of the Supreme Court in *Morge* to the duty of planning authorities seems to be directly contrary to an earlier European authority, which was not cited in argument to their Lordships as both parties were agreed that the *Woolley* approach was correct.

In *Commission v Ireland*,[105] the Irish system had a set of regulations that criminalised the activities prohibited by Article 12(1)(a) to (d), subject to the defence of having obtained a licence.[106] Unlike the equivalent English regulations, there was no additional duty in the Irish regulations for planning authorities to have regard to the Habitats Directive. The Commission cited two development projects as evidence of a failure to implement the Directive: the Lough Rynn hotel development, which was approved prior to a bat survey being carried out; and the Ennis Bypass, which was known to present an appreciable risk of disturbing resting sites, but was given planning consent before the issuing of a derogation.[107]

Advocate-General Léger stated (at paragraph 57): 'I believe that it follows from Article 12(1)(d) of the Habitats Directive that it was not possible for the Irish authorities to approve the Lough Rynn Estate development project, at least without a valid derogation...'

The ECJ endorsed the reasoning of the Advocate-General, holding:

> the Irish authorities require property developers to provide information on protected species only after development consent has been granted for the project concerned. Therefore, that procedure does not prevent certain developments which may be harmful to the environment.

> The Commission refers, in particular, to ... projects having negative impacts on bat populations (the Lough Rynn Estate project), horseshoe bat roosts (the Ennis Bypass project) ...

> In that regard, as noted by the Advocate General in points 53 to 61 of his Opinion, the authorisation of a project prior to the environmental impact assessment ... (the Lough Rynn Estate project), or the authorisation of other projects without a derogation, even though the preliminary assessment also concluded that that project would have negative impacts on the environment (the Ennis Bypass project ...), shows that the species listed in Annex IV(a) ... are subject to disturbances and to threats which the Irish rules do not make it possible to prevent.

> Consequently, as regards the projects put forward by the Commission in its application, it cannot be concluded that all measures have been taken to implement effectively the system of strict protection.[108] (emphasis added)

---

[104] *Commission v France* Case C-383/09.
[105] Case C-183/05.
[106] Specifically by regs 23(2) and 25(1) of the European Communities (Natural Habitats) Regs 1997, SI 94/1997.
[107] Case C-183/05 *Commission v Ireland*, Opinion of Léger AG at paras 52, 55, and 59.
[108] Ibid, paras 34–37, judgment at paras 34–37.

From this case, it would seem to follow that in order for the UK to comply with the Directive, English planning authorities must likewise inform themselves of the presence of any protected species before granting permission, and must make any permission subject to obtaining a prior derogation.

On Lord Brown's approach the authority is entitled to grant full permission to a development unless it concludes both that a disturbance is likely and that a licence would not be granted. Lord Brown's exception suggests that a pro-development council could simply cease to require that bat surveys be carried out in support of planning applications, so that it would not then be in a position to conclude that there would be harmful impacts to bats. It seems to us that such an approach would plainly not be in a 'spirit of sincere cooperation' with the EU, would tend to jeopardise the attainment of the objectives of the Directive, and would thus be unlawful under Article 4(3) TEU. Furthermore, it would run counter to the ruling in *Commission v Ireland* that the Irish planning authorities' practice of requiring information on protected species to be supplied only after planning consent had been granted indicated a failure to properly implement the Directive.[109] Moreover, a grant of full permission without making that permission subject to obtaining a derogation would be inconsistent with *Commission v Ireland*.

It might, of course, be argued that the European Court's expectation that Ireland and France should protect EPS by means of their town-planning system was unprincipled. Criminal penalties can, at least in theory, have a deterrent effect such as to prevent the prohibited conduct being carried out. So long as a system of protection is effective, it ought not to matter whether that protection is achieved through criminal penalties or administrative procedures.

The deterrent effect of any criminal law must depend upon the likelihood of detection or prosecution, the likelihood of conviction once a prosecution is brought, and the level of punishment inflicted on those who are caught. How does the UK measure up against these criteria? We consider that there are clear deficiencies in the UK legal framework. First, prosecutions may not be brought more than two years after the commission of the alleged offence.[110] This limitation period is a significant limit on liability because the police are under-resourced and can only undertake a limited number of investigations at any one time. The National Wildlife Crime Unit had just 12 members of staff in the 2009–10 financial year,[111] and many police forces lack officers who are dedicated to tackling wildlife crime on a full-time basis.[112]

---

[109] Ibid.

[110] 2010 Regs, reg 123(3).

[111] National Wildlife Crime Unit, *Annual Report 2010*, 14, available at: http://www.defra.gov.uk/paw/pdf/nwcu-annual-report10.pdf.

[112] See, eg Cheshire (http://www.cheshire.police.uk/advice–information/rural-and-environment/wildlife-crime.aspx), Northumbria (http://www.northumbria.police.uk/about_us/wildlife/wildlife-crimeofficer) and Norfolk–whose Wildlife Crime Officers perform their roles in addition to normal duties. Norfolk Constabulary also candidly declare that 'Wildlife crime is not a main core Police Priority' (http://www.norfolk.police.uk/safetyadvice/wildlifeprotection/tacklingtheproblems/wildlife-crimeofficers.aspx).

Secondly, we have already commented that the definition of 'disturbance' post-*Morge* is uncertain, and prosecutions will probably have to rely on contested expert evidence of fact such that unless the case was particularly blatant there would always be a 'reasonable doubt' as to whether the species was 'disturbed'. It could indeed be strongly argued that the law is too uncertain to form the basis of an information in the Magistrates Courts.

Thirdly, with regard to the level of punishment, the maximum penalty under Regulation 41(8) for disturbance is a six-month prison term and a fine of £5,000. This would be unlikely to deter a developer who stood to gain hundreds of thousands or millions of pounds from a development, especially if the developer was a company or an individual based overseas and was not liable to imprisonment.

Fourthly, there will be many instances where authorities are simply unaware that development potentially affecting EPS is proposed. As Nardell and Simpson point out, there are many categories of development which are permitted by statutory instrument, for which there is no requirement to apply to local planning authorities for permission.[113] Even where the authority's consent is required by law, Natural England's standing advice is that it wishes only to be consulted where an Environmental Impact Assessment is required, or where the proposed development either affects designated protected sites, or is likely to affect a species on which there is no standing advice.[114] This therefore 'leaves local planning authorities without Natural England's support to deal with many 'non-significant' EPS cases where Article 12(1) will still be breached',[115] and leaves Natural England in ignorance of such cases.

With these deficiencies in the legislative framework, one would expect detection and conviction rates to be poor and this is reflected in the data.

As it happens, bats provide a well-documented case study of the UK Regulations in action, partly because of the vigilance of the Bat Conservation Trust (BCT), which has a 'bat hotline' for members of the public to report incidents; and partly because under the Eurobats Agreement[116] the UK government gathers data on bat-related crimes.

In 2010, the BCT logged 301 incidents, which it considered represented a 'drop in the ocean' of actual incidents. It referred only 117 to the authorities for investigation, stating that it wishes to protect those who seek advice in the interests of preventing recurrences.[117] Of those incidents referred, 21 per cent related to disturbance, 12 per cent involved obstructions to roosts and 62 per cent involved damage to roosts. The police concluded that only 15 per cent of the cases had not involved any criminality, but they gave only three cautions and took no formal

---

[113] Nardell and Simpson, above n 17, 1171. The rights are granted by the Town and Country Planning (General Permitted Development) Order 1995.

[114] Natural England, *Standing Advice for Protected Species* (22 February 2011) para 5.

[115] Penny Simpson, above n 88, 3.

[116] Agreement on the Conservation of Bats in Europe, London, 4 December 1991.

[117] Bat Conservation Trust, *Bat Crime Review, 2003–2010*, 3 and 5 available at: http://www.bats.org.uk/publications_download.php/979/Bat_Crime_Review_2011.pdf.

action in respect of the other incidents. In 2010, only 28 per cent of incidents were not proceeded with on the basis of there being insufficient evidence, which suggests that the uncertain state of the law and the conception that it is not in the public interest to take action are main the causes of the low prosecution rate.[118] In respect of bat crimes, the BCT identify as the principal constraints the time limits, lack of police resources, the attitudes of the courts, and a reluctance to prosecute those who claim that they were acting on consultants' advice.[119]

The UK's report to the Sixth Meeting of the Parties to the Eurobats Agreement indicates that in the years 2006 to 2009 inclusive, there were five successful prosecutions arising out of 288 incidents. In 2009 there were 124 incidents of suspected bat crime investigated by the police, which resulted in three convictions of property developers, and two cautions. The fines were £1,500 or £2,000 in each case.[120] These figures indicate a conviction rate of around 2% of the incidents investigated.

However, bats are atypical in that crimes against them are one of six national priorities for the UK National Wildlife Crime Unit.[121] The great majority of EPS are afforded lesser priority. Aggregate figures for all wildlife crimes including domestically protected species and CITES cases show that the Unit processed 9,999 incidents in 2009–10, achieving 115 individual convictions with 523 ongoing investigations and 72 pending court cases at the end of the reporting period.[122] Of the incidents investigated, this is only a 1 per cent conviction rate.

Overall, the figures suggest that only a small fraction of reported disturbance of protected species is being punished, and it is likely that most incidents go unreported to the police. This is evidence that a primarily penal approach to implementing the Directive is ineffective in preventing the disturbance of EPS. The *Morge* decision will only increase the UK's reliance on the action of an over-stretched police force to prevent the disturbance of protected species.

For the above reasons, in our view the UK has failed properly to implement the Directive by putting in place a system of 'strict protection', and the *Morge* ruling not only failed to recognise this but will exacerbate the problem.

Towards a Principled Approach

What then do we consider would be the correct approach? First, we consider that the Regulations require detailed amendment so that there is sufficient certainty

---

[118] Ibid, 6–8.

[119] Ibid, 9.

[120] Defra, *National Report on the Implementation of the European Agreement on the Conservation of Populations of European Bats* (June 2010), 10–11.

[121] UK National Wildlife Crime Unit, *Annual Report 2010*, 2.

[122] National Wildlife Crime Unit, *Annual Report 2010*, number of incidents 11; disposal figures in table and footnote 13, 9.

about the test of 'disturbance' to be applied. Secondly, the developer must supply information about the ecological impact of the proposed works at the time when the application is made. Thirdly, while in principle it may be acceptable to have a division of roles between Natural England and planning authorities, developments must not be permitted to commence unless the appropriate authorities have—applying the correct test—either concluded that there will be no disturbance or issued a licence on the basis of the derogation criteria.

Whether the current division of functions between Natural England and the local planning authority is optimal must be open to doubt. While assessments of ecological impacts on species and their conservation status require scientific expertise, it might be considered that it should be for elected politicians rather than officers of Natural England to make the judgment whether there is a 'satisfactory alternative' to a scheme, and whether there is an 'imperative reason of overriding public interest' for it to go ahead. But given the current division of functions, how is the planning authority to ensure that no unlawful disturbance takes place? There are several possibilities that we discuss in turn:

(a) To refuse to grant permission unless Natural England had indicated that it was satisfied that there would be no disturbance or that it would license the prospective works. This would amount to a blanket policy which might be said to be accepting dictation by another agency and fettering the planning authority's own discretion.[123] It would also fail to ensure that a derogation was issued before works commenced. For those reasons, it would probably be unlawful.

(b) To refuse to grant permission unless Natural England had actually granted a licence, if the planning authority thought it necessary. Although this approach would satisfy the requirements of the Directive, it would amount to allowing Natural England to dictate the planning authority's decision, and so could be unlawful on domestic law principles.

(c) To grant full permission if the planning authority was satisfied that there was no disturbance, or that Natural England was likely to license the prospective works. This would not amount to being 'dictated to' by Natural England, as the planning authority would have made its own decision based on the Directive's derogation criteria, but it would not guarantee that there would be no disturbance, or that any necessary licence was obtained. Consequently, this approach would be insufficient.

(d) To grant permission if satisfied that there would be no disturbance or that Natural England was likely to license the prospective works, but on condition, in the latter case, that Natural England issued any licence that it thought necessary before the works could commence.

---

[123] By analogy with *Lavender v Secretary of State for Housing and Local Government* [1970] 1 WLR 1231.

It seems to us that option (d) is the approach most consistent with the European case law and with domestic law. This was the approach that appears to have been contemplated by Waksman J in *Woolley*, and by Ward LJ in *Morge*.[124] It is also the approach contemplated by central government policy Circular 06/2005, which reads:

> It is essential that the presence or otherwise of protected species, and the extent that they may be affected by the proposed development, is established before the planning permission is granted, otherwise all relevant material considerations may not have been addressed in making the decision ... Where this is the case, the survey should be completed and any necessary measures to protect the species should be in place, through conditions and/or planning obligations, before the permission is granted. In appropriate circumstances the permission may also impose a condition preventing the development from proceeding without the prior acquisition of a licence ...

> *the Directive's provisions are clearly relevant in reaching planning decisions, and these should be made in a manner which takes them fully into account.*[125] (emphasis added)

As the point was not at issue between the parties, this passage was not referred to the attention of the Justices of the Supreme Court in *Morge*. It might be said that this approach amounts to accepting dictation from another agency. In the case of *Lavender v Secretary of State for Housing and Local Government*, the defendant Secretary of State refused planning permission for a quarry on the basis that he would not allow a scheme that the Minister of Agriculture had objected to. The court held that this amounted to a fettering of the Secretary's discretion. However, although there is no direct authority on the point, it is strongly arguable that the reasoning in *Lavender* does not apply to our scenario. In that case, the Minister of Agriculture had 'no status save perhaps in a consultative capacity and certainly no status to make the effective decision'.[126] By contrast, the decision as to licensing is—as Lord Brown pointed out in *Morge*—properly one for Natural England. Furthermore, if a licence was necessary then the works could not be lawfully carried out without one, such that Natural England *would* hold an effective veto over the development. The planning authority would have considered the requirements of the Directive itself, made its own decision on the planning merits, and said that so far as it was concerned the works could go ahead. However, the planning condition would ensure that the developers approached Natural England for an assessment of the likelihood of disturbance, and that if Natural England thought there was a disturbance the works only went ahead with the benefit of a derogation from Article 12 of the Directive.

In any event, even if it did amount to a fettering of discretion there is a strong argument that a court should uphold the condition. It appears that Article 12(1)

---

[124] [2009] EWHC 1227 (Admin), [27] and [28]; [2010] EWCA Civ 608, [61], passage reproduced at p 59 above.
[125] Office of the Deputy Prime Minister, Circular 06/2005, *Biodiversity And Geological Conservation— Statutory Obligations And Their Impact Within The Planning System* (16 August 2005), paras 99 and 116.
[126] [1970] 1 WLR 1231 *per* Willis J, 1237.

of the Directive has direct effect.[127] Where a rule of national law prevents a Member State giving effect to a directly effective provision of EU law, that rule has to be read down or set aside.[128]

To what standard of proof must the planning authority be satisfied that there will not be a disturbance? In *Commission v Ireland*, Léger AG referred to the authorities' awareness of there being 'an appreciable risk' of disturbance,[129] and the Court held that in those circumstances there had been a failure to implement 'requisite measures'. It would seem from this that once the planning authority considers there to be a real risk of a prohibited activity, they must then go on to consider whether derogations would be needed.

Nothing in the Supreme Court's judgment in *Morge* prevents planning authorities from continuing to strictly follow approach (d),[130] it remains in accordance with national policy, and we consider that they must do so in order to comply with the Directive.[131]

Conclusion

The Supreme Court's ruling in *Morge* has not dispelled the fog of uncertainty that obscures the meaning of the word 'disturbance' in Article 12 of the Directive. It has missed the chance to mitigate the unspecific transposition of this article into domestic law. We have suggested that its new formulation begs more questions than it solves, and that the correct approach would have been to refer the whole question to the CJEU for a definitive ruling.

The main effect of the ruling has been to weaken the UK's system of protection for EPS by removing the obligations upon planning authorities to satisfy themselves before granting permission that a protected species would either not be disturbed, or that its disturbance would be lawfully licensed; and by authorising them to dispense with imposing a condition that the proposed activities be licensed

---

[127] *R v Secretary of State for Trade and Industry ex p Greenpeace Ltd (No 2)* [2000] 2 CMLR 94, [80] per Maurice Kay J; Associazione *Italiana Per Il World Wildlife Fund and Others v Regione Veneto*, Case C-118/94 (Art 12(1)(a) of the Habitats Directive); Case C-127/02 *Landelijke Vereniging tot Behoud van de Waddenzee, Nederlandse Vereniging tot Bescherming van Vogels v Staatssecretaris van Landbouw, Natuurbeheer en Visserij*, (Art 6 of the Habitats Directive); *World Wildlife Fund and Others v Autonome Provinz Bozen and others*, Case C-435/97 (EIA directive).

[128] Case C-213/89 *R v Secretary of State for Transport, ex p Factortame*.

[129] Case C-183/05, Opinion of Léger AG, para 61.

[130] Lord Brown and Lady Hale merely ruled that councillors were not legally 'required' to follow the approach outlined by Ward LJ ([2011] UKSC 2, [30] and [45]); not that it would be wrong for them to do so. We concur with Jason Lowther that it is important that local planning authorities are not 'lulled into complacency' by the ruling (see 'Determining the meaning of "disturbance" for European Protected Species', (2011) 23(2) *Journal of Environmental Law*, 319, 329.

[131] Accordingly, it appears to us that Nardell and Simpson's suggestion that authorities are entitled to take a 'broad brush approach' to disturbance and the derogation tests based on 'summary' advice is contrary to the scheme of the Directive (Nardell and Simpson, above n 17, 1168).

before works can commence. This was done without hearing full argument on the point, and apparently in ignorance of the contrary authority of *Commission v Ireland*, Case C-183/05, which has since been applied by the CJEU in *Commission v France*, Case C-383/09. It has removed what was previously a useful mechanism for preventing harm to the EPS, and has left only the criminal law to safeguard protected species from development. It has been argued here that this approach is inconsistent with the 'precautionary principle' and 'preventive principle' of EU environmental law, and that the criminal law is an ineffective mechanism for deterring the activities prohibited by the Directive. Consequently, by analogy with Case C-103/00 *Commission v Greece* and Case C-183/05 *Commission v Ireland*, it appears that the UK is in breach of its obligations under the European Treaties.

We have suggested that, as a matter of EU law, the correct approach for planning authorities is to only grant planning permission if they are satisfied either that there will be no disturbance or that the derogation criteria are likely to be met, and in the latter case only subject to a condition that necessary licences are issued by the licensing authority before the works commence.

4

How to Deal with Candidate SACs and Potential SPAs

GREGORY JONES QC AND NED WESTAWAY

… in order to ensure the restoration or maintenance of natural habitats and species of Community interest at a favourable conservation status, it is necessary to designate special areas of conservation in order to create a coherent European ecological network according to a specified timetable.[1]

Introduction

Directive 92/43/EEC on the conservation of natural habitats (the Habitats Directive) was a major step forward in European environmental law. The key provision is the establishment of a network of protected areas under the aspirational title 'Natura 2000'. Natura 2000 encompasses Special Protection Areas (SPAs) designated for wild and migratory birds under Directive 79/409/EEC[2] (now consolidated as Directive 2009/147/EC[3] the Wild Birds Directive), and Special Areas of Conservation (SACs) designated for habitats or species of importance under the Habitats Directive itself.

There is nothing to prevent Member States designating land as both an SPA and an SAC. In fact, the failure to additionally designate an existing SAC as an SPA (or vice versa) may breach European conservation law.[4] Due to the overlap, the Commission is not currently able to calculate the *combined* extent of Natura 2000 across Europe;[5] although the terrestrial network covers an area at least as large

---

[1] Recital to Council Directive 92/43/EEC on the conservation of natural habitats and of wild fauna and flora (the Habitats Directive) [1992] OJ L206/7.

[2] [1979] OJ L103/1.

[3] [2010] OJ L20/7.

[4] See Case C-535/07 *Commission v Austria* 14 October 2010, [24]: 'the legal regimes of the Birds and Habitats Directives are separate'.

[5] Vol 29 Natura 2000 Newsletter (December 2010) 8 available at: http://ec.europa.eu/environment/nature/info/pubs/docs/nat2000newsl/nat29_en.pdf.

as Spain and Italy combined[6] and an increasing area of protected marine sites is being designated by Member States.[7]

Two points are worth emphasising at the outset. First, the process of designation is incomplete. 'Nature and biodiversity' is one of four objectives of the Community's current Environmental Action Plan,[8] this aspires to fully establish the Natura 2000 network by the end of the plan period in 2012.[9] However, the EC's May 2010 'barometer' shows that in many Member States, including the UK, the network of both SPAs and SACs is inadequate and further designations are required.[10] Secondly, the duty to designate European conservation sites is in any event an ongoing duty. Article 11 of the Habitats Directive requires Member States to undertake surveillance of the conservation status of habitats and species; in the light of such surveillance new SACs, or changes and extensions to existing SACs, may be required. Article 12 of the Wild Birds Directive requires Member States to supply the Commission with triennial reports on implementation of the Directive's provisions, including the creation of SPAs in Article 3(2)(a). In *Commission v Austria*[11] the European Court of Justice (ECJ)[12] confirmed that there is an ongoing obligation to classify sites as SPAs, so that where outstanding features of natural interest only come to light later, a site is not precluded from European protection.

It is, therefore, a question of some importance what protection is afforded to conservation areas before they are designated as European sites. The protection for SPAs and SACs is contained in Article 6(2)–(4) of the Habitats Directive; these provisions apply to SPAs classified under the Wild Birds Directive[13] and Sites of Community Importance (SCIs) identified by the Commission under the third paragraph of Article 6(2) of the Habitats Directive, that Member States are obliged to designate as SACs. However, there is no protection in European law[14] for candidate SACs (cSACs), potential SPAs (pSPAs) or potential candidate sites. The protection of sites at this stage is largely a question of national policy. This chapter assesses the protection afforded to such sites and suggests that the lack of a principled European approach protecting potential Natura 2000 sites is surprising.

---

[6] 'Healthcheck for Europe's protected nature' available at: http://ec.europa.eu/environment/nature/info/pubs/docs/brochures/healthcheck.pdf.

[7] The UK, for example, submitted 15 new European marine sites to the Commission for consideration as SACs on 20 August 2010 and a further three were proposed by the Joint Nature Conservation Committee (JNCC) in July 2011.

[8] Decision No 1600/2002/EC of the European Parliament and the Council laying down the Sixth Community Environment Action Programme [2002] OJ L242/1.

[9] Ibid, Art (2)(a).

[10] See above n 5, 8–9.

[11] Case C-209/04 *Commission v Austria* [2006] ECR I-2755; [2006] Env LR 39.

[12] The official name of the Court, since the Lisbon Treaty came into force on 1 December 2009, is Court of Justice of the European Union (CJEU), although the original name European Court of Justice (ECJ) and variant European Union Court of Justice (EUCJ) are still used by some commentators, we shall use ECJ for pre-Lisbon decisions and CJEU for post-Lisbon decisions.

[13] Habitats Directive, Art 7.

[14] UK law has taken a different approach, as explained below.

The Designation Process

Article 4(1) of the Wild Birds Directive provides that

Member States shall classify in particular the most suitable territories in number and size as special protection areas for the conservation of [Annex I] species in the geographical sea and land area where this Directive applies.

SPAs are sites identified as important for the breeding, feeding or migration of rare or at risk species of birds in the EU. It is established that only ornithological criteria are relevant to the designation of SPAs.[15] '[E]conomic and recreational requirements' (within Article 2 of the Directive) are not relevant to the designation process.[16] In *Commission v Netherlands*[17] the ECJ held that Member States must classify as SPAs all sites which appear to be the most suitable for conservation.[18] The Dutch government had classified only half of the sites from an authoritative inventory of important bird areas as SPAs; it was held that this was 'manifestly less' than the number it ought to have classified, so there had been a breach of the Directive. A Member State has discretion in deciding what sites to classify as SPAs, but it is not unfettered and must accord with ecological reality.

The designation process for SACs under the Habitats Directive is multi-staged, with the European Commission given a coordinating role. Stage 1[19] is the drawing up by Member States of lists of SCIs within their borders containing either species prescribed in Annex II or Annex I habitat types. Annex III contains broad ecological criteria, such as population distribution, on which a relative assessment can be made. The list must be submitted for Stage 2[20] to the Commission, who in agreement with the Member State adopts a final list of SCIs. Member States must designate sites included on the list as soon as possible.[21] However, there remains scope for considerable delay before an SCI becomes an SAC; the Commission's list may be drawn up as late as three years after the Member State's Stage 1 submission.

The Member State's initial candidate lists should cover adequate territory[22] and must be based solely on ecological criteria.[23] In *First Corporate Shipping Ltd*[24] the ECJ emphasised the goal of creating a 'coherent European ecological network of

---

[15] Case C-355/90 *Commission v Spain (Santoña Marshes)* [1993] ECR I-4221, [26]–[27]; Case C-44/95 *R v SSE ex p RSPB* (Lappel Bank) [1996] ECR I-3805, [26].

[16] Ibid.

[17] Case C-3/96 *Commission v Netherlands* [1998] ECR I-3031.

[18] Ibid, [62].

[19] Habitats Directive, Art 4(1).

[20] Ibid, Art 4(2).

[21] Ibid, Art 4(4).

[22] Case C-71/99 *Commission v Germany* [2001] ECR I-5811.

[23] Case C-371/98 *R v SSETR ex p First Corporate Shipping Ltd* [2000] ECR I-9235; [2001] Env LR 34, [77]–[78].

[24] Ibid.

SACs'. In order to do this the Commission requires an 'exhaustive list' of potential sites of relevant ecological interest; were ecologically qualifying sites omitted from the list, the Commission's ability to achieve that goal would be undermined. Article 2(3) of the Habitats Directive, which provides that measures under the Directive 'shall take account of economic, social and cultural requirements', has no impact in relation to a Member State's selection of candidate sites.

Sites containing priority natural habitats or species *must* be listed as SCIs and consequently designated as SACs.[25] For other sites the situation was, at least until recently, less certain. Advocate General Léger in *First Corporate Shipping* considered that 'economic and social requirements may justify a site [other than one with a priority habitat or species] … not being designated as an SAC'.[26] In coming to this view, the Advocate General was influenced by the emphasis on sustainable development in the Habitats Directive: sustainable development is classically thought of as encompassing social and economic factors as well as environmental ones. However, in *Stadt Papenburg*[27] the CJEU held that a Member State could only refuse to agree with the Commission to designate an SAC on grounds of environmental protection. The CJEU followed Advocate General Sharpston's approach, who considered that economic considerations (and therefore sustainable development) were adequately catered for by the Article 6(4) procedure once a site is designated.

UK Designation

The UK initially took the view that SPAs and SACs could be adequately protected using the established system of Sites of Special Scientific Interest (SSSIs) notified under the Wildlife and Countryside Act 1981. This was optimistic in both the substantive and geographical scope of the protection afforded by the SSSI designation: to take just one example, the SSSI regime did not apply below the mean low-water mark. In 1994 regulations were adopted[28] that gave specific protection to 'European sites', these have been consolidated and updated by the Conservation of Habitats and Species Regulations 2010.

All European sites benefit from the protection derived from the Habitats Directive, including the appropriate assessment of plans or projects.[29] European sites are defined at regulation 8 of the 2010 Regulations as (a) SACs;[30] and

---

[25] Habitats Directive, pt 1 of Annex III.

[26] At [47]–[54].

[27] Case C-226/08 *Stadt Papenburg v Bundesrepublik Deutschland* [2010] Env LR 19, [33].

[28] Conservation (Natural Habitats etc) Regulations 1994.

[29] Conservation of Habitats and Species Regulations 2010, reg 21.

[30] Ie Sites of Community Importance on the Commissions final list (under Art 4(2) of the Habitats Directive) and SACs proposed exceptionally by the Commission on its own motion (under Art 5).

(b) SPAs and, importantly, cSACs until such time as those sites are confirmed as SACs or a is decision taken that they should not be designated SACs.[31]

Like other Member States, the UK is required to consider the criteria in Annex III of the Habitats Directive in selecting cSACs. There is no designation guidance for SPAs in the Wild Birds Directive; at national level the Joint Nature Conservation Committee (JNCC)[32] recommends the following initial selection guidelines (Stage 1):

— if the area is used regularly by 1 per cent or more of the Great Britain population of a species listed in Annex 1 of the Directive;
— if the area is used regularly by 1 per cent or more of the biogeographical population of a regularly occurring migratory species (other than those listed in Annex 1) in any season;
— if the area is used regularly by over 20,000 waterfowl or 20,000 seabirds in any season; and
— various combinations of criteria involving considerations such as popula-tion size and density, species range, breeding success, history of occupancy, multi-species areas, naturalness of site and severe weather refuges.

Stage 2 is to consider the most suitable areas in size and number on the basis of seven broad criteria: (1) population size and density, (2) species range, (3) breed-ing success, (4) history of occupancy, (5) multi-species areas, (6) naturalness and (7) severe weather refuges.

The UK SPA Review is currently under way, this is a broad assessment of the adequacy of the Natura 2000 network in the UK, considering where gaps need filling, especially in relation to cropped habitats. The ongoing review means that pSPAs are likely to be a changing and controversial topic in the UK and Gibraltar.

Undesignated SPAs: Direct Effect And Effectiveness

Article 288 of the Treaty on the Functioning of the European Union (TFEU) (ex Article 249 Treaty Establishing the European Community (TEC)) provides that directives 'shall be binding, as to the result to be achieved, upon each Member State to which it is addressed, but shall leave to the national authorities the choice of form and methods'. Where a Member State has failed to implement the provi-sions of a directive within the time limit provided and a provision is otherwise

---

[31] The Conservation (Natural Habitats etc) Regulations 1994, reg 8(1)(e); the same approach is taken in Ireland, see European Communities (Natural Habitats) Regulations 1997 and *Sweetman v An Bord Pleanála* [2009] IEHC 599, [26]ff. cSACs did not fall within the definition of European sites in the 1994 Regulations as originally enacted but were added by reg 2 of the Conservation (Natural Habitats, &c) (Amendment) (England) Regulations 2000.

[32] See http://www.jncc.gov.uk.

clear and binding, the CJEU may treat it as directly effective against the defaulting Member State.[33] Two *rationales* underlie direct effect: (i) ensuring the effectiveness of EC law and (ii) preventing Member States benefitting from their failure to comply with EC law (sometimes called Member State estoppel).

In *Basses Corbières*[34] France failed to designate any sites as SPAs in an area of the Pyrenees known for its rare birds including the Bonelli's Eagle, France sought to rely on Article 6 of the Habitats Directive to permit quarrying activities; the ECJ's assessment was as follows:

> 51 … a Member State cannot derive an advantage from its failure to comply with its Community obligation.

> 52 In that respect, if it were lawful for a Member State, which, in breach of the birds directive, has failed to classify as an SPA a site which should have been so classified, to rely on Article 6(3) and (4) of the habitats directive, that State might enjoy such an advantage.

> 53 Since no formal measure for classifying such a site as an SPA exists, it is particularly difficult for the Commission, in accordance with Article 155 of the EC Treaty (now Article 211 EC), to carry out effective monitoring of the application by Member States of the procedure laid down by Article 6(3) and (4) of the habitats directive and to establish, in appropriate cases, the existence of possible failures to fulfil the obligations arising thereunder. In particular, the risk is significantly increased that plans or projects not directly connected with or necessary to the management of the site, and affecting its integrity, may be accepted by the national authorities in breach of that procedure, escape the Commission's monitoring and cause serious, or irreparable ecological damage, contrary to the conservation requirements of that site.

> 54 Natural or legal persons entitled to assert before the national courts interests connected with the protection of nature, and especially wild bird life, which in this case means primarily environmental protection organisations, would face comparable difficulties.

> 55 A situation of this kind would be likely to endanger the attainment of the objective of special protection for wild bird life set forth in Article 4 of the birds directive, as interpreted by the case-law of the Court (see, in particular, Case C-44/95 *Royal Society for the Protection of Birds* [1996] ECR I-3805, paragraphs 23 and 25).

Article 6(2)–(4) of the Habitats Directive applies to sites classified as SPAs.[35] However, as France had not designated any SPAs in the Pyrenees, it was held that the Wild Birds Directive had been breached and the previous stricter provisions in Article 4(4) of that Directive applied. As interpreted by the ECJ Article 4(4) only allows harm to an SPA in exceptional circumstances, such as overriding reasons of public health or safety[36] and there is no derogation procedure as in Article 6

---

[33] See, eg Case 32/84 *Van Gend & Loos NV v Inspecteur der Invoerrechten en Accijnzen* [1985] ECR 779.
[34] Case C-374/98 *Commission v France (Basses Corbières)* ECR I-10799.
[35] By virtue of Habitats Directive, Art 7.
[36] See Case C-57/89 *Commission v Germany (Leybucht Dykes)* [1991] ECR I-883.

of the Habitats Directive. France was not entitled to rely upon the more relaxed provisions of the Habitats Directive given its failure to implement the Directive. Likewise, the failure by Spain to designate the Santoña Marshes, one of the most important Iberian ecosystems for aquatic birds, engaged Article 4(4) directly, this precluded most of the planned development at the site, including an important link road.[37]

The application of Article 4(4) where Member States have unlawfully failed to classify SPAs is a curious resurrection of an otherwise superseded legal provision. In *Basses Corbières* the ECJ justified applying the law in this way as it would incentivise Member States to classify sites so that they could benefit from the more relaxed derogations under the Habitats Directive.[38] This is a striking application of the principle of effectiveness: not only should Member States not frustrate the operation of EU law they should be actively encouraged to engage with it.

Candidate SACs: No Direct Effect but Duty of Cooperation

In contrast to the strictly protective approach outlined above, the CJEU has refused to extend the direct effect of the provisions of the Habitats Directive to candidate SACs. The issue arose in *Dragaggi*[39] where the Italian authority withdrew a dredging concession from a company on the grounds that it required appropriate assessment under Article 6 of the Habitats Directive. The area was on the list of SCIs submitted to the European Commission. The court held that the protection in Article 6 was not directly effective as it would contradict Article 4(5) and would preclude the Commission from excluding a site from the final list of SCIs were it to disagree with a Member State's assessment.[40] Advocate General Kokott put the same point more pithily: 'Direct applicability of those provisions would—unlawfully—anticipate the Commission's selection decision.' However, there is no obvious reason why an *interim* direct application of Article 6(2)–(4) to cSACs would bind the Commission's hand. If a decision were taken not to designate the site, those provisions would simply cease to apply. It seems to us that such an interpretation would more accurately reflect the underlying purposes of the Directive and the precautionary principle. Taking a more relaxed approach than Article 6(2)–(4) to the protection of candidate SACs may in fact prejudice the selection of those sites as SCIs and their eventual designation as SACs; the result of this could be that nature conservation interests do not receive the European protection that they deserve. This interpretation would be consistent with the

---

[37] *Commission v Spain*, above n 15.
[38] At [56].
[39] Case C-117/03 *Società Italiana Dragaggi* [2005] ECR I-167; [2005] Env LR 31.
[40] Ibid, [24]

CJEU's recent decision in *Stadt Papenburg*[41] that SCIs may only be selected on ecological grounds. It would also be consistent with the approach adopted under UK (and Irish) law, noted above, where cSACs are granted protection until a decision is taken on their candidacy.[42]

However, the ECJ in *Dragaggi* held that a Member State is nonetheless 'required to take protective measures appropriate for the purpose of safeguarding [the] ecological interest' of a cSAC.[43] The Advocate General, who came to a similar conclusion, considered that this was an expression of the principle of Member State cooperation in good faith, so that the Commission is able to select the 'best sites' from those submitted. The question arises what is the difference between appropriate protective measures as set out in *Dragaggi* and the protection afforded by Article 6(2)–(4). From a precautionary perspective, the right approach would be to protect cSACs *more strictly* than designated SACs. It ought not to be possible for plans or projects to be carried out in a cSAC that would prejudice the Commission's final selection of sites. Yet this is not the approach that is currently favoured by the CJEU. In two recent cases, the court has looked at what 'appropriate' protection means. In *Bund Naturschutz*[44] the ECJ considered the proposed construction of a motorway extension that would impact on a cSAC. The Court held that Member States may not authorise interventions 'which may pose the risk of seriously compromising the ecological characteristics' of a candidate site.[45] This is a high threshold and would clearly permit plans or projects in cSACs that would have a negative assessment under Article 6(3). *Doñana Natural Park*[46] related to similar circumstances and approved the test in *Bund Naturschutz*. After submission of the Natural Park as an SCI, the upgrading of a country road along the edge of the site was proposed. The Commission was particularly concerned about the effect of increased and quicker traffic on the Iberian lynx. However, the CJEU held that the Commission had failed to prove that the upgraded road put the lynx 'in great danger of being struck by vehicles'. Of course, appropriate assessment under Article 6(3) is in part designed to overcome a lack of information, but that provision did not apply to the Natural Park. The protection afforded by the CJEU to cSACs therefore appears to be significantly weaker than that under Article 6, and weaker still than that under Article 4(4) of the Wild Birds Directive. Given that Natura 2000 is supposed to be a coherent ecological network, this inconsistency in legal interpretation is puzzling and indeed, questionable. cSACs ought, one would think, to receive at least equivalent protection to SACs.

---

[41] See *Stadt Papenburg* above n 27.

[42] An analogy can be drawn with the application of the principle of effectiveness to unimplemented Directives whereby Member States may not take action that could seriously compromise attainment of the objectives of a Directive even before the date for transposition has expired (see, eg Case C-212/04 *Konstantinos Adeneler v Ellinikos Organismos Galaktos* [2006] ECR I-06057, [123]).

[43] See *Società Italiana Dragaggi* above n 39, [29].

[44] Case C-244/05 *Commission v Bund Naturschutz* [2006] ECR I-8445.

[45] Ibid, [46]–[47].

[46] Case C-308/08 *Commission v Spain* (*Doñana Natural Park*) 20 May 2010.

On 8 March 2011, the CJEU gave judgment in *Slovakian Bears*,[47] a case in which the Ministry for the Environment in Slovakia had refused a request by an environmental association, established in accordance with Slovak law, to be a party to administrative proceedings relating to certain derogations from the Habitats Directive. An administrative appeal brought by the association against the refusal had also failed. The association contended that this was in breach of Article 9(3) of the Aarhus Convention, which provides:

> 3. In addition and without prejudice to the review procedures referred to in paragraphs 1 and 2 above, each Party shall ensure that, where they meet the criteria, if any, laid down in its national law, members of the public have access to administrative or judicial procedures to challenge acts and omissions by private persons and public authorities which contravene provisions of its national law relating to the environment.

The CJEU was asked to give a preliminary ruling on whether inter alia the provisions of Article 9(3) had direct effect in EU law. The CJEU held that it did not, but added the following:

> 50 It follows that, in so far as concerns a species protected by EU law, and in particular the Habitats Directive, it is for the national court, in order to ensure effective judicial protection in the fields covered by EU environmental law, to interpret its national law in a way which, to the fullest extent possible, is consistent with the objectives laid down in Article 9(3) of the Aarhus Convention.

> 51 Therefore, it is for the referring court to interpret, to the fullest extent possible, the procedural rules relating to the conditions to be met in order to bring administrative or judicial proceedings in accordance with the objectives of Article 9(3) of the Aarhus Convention and the objective of effective judicial protection of the rights conferred by EU law, so as to enable an environmental protection organisation, such as the zoskupenie, to challenge before a court a decision taken following administrative proceedings liable to be contrary to EU environmental law (see, to that effect, Case C-432/05 *Unibet* [2007] ECR I-2271, paragraph 44, and Impact, paragraph 54).

UK Approach to cSACs, pSPAs and Proposed cSACs

The UK Government has adopted a more comprehensive policy approach than that required expressly by the provisions of the Habitats Directive. National policy guidance provides that both pSPAs and cSACs should be 'considered in the same way as if they had already been classified or designated'.[48]

---

[47] Case C-240/09 *Lesoochranárske zoskupenie VLK v Ministerstvo ivotného prostredia Slovenskej republiky* [2011] ECR I-0000.
[48] Para 6 of PPS9 (*Biodiversity and Geological Conservation*); consistent guidance is provided by the Scottish Executive, see, eg *Habitats Regulations Appraisal of Plans—Guidance for Plan-making bodies in Scotland* (Version 1.0) August 2010.

Paragraph 5 of Office of the Deputy Prime Minister (ODPM)[49] Circular 06/2005[50] reiterates that

> [a]s a matter of policy, the Government has chosen to apply the procedures described below [ie appropriate assessment etc] unless otherwise specified, in respect of Ramsar sites and potential SPAs (pSPAs), even though these are not European sites as a matter of law. This will assist the UK Government in fully meeting its obligations under the Birds Directive and Ramsar Convention.[51]

Under the *Basses Corbières* principle, pSPAs are protected by Article 4(4) of the Wild Birds Directive, but only to the extent that there has been a breach of that Directive through failure to classify the site. The implicit limits of this were discussed in *Humber Sea Terminal Ltd*[52] where Ouseley J distinguished between the effectiveness/estoppel principle in *Basses Corbières* and the application of UK policy. In *Humber Sea Terminal Ltd* a harbour revision order made by the Secretary of State affecting a pSPA was challenged. The claimant argued that the Secretary of State had misapplied European law by undertaking an appropriate assessment, rather than applying the stricter provisions of the Wild Birds Directive. The judge rejected this argument, holding that European law can only be relied upon if a successful allegation of breach of the Directive by failure to classify sites is made out. That was not argued by the claimant. Accordingly, the Secretary of State had properly followed national policy. Only where the national authorities have manifestly failed to designate an area could it be argued that the additional protections in Article 4(4) apply; this would require at the very least a strong case for designation, clear knowledge of that by the public authorities and a serious or repeated failure to act. The protection in UK policy that pSPAs will be treated as if they were European sites is of much wider application that the principle in *Basses Corbières*.

National policy does not stop there; paragraph 6 of Circular 06/2005 refers to *proposed* SACs (pSACs), and states that planning authorities should take note of this potential designation in their consideration of any planning applications that may affect the site. Presumably this encompasses SCIs that have yet to be included on a candidacy list submitted to the Commission.

Exactly when a potential or proposed site comes into existence is an important question given the policy protection that applies to these sites. On one view, any site put forward by anyone on the basis of ecological or ornithological criteria

---

[49] Under the then Rt Hon John Prescott MP, the ODPM had responsibility for Housing, Planning, Local Government and the Regions.

[50] At the time of writing, 10 September 2011, the Circular is under review.

[51] The UK Government's National Planning Policy Framework issued in March 2012 confirms this approach (if anything in stronger terms), stating that a European level of protection be extended to 'potential Special Protection Areas and *possible Special Areas of Conservation*' (emphasis added), as well as 'proposed Ramsar sites' and sites identified for compensatory measures for adverse effects on existing European sites (para 118).

[52] *Humber Sea Terminal Ltd v Secretary of State for Transport* [2005] EWHC 1289 (Admin); [2006] Env LR 4.

ought to be considered as a pSPA or pSAC. However, this could open the door to a good deal of confusion. Recent Planning Inspectorate (PINS) guidance advising planning inspectors of how to decide issues during planning appeals is at least clear; paragraphs 22 to 23 deserve to be quoted in full:

22. Parties to an appeal may sometimes argue that a particular area meets the criteria for a European site, eg a SPA or SAC, and ask the Inspector to conclude on whether such an area should be treated as if it were already a designated/classified site. It may be argued that Articles 6(2)–6(4) of the Habitats Directive apply to such sites as they do, according to Government policy, to pSPAs and Ramsar sites, and therefore that proposals that are likely to have a significant effect on the site should be subject to an appropriate assessment under Regulation 61 of the Habitats Regulations (covered under the Habitats Regulations Assessment section below).

23. It is for Government, not Inspectors, to determine whether a site should be treated as if it were already designated/classified. According to current UK practice, the Government considers that, prior to a site being fully designated/classified, it is subject to the assessment process set out in the Habitats Regulations following a ministerial announcement either of a formal public consultation on the proposed site, or that a site has been accepted as a pSPA, SCI or cSAC following a review exercise. If no such ministerial announcement has been made, regulation 61 of the Habitats Regulations does not apply to the proposal.[53] Inspectors will still need to consider the impact of the proposal according to the protection afforded by other legislation, such as eg the W&CA [Wildlife and Countryside Act 1981].[54]

The requirement for a ministerial announcement of some kind is rational enough: ministerial statements are a matter of public record, recorded in Hansard, easily dated and (usually) clear as to their terms. Also a ministerial announcement may be a decision amenable to judicial review,[55] which protects the rights to some extent of those prejudiced by such conservation classifications. However, the advice appears to be an innovation. PPS9 and Circular 06/2005 do not define 'potential' in pSPA, however it does not comfortably mean 'announced formally'. In the Sherwood Forest case, discussed below, the Nottinghamshire Wildlife Trust submitted that the word should be given its 'ordinary meaning'.[56] On a plain reading, the potential of a site suggests an inherent quality rather than a Minister's nascent intentions. A natural understanding of 'proposed' in pSAC is of course more compatible with the language of the guidance, but that only begs the question of why a different term was chosen.

[53] It is not clear how reg 61 of either the 1994 or 2010 Regulations is relevant in this context.

[54] Case Law and Practice Guide 4: Biodiversity (updated 24 January 2011), available at: http://www.planningportal.gov.uk/uploads/pins/pg4.pdf.

[55] The position is that a ministerial statement is amenable to judicial review where it has 'substantive legal consequences', see, eg *R (Hillingdon LBC) v Secretary of State for Transport* [2010] EWHC 626 (Admin); [2010] JPL 976 *per* Carnwath LJ at [48].

[56] See the Inspector's Report at [512].

Sherwood Forest

These issues arose in relation to a recent planning appeal about a waste incin-erator at Rufford Colliery, near Sherwood Forest in Nottinghamshire.[57] Natural England had promoted an application for an undefined part of Sherwood Forest to become an SPA. The application had reached Stage 1 of the JNCC process (the broad identification of areas) and was mentioned in the 2009 East Midlands Regional Plan. Natural England was satisfied that some part of Sherwood Forest would be likely to meet the Stage 1 criteria for classification as a SPA for woodlark and nightjar.[58] However, at the time of the appeals no part of the site was sub-ject to any nature conservation designations, formal consultation or ministerial declaration, nor had there been detailed ornithological surveys.

On the face of it there was no basis in law or policy for protecting the nature conservation interests of the Sherwood Forest. However the government, land-owners and the public would have been aware of the potential classification. In its proof of evidence on the issue, Natural England stated its view that

> These are sites whose potential has been placed in the public domain enabling decision-makers, developers and other interested parties to understand that these are sites to which the stated policy position on pSPAs applies.[59]

In June 2010, Natural England wrote general advice to local planning authorities around the Sherwood Forest, stating that the substantial breeding populations of nightjar and woodlark warranted 'at least [the forest's] identification as a potential SPA'.[60] The agency advised that a 'risk based approach' be adopted and that Local Planning Authorities (LPAs)

> satisfy themselves that planning applications contain sufficient objective information to ensure that all potential impacts on the breeding nightjar and woodlark population have been adequately avoided or minimised as far as is possible using appropriate measures and safeguards, at this stage, in order to ensure that any future need to review out-standing permissions under the 2010 Regulations is met with a robust set of measures in place.

An interesting feature of Sherwood Forest is that the boundaries of the hypo-thetical SPA were not defined, yet Natural England considered that these *could* be adequately fixed, were it necessary, by reference to ornithological criteria.

The Inspector took up Natural England's invitation to apply a 'risk based approach' and carried out a 'shadow assessment' (akin to an Article 6(3) assessment)

---

[57] Application reference APP/L3055/V/09/2102006, the Inspector's report was produced on 17 March 2011 and the Secretary of State made his decision to reject the appeal on the basis of the Inspector's report on 26 May 2011.

[58] Proof of Evidence (SPA Classification) of Neil Pike on behalf of Natural England, para 6.1.

[59] Ibid, para 4.4.

[60] Advice Note to Local Planning Authorities regarding consideration of the effects on the breeding population of nightjar and woodlark in the Sherwood Forest region, 28 June 2009.

of the proposed facility. His conclusion, which was accepted by the Secretary of State, was that harm to the integrity of the potential site would occur and that

> if Sherwood Forest were to be identified as a pSPA/SPA, permission for the ERF [Energy Recovery Facility] should not be granted unless no alternative solutions ware available and imperative reasons of overriding public interest indicate that the scheme should go ahead. However, it is not suggested that such reasons apply here.[61]

This approach represents an important extension of precautionary protection to conservation areas. It is well established that the conservation value even of unclassified or undesignated sites is a material consideration for relevant planning decisions. Also, failure to have regard to impacts on, say, a candidate SAC in an environmental statement may render an environmental impact assessment (EIA) invalid.[62] The Sherwood Forest case goes much further: it suggests that where there is a strong and well-publicised case for designating an area as a European site, the correct approach is to apply European protection, albeit in 'shadow' form. The effect is appropriate assessment by proxy.

The Sherwood Forest case was undoubtedly a *cause célèbre*, promoted by the national conservation agency. However there is no reason as a matter of principle why other parties could not achieve European protection for a site by appropriate high-profile campaigning. Had the Secretary of State in the Sherwood Forest case not assessed conservation value in line with European law, he would arguably have been acting unlawfully or irrationally, although the success of a challenge on such grounds would not be at all certain.[63]

While reliance may be placed upon the potential status as a European site, it ought not to provide a reason to delay designation or classification indefinitely. National authorities that do this may be required to grant planning permission and to pay compensation to the developer if they subsequently retract it because of belated designation.[64]

The depth and scope of the approach adopted in respect of Sherwood Forest is striking, it applies the precautionary principle and appears to go further than both EU jurisprudence and national policy. This reflects a principled approach in an area where there is a lack of formal guidance.

Unlike many areas of European environmental law, the UK was a key proponent of greater protection for wild birds, and the Wild Birds Directive can be seen

---

[61] At [1155].

[62] *Seaport Investments Ltd's Application for Judicial Review* [2007] NIQB 62; [2008] Env LR 23, [31] where Weatherup J found it 'striking' that there was no reference to cSACs in the environmental statement.

[63] A related challenge was unsuccessful in *Bown v Secretary of State for Transport, Local Government and the Regions* [2003] EWCA Civ 1170; [2004] Env LR 26, though there the argument was that a site should have been (rather than should be) designated as an SPA.

[64] See the discussion in *Lafarge Redland Aggregates Ltd v Scottish Ministers* 2001 SC 298; [2001] Env LR 27.

to be modelled to a large extent on British legislation.[65] The approach that has been adopted by the UK Government in relation to cSACs, pSPAs, pSACs and possible pSPAs, such as Sherwood Forest, continues this pattern. The principles that appear to underpin this approach are:

(a) *Effectiveness*: Member States must 'facilitate the achievement of the Union's tasks and refrain from any measure which could jeopardise the attainment of the Union's objectives';[66] those objectives include establishing Natura 2000 and maintaining a high level of environmental protection; by providing strong protection to potentially important sites the UK approach ensures that those objectives are not undermined;

(b) *The precautionary principle*:[67] an absence of established evidence about the conservation value of a site is not a reason for allowing harmful projects in circumstances where its potential status as an SAC or SPA is recognised;

(c) *Member State estoppel*: to the extent that inadequate or incomplete classification or designation of sites is a failure of the state, the UK is precluded from relying upon this to avoid the application of European habitat law; and

(d) *Equivalence and consistency*: national policy protection for pSPAs may be weaker than that in the ECJ case of *Basses Corbières* but UK law provides stronger protection for cSACs than the European position in *Bund Naturschutz* and affords protection to pSACs that do not receive any express protection in European law. It is appropriate that there be a consistent basis for the protection of sites forming part of Natura 2000 which is intended to be a coherent network.

This suggests that the UK's approach to candidate and potential European sites may eventually find expression in European law or Commission guidance—of which there is as yet none on this topic. Sweden, it may be noted, also extends the provisions of Article 6 to all proposed SACs and SPAs.[68] Given that the EU missed its Action Plan target of halting biodiversity loss in Europe by 2010,[69] this is an area where further European harmonisation and central guidance would be desirable.

---

[65] See N Haigh (ed) *Manual of Environmental Policy: The EU and Britain* (Elsevier, updated 2010) 9.2–9.5.

[66] See Art 4(3) TEU (ex Art 10 TEC).

[67] See Art 191(2) TFEU.

[68] See the opinion of Advocate General Kokott in *Dragaggi* [2005] ECR I-167, [15].

[69] See, eg Commission report COM (2010) 548 (final) on the 2010 Assessment of Implementing the EU Biodiversity Action Plan, 8 October 2010.

Conclusion

The Sherwood Forest case may represent a high water mark of purposive interpretation in this area, it is non-binding and it goes further than the published PINS guidance on the subject. Alternatively, it may open the way for environmental NGOs and independent experts to promote and campaign for the designation or classification of sites, and then to argue that a 'shadow' assessment ought to be undertaken of any plans or projects likely to harm them. In any event, this is an area, at least at national level, where further developments can be expected. If the matter does get tested in the courts, an unusual feature of the litigation will be that European authorities suggest a more conservative approach.

Chapter 7 Conclusion

5

The Meaning of 'Any Plan or Project' Under Article 6(3)

STEPHEN TROMANS QC

Introduction

We begin with the terms of Article 6(3) of the Directive:

> Any plan or project not directly connected with or necessary to the management of the site but likely to have a significant effect thereon, either individually or in combination with other plans or projects, shall be subject to appropriate assessment of its implications for the site in view of the site's conservation objectives. In the light of the conclusions of the assessment of the implications for the site and subject to the provisions of paragraph 4, the competent national authorities shall agree to the plan or project only after having ascertained that it will not adversely affect the integrity of the site concerned and, if appropriate, after having obtained the opinion of the general public.

To put it in context, the Habitat Directive's overarching aim, set out at Article 2(1), is

> to contribute towards ensuring biodiversity through the conservation of natural habitats and of wild flora and fauna in the European territory of the Member States to which the Treaty applies.

Article 6 of the Directive determines the relationship between conservation and land use, requiring inter alia, that: Member States establish necessary conservation measures for special areas of conservation (Article 6(1)); and that Member States take appropriate steps to avoid the deterioration of natural habitats and the habitats of species as well as disturbance of the species for which the areas have been designated (Article 6(2)). A number of points can be made immediately, simply on the wording of Article 6(3) as it appears on its face. It is comprehensive—'*any* plan or project' (emphasis added). This is in contrast to the approach in the EIA Directive,[1] with its lists of types of Annex I and II projects. Nor is there

---

[1] Council Directive of 27 June 1985 on the assessment of the effects of certain public and private projects on the environment 85/337/EEC, OJ L175, 05/07/1985 P 0040–0048 as amended by 97/11/EC and 2003/35/EC.

any attempt to elaborate on what is meant by a 'plan' in the same way as the SEA Directive.[2]

The only exception relates to plans or projects which are either directly concerned with the management of the site or are necessary to the management of the site. The key test is the likelihood of the plan or project having a significant effect on the site. What is considered in appropriate assessment is 'the implications' of the plan or project for the site. This contrasts with the assessment of 'effects' under the Environment Impact Assessment (EIA) regime, and emphasises the breadth of the assessment required, implications being a broader and more open textured concept than effects. At the same time it is the possible effect on the integrity of the site which is the critical test.

The provision bites in the restriction on the competent national authority 'agreeing' to the plan or project—again a broader concept than granting development consent for EIA purposes (the decision which entitles the developer to proceed with the project).

Because, unlike EIA, the requirements of Article 6(4) are concerned with substantive protection and not with procedure as such, the European case law has emphasised the constraints on the application of the 'adverse effect on integrity' test in order to achieve effective application of the Directive.

In view of this, it should come as no surprise that both the Commission and the European Court of Justice (ECJ)—now the Court of Justice of the European Union (CJEU)—have emphasised the breadth of the terms 'plan or project' in order to further these objectives.[3]

The Commission's Approach

The European Commission's published guidance, *Managing Natura 2000 sites: The provisions of Article 6 of the 'Habitats' Directive 92/43/EEC*, noting that the Directive does not explicitly define 'plan' or 'project', states that due consideration must be given to general principles of interpretation and advances two arguments for a 'very broad' interpretation of 'plan' or 'project': the Habitats Directive does not circumscribe the scope of either 'plan' or 'project' by reference to particular categories of either; and, the more narrowly 'plan' and 'project' are defined, the more potentially restricted is the means to balance a conservation interest against a damaging non-conservation interest.

The guidance further states at paragraph 4.3 that: 'the key limiting factor is whether or not [plans or projects] are likely to have a significant effect on a site'.

---

[2] Directive 2001/42/EC of the European Parliament and of the Council of 27 June 2001 on the assessment of the effects of certain plans and programmes on the environment, OJ L197, 21/7/2001, 30–37.

[3] See Scott, ch 6 in this volume at pp 103–06.

This is the guiding principle adopted by the courts. How wide can the concept of a 'project' then extend? It is clearly a very broad concept, capable of encompassing many forms of human activity. Physical development can, of course, constitute a 'project' but its meaning, as can be seen from the case law, is much broader than that. A project can be something very large in scale, or potentially something very small. Article 6(3) does however imply that a 'project' is something which the competent authorities might be expected to 'agree' to, or not agree to. As with 'development consent' in an EIA, it may raise the question of whether the Member State has fully transposed the Directive by having in place mechanisms which would enable it to conduct an Appropriate Assessment (AA)[4] for a 'project' and to 'say no' if the result of that AA so requires.

The definition of 'project' is not only important for triggering the application of Article 6(3). It is also important to be able to define and describe the parameters of what constitutes the project in order to be able to conduct a proper AA of its implications for the site concerned.

Support for a broad definition of 'project' is reinforced by analogy with the EIA Directive 85/337/EEC which operates in a similar context and defines a 'project' (at Article 1(2) of Directive) as: the execution of construction works or of other installations or schemes (first indent); and other interventions in the natural surroundings and landscape including those involving the extraction of mineral resources (second indent).

The Case Law

Some clarification as to the definition of 'plan or project' was provided by the ECJ in the *Waddenzee* case.[5] The case concerned mechanical fishing for cockles by means of trawling metal cages over the seabed.[6] The court found the fishing to be an activity within the concept of 'project' as defined in the second indent of Article 1(2) of Directive 85/337. The ECJ (at paragraph 24) approached the question of defining 'plan' or 'project' by analogy with the definition of 'project' in Article 1(2) of Directive 85/337, both being intended to prevent activities which are likely to damage the environment from being authorised without prior assessment of their potential impact.[7]

---

[4] See Scott ch 6 in this volume and Stookes ch 8 in this volume.

[5] Case C-127/02 *Landelijke Vereniging tot Behoud van de Waddenzee v Staatssecretaris van Landbouw (Coöperatieve Producentenorganisatie van de Nederlandse Kokkelvisserij UA, intervening)* [2004] ECR I-7405.

[6] This was not just simple fishing—it involved very substantial disturbance of the seabed, with powerful jets of water and the scraping of the top 4–5 cm into a cage.

[7] See Scott, ch 6 in this volume, pp 103–06.

The court also referred to the *Managing Natura 2000 Sites* guidance as making it clear (at paragraph 41) that

> the triggering of the environmental protection mechanism provided for in Article 6(3) of the Habitats Directive does not presume ... that the plan or project considered definitely has significant effects on the site concerned out follows from the mere probability that such an effect attaches to that plan or project.

These questions were, to an extent, revisited in Case C-241/08 *Commission v France* in which it was confirmed that a plan or project not necessarily directly connected with the management of the relevant site, nonetheless fell within the requirements of the Directive. The ECJ held (at paragraph 54) that

> In order to ensure fully the attainment of the conservation objectives referred to in the Habitats Directive, it is therefore necessary, in accordance with Article 6(3) of the Habitats Directive, that each plan or project, not directly connected with or necessary for the management of the site, which is likely significantly to affect the site be subject to an individual assessment of its implications for the site concerned in view of the site's conservation objectives.

Turning to domestic case law, in *R (Edwards and others) v Environment Agency and others*,[8] the House of Lords reviewed the approach of the ECJ in *Waddenzee*. In considering the definition of 'project' in the context of an application to vary an existing operation by allowing a different type of fuel to be burnt in a cement kiln, Lord Hoffman (at paragraph 51, obiter) had regard to the definition of project at Article 1(2) of Directive 85/337—the execution of construction works or other installations or schemes—which he stated 'appears to contemplate something new and not merely a change in the way existing works are operated'. Lord Hoffman referred to the German version '*die Errichtung von baulichen oder sonstigen Anlagen*' to support this analysis. '*Errichtung*' means 'erection' or 'construction' and '*Anlage*' means 'installation' or 'plant'.

In the context of the EIA Directive, this approach is logical, in that the Directive itself draws a distinction between the listed types of project and changes to and extensions of projects within those categories which are already authorised, executed or in the process of being executed (Annex II, paragraph 13, second indent). These are within the scope of the Directive if they may have significant adverse effects on the environment. However, it may be noted that Lord Mance and Lord Brown of Eaton-under-Heywood took a wider view of the term 'project' as covering a plan to change to tyre burning: see paragraphs 83 to 87 and 76.

Naturally, since the Habitats Directive does not draw that distinction, it may well be necessary, in order to give effect to the Directive, to undertake AA on changes to existing projects. A change of fuel for example, in an existing power station, could have implications for European sites in terms of substances emitted and their deposition on that those sites.

---

[8] *R (Edwards and others) v Environment Agency and others (No 2)* [2008] UKHL 22; [2008] 1 WLR 1587.

The English courts returned to consider this issue in more depth in *Wightlink*,[9] in which the High Court examined, inter alia, whether a proposal to introduce a new class of ferry onto the route between Lymington and Yarmouth was a plan or project within the meaning of the Habitats Directive. Owen J found the decision in *Waddenzee* to be of assistance in three respects (at paragraph 72) in that it: (1) provided confirmation as to the breadth of approach to be adopted in interpreting Article 6(3); (2) provided guidance as to the test to be applied; and (3) was based on an analogous factual situation. In the first respect, Owen J referred to the guidance in *Managing Natura 2000 Sites* that the words 'plan' and 'project' be given a 'very broad' definition and recalled that *Waddenzee* made it clear that Article 6(3) should be interpreted in light of its broad objective—a high level of protection for the environment—and that it integrated the precautionary principle. The guidance as to the test to be applied was that (at paragraph 76) where an action could potentially have an impact on the environment or on a European site, it should be considered to be a 'plan or project'.

Notwithstanding that the questions are inevitably fact-sensitive, Owen J was satisfied (at paragraph 77) that the distinction between the direct effect of the dredging considered in *Waddenzee* and the indirect effect of the new ferries in the matter before him, was not significant. Activity giving rise to adverse effects on protected sites would be a plan or project for the purposes of Article 6(3) of the Directive whether directly or indirectly. The size and displacement of the ferries, their method of propulsion and steering, and their operation in narrow tidal channels, meant that they could physically disturb the bed and banks and cause erosion to the protected mudflats and salt-marshes.

Owen J was less inclined to follow the obiter views of the House of Lords in *Edwards* on the meaning of 'project' (as above) in the context of this case, noting that Lord Hoffman had said that if the decision on the relevant point had been necessary for the determination of that appeal he would have proposed a reference to the ECJ. He noted (at paragraph 80) Lord Mance's view in *Edwards* that a change to burning tyres probably would have constituted a project, and that Lord Brown said he inclined to the same view.

Owen J also firmly rejected any distinction between direct (intended) effects of an activity as in *Waddenzee* and indirect side effects as in this case. The question is whether the activity gives rise to a risk of adverse effects, whether directly or indirectly. That must be correct so, for example, if houses are built in proximity to a protected bird habitat, and an indirect effect is that home-owners may keep dogs or cats which disturb or predate birds, that is an effect of the project, despite its indirect nature. Moreover, it should not be assumed that a 'project' (or 'plan') has to involve some physical disturbance of the environment in order to be caught. What if the claimant yachtsmen in *Wightlink* planned a regatta in close proximity to mudflats on which birds were roosting or feeding at a critical time of the year?

---

[9] *R (Akester and another on behalf of the Lymington River Association) v Department for the Environment, Food and Rural Affairs and another* [2010] EWHC 232 (Admin).

Is there any reason why that would not be a plan or project requiring appropriate assessment?

The CJEU has returned to the subject in the recent decision of the First Chamber in Case C-50/09 *Commission v Ireland* (3 March 2011). In that case in the context of the EIA Directive, the Court held that demolition works fall within that Directive, despite the general absence of any express reference to demolition in the Annexes. Again, a purposive approach was taken, in that the references in the Directive to protection of 'the cultural heritage' and to 'landscapes of historical, cultural or archaeological significance' would otherwise be purposeless (paragraph 98). Demolition could in any event be described as 'other interventions in the natural surroundings and landscape'. It was thus no surprise that the same approach was used in *R (Save Britain's Heritage) v Secretary of State for Communities and Local Government*, on appeal from the decision of HH Judge Pelling QC[10] when the Court of Appeal[11] ruled that the demolition of buildings and other structures is capable of constituting a project falling within Annex II of the EIA Directive, and as a result, paragraph 2(1)(a) to (d) of the Town and Country Planning (Demolition—Description of Buildings) Direction 1995 (the Direction) is unlawful and should not be given effect.

In the context of habitats protection, a project (or indeed a plan) may well contain or entail demolition or its equivalent in the natural environment, that is removal of landscape features such as trees, hedges, wetland, or relevant man-made features which are important in terms of habitat.[12] Hence *Commission v Ireland* represents an important clarification.

Plans

The other aspect of the 'plan or project' formula is of course 'plan'. Unlike the SEA Directive there is no elaboration on what is a 'plan or programme' for the purposes of the Habitats Directive. Nor need there be if, as for 'project', the essential test is the effect of the proposed activity rather than its precise nature or status.

---

[10] *R (Save Britain's Heritage) v Secretary of State for Communities and Local Government* [2010] EWHC 979 Admin.

[11] [2011] EWCA Civ 334. The court comprised the Chancellor, Toulson LJ and Sullivan LJ.

[12] In *Carla Homes No 1* [2010] EWHC 2866 (Admin) the court held in an obiter comment that a decision to revoke the Regional Spatial Strategy is a 'plan' for the purposes of Directive 2001/42/EC of the European Parliament and of the Council of 27 June 2001 on the assessment of the effects of certain plans and programmes on the environment, is known as 'the Strategic Environmental Impact Assessment or "SEA" Directive.'

Certainly the European Court will accord 'plan' a broad meaning under the Habitats Directive.[13] In Case C-256/98, *Commission v France*, Advocate General Fennelly, in a passage not disapproved by the Court said (paragraph 33):

> In the context of Article 6(3), the term 'plan' must in my view be interpreted extensively. The sites likely to be affected by such plans are, by definition, sites of Community importance, which benefit from the protection regime established in accordance with Article 6(1) and (2); the adoption of a narrow interpretation of the term 'plan' would be contrary to both the wording of Article 6(3) ('[any] plan or project'), and the conservation objectives which the designation of SACs seeks to pursue. As the possible future development of a site depends primarily on the assessment, it seems to me that the obligation *ratione materiae* to carry out a site assessment must therefore cover all development activities with the exception of those which are unlikely to have any significant effect, either individually or in combination with other development activities, on the site's conservation objectives. This is consistent with the principle of Community law that exceptions to the general rule (here, development activities which do not require a site assessment) are to be interpreted restrictively.

Managing Natura 2000 Sites includes (at paragraph 4.3.2) 'land-use plans' (both in the sense of regional spatial plans and detailed plans serving as frameworks for development consent) and 'sectoral plans' (for example, transport network plans, waste management plans and water management plans) as obviously coming within the scope of Article 6(3) of the Directive so far as they are likely to have a significant impact on a relevant site. However, a distinction is drawn between 'plans' where there is a clear and direct link between the content thereof and likely significant effects on a site, and 'plans' which are in the nature of policy statements showing general political will or intention. It suggests that it would not be appropriate to treat the latter as 'plans' for the purposes of Article 6(3). Taking a purposive approach, the issue should perhaps be whether the 'plan' is such as to have implications for protected sites. On that basis, even a general, non-site specific policy statement could have such implications in certain cases.

In Case C-6/04 *Commission v UK* the ECJ found that the UK had, in a number of respects, failed to faithfully transpose the Habitats Directive. One of these failings was in respect of land use plans. The Commission's case was that although land use plans do not as such authorise development and planning permission must be obtained for development projects in the normal manner, they have great influence on development decisions. Therefore land use plans must also be subject to appropriate assessment of their implications for the site concerned.

The UK accepted that land use plans can be considered to be 'plans and projects' for the purposes of Article 6(3) of the Habitats Directive, but disputed that they can have a significant effect on sites protected pursuant to the Directive. It submitted that they do not in themselves authorise a particular programme to

---

[13] In *Terre Wallonne Asbl & Inter-Environnement Wallonie Asbl v Région Wallonne* (Joined Cases C-105/09 and C-110/09) [2011] Env LR D8 the CJEU held that the SEA Directive applied to a nitrate management plan.

be carried out and that, consequently, only a subsequent consent can adversely affect such sites. It was therefore sufficient to make only that consent subject to the procedure governing plans and projects.

The problem with this argument is that, as already noted, the Directive is not just concerned with 'effects' of a plan on a site, but with its 'implications' for the site. Further, as the Court pointed out, the AA system rests on a highly precautionary approach to the potential of a plan of project for adverse effects on a site's integrity. Given the statutory importance accorded to the development plan under the UK planning system, the possible implications of such plans for sites could not be so easily dismissed:

> 54. As to those submissions, the Court has already held that Article 6(3) of the Habitats Directive makes the requirement for an appropriate assessment of the implications of a plan or project conditional on there being a probability or a risk that it will have a significant effect on the site concerned. In the light, in particular, of the precautionary principle, such a risk exists if it cannot be excluded on the basis of objective information that the plan or project will have a significant effect on the site concerned (see, to this effect, Case C-127/02 *Waddenvereniging and Vogelbeschermingsvereniging* [2004] ECR I-7405, paragraphs 43 and 44).
>
> 55. As the Commission has rightly pointed out, section 54A of the Town and Country Planning Act 1990, which requires applications for planning permission to be determined in the light of the relevant land use plans, necessarily means that those plans may have considerable influence on development decisions and, as a result, on the sites concerned.
>
> 56. It thus follows from the foregoing that, as a result of the failure to make land use plans subject to appropriate assessment of their implications for SACs, Article 6(3) and (4) of the Habitats Directive has not been transposed sufficiently clearly and precisely into United Kingdom law and, therefore, the action brought by the Commission must be held well founded in this regard.

In the curious case of Mr Boggis,[14] the claimant argued that confirmation of a Site of Special Scientific Interest (SSSI) which precluded a list of operations likely to damage a geological feature (a cliff face the interest of which lay in its erosion) was a project or a 'plan' that should have been subject to AA. The Court of Appeal rejected that argument in somewhat round terms (see Sullivan LJ at paragraphs 20 and 22):

> 20. By no stretch of the imagination could the notification or confirmation of an SSSI, whether or not it included the 'erection, maintenance and repair of sea defences or coast protection works …' among the list of OLDs [operations likely to damage] under subsection 28(4)(b), be described as an '*intervention* in the *natural* surroundings and landscape …' The notification and confirmation (to simplify matters I will refer only to notification when dealing with this issue) of an SSSI is not an intervention at all, it is a means of ensuring that any such intervention takes proper account of the features

---

[14] *R (Boggis and Easton Bavents Conservation) v Natural England and Waveney District Council* [2009] EWCA Civ 1061; [2010] Env LR 13.

that are of special interest in the SSSI. Moreover, even if notification could sensibly be described as an 'intervention', paragraph 19 of the OLDS, which prohibits the erection etc, without consent of artificial sea defences, could not possibly be described as an intervention in the 'natural' surroundings. Any 'intervention' would be the prevention (without consent) of man's attempts to intervene in the natural surroundings.

22. Is notification of an SSSI a 'plan' for the purposes of Article 6.3? Blair J. held that normally it was not (para 101 judgment). He was right to do so. I will consider below whether the qualification 'normally' was justified. This case is concerned with the notification of SSSIs, but when considering whether such a notification amounts to a plan for the purposes of Article 6.3 it is important to bear in mind that SSSIs are only one among many areas or features that may be designated because of their special environmental qualities. By way of example, the Secretary of State lists buildings that are of special architectural or historic interest, schedules ancient monuments that are of national importance, and designates areas of archaeological importance that appear to him to merit treatment as such. Local planning authorities designate as Conservation Areas those parts of their area that are of special architectural or historic interest the character or appearance of which it is desirable to preserve or enhance. Natural England has power to designate Areas of Outstanding Natural Beauty (AONBs) and, subject to confirmation by the Secretary of State, National Parks.

23. The common thread running through all of these provisions is that they 'flag up' the special interest of the feature, and impose, or enable the imposition, of more stringent controls than would otherwise be imposed by the 'normal' planning process over any activities which might harm it, thereby ensuring that before any plan or project that is likely to have an adverse impact upon it is authorised, full account will have been taken of that which is of special interest. [Counsel for Mr Boggis] submitted, consistently with his submission that notification of an SSSI was a plan, that some, at least, of these other designations would also be plans for the purposes of Article 6.3. I do not accept that submission: such notifications are not themselves plans, they are a means of ensuring that land use and other plans take proper account of environmental features of special interest.

Sullivan LJ was able without too much difficulty to distinguish such notifications from the land use plans considered by the ECJ in Case C-6/04 to constitute 'plans':

26. The Development Plan does not define those activities for which planning permission must be obtained—that is the function of Part III of the 1990 Act and the General and Special Development Orders made under the Act—it describes the circumstances in which planning permission is likely to be permitted or refused for those activities which do require planning permission. Sites are allocated for housing and other forms of development, and there are policies to the effect that 'permission will normally be granted/refused for ….' Thus, Development Plans effectively create a powerful statutory presumption in favour of, or against, permitting certain types of development in particular locations.

27. The list of OLDs in a notification of an SSSI, setting out those operations which must not be carried out unless one of the conditions in section 28E(3) is fulfilled, or planning permission is granted (section 28P(4)(a)), is no more a 'plan' than is the requirement

to obtain Conservation Area Consent for certain operations in a Conservation Area. [Counsel for Mr Boggis] placed great emphasis on the totality of the notification 'package' which, by virtue of subsection 28(4) included the

'Statement of [English Nature's] views about the management of the land (including any views [English Nature] may have about the conservation and enhancement of that flora or fauna or those features).'

28. However, the statement of English Nature's views was just that, a statement of its views with no further statutory significance. The statement made it clear that it did not constitute consent for any of the OLDs. For those OLDs requiring planning permission, including the erection etc. of sea defences, the views of English Nature could not in any event be determinative of the question whether the operation would be able to be lawfully carried out. While a grant of planning permission would obviate the need for a consent under section 28E(3)(a), the converse is not the case. The views of English Nature, whether expressed in the statement or otherwise, would be one, but only one, of the material considerations to be considered by the local planning authority, or on appeal the Secretary of State. The lack of any 'bite' in a statement of views under sub-section 28(4) is confirmed by the other provisions in the 1981 Act relating to the management of the SSSIs: section 28J which enables English Nature to formulate 'Management Schemes'; and section 28K which enables English Nature to serve 'Management Notices' if owners or occupiers do not give effect to Management Schemes.

29. For all these reasons I consider that a notification 'package' under section 28 of the 1981 Act is most certainly not a plan for the purposes of Article 6.3 of the Habitats Directive, and would delete the qualification 'normally' in paragraph 101 of Blair J's judgment

It is fair to say that the Court of Appeal were not generally sympathetic to the merits of Mr Boggis' case, in that he was attempting to facilitate retention of works (DIY-coast protection) which were unlawful. As Sullivan LJ put it at paragraph 41:

No application has been made for either a planning permission or a consent under section 16, and in my view the court should be slow to grant relief which is, in reality, intended to facilitate the retention of works that are unlawful. I am not unsympathetic to the plight of the First Respondent and the other residents who can see the cliff face remorselessly approaching the boundaries of their properties. But they are, with respect, aiming at the wrong target in challenging the confirmation of the SSSI. Their only lawful course is to apply for planning permission and a section 16 consent for the sacrificial sea defence. On such an application the Interested Party, or on appeal, or if the application is called in, the Secretary of State, will be able to look at the problem in the round, giving due weight both to their rights under Article 8 of the ECHR, and to the special scientific interest of the SSSI, as two, among what are likely to be many other, material considerations.

It may, however, be that Sullivan LJ's analysis takes matters a step too far. A management statement, whilst it may lack 'statutory bite', may well have implications for a site if it is followed. It needs to be remembered that the Directive itself contains a specific exception relating to plans or projects which are either directly concerned with the management of the site or are necessary to the management of the site. So the statement in a notification may well be a 'plan', but would not require AA if they are directly concerned with management of the European site or are necessary for such management—by which must be inferred management of the nature conservation interest for which the site was designated.

Conclusion

In conclusion, therefore, whilst the concepts of 'project' and 'plan' have received quite substantial judicial attention, issues still emerge. Indeed, there is currently an appeal from Northern Ireland pending before the Supreme Court concerning the extent to which ministerial planning statements should be regarded as 'plans or programmes' for the purposes of the SEA Directive[15] which might have implications for the obligation to carry out appropriate assessments under the Habitats Directive.

This is perhaps not surprising given the very serious constraining effect of Article 6(3) on any plan or project on which it bites. The issue is therefore at the frontier of habitat conservation, and there will be a general tendency, driven by the principle of effectiveness, to push the frontier ever outward. The golden rule which emerges is that the concepts will be construed and applied as broad enough to match the potentially harmful impacts of the activity concerned, but it remains the fact that the Habitats Directive aims to catch 'plans' and 'projects', not simply all human activity. Hence the words must be given some meaning.

---

[15] The Court of Appeal in Northern Ireland held that they were not, see *Re Central Craigavon Lt (CCL)* [2011] NICA 17.

6

Appropriate Assessment: A Paper Tiger?

PETER SCOTT

Introduction

Mao Tse Tung's acidic comment that: 'US imperialism is a paper tiger'[1] presented a view of contemporary US military power which contrasted vividly with Nikita Khruschev's alleged rejoinder in 1962: 'but a Paper Tiger armed with atomic teeth'.[2] The thesis of this chapter is that the requirement for an 'appropriate assessment' under the Habitats Directive, as it has been interpreted in case law and applied by public authorities in the United Kingdom, is characterised on the one hand by scepticism as to its effectiveness to deliver the outcomes required by the legislation, and on the other hand, by a perception that the invocation of the process can have a 'nuclear' impact on sustainable development simply because of the impossibility of demonstrating a positive conclusion.

Under Article 6(3) of the Habitats Directive: 'any plan or project not directly connected with or necessary to the management of the site but *likely* to have a significant effect thereon, either individually or in combination with other plans or projects, shall be subject to appropriate assessment of its implications for the site in view of the site's conservation objectives'(emphasis added). In her seminal opinion in the *Waddenzee* case,[3] Advocate General Kokott analysed the meaning of the word 'likely' in Article 6(3) of the Directive by reference to its meaning in nine different language versions. She concluded that

---

[1] 'US Imperialism is a Paper Tiger', 14 July 1956. Part of a talk with two Latin-American public figures, see Selected Works of Mao Tse Tung available at: http://www.marxists.org/reference/archive/mao/selected-works/volume-5/mswv5_52.htm. The phrase was picked up over half a century later by Osama bin Laden: 'As I said, our boys were shocked by the low morale of the American soldier and they realized that the American soldier was just a paper tiger.' Interview with ABC reporter John Miller (May 1998). More recently, on 10 November 2011, US Defence Secretary Leon Panetta said the US military would turn into a 'paper tiger' if it were to suffer a $1 trillion dollar budget cut over the next decade: 'It's a ship without sailors. It's a brigade without bullets. It's an air wing without enough trained pilots. It's a paper tiger.'

[2] See, eg Major Nicholas P Vaslef, 'Myth of the Monolith' *Air University Review,* January–February 1968 available at: http://www.au.af.mil/au/cadre/aspj/airchronicles/aureview/1968/jan-feb/vaslef.html.

[3] *Landelijke Vereniging tot Behoud van de Waddenzee v Staatssecretaris van Landbouw Natuurbehher en Visserij* [2005] All ER (EC) 353; [2004] ECR I-7405; [2005] 2 CMLR 31; [2005] Env LR 14.

73. ... the criterion must be whether or not reasonable doubt exists as to the absence of significant adverse effects. In assessing doubt, account will have to be taken, on the one hand, of the likelihood of harm and, on the other, also of the extent and nature of such harm. *Therefore, in principle greater weight is to be attached to doubts as to the absence of irreversible effects or effects on particularly rare habitats or species than to doubts as to the absence of reversible or temporary effects or the absence of effects on relatively common species or habitats.*

74. Therefore, an appropriate assessment is always necessary where *reasonable doubt exists* as to the absence of significant adverse effects. (emphasis added)

In its judgment, the ECJ took a similar approach, although in keeping with its general convention it made no express reference to the Advocate General's opinion in the particular case under consideration. The Court ruled

44. In the light, in particular, of the precautionary principle, which is one of the foundations of the high level of protection pursued by Community policy on the environment, in accordance with the first subparagraph of Article 174(2) EC, and by reference to which the Habitats Directive must be interpreted, such a risk exists if it cannot be excluded on the basis of objective information that the plan or project will have significant effects on the site concerned (see by analogy, inter alia Case C-180/96 *United Kingdom v Commission* [1998] ECR I-2265, paragraphs 50, 105 and 107). Such an interpretation of the condition to which the assessment of the implications of a plan or project for a specific site is subject, which implies that in case of doubt as to the absence of significant effects such an assessment must be carried out, makes it possible to ensure effectively that plans or projects which adversely affect the integrity of the site concerned are not authorised, and thereby contributes to achieving, in accordance with the third recital in the preamble to the Habitats Directive and Article 2(1) thereof, its main aim, namely, ensuring biodiversity through the conservation of natural habitats and of wild fauna and flora.

45. ... the first sentence of Article 6(3) of the Habitats Directive must be interpreted as meaning that any plan or project not directly connected with or necessary to the management of the site is to be subject to an appropriate assessment of its implications for the site in view of the site's conservation objectives if it cannot be excluded, on the basis of objective information, that it will have a significant effect on that site, either individually or in combination with other plans or projects.

The restriction which this analysis imposed on the implementation of plans and projects has been generally recognised as one of the most stringent available to governmental or private objectors to plans or projects in the vicinity of European sites. The ECJ and its Advocate General was also required to address the meaning of the phrase 'plan or project' for the purposes of Article 6(3). Again, a teleological approach was taken by both the Court and Advocate General Kokott. In her opinion to the Court, Advocate General Kokott applied a precautionary approach which recognised the high level of protection which needed to be afforded to Europe's most sensitive environmental features. She advised that:

30. *For unintentional damage to Natura 2000 sites to be avoided effectively, all potentially harmful measures must, where possible, be subject to the procedure laid down in Article 6(3) of the habitats directive. Therefore, the terms 'plan' and 'project' should be interpreted*

broadly, not restrictively. This is also consistent with the wording, which expressly refers to any plan or project in almost all language versions.

31. The question how the words 'plan' and 'project' should be defined in detail may be left open here since mechanical cockle fishing was regarded as a plan or project when it commenced—a matter on which none of the parties has cast doubt. On account of its wide-ranging effects on the upper layer of the seabed it is in principle comparable, in terms of its environmental impact, with the extraction of mineral resources. In that respect it would therefore have to be regarded as another intervention and thus as a project within the meaning of Article 1(2) of the directive on environmental impact assessment. That provision defines a project as the execution of construction works or of other installations or schemes or other interventions in the natural surroundings and landscape including those involving the extraction of mineral resources. Without wishing to apply this definition of 'project' definitively to the habitats directive, it is at least appropriate and adequate in the present case. In this case the question whether the authorisation relates to one or several projects, or even to a plan coordinating various projects, can be left open. It makes no difference as regards the legal consequences. (emphasis added)

The approach of the ECJ was more prosaic. Having noted the absence of a definition of 'plan or project' in the Habitats Directive, it referred to the Environmental Impact Assessment (EIA) Directive[4] in which definitions are provided for the meaning of 'plan or project' for the purposes of that directive. In so doing, the ECJ focused on the sixth recital of the EIA Directive. I pause here to observe that it is, of course, well established that the ECJ often attaches great importance to the preamble or recitals of a Directive as an interpretative aid in establishing the meaning of the Articles which follow.[5] However, in this instance, the Court went further by referring to the recitals from another (albeit one that is arguably related) directive in order to interpret the meaning of Article 6(3) of the Habitats Directive:

24. [T]he sixth recital in the preamble [to the EIA Directive] which states that development consent for projects which are likely to have significant effects on the environment should be granted only after prior assessment of the likely significant environmental effects of these projects has been carried out, defines 'project' as follows in Article 1(2):

'— the execution of construction works or of other installations or schemes,

— other interventions in the natural surroundings and landscape including those involving the extraction of mineral resources.'

---

[4] Council Directive 85/337/EEC of 27 June 1985 on the assessment of the effects of certain public and private projects on the environment, [1985] OJ L175, 40.

[5] For an example see Case C-173/99 *BECTU* [2001] ECR I-4881, paras 37–39. For a useful analysis of the ECJ's approach to the use of recitals as interpretative aids, see Daniel Denman, Head of the UK Cabinet Office Legal Advisers, 'EU Legislation', a paper presented to the Constitutional and Administrative Law Bar Association (ALBA) on 3 December 2008 available at: http://www.adminlaw.org.uk/docs/EU%20LAW-%20Denman.pdf.

25. An activity such as mechanical cockle fishing is within the concept of 'project' as defined in the second indent of Article 1(2) of Directive 85/337.

26. Such a definition of 'project' is relevant to defining the concept of plan or project as provided for in the Habitats Directive, which, as is clear from the foregoing, seeks, as does Directive 85/337, to prevent activities which are likely to damage the environment from being authorised without prior assessment of their impact on the environment.

27. Therefore, an activity such as mechanical cockle fishing is covered by the concept of plan or project set out in Article 6(3) of the Habitats Directive.

Initial reactions to the *Waddenzee* judgment amongst the legal profession and professional ecologists concerning (a) the threshold of confidence perceived to be required for a positive appropriate assessment and (b) the large extension to the meaning of 'plan or project' which had been generally held and applied in the UK up to that time. However, as practice and case law have developed in the area, there has been a blurring of the original certainties and, in some cases, some quite striking contradictions, which can inform developers' and projectors' approach to these situations, as well as the tactics of objectors regulators and consultees.

Waddenzee and the High Water Mark

The threshold of confidence of no likely adverse effect on integrity is defined in the judgment of the ECJ in *Waddenzee* in wording which is in part definitional, and in part illustrative. Each of these elements is capable of being examined to a large extent independently of the other. The apparent certainty of ascertainment of 'best scientific information available' has, in the event, also provided an unexpected degree of subjectivity in the decision-making process. Paragraphs 54 and 61 of the *Waddenzee* judgment highlighted this particular issue:

54. Such an assessment therefore implies that all the aspects of the plan or project which can, either individually or in combination with other plans or projects, affect those objectives must be identified in the light of *the best scientific knowledge in the field*. (emphasis added)

While it may be an assumption among legislators that such best scientific knowledge is ascertainable, long experience of litigation in fields of some scientific controversy suggests that the concept may frequently be elusive. The ECJ had found in *Waddenzee* that

61. The competent national authorities, taking account of the appropriate assessment of the implications of mechanical cockle fishing for the site concerned in the light of the site's conservation objectives, are to authorise such an activity only if they have made certain that it will not adversely affect the integrity of that site. That is the case where *no reasonable scientific doubt* remains as to the absence of such effects. (emphasis added)

This adds a further gloss to the converse of the best scientific knowledge, with associations for English lawyers of the criminal burden of proof. It also carries with it an implication that there should be no reasonable doubt within the scientific community as a whole. However, it is plain simply by a first reading of paragraph 61 of the *Waddenzee* judgment that, where there are two reputable inconsistent scientific views amongst leading scientists as to whether there was a likelihood of a significant adverse effect on the Special Protection Area's (SPA's) integrity, the decision-maker would be bound to conclude that there was a reasonable scientific doubt.

Getting the application of the precautionary principle right is critical because the importance of the precautionary principle will not diminish. Indeed, as Trouwborst recognises '[the] considerable uncertainty concerning the impacts of climate change on species and habitats' means that 'the precautionary principle comes into play'.[6] This is particularly the case when one considers the uncertainty related to ensuring the necessary connectivity of habitats in order to maintain 'good conservation status' for certain species and habitat types. Having noted the inherent difficulty in predicting precisely for what populations, locations and points in time, the required measures must be applied, Trouwborst suggests that a proper application of the precautionary principle to the obligations contained within the Habitats Directive would mean that EU Member States are obliged 'proactively [to] create comprehensive ecological infrastructure ensuring mobility for all species groups, rather than reserving connectivity measures for cases in which scientific studies have conclusively established that species X in site Y is in *dire straits* due to climate change'.

Judicial Confidence in Relation to Scientific Uncertainty

R (Boggis and Anor) v Natural England

It has proved that the application *Waddenzee* test is in practice dependent upon the approach judges are prepared to take in judicial review proceedings to conflicting scientific views. Presented with two such views in *R (Boggis and Anor) v Natural England*[7] Blair J was required to consider material before him in respect

---

[6] A Trouwborst, 'Conserving European Biodiversity in a Changing Climate: The Bern Convention, the European Union Birds and Habitats Directives and the Adaptation of Nature to Climate Change', (2011) 20 *Review of European Community and International Environmental Law*, 62–67.

[7] *R (Boggis) v Natural England* [2009] EWCA Civ 1061; [2010] PTSR 725; [2010] 1 All ER 159; [2010] Env LR 13; [2010] JPL 571; *The Times*, 8 December 2009, reversed on appeal [2009] EWCA Civ 1061; [2010] PTSR 725; [2010] 1 All ER 159; [2010] Env LR 13; [2010] JPL 571; *The Times*, 8 December 2009 (Administrative Court).

of a decision of English Nature—or Natural England as it became—to confirm an area as a Site of Special Scientific Interest (SSSI).[8] One of the purposes of this decision was to facilitate the erosion of part of the Suffolk coast. Mr Boggis sought to quash the decision by reference to Article 6(3) notwithstanding the view of the expert employed by Natural England that rising sea levels would make the issue of coastal defence irrelevant to the fate of the European sites just north of the defended coast.

After reviewing a report by two Natural England officers to justify a decision reached without consideration of the issue of potential impact on European sites, and a contradicting report by Professor Vincent of the University of East Anglia, Blair J concluded:

> My reading of the evidence I have seen is that Natural England may well be right to say that the effect on the SPA will be neutral whether or not the sea defences are maintained ... However I consider that on the evidence before the Court on this hearing, the risk cannot be objectively excluded. In case of doubt, an appropriate assessment must be carried out (see the decision in *Waddenzee* at para 44).

Blair J's reading and application of the legal framework appear to the writer to correspond precisely to the received wisdom immediately following *Waddenzee*. By contrast, Sullivan LJ giving the judgment in the Court of Appeal in respect of the appeal by English Nature against the judgment of Blair J, dealt with the issue in a very different way. The consequence was that Natural England's preferred view of the science and of the application of that science was effectively not susceptible of challenge by judicial review. Sullivan LJ also suggested that there were significant evidential preconditions to a challenge on the basis of appropriate assessment.

> Whether a breach of Article 6.3 is alleged in infraction proceedings before the ECJ by the European Commission (see *Commission of the European Communities v Italian Republic* Case C-179/06, para 39), or in domestic proceedings before the courts in member states, a claimant who alleges that there was a risk which should have been considered by the authorising authority so that it could decide whether that risk could be 'excluded on the basis of objective information', must produce credible evidence that there was a real, rather than a hypothetical, risk which should have been considered.

How substantial a burden this is can be judged from the fact that that notwithstanding the scientific report submitted by the claimant and representations prior to confirmation in relation to lawfulness vis à vis the European sites, Sullivan LJ, taking a different view of the facts from Blair J, held that

> In the present case there was no such evidence prior to confirmation. It simply did not occur to anyone, including Natural England, that there was a risk to the Special

---

[8] Originally notified under the National Parks and Access to the Countryside Act 1949, SSSIs have been re-notified under the Wildlife and Countryside Act 1981. Improved provisions for the protection and management of SSSIs were introduced by the Countryside and Rights of Way Act 2000 (in England and Wales).

Protection Area (SPA) which required an assessment under Article 6(3). Nor was there such evidence after confirmation. Professor Vincent very properly disclaimed any expertise in nature conservation. It follows that, even if the notification/confirmation of the SSSI was a plan or project for the purposes of Article 6.3, there was no breach of that Article.

By constructing a distinction between 'hypothetical' and 'real' risk, Sullivan LJ effectively reduced the level of confidence which any decision-maker was required to obtain in order to conclude that no appropriate assessment was required, and this decision therefore is particularly significant.[9]

R (Akester) v DEFRA and Others

In *R(Akester) v DEFRA and others*[10] (or *Wightlink* as it is also known) local residents applied for judicial review of a decision of the ferry operator, Wightlink, to introduce a new class of ferry on a route between the mainland and the Isle of Wight. Wightlink, although a private company, was the owner of and statutory harbour authority for the ferry terminal comprising Lymington Pier. It had introduced a new, substantially larger ferry on the route between Lymington and Yarmouth. The claimants sought declaratory relief against the first defendant government department (DEFRA) and Wightlink. They argued that the decision by Wightlink to operate the new ferry was unlawful because it was made and implemented in breach of Directive 92/43 and the Conservation (Natural Habitats, &c) Regulations 1994. The first issue that the High Court had to determine was whether the proposal to introduce the new ferries was a 'plan or project' within the meaning of Article 6(3). The Court found that it was.[11] But Owen J was also presented with differing scientific views as to whether the activities were likely to have significant environmental effects on the SPA. The judge was clear that, provided the decision-maker[12] clearly adopted the opinion they had commissioned from ABPMER[13] of no likely significant effect, they would be entitled to reject the contrary view held by HR Wallingford[14] and the objection of Natural England which was based on the Wallingford reports.[15]

Any discussion on the threshold of confidence as to the relevant science would not be complete without noting the approach of Sullivan J (as he then was) to

---

[9] These issues are further discussed in Peter Scott: 'Interpretations of Article 6(3) of the Habitats Directive' (2010) 21 *Journal of Water Law* 33.

[10] *R (Akester and Anor) v DEFRA & Wightlink Ltd* Owen J 16 February 2010; [2010] EWHC 232 (Admin); [2010] Env LR 33; [2010] ACD 44; [2010] NPC 19

[11] See Tromans, ch 5 in this volume at p 95.

[12] In that case, Wightlink, the company which ran the ferry service in question.

[13] ABPmer is a marine environmental consultancy.

[14] HR Wallingford is a consultancy specialising in, amongst other things, engineering and environmental hydraulics and water management.

[15] On the weight that can be given by planning authorities to the views of Natural England see George and Graham, ch 3 in this volume at pp 58–60.

off-site mitigation. This is addressed below.[16] It has, however, provided applicants and decision-makers with scope in many cases to come to conclusions as to plans or projects without undertaking appropriate assessment at all.

Conservation Objectives

Another formulation of the threshold in *Waddenzee* rotates around the axis of the conservation objectives of the European site in question:

> 46. As is clear from the first sentence of Article 6(3) of the Habitats Directive in conjunction with the 10th recital in its preamble, the significant nature of the effect on a site of a plan or project not directly connected with or necessary to the management of the site is linked to the site's conservation objectives.

> 47. So, where such a plan or project has an effect on that site but *is not likely to undermine its conservation objectives*, it *cannot* be considered likely to have a significant effect on the site concerned.

> 48. Conversely, where such a plan or project is likely to undermine the conservation objectives of the site concerned, it must necessarily be considered likely to have a significant effect on the site. As the Commission in essence maintains, in assessing the potential effects of a plan or project, their significance must be established in the light, inter alia, of the *characteristics and specific environmental conditions* of the site concerned by that plan or project. (emphasis added)

By contrast, the opinion of Advocate General Kokott differed slightly in its approach to the conservation objectives:

> 84. However, I must concur with the Commission in so far as it refers to the conservation objectives of the site. These objectives demonstrate its importance within Natura 2000. Therefore, each of these objectives is relevant to the network. If adverse effects resulting from plans and projects were accepted on the grounds that they merely rendered the attainment of these objectives difficult but not impossible or unlikely, the species numbers and habitat areas covered by Natura 2000 would be eroded by them. It would not even be possible to foresee the extent of this erosion with any degree of accuracy because no appropriate assessment would be carried out. These losses would not be offset because Article 6(4) of the habitats directive would not apply.

> 85. Thus, in principle any adverse effect on the conservation objectives must be regarded as a significant adverse effect on the integrity of the site concerned. Only effects which have *no impact* on the conservation objectives are relevant for the purposes of Article 6(3) of the habitats directive.

> 86. The answer to this part of the third question must therefore be that any effect on the conservation objectives has a significant effect on the site concerned. (emphasis added)

---

[16] See Stookes, ch 8 in this volume at pp 144–49.

Ironically, in relation to essentially the same facts as in the *Boggis* proceedings, the Environment Agency Suffolk Coastal District Council Waveney District Council and Suffolk County Council as Shoreline management plan authorities adopted an appropriate assessment which clearly concluded that there would be (not merely was likely to be in the *Waddenzee* sense) a significant adverse impact on the integrity of the Special Protection Area concerned, and therefore proposed an Article 6(4) case for a derogation in relation to imperative reasons of overriding public interest (IROPI)[17] and no satisfactory alternative. While Sullivan LJ would have held for Natural England in any event in denying 'plan or project' status to the SSSI confirmation, the views he expressed in relation to the issue of the science may need to be revisited in due course.

However, the same statement of case for derogation presents one of the most striking instances of interpretation of the *Waddenzee* judgment. The conservation objectives of the Special Area of Conservation in relation to the coastal lagoons also affected by proposed managed retreat or abandonment of defended positions make reference to 'subject to natural change'. This is interpreted by the coast defence authorities in the sense that the abandonment of defence of shingle banks allows natural processes to destroy the lagoons but does not constitute any threat to their integrity. Lagoons are defined as ephemeral phenomena, whose planned loss from Natura 2000 as a result of plans and projects involving managed retreat requires that no measures are taken to defend them, and that (because Article 6(4) is not engaged at all) there is no need for the provision of any replacement habitat. The previous and historic practice of building up the shingle banks with beach material is condemned as contrary to the nature conservation interest of the SAC in being potentially harmful to the establishment of tern nesting habitat on the shingle bank itself, even though it had been previously established that measures could be taken to minimise the adverse impact in this respect.[18]

Until recently only the first branch of the *Waddenzee* rule was given particular attention, but the view that both branches are equally important is now becoming more prevalent, and the use of both branches introduces more elements which applicants for consents can address in their efforts to persuade decision-makers that the threshold is not crossed, or in the case of the reinterpretation of the obligations in relation to coastal lagoons, could not constitute an adverse impact on the integrity of the site.

Choice of Decision-maker

The selection of the most likely decision-maker to agree with the applicants' optimistic view of the impact of the proposals can be crucial; this is because each

---

[17] See Clutten and Tafur, ch 10 in this volume.
[18] See further Peter Scott, '*Boggis v Natural England* and endangered water habitat' (2009) 20 *Journal of Water Law* 195.

question in the branches has to be addressed by the decision-maker itself, and cannot be delegated to another body, for example the nature conservation body. This is most useful to applicants who can apply to a body which is perceived as being more sympathetic or realistic in its assessments than the nature conservation body, which could include the local planning authority or a government department.

Clearly an applicant who proceeds by way of notice to the nature conservation body or to a body which maintains a joint position in relation to the underlying SSSI confronts the nature conservation body itself, and is in a position of much greater difficulty than one who proceeds by way of application to a body which is prepared to accept a different view from that of the nature conservation body, or which is minded not to seek to challenge the applicant's expert report by way of commissioning its own study: such a course of action was encouraged by planning policy guidance in relation to environmental impact assessment.

In relation to any other decision-maker, an applicant who presents, whether in the form of an environmental impact assessment or otherwise, a full assessment of impact on the European site thereby provides to the decision-maker a basis upon which it can make a screening decision or determination of no likely adverse effect which is likely not to be susceptible to judicial review.

The only context in which there is clearly no option for the applicant for consent to avoid an Article 6(4) decision by a particular decision-maker appears to be one in which as many as 11 different decision processes are consolidated in the hands of one decision-maker, as for example, with the central bodies of Northern Ireland and Wales in recent years.[19] Applicants may consider it less likely that a central body will dissent from the advice of its own nature conservation body without the benefit of an independent inspector's report than that an independent authority with democratic structure and expertise in a particular field may exercise a robust judgement in response to representations, whether or not supported by evidence or scientific research papers.

Building in Control Measures and Pilots

One other route by which to achieve a positive appropriate assessment is through the combination of development proposals with mechanisms capable of ensuring that their impact is so controlled as not to impact on the integrity of the site. Following the *Waddenzee* judgment, the concept of a pilot project to demonstrate

---

[19] In this connection it may be noted that under the Marine and Coastal Access Act 2009 the Welsh Assembly Government (WAG) opted not to implement IFCAs but to bring all fisheries functions in house, stating that such measures were necessary in part to avoid infraction proceedings on the basis of the actions of other bodies, see WAG, 'A Proposal for the Future Management and Enforcement of Sea Fisheries in Wales' 6 June 2008 at para 6.

the consistency of the proposal with Article 6(3) was, at least in certain areas, discouraged by nature conservation agencies, who alternatively urged that pilots be conducted outside European sites—which, of course, flew in the face of the decided case law that the issue had to be judged with regard to the specific conditions of the site in question.

In my view, the French text of Advocate General Kokott's opinion endorsed the concept of pilot projects. The author originally translated this as follows:

> 108. … Measures targeted at reducing or avoiding the damage can equally play a role. In the case of scientific uncertainty one can properly obtain new information on the effects through scientific observation and, consequently, to carry out a pilot installation of the plan or project.

The long-delayed official translation, I believe, misses the point:

> 108. … Measures to minimise and avoid harm can also be of relevance. Precisely where scientific uncertainty exists, it is possible to gain further knowledge of the adverse effects by means of associated scientific observation and to manage implementation of the plan or project accordingly.

It appears to me that controlled pilot projects should be an essential part of the ascertainment of no adverse impact on the integrity of the site, and indeed are essential to the achievement of high level policy objectives which require the utilisation of European sites, as for instance in the development of sustainable molluscan aquaculture in estuaries in England and Wales necessary to meet European and UK policy in that regard. The term 'adaptive management' may be equated in many respects with that of a 'pilot project'.

Diversion of Pressure and Other Strategies

Such control mechanisms may be regarded as more reliable in terms of verifiably achieving their objectives than devices such as the development of Suitable Accessible Natural Greenspace (SANG), designed to divert additional pressure on Thames Heath's SPA by creating alternative attractive green spaces for recreation, rather than seeking to control directly the use of public access through and within European sites. In my opinion, the UK has signally failed to address the impacts of public rights generally on European sites, with the exception since *Waddenzee* of some rights of public fishery.[20]

Even less reliable measures of control have been recently relied upon by the Eastern Sea Fisheries Joint Committee (and its successor the Eastern Inshore

---

[20] In relation to such issues the approach of the devolved administrations in Scotland and Wales have, in my experience, tended in the one case to be more draconian and in the other to be less strict, than the approaches favoured by English authorities, despite the general state of lack of information in respect of conservation objectives of marine sites not being greatly different.

Fisheries and Conservation Authority) and Natural England in relation to an infraction complaint relating to a controversial fishing method involving the use of propeller wash to blow substrate off cockle populations.[21] In that instance, expert analysis of aerial photographic evidence of damage caused by the particular type of fishing methodology employed accompanied by detailed environmental reports in relation to its impact were rejected as unpersuasive on the ground that the data was gathered remotely rather than on the ground, and because it was said that any damage to the integrity of the site was avoided by the proposal that the fishermen abide by a voluntary 'code of best practice'—a code which had been widely disregarded and was to be unmonitored by the authorities. It was claimed that such a code of conduct had worked well in another fishery where the fishing technique in question was not used.

Variability of Implementation

It is perhaps unsurprising that where a nature conservation agency advises against approval of a project with implications for a European protected site, it has an expectation that the decision-maker will conclude a negative appropriate assessment, even when the nature conservation agency is unable to provide scientific evidence to support its conclusion. When the most severe criteria are applied, any development which changes the ecological balance of an area can be rejected by the nature conservation agency and by authorities which defer to or opt to adopt the view of the agency as their own.[22] Given that it is extremely difficult for any development proposal not to have some implications for ecology, the potential even for truly sustainable development within such areas appears at least in theory to be very limited.

A challenge based upon appropriate assessment will be likely to be successful where a decision-maker is predisposed in favour of the project and takes a different view of the weight of the scientific evidence from the nature conservation agency or objectors. Similar outcomes are possible where the decision-maker is favourably inclined towards measures of control of the project to give assurance of the absence of adverse effect on the integrity of the site. Ironically, the challenge

---

[21] Complaint by the author to the European Commission: correspondence and reports at the time of writing are subject to an access to environmental information under the Environmental Information Regulations 2004 request to Natural England.

[22] For example, Natural England has insisted that an appropriate assessment must be determined as negative where there is any reduction of food source for one species of bird even where the proposal provides increases of food sources for other species of European interest which should arguably be accepted as more than mitigating and in fact achieving, on balance, a benefit to the integrity of the site.

by Hart District Council to the housing proposals linked with SANGs[23] failed as a result of a more relaxed view of Article 6(3) by the nature conservation agency.

In many cases, if the nature conservation agency does not maintain an objection in relation to appropriate assessment, a closely-argued and more detailed objection risks being disregarded by the decision-maker precisely because the nature conservation agency has not sustained an objection, even where the third party objection is well informed and researched. This is precisely illustrated by the fate of Hart's challenge in what became known as the *Dilly Lane* case. The background is precisely that after public inquiry Natural England had withdrawn an objection to an appeal against refusal of permission for 170 houses following a proposal for provision of alternative recreational facilities described as 'equally attractive for recreational purposes', and advised Hart that they could conclude that no significant adverse effect on integrity was likely, and that no appropriate assessment at all was required. An inspector nevertheless concluded that significant adverse effects could not be discounted and that an appropriate assessment was required, and recommended refusal. The Secretary of State nevertheless allowed the appeal, giving 'great weight' to Natural England's withdrawal of its objection.

It is instructive that Natural England's pre-inquiry position was that 'it has been concluded that *on balance* a competent authority … would *probably* be in a position to conclude that the effects on the SPA arising from this development would be avoided, if the proposals are put into place' (emphasis added). Following its position Natural England did not give evidence at the inquiry.

The assertions of Natural England as to the likely effectiveness of the SANGs were seriously challenged by the Inspector, who concluded:

> Having regard to the conservation objectives for the SPA I am unable to conclude that the proposed package of measures could lead to a judgment of no likely significant effect on the SPA. The probability of the proposals having a significant effect on the SPA in combination with other plans or projects cannot be discounted. It follows that an appropriate assessment should be carried out in order to ascertain if the proposal would adversely affect the integrity of the site.

The inspector concluded that there was inadequate information to inform an appropriate assessment, and that there were alternative sites in the south-east where the housing in question could be provided.

Sullivan J dealt with Hart's challenge to the Secretary of State's decision by concluding simply that avoidance or mitigation measures forming part of a plan or project could lawfully be considered at the screening stage. He rejected the view expressed in paragraph 2.6 of the European Commission's methodological guidance[24] that screening should be carried out in the absence of mitigation measures as having no authority. He also rejected the Advocate-General's opinion

---

[23] *R (Hart District Council) v Secretary of State for Communities and Local Government* [2008] EWHC 1204; [2008] 2 P & CR 16. See Ricketts and Bischoff, ch 7 in this volume at p 122.

[24] Assessment of plans and projects significantly affecting Natura 2000 sites Methodological guidance on the provisions of Article 6(3) and (4) of the Habitats Directive 92/43/EEC.

in the *Waddenzee* case that in principle, avoidance or minimisation should be irrelevant in determining the need for an appropriate assessment. Sullivan J took this as being expressed in the context of a question from the Raad van State which referred to 'the possibility' of measures to minimise damage being taken into account. However, this interpretation is inconsistent with the Advocate-General's further eminently reasonable comment: 'It appears doubtful that such measures could be carried out with sufficient precision in the absence of the factual basis of a specific assessment.' Sullivan J then went on to consider the hypotheses that the decision-maker agrees or disagrees with the conclusions of the applicants' study of deflected pressure. He concluded that in the one case it can conclude at the screening stage that there is no need for an appropriate assessment, and in the other it requires an appropriate assessment.

Consequently, following *Hart* it must be concluded that a decision-maker need not require an appropriate assessment where a report is submitted by the applicant that adverse effects on the integrity of the site can be avoided by alternative measures outwith the European site.[25] Given the author's experience of totally different approaches by nature conservation agencies to projects in the same location, there is a concern that the operation of appropriate assessment may be subject to variation according to the predilection of each decision-maker as to the outcome of the project. The attitude of the Sea Fishery Committee and Natural England in respect of the recent infraction complaint referred to showed a determination to interpret the evidence and the alleged efficacy of a 'control' mechanism in such a way as to permit a positive appropriate assessment even against investigation of an infraction by the European Commission.

Similarly, the SANGs mechanism represents an off-site strategy of mitigation, under which developers who contribute to the cost of SANGs obtain consents and developers who do not, even in relation to small scale development, are refused. However, while strategies for the displacement of recreational pressures have thus been accepted as legitimate to avoid the engagement of Article 6(3);[26] in other areas of economic activity this is not the case.[27]

Conclusion

At the present time, the interpretation of the obligations of decision-makers under Article 6(3) in the English courts has provided public authority decision-makers

---

[25] Sullivan J also suggested that the methodological guidance was primarily, if not exclusively, concerned with the execution of mitigation measures within the site.

[26] Particularly evident in the decisions of Sullivan J (as he then was) and LJ (as he his now) cited above.

[27] In the author's perception and experience such approaches are not favoured in relation to activities to which a particular conservation agency is unsympathetic or which is not (as in the case of housing) supported by political and planning policies and by significant constituent interests.

with a significant 'margin of appreciation' in the application and disapplication of the high and strict level of protection laid down by the ECJ in *Waddenzee*. In practice, it may be perceived that decision-makers are adopting still wider interpretations of that discretion.[28]

It would indeed be ironic if, at least in relation to developments outwith a European site[29] the greatest threat to their continuance and viability might not be appropriate assessment but Article 12 of the Habitats Directive. If the decision of the Supreme Court in *R (Morge) v Hampshire County Council*[30] were applied to projects in relation to which there is a choice of available locations and where the projector clearly understands and objectively assesses the probability of killing European protected species, then such a project would have difficulty in establishing the preconditions of derogation under Article 16.

Given the sweeping discretions conferred on decision-makers by judicial inter-pretation, and the lack of judicial dissent above first instance, a reference to the ECJ for preliminary determination is not anticipated. It is, therefore, arguable that the original full strength of the *Waddenzee* principles is likely to be applied only selectively in England and Wales in the absence of infraction proceedings. For that reason the analogy suggested by the title of the paper may be apposite in some areas of activity in England and Wales, but not in others where Article 6(3) still has very sharp teeth.

---

[28] As has been seen in relation to SANGs and the Suffolk coastal complaint, and the Wash infraction proceeding referred to above.

[29] See, eg wind farms in relation to European Protected Species such as bats.

[30] *R (Morge) v Hampshire County Council* [2011] UKSC 2; [2011] 1 WLR 268; [2011] PTSR 337; [2011] 1 All ER 744; [2011] Env LR 19.

7

SANGs: The Thames Basin Case Study

SIMON RICKETTS AND SARAH BISCHOFF

Introduction

The requirements of the Habitats Directive are strict. Whether or not Stookes is correct in his assessment that there is 'inherent conflict within the Directive between habitat and species conservation and improvement and the pursuit of plans and projects', there is certainly a real tension between the two.[1] This tension has led to one particularly creative approach being applied to the concept of 'mitigation'. Its origins lay in the particular problems posed by the Thames Basin Heaths Special Protection Area (the Thames Basin Heaths SPA) but its solution known as the Suitable Alternative Natural Greenspace (SANG) has since been widely applied.[2]

The Thames Basin Heaths SPA is an area of open heathland, scrub and woodland located across Surrey, Hampshire and Berkshire that supports important bird breeding populations. It is here that pressure for new housing in the South East and the implications for the protected birds of all those new dog-walking home-owners and their wandering cats collided head on.

This chapter examines the SANG mechanism that has been developed at a regional level to standardise the mitigation to be provided by local authorities and developers in connection with development in the vicinity of the Thames Basin Heaths SPA. It reviews its evolution in terms of policy and its consideration by the courts and by the Secretary of State and inspectors, and considers the possible implications of the Localism Act 2011 for its future use.

A SANG is effectively an existing open space that is due to undergo enhancements financed by local authorities and developers to attract more visitors by providing an enjoyable natural environment for recreation as an alternative to the use for recreation of an SPA. The basic principle of the SANG is that there is a 'zone of influence' of 400 metres to 5 kilometres as the crow flies, measured

---

[1] See Stookes ch 8 in this volume at pp 140–41.
[2] The SANG mechanism is cited by Waite as an example of the application of a concept which he calls 'The Principle of Equilibrium in Environmental Law', see Waite ch 13 in this volume at p 245.

from the perimeter of the SPA to the primary point of access to 'the curtilage of the dwelling'.

Within the zone of influence, provision and ongoing management of SANG, paid for by way of developer contributions, should be sought by local authorities in relation to new residential development to ensure that there is no 'likely significant effect' on the SPA. Coordination at a higher borough/district level has been particularly important given that some 15 borough or district councils in South East England fall within the zone of influence.

The Evolution of SANG: The South East Plan and the Thames Basin Heaths SPA

Thames Basin Heaths SPA

The Thames Basin Heaths SPA[3] is a composite site which, together with the nearby Wealden Heaths SPA and Ashdown Forest SPA, forms part of a network of 8,400 hectares of complex heathland in southern England. It once was continuous heathland, scrub and woodland, but is now fragmented into separate blocks by roads, urban developments and farmland. The SPA borders major centres of population and, as a result of housing pressures, concern grew over increased leisure use of the SPA, mainly through dog walkers on the heathlands causing disturbance to the protected ground-nesting birds.

The SPA was designated in 2005 to protect three bird species in particular: the Dartford warbler, the nightjar and the woodlark. The key stages in the evolution of the SANG mechanism in relation to the Thames Basin Heaths SPA can be summarised as follows:

9 March 2005: The Thames Basin Heaths was designated as an SPA. Natural England begins to draft a delivery plan, setting out mitigation standards for residential development near the SPA, consisting of an exclusion zone and the provision of a SANG.

May 2006: English Nature published its Draft Delivery Plan (DDP) for future housing development in the vicinity of the Thames Basin Heaths SPA. This document, prepared partly in response to the ruling of the European Court of Justice (ECJ) in October 2005[4] that made it clear that the Habitats Directive applied to development plans, had no statutory status but aimed to provide a consistent way for competent authorities within the SPA to meet the requirements of the Habitats Directive. It set out mitigation standards for residential developments near the SPA and introduced the concept of development-free buffer zones and

---

[3] See http://jncc.defra.gov.uk/page-2050.
[4] Case C-6/04 *Commission v UK* [2005] ECR 1-9017.

the provision of SANG. On the basis that recreational activity, particularly dog walking, has a detrimental impact on ground-nesting bird populations, and that additional residential development within 5 kilometres of the edge of the SPA would exacerbate such pressures, the DDP sought to stop all new residential development within 400 metres of the SPA (the exclusion zone). It also recommended a number of mitigation measures which had to be implemented by any development within 400 metres and 5 kilometres from the edge of the SPA (the buffer zone). The primary measure named was the provision of SANG: the DDP stipulated that within 400 metres and 2 kilometres, 16 hectares of SANG would have to be provided per 1,000 of new population, while between 2 kilometres and 5 kilometres, 8 hectares of SANG would need to be provided per 1,000 of new population.

The proposals attracted significant objection, particularly from the house-building industry.

November 2006 to March 2007: The Examination in Public (EIP) of the Draft South East Plan took place. The South East Plan sought to allocate a target figure of 29,000 new dwellings each year, spread broadly across the South East.

Peter Burley, a Principal Planning Inspector with the Planning Inspectorate, was appointed as assessor to report to the EIP Panel on the strategic implications of the Thames Basin Heaths SPA for the South East Plan and future housing development and to consider whether the DDP is a sound solution for the area.

February 2007: Peter Burley's report to the EIP Panel was published. He found that the requirements of the DDP and in particular its concentration on the provision of SANG for all new housing development within 5 kilometres of the SPA, had resulted in delays in the provision of new housing in the area and in some areas had caused a virtual moratorium on new house building. This had created considerable concerns within the house-building industry and amongst the affected local authorities.

The Inspector found that the DDP confused avoidance with mitigation measures, leading to the incorrect advice that no appropriate assessment was needed where SANG was provided. He considered that the provision of SANG would undoubtedly reduce the impact of the developments on the SPA. However, SANG did not eliminate all risk (as, for example, dog walkers could still choose to use the SPA rather than a SANG), and so did not eliminate the need for an appropriate assessment.

The Inspector further found that the disproportionate blanket inclusion of all housing development within 5 kilometres of the edge of the SPA was unsound. He stated that the DDP had incorrectly applied the 'in combination with other plans or proposals' test by considering each application in combination with the remaining 40,000 homes anticipated in the South East Plan. The Inspector also criticised the DDP's excessive requirements for SANG and its failure to give sufficient weight to other avoidance and mitigation measures, particularly access management. He considered that the mitigation strategy only needed to cover larger developments of more than 10 houses within 5 kilometres of the SPA or smaller developments of less than 10 houses within one kilometre of sensitive areas of the SPA. Developments of over 50 houses within 5 to 7 kilometres should be individually assessed. He also considered that the level of SANG should be reduced to 8 hectares per new 1,000 population and that more general guidance should be provided.

He recommended that a strategic partnership involving affected local authorities, the South East England Regional Assembly (SEERA) and Natural England should be set up to coordinate a strategy and channel funding to the SPA. In the longer term a joint development plan document should be drawn up to include a long-term avoidance and mitigation strategy, and also include access management and habitat management plans. Work should be undertaken to identify and establish a definite list of land available for use as SANG. A standard contribution for SANG should also be calculated.

In relation to the South East Plan, he considered that to give adequate time for SANG to be brought forward, it might be necessary to phase new housing development so that a larger proportion came forward after 2016. He also noted that there was little evidence that the provision of SANG together with other measures would be sufficient to mitigate the impact on the SPA, so that until more quantifiable evidence was firmly established, no further housing (above that allocated in the South East Plan) should be allocated within the area.

October 2007: A partnership for the protection of the SPA was established, including local authorities within the SPA and SEERA.

May 2008: Natural England's Guidelines for the Creation of Suitable Accessible Natural Greenspace were published. Relating specifically to the means of providing mitigation for housing within the Thames Basin Heaths Planning Zone, this document set out the features which had been found to attract visitors to the Thames Basin Heaths SPA, and which therefore should be replicated in SANG. It provided guidelines on the type of site which should be identified as SANG and measures which can be taken to enhance sites so that they may be used as SANG.

The Guidelines state that SANG may be created from:

— existing open space of SANG quality with no existing public access or limited public access, which for the purposes of mitigation could be made fully accessible to the public;
— existing open space which is already accessible but which could be changed in character so that it is more attractive to the specific group of visitors who might otherwise visit the SPA; and
— land in other uses which could be converted into SANG.

It sets out the following 'must haves' which are essential in all SANG:

— For all sites larger than 4 hectares there must be adequate parking for visitors, unless the site is intended for local use, that is within easy walking distance (400 metres) of the developments linked to it. The amount of car parking space should be determined by the anticipated use of the site and reflect the visitor catchment of both the SANG and the SPA.

— It should be possible to complete a circular walk of 2.3 to 2.5 kilometres around the SANG.
— Car parks must be easily and safely accessible by car and should be clearly sign-posted.
— The accessibility of the site must include access points appropriate for the particular visitor use the SANG is intended to cater for.
— The SANG must have a safe route of access on foot from the nearest car park and/or footpath/s.
— All SANG with car parks must have a circular walk which starts and finishes at the car park.
— SANG must be designed so that it is perceived to be safe by users; it must not have tree and scrub cover along parts of the walking routes.
— Paths must be easily used and well maintained but most should remain unsurfaced to avoid the site becoming too urban in feel.
— SANG must be perceived as semi-natural spaces with little intrusion of artificial structures, except in the immediate vicinity of car parks. Visually-sensitive way-markers and some benches are acceptable.
— All SANG larger than 12 hectares must aim to provide a variety of habitats for users to experience.
— Access within the SANG must be largely unrestricted with plenty of space provided where it is possible for dogs to exercise freely and safely off lead.
— SANG must be free from unpleasant intrusions (for example, sewage treatment works, smells and so on).

The Guidelines also require SANG to have at least one of the following features:

— An owner should be able to take dogs from the car park to the SANG safely off the lead.
— Where possible, SANG should have a gently undulating topography.
— Access points should have signage outlining the layout of the SANG and the routes available to visitors.
— SANG should provide a naturalistic space with areas of open (non-wooded) countryside and areas of dense and scattered trees and shrubs. The provision of open water on part, but not the majority of sites is desirable.
— Where possible SANG should have a focal point such as a view point, monument or similar.
— In addition, it would be beneficial, although not necessary, that the SANG is clearly sign-posted or advertised in some way, and that there are leaflets and/or websites advertising its location to potential users. It would be desirable for leaflets to be distributed to new homes in the area and be made available at entrance points and car parks.

6 May 2009: The final version of the South East Plan was published. Policy NRM6 on the Thames Basin Heaths SPA states:

New residential development which is likely to have a significant effect on the ecological integrity of Thames Basin Heaths Special Protection Area (SPA) will be required to demonstrate that adequate measures are put in place to avoid or mitigate any potential adverse effects. Such measures must be agreed with Natural England.

Priority should be given to directing development to those areas where potential adverse effects can be avoided without the need for mitigation measures. Where mitigation measures are required, local planning authorities, as Competent Authorities, should work in partnership to set out clearly and deliver a consistent approach to mitigation, based on the following principles:

  i.   a zone of influence set at 5km linear distance from the SPA boundary will be established where measures must be taken to ensure that the integrity of the SPA is protected.
  ii. within this zone of influence, there will be a 400m 'exclusion zone' where mitigation measures are unlikely to be capable of protecting the integrity of the SPA. In exceptional circumstances, this may vary with the provision of evidence that demonstrates the extent of the area within which it is considered that mitigation measures will be capable of protecting the integrity of the SPA. These small locally determined zones will be set out in local development frameworks (LDFs) and SPA avoidance strategies and agreed with Natural England.
  iii. where development is proposed outside the exclusion zone but within the zone of influence, mitigation measures will be delivered prior to occupation and in perpetuity. Measures will be based on a combination of access management, and the provision of Suitable Accessible Natural Greenspace (SANG).

Where mitigation takes the form of provision of SANG the following standards and arrangements will apply:

  iv. a minimum of 8 hectares of SANG land (after discounting to account for current access and capacity) should be provided per 1,000 new occupants.
  v.   developments of fewer than 10 dwellings should not be required to be within a specified distance of SANG land provided it is ensured that a sufficient quantity of SANG land is in place to cater for the consequent increase in residents prior to occupation of the dwellings.
  vi. access management measures will be provided strategically to ensure that adverse impacts on the SPA are avoided and that SANG functions effectively.
  vii. authorities should cooperate and work jointly to implement mitigation measures. These may include, inter alia, assistance to those authorities with insufficient SANG land within their own boundaries, cooperation on access management and joint development plan documents.
 viii. relevant parties will cooperate with Natural England and landowners and stakeholders in monitoring the effectiveness of avoidance and mitigation measures and monitoring visitor pressure on the SPA and review/amend the approach set out in this policy, as necessary.
  ix. local authorities will collect developer contributions towards mitigation measures, including the provision of SANG land and joint contributions to the funding of

access management and monitoring the effects of mitigation measures across the SPA.

x. large developments may be expected to provide bespoke mitigation that provides a combination of benefits including SANG, biodiversity enhancement, green infrastructure and, potentially, new recreational facilities.

Where further evidence demonstrates that the integrity of the SPA can be protected using different linear thresholds or with alternative mitigation measures (including standards of SANG provision different to those set out in this policy) these must be agreed with Natural England.

The mechanism for this policy is set out in the TBH Delivery Framework by the TBH Joint Strategic Partnership and partners and stakeholders, the principles of which should be incorporated into local authorities' LDFs.

The supporting text to the policy states:

Natural England has identified that net additional housing development (residential institutions and dwellings) up to 5 km from the designated sites is likely to have a significant effect (alone or in combination with other plans or projects) on the integrity of the SPA. Initial advice from Natural England is that an exclusion zone of 400 metre linear distance from the SPA is appropriate. The district level housing allocations for the sub-region presuppose that an effective approach to dealing with the effects of development on the SPA can be found. Local authorities that are affected by the designation should deal, in their LDDs [Local Development Documents], with the issue of the effects of development on the SPA, and put forward a policy framework to protect the SPA whilst meeting development requirements. The focus of this policy is on avoidance and mitigation of the effects of residential development. This does not obviate the need for possible Habitats Regulation Assessment on other forms of development.

Nor do the provisions of this policy exclude the possibility that some residential schemes (and, in particular, relatively large schemes) either within or outside the 5 km zone might require assessment under the Habitats Regulations due to a likely significant effect, alone or in combination with other plans or projects, and subject to advice from Natural England.

Applications for all non-residential development will need to be subject to Habitats Regulations Assessment where they are likely to have a significant adverse impact on the integrity of the Thames Basin Heaths SPA.

To assist local authorities in the preparation of LDDs and to enable development to come forward in a timely and efficient manner, Policy NRM6 sets out the extent of mitigation measures required, based on current evidence. The evidence available indicates that effective mitigation measures should comprise a combination of providing suitable areas for recreational use by residents to buffer the SPA and actions on the SPA to manage access and encourage use of alternative sites. Such measures must be operational prior to the occupation of new residential developments to ensure that the interests of the SPA are not damaged. Local Authorities and Natural England will need to cooperate so that the effect of mitigation measures can be monitored across the SPA.

Where developers propose a bespoke solution, this will be assessed on its own merits under the Habitats Regulations. The SANG requirement for bespoke solutions may vary according to the size and proximity of development to the SPA; early consultation with Natural England and the local planning authority is encouraged.

Should it become apparent during the lifetime of this Plan that alternative arrangements may need to apply, these must be brought forward with the agreement of Natural England.

One route would be the publication of supplementary guidance to this Plan by Natural England to set out alternative arrangements or further details.

2009: The Thames Basin Heaths Joint Strategic Partnership published and endorsed the Thames Basin Heaths Special Protection Area Delivery Framework (SPA Delivery Framework).

The SPA Delivery Framework aims to create a consistent and long-term approach among local authorities within the SPA to balance the delivery of housing and the protection and enhancement of the natural environment of the SPA. It is intended to be consistent with policy NRM6 of the South East Plan and takes into considerations the findings of Peter Burley. The Framework requires local authorities to refer to it in the preparation of local or joint development plan documents and supplementary planning documents. It also states that local authorities should ensure that appropriate references are made to the provision of SPA-related avoidance measures in their local development frameworks and supporting implementation documents in line with policy within the South East Plan. However, it is clear in stating that adopting the principles set out in the SPA Delivery Framework in development plan documents or supplementary planning documents does not negate the need to undertake appropriate assessment under the Habitats Regulations of the land use plans which adopt the measures set out in the SPA delivery framework.

It also makes recommendations as to the type and extent of residential development that may have a significant effect (alone or in combination with other development) on the SPA, and sets out key criteria for the delivery of avoidance measures. The Framework reiterates the presumption against development within 400 metres of the SPA perimeter (as the crow flies), and states that an appropriate assessment will have to be carried out if any development is proposed within this exclusion zone to demonstrate that the development will not have an adverse effect on the SPA, and/or the acceptance of any avoidance measures provided. Applications for large scale development proposals beyond the 5 kilometre limit should be assessed on an individual basis and, where appropriate, a full appropriate assessment may be required to ascertain whether the proposal could have an adverse effect on the SPA.

In terms of avoidance measures, a three-pronged approach is introduced, consisting of the provision of SANG, access management and habitat management.

In relation to SANG, the SPA Delivery Framework states that SANG should draw new residents away from the SPA and should be delivered by local authorities (or groups of local authorities). SANG provision should be funded by developer contributions collected at local or cross authority level, and the calculation of costs should take account of acquisition costs, upgrading costs and maintenance and management costs in perpetuity. Alternatively, SANG may be provided by developers for individual developments. SANG should be provided on the basis of at least 8 hectares per 1,000 population, and the size of site suitable for use as a SANG, though dependent on site characteristics and location, should be of at least 2 hectare and located within a wider open space or network of spaces.

27 May 2010: Eric Pickles, Secretary of State for Communities and Local Government, published a letter to all local planning authorities, confirming the new government's intention to revoke all regional spatial strategies including the South East Plan. The letter is intended to be a material consideration in preparation of planning documents and determination of planning applications.

6 July 2010: The South East Plan and other regional spatial strategies were purported to be revoked with immediate effect.

9 December 2010: The Bi-annual Thames Basin Heaths Joint Strategic Partnership meeting took place. At the meeting, the possible implications of the emerging Localism Bill for the Thames Basin Heaths SPA and the function and role of the Joint Strategic Partnership Board were considered. The minutes of the meeting note that the approach to localism in the Bill (which had not at that stage been published) appears to allow for developments to be approved by new routes, for example by way of a neighbourhood development order. It further notes that how localism will work in practice is unclear, particularly in how the Habitats Regulations will be adapted to reflect this, or how compliance will be enforced. It concludes that the change in approach as to who can give consent for new development and how that consent is given has implications for the future role and composition of the Joint Strategic Partnership and the projects it is currently pursuing. It observes that is uncertain what this may mean for funding streams for projects if development is further delayed by this process. Of particular concern are the implications on the SPA of the neighbourhood planning approach, where no consent is needed from the relevant local authority where schemes demonstrate compliance with an adopted neighbourhood plan and have local support.

In addition, the Joint Strategic Partnership proposed that its terms of reference are amended to take account of the abolition of the South East of England Regional Assembly (a full voting member) and the Government Office for the South East (an advisory member).

The draft amended terms of reference also made reference to the Joint Strategic Partnership providing a vehicle for joint working, liaison and the exchange of information between local authorities and other organisations affected by the SPA. In particular:

— the Joint Strategic Partnership Board will act as an advisory body for local authorities affected by the SPA, and retain an overview of and monitor the implementation of, measures to avoid the impact of development on the SPA (including local authority policy/avoidance strategies, coordinating the provision of SANG and strategic access management and monitoring measures);

— the Strategic Access Management and Monitoring Board will have responsibility for oversight of the contact with Natural England and directing the strategic access management and monitoring project;

— the Thames Basin Heaths Officer Group will provide a forum for officers to discuss and share information about Thames Basin Heaths policy and implementation issues, including local authority policy and avoidance strategies, the coordination of SANG and the implementation of the strategic access management and monitoring project; and

— the Access Management and Monitoring Partnership will provide advice about strategic access management and monitoring measures and for the implementation of those measures.[5]

7 February 2011: Following two sets of judicial review proceedings brought by Cala Homes, the South East Plan and other regional spatial strategies again constitute part of the development plan until formally abolished by the Localism Bill coming into force. However, the Government's intention to abolish the South East Plan and other regional strategies continues to be a material consideration for the purpose of determining planning applications and appeals.

Application of Policy NRM6 and SPA Delivery Framework by Individual Authorities

Bracknell Forest Borough Council

In February 2008, Bracknell Forest Borough Council adopted its Core Strategy. Policy CS14 of the Core Strategy states that

> The Council will carry out an assessment of the effects of a development proposal on the conservation objectives of the Thames Basin Heaths SPA where there is a risk of the proposal having a significant impact on the integrity of the site, either alone or in combination with other proposals. Proposals leading to a net increase in residential dwellings, within a straight-line distance of 5 kilometres from the SPA boundary, are likely to have a significant effect. The Council will not permit development which, either alone or in-combination with other development, has an adverse effect upon the integrity of the SPA. Development outside the 400-metre zone will be permitted where it can demonstrate that it can remove any adverse effect by contributing towards avoidance and mitigation measures in line with the SPA Technical Background Document. The effective avoidance and/or mitigation of any identified adverse effects must be demonstrated and secured prior to approval of the development.

The SPA Technical Background Document to the Core Strategy sets out the specific avoidance and mitigation measures which Bracknell Forest Borough Council considers are necessary to remove the adverse effects which may arise from the

---

[5] This advice is available at: http://www.surreyheath.gov.uk/planning/tbh/meetings.htm.

policies within the Core Strategy Development Plan Document (DPD). These measures, to be funded by developers' financial contributions, include enhancements to Council-owned open space, visitor management on the SPA, and education strategies. Large developments are also encouraged to provide bespoke solutions. An SPA Implementation Strategy was approved in June 2007, which allowed Bracknell Forest Borough Council to implement the measures set out within the SPA Technical Background Document, specifically through the collection of financial contributions.

Subsequently, Bracknell Forest Borough Council published Open Space Management Plans in consultation with Natural England, which set out the precise works proposed to areas of open space and the order of priority for these enhancements.

Natural England agreed that Bracknell Forest Borough Council's current avoidance and mitigation strategies, set out in the SPA Technical Background Document and the SPA Implementation Strategy, would adequately protect the SPA from harm caused by new development. As such, if a planning application were to be submitted together with a financial contribution towards strategic avoidance and mitigation measures, (subject to other planning considerations) the application could be approved.

Following the SPA Delivery Framework and the publication of the South East Plan, Bracknell Forest Borough Council revised its avoidance and mitigation strategy. It published a Thames Basin Heaths Special Protection Area Avoidance and Mitigation Supplementary Planning Document, which was consulted on in November 2009 and which was to provide updated guidance in line with the regional policy and guidance to the construction industry, environmental interest groups, the council and the public on how new residential developments impact the Thames Basin Heaths SPA and how such impacts could be avoided or mitigated. SANG contributions were calculated at a level of £2,636 per net additional dwelling, although the figure could be reduced to reflect any in-kind mitigation measures agreed with the developer.

Bracknell Forest Borough Council stated on its website that

> due to changes in planning policy at the national and regional levels, the Thames Basin Heaths Special Protection Area Avoidance and Mitigation Supplementary Planning Document is being further revised taking account of all the consultation comments and the new policy framework. It is intended that there will be a further consultation in September 2011. It is anticipated that the final version of the SPD will be adopted by the end of 2011.

As part of Bracknell Forest Borough Council's avoidance and mitigation measures, Bracknell Forest Borough Council is now seeking SPA developer contributions made up of SANG contributions and strategic access management and monitoring contributions, on all new planning applications validated from 14 July 2011 until the adoption of the Thames Basin Heaths SPA Avoidance and Mitigation Supplementary Planning Document.

Rushmoor Borough Council

Rushmoor Borough Council submitted its core strategy to the Secretary of State in March 2011 and an independent examination took place in June with the inspector's report due in August 2011. Policy CP13 of the draft Core Strategy states that

> New development which is likely to have a significant effect on the ecological integrity of the Thames Basin Heaths Special Protection Area (SPA) will be required to demonstrate that adequate measures are put in place to avoid or mitigate any potential adverse effects. The mechanism for delivering this policy is set out in the Council's Thames Basin Heaths Special Protection Area Avoidance and Mitigation Strategy and in the Thames Basin Heaths Delivery Framework prepared by the Thames Basin Heaths Joint Strategic Partnership. No residential development resulting in a net gain of units will be permitted within 400m of the SPA boundary, unless in agreement with Natural England an Appropriate Assessment demonstrates that there will be no adverse effect on the SPA. Where mitigation measures are applicable, as set out in the Delivery Framework, the following standards will apply unless an alternative strategy has been agreed:
>
> — A minimum of 8 hectares of SANG land (after discounting to account for current access and capacity) should be provided in perpetuity per 1,000 new occupants either through contributions towards the provision of SANG identified by the Borough Council, or through on site SANG agreed with Natural England;
> — Contributions towards Strategic Access Management and Monitoring measures.

Rushmoor Borough Council has also prepared a draft Thames Basin Heaths SPA Avoidance and Mitigation Strategy, to provide guidance to developers in Rushmoor on the provision of avoidance measures. This strategy is designed to support the Thames Basin Heaths SPA policy in the East of England Plan and the emerging core strategy policy, by

(a)   identifying two sites suitable be used as SANG: Southwood Woodlands and Hawley Meadows (which is shared between Rushmoor, Hart and Surrey Heath Councils); and

(b)   requiring developer contributions towards strategic access management and monitoring measures, on a per bedroom measure.

Accordingly, in Rushmoor it seems to be 'business as usual' as far as SANG is concerned.

The Royal Borough of Windsor and Maidenhead

In July 2010, the Royal Borough of Windsor and Maidenhead adopted the first part of a supplementary planning document to address the impacts of residential development on the Thames Basin Heaths SPA. This first part, which is a material consideration in the assessment and determination of planning permissions, sets out how new residential developments are required to avoid and mitigate the impacts of their development on the SPA. It employs the two-pronged approach to mitigating against the potential adverse effects of residential development on the SPA set out in the East of England Policy NRM6; requiring the provision of SANG and the provision of financial contributions towards strategic access management and monitoring.

The second part, yet to be adopted, is expected to set out the level of developer contributions payable towards a SANG, measured per unit of residential accommodation. However, as the Royal Borough of Windsor and Maidenhead has not yet been able to identify and deliver a suitable site for use as a SANG, the second part is as yet outstanding.

Dorset Heathlands

It is also noteworthy that a very similar approach to that taken in the Thames Basin Heaths SPA has been taken in relation to the Dorset Heathlands. The impact of intensified residential development on the protected heathlands were noted by Natural England, which advised

> that development within 400 m of the heathlands was likely to have a significant effect upon the European site, either alone or in combination with other developments, so that local authorities undertaking an appropriate assessment would in most cases not be able to be certain that any adverse effects could be avoided or alleviated; and:

> that in relation to development within 400 m and 5 km of the heathlands, local authorities undertaking an appropriate assessment would still identify a significant adverse effect in combination with other proposals, but that avoidance or mitigation measures to divert recreational pressures away from the heathlands could allow development to be approved.

As a result of Natural England's findings, the Dorset Heathlands Interim Planning Framework 2010–2011 was put into place. It seeks to protect the area between 400 metres and 5 kilometres from the boundary of the protected heath by setting out the interim approach to the mitigation of the harmful effects of residential development in South East Dorset on Dorset's lowland heaths. It was originally envisaged to be in place only until the end of 2011, by which time affected local planning authorities had agreed to have in place a joint Heathlands Development Plan Document as part of their Local Development Frameworks. The Heathlands Development Plan Document was submitted to the Secretary of State in February 2011, following extensive joint consultation by Bournemouth, Christchurch, East Dorset, Purbeck and Poole Councils in 2007. However, the timing for adoption has been pushed back to 2014 for unknown reasons. Although currently, the Interim Planning Framework continues to operate, in early 2012, the affected local authorities published and consulted on the Dorset Heathlands Planning Framework Supplementary Planning Document 2012–2014, which proposes to convert the Interim Planning Framework into a supplementary planning document to form part of the local development framework for each authority. The Supplementary Planning Framework contains a revised mitigation programme required to permit the predicted level of housing up to 2014 to come forward. Once adopted, the Supplementary Planning Framework will address the impacts of residential development on the Dorset Heathlands, until the Dorset Heathlands Development Plan Document is finalised and adopted.

Consideration of SANG Principles by the Courts

Millgate Developments Ltd v The Secretary of State for Communities and Local Government[6]

This case concerned a challenge under section 288 of the Town and Country Planning Act 1990 to the decision of an inspector to dismiss an appeal for the demolition of two houses and the erection of two blocks of seven apartments, located 1.4 kilometres from Crowthorne Woods (which forms part of the Thames Basins Heath SPA). The inspector's grounds for refusal centred on the failure to make provision for any SANG as the proposal could, in combination with other plans and projects, have a significant adverse effect on the integrity of the SPA.

Millgate Developments Ltd (Millgate) submitted that the inspector had misdirected himself because he had taken the wrong approach to the issue of SANG and had failed to consider the argument that because of the existence of alternative green spaces in the locality, the proposed development would not have an effect on the special protection area.

The claim was refused and it was held that there was no error in the Inspector's decision. The inspector had been right in rejecting Millgate's case because the open space they relied upon had not made it to a final list of suitable alternative green spaces and the other alternatives were too far away to be an attractive alternative to future occupants of the development.

Hart District Council v Secretary of State for Communities and Local Government, Luckmore Ltd and Barratt Homes Ltd[7]

This case concerned a challenge to the Secretary of State's decision to grant of planning permission to construct 170 houses on a greenfield site at Dilly Lane, Hartley Wintney, and to undertake associated improvements to a footpath and the creation of a SANG on an adjoining piece of land. The site lies approximately 1.5 kilometres from the edge of Hazeley Heath in Hart District, which forms part of Thames Basin Heaths SPA. It was proposed that the SANG would avoid any net effect of an increased local population on the SPA by providing alternative

---

[6] *Millgate Developments Ltd v The Secretary of State for Communities and Local Government* [2008] EWHC 1906 (Admin).

[7] *Hart District Council v Secretary of State for Communities and Local Government, Luckmore Ltd and Barratt Homes Ltd* [2008] EWHC 1204.

recreational space for new residents and existing residents. The Secretary of State had granted planning permission against his inspector's recommendation and contrary to the views of the local planning authority and English Nature.

The case centred on whether the avoidance or mitigation measures (in this case, the SANG) could be taken into account at the first 'screening' stage or whether they could only be taken into account at the second, appropriate assessment stage in assessing whether a plan or project was likely to have a 'significant effect' on the SPA. Sullivan J (as he then was) rejected the challenge and held that the mitigation measures could be taken into account at the screening stage. If certain features were to be incorporated into a project, there was no sensible reason why they should be ignored at the initial assessment stage merely because they were directed at combating the likely effects of the project on the SPA. Sullivan J commented that anything requiring the proponent of a project to consider mitigation measures at an early stage should be encouraged. The underlying principle was that the Habitats Directive was intended to be 'an aid to effective environmental decision-making, not a legal obstacle course'. If, having considered the scientific evidence, the Secretary of State was satisfied that the mitigation measures would avoid a net increase in visitors to the SPA and therefore avoid any effect it would have been 'ludicrous' to require an appropriate assessment on the basis that the development without SANG would be likely to have significant effects, only to then reassemble the project with the mitigation in place at the appropriate assessment stage.

Planning Appeal Decisions Where SANG Provision has been an Issue

Paul Hedges v Hart District Council

This appeal concerned the refusal of planning permission for the demolition of an existing dwelling and the erection of eight three-bedroom houses and one four-bedroom house within 650 metres of the Thames Basin Heaths SPA. One of the main issues considered was the effect on the proposal on the Thames Basin Heaths SPA. It is of particular interest because the appeal was decided on 24 November 2010, and the Inspector specifically referred to the mitigation measures set out in policy NRM6 of the South East Plan, stating that although it was the Government's intention to abolish regional spatial strategies, including the South East Plan, Policy NRM6 was consistent with the approach adopted by Natural England and the local plan policies of the Hart District Local Plan (which also opposed proposals that would adversely affect the nature conservation value of the SPA and opposed development that would have a significant adverse effect on plant or animal special or their habitats).

The Inspector noted that the SPA was particularly sensitive to increased recreational pressures from visitors walking (either on their own or with dogs), and that as a result of the SPA extending across 11 authorities, the Thames Basin Heaths SPA Joint Strategic Partnership Board had adopted the SPA Delivery Framework to ensure consistency of approach. She noted that the appellant had submitted a unilateral undertaking under section 106 of the Town and Country Planning Act 1990, pursuant to which it covenanted to make a financial contribution towards a SANG in the form of a new country park located about 2.5 kilometres from the development site. At the hearing, Hart District Council confirmed that the proposed contribution towards the SANG would provide adequate mitigation for the proposal, despite the development site being closer to the SPA than to the SANG. This was because the Council considered that the SANG would attract other residents within the locality and thereby relieve the pressure for recreational uses within the SPA. In light of this and subject to the planning obligation being submitted by the appellant, the Inspector found that the proposal would provide adequate mitigation in relation to the SPA and that it would not harm the integrity of the SPA, complying with Policy NRM6 of the South East Plan and local plan policies.

Taylor Wimpey UK Ltd and Homes and Communities Agency v Bracknell Forest Borough Council (Ref: APP/R0335/A/08/2084226)

This case concerned an appeal by Taylor Wimpey UK Limited (Taylor Wimpey) and the Homes and Communities Agency (HCA) against Bracknell Forest Borough Council's (BFBC) refusal to grant outline planning permission to erect 781 dwellings including 336 affordable dwellings, and associated development including the remodelling of Ramslade House[8] to provide community facilities with ancillary uses, new community/commercial floorspace and landscaping, parking and vehicular access. At the time of the inquiry, the South East Plan, including Policy NRM6 on the Thames Basin Heaths SPA, existed in draft form. Planning permission for 730 dwellings already existed and had been implemented. The development site, a former RAF training facility, fell within the 5 kilometre zone within which mitigation to avoid impacts on the SPA was considered necessary.

One of the 11 reasons for refusal was that following an appropriate assessment, BFBC felt that it was unable to satisfy itself that the proposal (in combination with other projects) would not have an adverse effect on the integrity of the Thames Basin Heaths SPA. It thus felt that it had to refuse permission. The inspector and the Secretary of State considered whether or not the appeal proposal had an adverse effect on the integrity of the SPA.

---

[8] Ref: APP/N1730/A/10/2133568.

As the site was within 5 kilometres of the SPA (but fell outside the 400 metre exclusion zone), it was clear that mitigation was required to avoid impacts on the SPA. While the inspector and the Secretary of State were satisfied that Natural England's quality criteria for a SANG could be met, they were concerned over a shortfall in provision on the site of 2 hectares of SANG. It appeared that the appellants had calculated that the SANG would extend to some 12.07 hectares, a shortfall of 2.36 hectares from the calculation made by the inspector based on the SPA Delivery Framework requirement that SANG should be provided on the basis of at least 8 hectare per 1,000 population, assuming 2.4 persons per dwelling. To overcome this shortfall, the inspector reported that the appellants argued that the HCA owned part of South Hill Park and would be prepared to make a compensatory financial payment towards off-site SANG provision, although any such ownership would need to be discounted.

However, the inspector was not satisfied that land at South Hill Park would satisfactorily compensate for the under-provision of SANG on site, mainly because that site was already heavily used, was a very formal park, with little apparent potential for changes to habitat type or structure to increase its semi-natural feel and appearance and thus increase its attractiveness to SPA users. Additionally, it appeared that this park catered for people within walking distance but that it was not considered to be attractive enough (even with enhancements) to encourage people to drive to it instead of the SPA. Even with the introduction of anti-pet covenants in the leases to the apartments at the proposed development site, it was not considered that the secondary mitigation measures would make up for the shortfall of 2 hectares in SANG. The Secretary of State agreed with the Inspector's recommendations and dismissed the appeal.

Bracknell Forest Borough Council v Princesgate Estates Plc[9]

This appeal was determined prior to the adoption of the SPA Delivery Framework, and concerned an appeal against refusal of planning permission for a scheme of housing to replace four detached bungalows with ancillary garages and hardstanding, located about 1.3 metres from the boundary of the Thames Basin Heaths SPA. Natural England and Bracknell Forest Borough Council (BFBC) had advised that the proposed increase in the number of dwellings on the site would be likely to have a significant effect on the integrity of the SPA, in combination with other dwellings proposed near to the SPA.

The scheme was supported by a set of executed unilateral undertakings under section 106 of the Town and Country Planning Act 1990, which, in the event that permission was granted, would provide for financial contributions towards (among other things) the cost of providing alternative open space in Bracknell and other measures to mitigate the impact of development on the Thames Basin

---

[9] Ref: APP/R0335/A/06/2026308.

Heaths SPA. The financial contribution was based on the policy contained in an SPA technical background paper published by BFBC (which predicted the type and level of impacts arising from the Council's Core Strategy and incorporated a package of strategic measures necessary to avoid or mitigate the effects of residential development within 5 kilometres of the SPA), and an emerging supplementary planning document, entitled 'Limiting the Impact of Development' (which set out the costs of implementing the avoidance and mitigation strategy, stating that the costs would be funded through contributions secured by residential developments near the SPA). During the course of the appeal, this document was approved.

The Inspector found that the provisions of the unilateral undertakings would mitigate the effect of the development and that there would be no adverse impact on the integrity of the SPA.[10]

Rectory Homes Ltd v Royal Borough of Windsor and Maidenhead[11]

Again in this appeal, the SPA Delivery Framework had not yet been adopted and the Inspector had to consider the effect of development proposed 1.5 kilometres away from the Thames Basin Heaths SPA on the integrity and quality of the SPA. In this case, the development which was the subject of the appeal consisted of the demolition of an existing dwelling and the erection of another dwelling.[12] The Inspector considered that the proposed development, both alone and in combination with other projects, would only result in a marginal increase in the use of the SPA and so did not have a detrimental impact on the integrity and quality of the Thames Basin Heaths SPA. Even in the absence of mitigation measures, such as SANG, it was difficult for a local planning authority to demonstrate harm to the SPA where the proposed development comprises a single dwelling house.

Conclusion

The SANG mechanism addresses a problem that threatened to make housing provision within a large area of the South East very difficult indeed and streamlines

---

[10] The details of management plans of the alternative green spaces were yet to be finalised at the time the Inspector gave his decision, so that there was an issue as to whether they would be in place before the contributions by the developer would need to be accepted by the Council. The Inspector held that this issue could be overcome by a condition limiting the commencement of the development until the relevant management plans were finalised, and that therefore there would be no adverse impact on the SPA.

[11] Ref: APP/T0355/A/06/2016346.

[12] The two dwellings were to be erected on the site of a previous dwelling, but one dwelling had already been completed at the time of the inquiry under another planning permission so that the Inspector only considered the erection of one detached dwelling.

authorities' application of the tests in the Habitats Directive, which would otherwise be very difficult to apply on a piecemeal basis. The coordination across affected local authorities has withstood the planned announcements of the abolition of regional spatial strategies and the closure of regional offices, and SANG has proven to be a necessary and pragmatic solution to a fundamental conflict between habitats protection and the need for housing. However, developers still gripe at the cost and land-hungry nature of the requirements and the rigidity with which they are applied, as is demonstrated in the reasoning of the inspector and Secretary of State in Taylor Wimpey's appeal against Bracknell Forest Borough Council's refusal of planning permission.

On the other hand, there are equivalent concerns that the mere availability of SANG may not in practice prevent adverse effects arising on the SPA as a result of new development, but is instead a simple and convenient hoop-jumping exercise designed to circumvent the strict requirements of the Habitats Directive by way of financial payments.

On the assumption that SANG is a useful mechanism, what are the likely implications of the Localism Act 2011?

Most obviously, the proposed abolition of the South East Plan will mean that authorities are no longer bound by policy NRM6. At present it appears likely that authorities will continue the approach but in theory there is little to prevent individual authorities choosing to go their own way. Nor do we now have a regional planning body, in the form of SEERA, to ensure that authorities act in a coordinated manner, although again, in practice, the authorities in relation to the Thames Basin Heaths SPA continue to work together as before. The duty to cooperate that will be introduced by the Localism Bill, may also do its bit in this regard.

Authorities will need to be alert to the implications of the new consenting procedures, given that residential development will be able to come forward in certain situations by way of the proposed neighbourhood development order procedures.[13] As mentioned, the Thames Basin Heaths Joint Strategic Partnership is already concerning itself with the issues raised by the new local tier of planning.

Local Planning Authorities also need to consider the position of SANG contributions in light of the Coalition Government's commitment to preserve the Community Infrastructure Levy introduced by the previous Government. 'Infrastructure' for the purposes of the Community Infrastructure Levy under the Planning Act 2008 includes 'sporting and recreational facilities' and 'open spaces', and the Localism Act 2011 amends elements of the previous Government's proposed Community Infrastructure Levy system, so that receipts from the Community Infrastructure Levy can be spent on ongoing maintenance of infrastructure, and not just its initial provision. We believe it to be likely that

---

[13] The proposed 'community right to build' procedure does not raise the same issue as it will not be available where the development would be likely to affect a European-designated nature conservation site.

Simon Ricketts and Sarah Bischoff

SANG contributions and contribution towards strategic access management and monitoring measures will fall within the type of project for which the Community Infrastructure Levy applies, although the Thames Basin Heaths Joint Strategic Partnership Board is reportedly unsure as to the extent to which SANG provision and management amounts to 'infrastructure' within the meaning of the Planning Act 2008. The significance is that regulation 123 of the Community Infrastructure Regulations 2010 provides that local authorities will not be able to secure contributions under section 106 agreements through application of tariff-type policies for infrastructure covered by the Community Infrastructure Levy from April 2014. As such, to the extent that SANG provision and management does amount to 'infrastructure', it will be essential to the continuing use of the SANG mechanism that authorities have their Community Infrastructure Levy (CIL) charging schedules approved by April 2014 so that developer-contributions towards the provision and maintenance of SANG can still be secured.

8

The Habitats Directive:
Nature and Law

PAUL STOOKES

Nature, natural, and the group of words derived from them, or allied to them in etymology, have at all times filled a great place in the thoughts and take a strong hold on the feelings of mankind. That they should have done so is not surprising, when we consider what the words, in their primitive and most obvious signification, represent; but it is unfortunate that a set of terms which play so great a part in moral and metaphysical speculation, should have acquired many meanings different from the primary one, yet sufficiently allied to it to admit of confusion. The words have thus become entangled in so many foreign associations, most of a very powerful and tenacious character, that they have come to excite, and to be the symbols of, feelings which their original meaning will by no means justify, and which have made them one of the most copious sources of false taste, false philosophy, false morality, and even bad law.[1]

Introduction

In his essay *Nature, the Utility of Religion, and Theism* (1850–58) John Stuart Mill sought to ascertain precisely what 'Nature' meant. He concluded that it either denotes the entire system of things or things as they would be without human intervention. He then disregards both as either 'unmeaning', or irrational and immoral. Mill ends his essay by noting that

> the scheme of Nature regarded in its whole extent, cannot have had for its sole or even principal object, the good of human or other sentient beings … and the duty of man is to co-operate with the beneficent powers, not by imitating but by perpetually striving to amend the course of nature and bring that part of it over which we can exercise control more neatly into conformity with a high standard of justice and goodwill.[2]

---

[1] John Stuart Mill, (1806–73), *Nature, the Utility of Religion, and Theism*, (2nd edn) (Longman Green, 1850–58) 3.

[2] Ibid, 64–65.

The interpretation of 'Nature' by JS Mill has an anthropocentric basis. This is comparable with the objectives of the Habitats Directive 92/43/EEC which offers an initial ecocentric stance but has one eye firmly fixed on human self-interest. For instance, the recital to the Directive states that 'the preservation, protection and improvement of the quality of the environment, including the conservation of natural habitats and of wild fauna and flora, are an essential objective'. Yet its main aim is 'to promote the maintenance of biodiversity, taking account of economic, social, cultural and regional requirements' with 'contribution to the general objective of sustainable development'.

The Directive recognises that natural habitats are continuing to deteriorate and wild species are seriously threatened. It notes that in view of the threats to certain habitats and species, those habitats and species should have priority in order to favour the early implementation of measures to conserve them. It relies upon the designation of Special Areas of Conservation (SACs) to further conservation objectives and to prevent the deterioration of habitats. Once designated, the Directive seeks to protect the SACs by requiring an appropriate assessment of any plan or project likely to have a significant effect on the conservation objectives of that SAC. Society can therefore preserve biodiversity, natural habitats and species if it chooses to do so. Equally, it can place human or public interest before nature conservation.[3]

Inherent Conflict

There is inherent conflict within the Directive between habitat and species conservation and improvement and the pursuit of plans and projects. Waite suggests that 'a principle of Equilibrium' may be applied to environmental law in general and to the application of the Habitats Directive in particular.[4] But can such a balance be achieved? Ludwig Krämer in *EC Environmental Law*[5] notes that it was not really possible to transform designated habitats into 'nature museums' without change, but then cites the EC's 'Communication on rational use and conservation of wetlands',[6] that 'almost everywhere in Western Europe habitats and nature protection sites are shrinking slowly, but dramatically due to road and other infrastructure construction, urbanisation, intensive farming activity, irrigation and holiday and leisure activities.[7] This is evident in the UK by reference to the judicial proceedings discussed below.

---

[3] See Clutten and Tafur, ch 10 in this volume.
[4] See Waite, ch 13 in this volume at pp 248–50.
[5] Ludwig Krämer, *EC Environmental Law* (6th edn) (Sweet & Maxwell, 2006) para 5-14.
[6] COM (1995) 189 (29 May 1995).
[7] Krämer adds that: 'Perhaps the most eloquent example is the French habitat Carmargue which lost, between 1942 and 1984, about 1,000 hectares per year of its natural surface, see A Tamisier, *Camargue, milieux et paysages evolution de 1942 et 1984* (Arles, 1992).

By 20 August 2010 there were 613 SACs in the UK collectively covering over 2.6 million hectares.[8] This is just over 10,000 square miles and equivalent to around 10 per cent of the land area in the UK. There is a further 2.9 million hectares of candidate and possible SACs currently proposed although these are primarily offshore sites.[9] This simplistic quantitative summary merely suggests that UK habitat designation is not of marginal interest but involves sizeable land areas. Yet designation does not provide absolute protection and does allow human intervention. Whether or not such intervention is permitted is determined by an appropriate assessment. The development of domestic jurisprudence has raised questions (and some eyebrows) as to who, what, why and how appropriate assessment is carried out. The problem is that inconsistency in approach leaves uncertainty in application. Moreover, in the absence of any obligation to review whether the predictions contained in an appropriate assessment are accurate or, indeed, whether decisions should be revisited in their entirety when found to be wanting for environmental credibility; getting it right in the first place is critical. Put another way, is our domestic process for habitats protection susceptible to Mill's complaint of being 'bad law' for nature?

Lappel Bank: Justice Delayed

In *R v Secretary of State for the Environment ex p RSPB*[10] (the *Lappel Bank* case) the House of Lords was faced with uncertainty and competing arguments about the lawfulness of a proposed designation of a Special Protection Area (SPA) under the Wild Birds Directive 79/409/EEC (that is an SAC). The proposed site was due to be developed as a port and so the House of Lords sought a preliminary ruling from the European Court of Justice (ECJ) as to whether economic interests could be taken into account in the SPA designation. If not, the Lords asked whether economic requirements which may constitute imperative reasons of overriding public interest of the kind referred to in Article 6(4) of the Habitats Directive could be taken into account for the purpose of an appropriate assessment. The House of Lords invited the ECJ to treat the reference as a priority but then refused to grant an interim injunction to the RSPB to protect the site until the ECJ's ruling. The injunction was refused because the RSPB would not, or

---

[8] See, eg the Joint Nature Conservation Committee (JNCC), http://jncc.gov.uk/page 1456. JNCC explains that SACs are described as sites that have been adopted by the European Commission and formally designated by the relevant Member State. There are also Sites of Community Importance (SCIs) which are sites which have been adopted by the EU but not formally designated by the Member State and Candidate SACs (cSACs) which are sites that have been submitted to the EC by the Member State, but not formally adopted. As to protection afforded to cSACs see, Jones and Westaway ch 4 in this volume.
[9] http://jncc.gov.uk/page 1456.
[10] *R v Secretary of State for the Environment ex p RSPB* [1997] Env LR 431.

could not provide an undertaking in damages to cover the potential financial loss to the port and the council caused by any delay while the ECJ considered the reference should the court ultimately have found that the Secretary of State was right all along. In Case C-44/95 *R v Secretary State of the Environment ex p RSPB*,[11] the ECJ subsequently ruled that

> 41. Economic requirements, as an imperative reason of overriding public interest allowing a derogation from the obligation to classify a site according to its ecological value, cannot enter into consideration at that stage. But that does not, as the Commission has rightly pointed out, mean that they cannot be taken into account at a later stage under the procedure provided for by Article 6(3) and (4) of the Habitats Directive.

> 42. The answer to the second part of the second question must therefore be that Article 4(1) or (2) of the Birds Directive is to be interpreted as meaning that a Member State may not, when designating an SPA and defining its boundaries, take account of economic requirements which may constitute imperative reasons of overriding public interest of the kind referred to in Article 6(4) of the Habitats Directive.

By the time the ECJ gave its ruling the developer had concreted over the very site due to be designated an SPA. No financial implications to the port or the council but loss of a proposed SPA which, according to the ECJ, would have been entitled to have been designated without reference to economic interests. If such designation had occurred, any development of the site would then have required an appropriate assessment under Article 6(4) the Habitats Directive.

The habitat loss aside, the greatest concern arising from the *Lappel Bank* fiasco is that the courts still, in the main, require an undertaking in damages from applicants seeking to secure urgent interim relief. Indeed, Part 25A of the Civil Procedure Rules requires this. Such a requirement may be acceptable in commercial contractual disputes without an environmental aspect to the claim as in *American Cyanamid v Ethicon Ltd*.[12] In those instances there is more likely to be equality of arms. However, an undertaking in damages as a prerequisite to an injunction in environmental cases is likely to be unfair, inequitable and prohibitively expensive where the applicant will often be bringing proceedings with little or no financial resources and will often be ranged against corporate or public bodies with budgets for legal and other expertise. This requirement for an undertaking is arguably in breach of Article 9(4) of the Aarhus Convention 1998. Indeed, the United Nations Aarhus Compliance Committee Findings for Communication ACCC/2008/33 (advance final copy, December 2010) concluded that the undertakings requirement

> leads to the situation where injunctive relief is not pursued, because of the high costs at risk, where the claimant is legitimately pursuing environmental concerns that involve the public interest. Such effects would amount to prohibitively expensive procedures that are not in compliance with article 9, paragraph 4. [paragraph 133]

On the substance of the Habitats Directive, the *Lappel Bank* case highlights the perhaps obvious point that for habitats to be afforded protection, the

---

[11] Case C-44/95 *R v Secretary State of the Environment ex p RSPB* [1996] ECR I-3805.
[12] *American Cyanamid v Ethicon Ltd* [1975] AC 396.

Directive must first be engaged. This requires designation as an SAC. Without designation, a proposal may proceed with serious, irreversible adverse consequences and where economic factors including loss of profit and inequality of arms may easily override the environmental concerns. But for RSPB not being able to provide an undertaking in damages for an injunction to stay the development while the ECJ considered its case, the nature site may not have been destroyed and subsequently developed. Ultimately, the Secretary of State chose economic interests over nature interests. The ECJ's view in *Lappel Bank* was soon afterwards affirmed in Case-C371/98 *R v Secretary of State for the Environment, Transport and the Regions ex p First Corporate Shipping Ltd*[13] in which the court held that when selecting and defining SACs regard must only be had to conservation issues and not to economic, social, cultural or other matters.

Approach of the UK Courts to the Habitats Directive

The UK domestic courts continued to tread an uncertain habitats path after *Lappel Bank*.[14] In *WWF-UK v Secretary of State for Scotland*[15] (Court of Session) the applicant challenged the exclusion of certain highland areas in Scotland (the Cairn Gorm) from being within an SPA and SAC and also challenged the permission to develop a funicular railway adjacent to those habitat sites. The Court of Session dismissed the claim finding that, among other things, the identification of sites and the drawing of boundaries were linked processes involving the exercise of discretion by the Secretary of State. The Court held that there was no requirement that all contiguous or geographically linked qualifying habitats or species needed to be included within a site, and that the Habitats Regulations 1994 transposing the Directive did not require an absolute guarantee that the integrity of a site would not be adversely affected.

In contrast, in Case C-127/02 *Landelijke Vereniging tot Behoud van de Waddenzee v Staatssecretaris van Landbouw, Natuurbe- heeren Visserij* (*Waddenzee*),[16] the ECJ took a more inclusive and precautionary approach to the issue. In particular, it ruled at paragraph 45 that

> Article 6(3) of the Habitats Directive must be interpreted as meaning that any plan or project not directly connected with or necessary to the management of the site is to be subject to appropriate assessment of its implications for the site in view of the site's

---

[13] Case-C371/98 *R v Secretary of State for the Environment, Transport and the Regions ex p First Corporate Shipping Ltd* [2000] ECR I-9235.

[14] Edwards sees this as a symptom of the absence within British administrative law of 'an established doctrine on the intensity of judicial review' see, Edwards, ch 12 in this volume at p 211.

[15] *WWF-UK v Secretary of State for Scotland* [1999] Env LR 632.

[16] Case C-127/02 *Landelijke Vereniging tot Behoud van de Waddenzee v Staatssecretaris van Landbouw, Natuurbe- heeren Visserij* [2004] ECR I-9405.

conservation objectives if it cannot be excluded, on the basis of objective information, that it will have a significant effect on that site, either individually or in combination with other plans or projects.

The *Waddenzee* case helped to clarify the priority of precaution and nature conservation under the Habitats Directive.[17]

Once an SAC has been designated, conservation and improvement of habitats and species can be pursued although there is not a complete bar on planning applications being made in respect of the designated land. In *R (Merricks) v Secretary of State for Trade & Industry*[18] the applicant challenged a permission to develop a 26-turbine wind farm on Romney Marsh in Kent. The appropriate assessment was undertaken by the Secretary of State and published after the planning inquiry. In judicial review proceedings, the claimant argued that both the Inspector and Secretary of State underplayed the *Waddenzee* requirement for precaution and that there were further factors to be taken into account. It was submitted by the claimant that in carrying out the assessment the Secretary of State failed to fill in gaps in the evidence in relation to the impact of birds or failed to explain why it was not necessary to fill the gaps. The application was dismissed. The Court of Appeal held that the correct approach to *Waddenzee* had been used and, further, that proceedings should not advance simply on the basis of new evidence as to bird mortality and criticism of the risk assessment undertaken by the developer. The Court of Appeal recognised that the Bewick swan population was not large and was a species of great importance but noted that 'the actual recorded figures of swans of any sort dying through collision with wind turbines are remarkably low'. The Court was content that the appropriate assessment could be carried out and then published *after* the public inquiry even though it would then not be subject to the scrutiny and public participation which is one of the aims of the appropriate assessment process.

Mitigation

The High Court in *R (Hart DC) v Secretary of State for Communities & Local Government*[19] considered the question as to whether it is permissible to consider mitigation measures at the screening stage of an appropriate assessment. The screening procedure is found in regulation 48 of the Conservation (Natural Habitats, &c) Regulations 1994 (now 2010) and in particular, regulation 48(2) 'that the person applying for any such consent, permission or other authorisation shall provide such information as the competent authority may reasonably require

---

[17] See, Scott, ch 6 in this volume at pp 104–07.

[18] [2007] EWCA Civ 1034.

[19] *R (Hart DC) v Secretary of State for Communities & Local Government* [2008] EWHC 1204 and see Ricketts and Biscoff, ch 7 in this volume at pp 132–33.

for the purposes of the assessment or to enable them to determine whether an appropriate assessment is required'.[20] In *Hart* the Planning Inspector hearing an appeal found that there was inadequate information to enable an appropriate assessment to be carried out. The Secretary of State disagreed and decided that she could proceed to grant planning permission without having to undertake an appropriate assessment. The applicant Council challenged the decision on the basis that the Secretary of State erred in accepting mitigation measures at the screening stage. Sullivan J dismissed the application, finding at paragraph 76 that

> there is no legal requirement that a screening assessment under Regulation 48(1) must be carried out in the absence of any mitigation measures that form part of a plan or project. On the contrary, the competent authority is required to consider whether the project, as a whole, including such measures, if they are part of the project, is likely to have a significant effect on the SPA. If the competent authority does not agree with the proponent's view as to the likely efficacy of the proposed mitigation measures, or is left in some doubt as to their efficacy, then it will require an appropriate assessment because it will not have been able to exclude the risk of a significant effect on the basis of objective information (see *Waddenzee* above).

The Court's view in *Hart* that mitigation measures may reasonably be taken into account as part of the initial screening process is of concern and sits uncomfortably with the fact that mitigation measures will often be critical aspects of the proposal that require detailed assessment and should be subject to public scrutiny. To exclude such assessment and comment appears at odds with the purpose of the Directive and the precautionary principle.

Mitigation in screening has received judicial attention in relation to an environmental impact assessment (EIA) under the EIA Directive 85/337/EEC. Indeed, the European Commission 2000 guidance: 'Managing Natura 2000 sites: The provisions of Article 6 of the "Habitats" Directive 92/43/EEC' provides at paragraph 1.1 that the term 'assessment' for carrying out an appropriate assessment is used as in an EIA. The starting point for an EIA is the Directive itself which under Article 5(3) requires that 'the information to be provided by the developer as part of its environmental statement shall include *at least ... a description of the measures envisaged in order to avoid, reduce and, if possible, remedy significant adverse effects*' (emphasis added).

In *Berkeley v Secretary of State for the Environment*,[21] Lord Hoffman highlighted that a key purpose of the Directive was that it required

> 8. ... not merely that the planning authority should have the necessary information, but that it should have been obtained by means of a particular procedure, namely that of an EIA. And an essential element in this procedure is what the Regulations call the 'environmental statement' by the developer should have been 'made available to the public' and the public should have been 'given an opportunity to express an opinion'.

---

[20] See Scott, ch 6 in this volume at pp 115–16.
[21] *Berkeley v Secretary of State for the Environment* [2001] 2 AC 603.

In essence, without an environmental statement and the proposal being regarded as EIA development, the opportunity for public participation to the standard required by the Directive is lost. Thus, a negative EIA screening opinion relying upon mitigation measures that are assumed to be effective not only avoids any comprehensive environmental assessment of the proposal and the mitigation measures proposed it also prevents the public from engaging in the 'early and effective participation' required under Article 6 of the EIA Directive. The twin concepts of mitigation and public participation were brought together in *British Telecommunications Plc v Gloucester CC*[22] in which the High Court stated at paragraph 71 that

> There is no doubt that it is for the planning authority to decide in the first instance whether or not there are likely to be significant effects on the environment such as to warrant an environmental statement. Can they conclude that there would be significant effects, save for the fact that they have required (or at least will require) the developer to take mitigating steps whose effect to render such effects insignificant? In my judgement they cannot. Paragraph 3 of Sch 2, which sets out the information required (and in turn reflects Art 5 of the Directive read with Appendix IV) requires amongst other things that there is a description of the measures envisaged to 'avoid, reduce and if possible remedy' adverse effects. The purpose is surely to enable public discussion to take place about whether the measures will be successful, or perhaps whether more effective measures can be taken than those proposed to ameliorate the anticipated harm. In my opinion, therefore, the question whether or not there are likely to be significant environmental effects should be approached by asking whether these would be likely to result, absent some specific measures being taken to ameliorate or reduce them. If they would, the environmental statement is required and the mitigating measures must be identified in it.

In *R (Lebus) v South Cambridgeshire DC*,[23] the High Court adopted the *BT* approach and held at paragraph 46 that

> It was not appropriate for a person charged with making a screening opinion to start from the premise that although there may be significant impacts, these can be reduced to insignificance as a result of implementation of conditions of various kinds. The appropriate course in such a case is to require an environmental statement setting out the significant impacts and the measures which it is said will reduce their significance.

Further, in *Gillespie v First Secretary of State & Bellway Urban Renewal Southern*,[24] at first instance, Richards J (as he then was) concluded at paragraph 79:

> The correct approach [on the part of the First Secretary of State] would have been to hold that significant effects were likely and that an EIA was therefore required, leaving the suitability and effectiveness of the proposed remediation measures to be discussed and assessed in the context of the EIA procedures.

---

[22] *British Telecommunications Plc v Gloucester CC* [2000] EWHC 1001.
[23] *R (Lebus) v South Cambridgeshire DC* [2002] EWHC 2009.
[24] *Gillespie v First Secretary of State & Bellway Urban Renewal Southern* [2003] EWHC 8.

Inconsistency has, however, arisen since *Gillespie* went to the Court of Appeal, under the title *Bellway Urban Renewal Southern v Gillespie*,[25] and the issue received a 'gloss' from each of the three sitting judges. Pill LJ, one of the Lord Justices in *Gillespie* considered the question again in *R (Catt) v Brighton & Hove CC*,[26] in which the Council had concluded that an EIA was not required for a series of temporary planning permissions to use and develop Withdean Stadium by Brighton & Hove Albion Football Club. Pill LJ concluded that

> 35. I repeat my statements in *Gillespie*, at paragraph 36, that the decision maker is not 'obliged to shut his eyes to the remedial measures submitted as a part of the planning proposal', and that 'in making his decision, the Secretary of State [the planning authority] is not required to put into separate compartments the development proposal and the proposed remedial measures and consider only the first when making his screening decision'. Laws LJ was considering the facts in *Gillespie* and I do not consider he was asserting a general principle that, only when remedial measures are 'uncontroversial', can they be taken into account when giving a screening opinion.

The claimant's case in *Catt* was that the mitigation (not remedial) measures relied upon were controversial; not least because one of the measures was abandoned within a few months of planning permission being granted because it was unfit for purpose. Soon after *Catt* the Court of Appeal in *R (Dicken) v Aylesbury Vale DC*[27] drew a distinction between a 'separate or free-standing remedial system' and the mitigation measures under consideration which were 'part and parcel of the proposed development itself'. Laws LJ, delivering the judgment in the Court of Appeal, stated at paragraph 16:

> But if in truth there is nothing of substance to dispute, having regard, it may be, to plainly effective remedial measures, whether or not part and parcel of the development itself, then as I see it there is no requirement for an EIA.

In *R (Birch) v Barnsley MBC*,[28] the Court of Appeal appears to have returned to the *Lebus* position with Sullivan LJ finding that

> 22. ... The approach adopted in the screening opinion, which merely stated that the impacts 'should be ... controllable' was not merely inadequate, it was contrary to the underlying purpose of the Regulations (see *R (Lebus) v South Cambridgeshire District Council* [2002] EWHC 2009 (Admin) at paragraph 45 and *Bellway v Gillespie* [2003] EWCA Civ 400 per Laws LJ at paragraph 46.

> 23. An EIA was required so that the proposed controls could be identified and their adequacy thoroughly tested through the EIA process. In the absence of a condition in the planning permission prescribing, perhaps by reference to the Protocol, some minimum standard for the material to be spread, it would necessarily be a question of fact and degree whether the material which was being spread was still waste or had ceased to

---

[25] *Bellway Urban Renewal Southern v Gillespie* [2003] EWCA Civ 400.
[26] *R (Catt) v Brighton & Hove CC* [2007] EWCA Civ 298.
[27] *R (Dicken) v Aylesbury Vale DC* [2007] EWCA Civ 851.
[28] *R (Birch) v Barnsley MBC* [2010] EWCA Civ 1180.

be waste. The Protocol would certainly be relevant for the purpose of answering that question and might well be adopted by the decision-maker as the relevant standard. But not having been expressly incorporated into the planning permission, it could not be assumed that it would necessarily be determinative.

24. It is precisely this kind of issue—what controls or conditions are necessary in order to ensure that there will be no cumulative impact—that should have been considered in an EIA. I would also accept Mr Hyam's submission that the council's 'wait and see, and serve an enforcement notice if necessary' approach is the very antithesis of the precautionary principle which underlies the Directive. Recital 1 to the Directive is in this term:

'Whereas the 1973 and 1977 action programmes of the European Communities on the environment, as well as the 1983 action programme, the main outlines of which have been approved by the Council of the European Communities and the representatives of the Governments of the Member States, stress that the best environmental policy consists in preventing the creation of pollution or nuisances at source, rather than subsequently trying to counteract their effects; whereas they affirm the need to take effects on the environment into account at the earliest possible stage in all the technical planning and decision making processes; whereas, to that end, they provide the implementation of procedures to evaluate such effects;'

Returning to the Habitats Directive, the *Hart* approach to mitigation in screening appears to follow the *Catt* and *Dicken* line. Yet this arguably undermines the purpose of the Directive. In *Hart* the High Court appeared to reject EC guidance as to how mitigation measures should be dealt with although this appears highly relevant. The EC Guidance 2000: The provisions of Article 6 discuss at paragraph 4.5.2 how mitigation is a central part of the appropriate assessment process. More recent guidance 'The Habitats Directive and non-energy mineral extraction' (July 2010) emphasises throughout the importance of mitigation and that a precautionary approach should be taken to screening for appropriate assessment. Paragraph 5.3.1 provides for instance, that

When doing this initial evaluation it is important to recall that the emphasis is on there being a 'likelihood' of potentially significant effects—not a certitude. This shows the precautionary nature of this initial test. If there is any doubt over whether the effects are likely to be significant or not then an Appropriate Assessment must be undertaken to ensure that these potential effects can be studied in full. The lack of information or data cannot be used as a reason for not carrying out an Appropriate Assessment (*cf* The European Court of Justice (C-127/02 *Waddenzee*).

While paragraph 5.5.3 states that

measures are aimed at minimising or even cancelling the negative impact of a project. Avoidance or reduction of impacts at source should be the preferred options (EC 2000). Mitigation measures are an integral part of the specifications of a plan or project and should be considered during the appropriate assessment.

To seek to avoid an appropriate assessment by reliance upon mitigation measures that will be assumed to be effective is an unduly exclusionary approach to the Directive that is contrary to the precautionary principle. Indeed, the appropriate assessment should discuss, analyse and offer for public consultation those very mitigation measures that are said to suggest that the likely significant effects may not be so likely after all.[29]

Competent Authority

The Habitats Directive does not state who should carry out the Article 6 appropriate assessment. The EU Commission's guidance on Article 6(3) (EC, 2000) states at paragraph 1.1 that it is 'the responsibility of the competent authority in each Member State to make the key decisions within the Article 6(3) and (4) assessments'. Who the competent authority may be is largely left to the Member State. In *R (Akester and another) v Defra*[30] the claimants argued that the decision to introduce a new larger ferry on a service from the UK mainland to the Isle of Wight was unlawful. The ferry route affected an SAC. Wightlink Ltd was the ferry operator. It was also, as the statutory harbour authority, the regulator. The High Court held that, among other things: (i) the introduction of the ferries was a project within the ambit of Article 6(3); (ii) as harbour authority, Wightlink was responsible for carrying out an appropriate assessment, notwithstanding that it was also the ferry operator; (iii) a decision maker would have been bound to conclude that the risk of significant effects on the protected sites could not be excluded; and (iv) this prompted the requirement for an appropriate assessment.

The concern as to who undertakes the appropriate assessment for the Habitats Directive is brought into focus in *Akester* in which the operator seeking the permission and securing financial gain from the project is also the harbour authority granting the permission and accordingly the competent authority acting on behalf of the Member State. There is not only the potential conflict of interest arising but also a question as to whether there is adequate expertise available to the competent authority.

An underlying concern about habitats' protection in the UK, and one that has not been tested, is that no one appears to really know (or attempts to check) whether the appropriate assessments carried out are, in fact, effective. Not the developer, the competent authorities, Defra, or the European Union. There is no systematic review, analysis, or monitoring requirement for the assessment. There appears to be no follow up to ensure that mitigation measures are being implemented. The assessments themselves are undertaken by a wide range of organisations many of whom will be ill-equipped and not competent to carry on what

---

[29] Para 53 of revised guidance on EIA for Scotland: Circular 3/2011 which accepts the precautionary approach to mitigation measures taken in *Lebus* and more recently, *Birch v Barnsley* available at: http://www.scotland.gov.uk/Publications/2011/06/01084419/0. Although amended EIA guidance is still due in England and Wales, Circular 3/2011 adopts near-identical wording to the draft amended Circular on EIA published by the Department of Communities and Local Government in 2006.

[30] *R (Akester and another) v Defra* [2010] EWHC 232 (Admin).

should involve highly specialist and complex analysis. The assessment will often refer to environmental statements prepared by the developer or its consultant as part of the planning application process; leaving a question as to the independence and integrity of any assessment. What was the overriding imperative for Wightlink in *Akester*, or for the Secretary of State in *Hart*? When review was sought in *Merricks* it was denied.

Conclusion

In conclusion, it cannot really be said that the Habitats legislation is of itself 'bad law', although there are now some instances of bad application of that law. Furthermore, it is fair to say that there is a high standard of justice which, from time to time, considers the bad application of the law. However, that standard of justice has been found to be prohibitively expensive for many,[31] inadequate in certain aspects such as when seeking urgent interim protection of habitat sites and arguably wrongly applied when considering the concepts of precaution and mitigation. Finally, it is of concern that JS Mill, and many of us today, think it acceptable that we should strive to amend the course of nature and seek to exercise and control it so as to bring it into conformity with our 'high standard of justice and goodwill'. Arguably, this could be said to be the underlying principle behind the land use planning system. There may be an argument that we should instead follow nature's path and let us be led away from our own false taste, false philosophy and false morality. If carried out effectively and thoroughly, appropriate assessment under the Habitats Directive may be a way along nature's path. And perhaps this is what JS Mill implied all along.

---

[31] See, eg the Findings & Recommendations of the UN Aarhus Compliance Committee for Communication ACCC/C/2008/33 (December 2010) at para 141 that the UK is failing to ensure that the costs for all court procedures subject to Art 9 are not prohibitively expensive available at: http://www.unece.org.

9

Adverse Effects on the Integrity of a European Site: Some Unanswered Questions

GREGORY JONES QC

Introduction

According to its Preamble, the Council Directive on the conservation of natural habitats and of wild fauna and flora (the Habitats Directive) aims to contribute towards ensuring biodiversity though the conservation of natural habitats and wild flora and fauna. One important way it does so is by the designation, maintenance and protection of Special Areas of Conservation (SACs).[1] Consequently, there is a strong presumption contained in Article 6(3) that any 'plan or project' (PoP) which would adversely affect the integrity of an SAC should not be permitted. Article 6(3) provides that

> Any plan or project not directly connected with or necessary to the management of the site but likely to have a significant effect thereon, either individually or in combination with other plans or projects, shall be subject to appropriate assessment of its implications for the site in view of the site's conservation objectives. In the light of the conclusions of the assessment of the implications for the site and subject to the provisions of paragraph 4, the competent national authorities shall agree to the plan or project only after having ascertained that it will not adversely affect the integrity of the site concerned and, if appropriate, after having obtained the opinion of the general public.

That presumption is rebutted only by the exceptional circumstances set out in Article 6(4).[2] Article 6(3) of the Habitats Directive requires: first, that any PoP[3] which is 'likely to have a significant effect' on an SAC must be subject to an appropriate assessment (AA) by a competent national authority (the AA stage); and secondly,

---

[1] As to the designation process and the protection afforded to emerging SACs, see Jones and Westaway, ch 4 in this volume.

[2] They are derogations from the general rule in Art 6(3) of the Habitats Directive that authorisation can only be granted to plans or projects not affecting the integrity of the site concerned. Accordingly, they are interpreted in a restrictive way by the courts. On IROPI see Clutton and Tafur, ch 10 of this volume.

[3] For a discussion of the meaning of 'PoP' see Tromans, ch 5 in this volume.

that the authority may only approve a PoP where it has ascertained that it would not adversely affect the integrity of the site concerned (the decision-making stage). If the conclusion is that it would, that is called a 'negative assessment'.[4] This reflects the generally protective approach of EU environmental law.

The General Approach to EU Environmental Protection

The stated objective of the Directorate-General for the Environment is 'to protect, preserve and improve the environment for present and future generations'. Article 191(2) of the Treaty on the Functioning of the European Union provides that

> Union policy on the environment shall aim at a high level of protection taking into account the diversity of situations in the various regions of the Union. It shall be based on the precautionary principle and on the principles that preventive action should be taken, that environmental damage should as a priority be rectified at source and that the polluter should pay.

The 'precautionary principle' thus applies to both elements of Article 6(3). So, for example, it is not enough that there is no evidence of adverse effects; the competent authority must be positively satisfied, or 'certain' there are no adverse effects, or to use the words of the court in *Waddenzee*,[5] that is, 'where no reasonable scientific doubt remains as to the absence of such effects' upon the integrity of the SAC. The application of the precautionary principle sets the contextual basis of the approach likely to be adopted by the Court of Justice of the European Union (CJEU) in its interpretation of the Habitats Directive.

Article 6(3)

At the outset it is useful to note the wording used for the two parts of Article 6(3). The trigger for an AA is a decision that the PoP is 'likely' to have 'significant environmental effects' on the SAC. The word 'likely' has a stricter meaning in EU environmental law than its ordinary English meaning would suggest. The high water mark of this European precautionary approach to the meaning of 'likely' in this context is to be found in the opinion of Advocate General Kokott in *Waddenzee*.[6] In her

---

[4] See Art 6(4).
[5] Case C-127/02 *Landelijke Vereniging tot Behoud van de Waddenzee v Staatssecretaris van Landbouw, Natuurbeheer en Visserij* (Waddenzee) [2004] ECR-7405.
[6] Ibid.

opinion to the court she stated that 'an appropriate assessment is always necessary where *reasonable doubt exists* as to the absence of significant adverse effects'.[7] The court itself answered the question posed by the reference as follows:

> The first sentence of Article 6(3) of Directive 92/43 must be interpreted as meaning that any plan or project not directly connected with or necessary to the management of the site is to be subject to an appropriate assessment of its implications for the site in view of the site's conservation objectives *if it cannot be excluded, on the basis of objective information*, that it will have a significant effect on that site, either individually or in combination with other plans or projects. (emphasis added)

For the AA stage the threshold of confidence required by the court was that

> all the aspects of the plan or project which can, either individually or in combination with other plans or projects, affect those objectives must be identified *in the light of the best scientific knowledge in the field*.[8] (emphasis added)

Two points arise from these two passages. First, the test for 'likely' is only satisfied *if it cannot be excluded, on the basis of objective information* that there will be significant effects upon the site.[9] To an English common law lawyer this formulation of the test appears to be more akin to the criminal standard of proof of 'beyond all reasonable doubt'[10] than the civil standard or whether something is 'more likely than not'. Secondly, the court referred to the effect of the proposed development upon the site's *conservation objectives*. This does not appear in Article 6(3) itself. However, the Preamble to the directive states:

> Whereas an appropriate assessment must be made of any plan or programme likely to have a significant effect *on the conservation objectives* of a site which has been designated or is designated in future. (emphasis added)

---

[7] Para 74 opinion. (emphasis added)

[8] At para 54 of the judgment. See Scott, ch 6 in this volume.

[9] In *Cornwall Waste Forum St Dennis Branch v Secretary of State for Communities and Local Government* [2012] EWCA Civ 379 Carnwath LJ discussed, without deciding, the correct meaning of the two-stage approach: '7. I note here a criticism made by Mr Phillips (for SITA) of the judge's summary of the two stage-approach. He [the Judge] had said (para 12): "First, consideration ... is given to whether it can be shown that no adverse effect can possibly result. This is a negative consideration; that is to say if it is not possible to say that no adverse effect might be occasioned then appropriate assessment must be made. That appropriate assessment will then decide whether the project is likely to have a significant effect on the site." This, says Mr Phillips, misstates the test at both stages. At stage one, the test is not whether *no adverse effect* can *possibly* result, but whether there is a *likelihood* of *significant* effects. Conversely, at stage two, likelihood of significant effects is not the question; this has been decided at stage one. The question is the implications of those effects in relation to the conservation objectives of the site. He makes a similar criticism of the judge's comments at para 36 (—the approach should be that if it is not possible to rule out any adverse effects then appropriate assessment should be made ...) 8. While I see some force in this criticism, it is clear that the first stage sets a lower hurdle that the strict wording might be thought to imply. This appears from the decision of the European Court in *Waddenzee* (2004) Case 127/02. According to that judgment (para 45), an—appropriate assessment will be required in relation to any project: "if it cannot be excluded on the basis of objective information that it will have a significant effect on that site ... " 9. In any event the arguments in the present case have turned not on the nature of the test, but on allocation of responsibility for applying'.

[10] For a concise and masterly exposition of the criminal standard of proof see JC Smith, *Criminal Evidence* (Sweet & Maxwell, 1995) 35–37.

It is well established that the preambles or recitals to directives are acknowledged as relevant to the correct interpretation of European law.[11] However, it is perhaps curious in the present instance that the same wording from the Preamble was not directly transposed into the part of Article 6(3) to which it relates. The consequence of this interpretation of Article 6(3) means that the trigger for AA under the Habitats Directive is different to that for an environmental impact assessment under the Environmental Impact Assessment Directive[12] (EIA Directive) required for certain projects that development is likely to have a significant impact on the environment. This means that it is possible that an EIA might be required where an AA is not. This is because the development might have significant environmental effects generally, say in respect of aspects of the environment not covered by the conservation objectives of the SAC. The trigger for the EIA Directive is directed to *all* likely significant environmental effects arising from the project.[13]

What then is the significance of the word *integrity*? It does not appear in the first part of Article 6(3). Can a distinction thus be drawn between an adverse effect upon the SAC and its conservation objectives and an adverse effect upon the *integrity* of the SAC? Is it possible to say that although a development may have an adverse effect upon the SAC and its objectives, it may not have an adverse effect upon the *integrity* of the SAC? If the development causes damage only to particular plants or wildlife amounting only to a so-called 'local' or short-term impact will it not affect the *integrity* of the SAC?

The First Part of Article 6(3)

Before addressing in further detail the second part of Article 6(3) it is helpful to examine the first part of Article 6(3). Plainly, the duration of an effect is a relevant factor when considering the likely significance of any effect on an SAC. It is, of course, not determinative. A very short effect may be significant; likewise, an effect of long duration may not be significant. By analogy, an environmental impact assessment following good practice will be expected to assess environmental

---

[11] See, eg Case C-83/96 *Provincia Autonoma di Trento v Dega* [1997] ECR I-5001 paras 15–19 and Case C-178/91 *Ponente Carni and Cispanda Construzioni* [1993] ECR I 1915 paras 19–20.

[12] Council Directive 85/337/EEC of 27 June 1985 on the assessment of the effects of certain public and private projects on the environment.

[13] The other main difference, of course, is that the EIA Directive gives no direction as to whether or not consent should be granted for a development. By contrast, the Habitat's Directive gives directions as to the circumstances in which consent may or may not be granted (see the opinion of Advocate General in Case 209/04 *Commission v Austria* [2006] I-02755).

affects over different periods of time.[14] The fact that an effect may be temporary does not mean that it cannot be significant or adverse.

In *Waddenzee* the Court of Justice of the European Union (CJEU) recognised that in carrying out the first stage of Article 6(3) any assessment of the significant likely effects of a project not directly concerned with the management of the site was linked to the SAC's *conservation objects*. As previously stated, were a PoP to have an effect on the site but one which not likely to undermine its conservation objects, it would not be considered likely to have a significant effect on the site, and the converse is true. This is because in assessing significance for the purpose so the Habitats Directive (and the English Habitats Regulations) one is looking to see what the impacts would be upon the elements that make the SAC special and worthy of conservation.

The Second Part of Article 6(3)

The second part of Article 6(3), of course, expressly refers to the *integrity* of the site. The meaning of *integrity* of the SAC is clearly important because it is only when it is established what the integrity comprises in a particular case can one possibly ascertain whether that integrity would be adversely affected. *The Shorter Oxford English Dictionary on Historical Principles*[15] defines 'integrity' as 'the condition of having no part or element taken away or lacking, undivided state, completeness'. But dictionary definitions are of limited assistance in the interpretation of EU legislation.

Integrity as the Capacity for Self-Repair

According to the European Commission's Guidance, 'Managing Natura 2000'[16] at paragraph 4.6.3, the integrity of a site involves its ecological functions; the site may be described as having a high degree of integrity where its capacity for self-repair and self-renewal under the dynamic conditions is maintained, and a minimum of management support is required. This suggests that a site's capacity for 'self-repair and self-renewal' may be relevant to the question as to whether the development would adversely affect the integrity of the site.

---

[14] See Tromans and Fuller, *Environmental Impact Assessment–Law and Practice* (Lexis Nexis, 2003) para 9.77.

[15] (6th edn) (Oxford University Press, 2007).

[16] http://ec.europa.eu/environment/nature/natura2000/management/guidance_en.htm.

Integrity as the Maintenance of the Coherence of the Site's Ecological Structure and Function

In its guidance on the 1994 version of the Habitats Regulations, Habitats Regulations Guidance Note 1 (HRGN1) Natural England writes:[17]

> VI. Integrity of the Site
>
> 22. Having regard to English Nature's advice, other consultation responses and any other information available, the competent authority should decide whether the plan or project, as proposed, would adversely affect the integrity of the site, in the light of its conservation objectives. That is, whether the plan or project would adversely affect the *'coherence of the site's ecological structure and function, across its whole area, or the habitats, complex of habitats and/or populations of species for which the site is or will be classified'* (PPG 9 box C10). An adverse effect on integrity is likely to be one which prevents the site from making the same contribution to favourable conservation status for the relevant feature as it did at the time of its designation.
>
> 23. The form of words used in Regulation 48(5) implies that a precautionary approach should be taken in considering effects on integrity, in line with the Government's principles for sustainable development (see *Sustainable Development: the UK strategy* page 33). Regulation 48(5) says that (subject to Regulation 49) projects may only proceed if the competent authority has ascertained that it will not adversely affect the integrity of the European site.

This guidance equates integrity with the 'coherence of the site's ecological structure and function'. According to the guidance this is to be judged 'across its whole area, or the habitats, complex of habitats and/or populations of species for which the site is or will be classified'.

Conservation Objectives

As we have seen, Article 6(3) itself talks only of adverse affects on the SAC site. The Preamble states that an AA is required where the development is 'likely to have a significant effect *on the conservation objectives* of a site'. (emphasis added) In *Waddenzee* the court held that a PoP 'is to be subject to an appropriate assessment of its implications for the site *in view of* the site's conservation objectives'. (emphasis added) and that all those aspects which might '*affect those objectives* must be identified' (emphasis added) in the AA. It is true that these statements refer to the need for and content of the AA but it would be bizarre if the AA were to be addressed to the likely significant impacts caused by the proposal upon the SAC's conservation objectives, but that the integrity test were to be addressed simply on the impact on the SAC. If this were the case the AA might not be comprehensive enough to detect all those matters which might affect the SAC. The

---

[17] http://www.ukmpas.org/pdf/practical_guidance/HRGN1.pdf.

answer, presumably, is that the SAC is designated in order to achieve the expressed conservation objectives so that there can only be an adverse affect upon the SAC (as opposed say to the environment in general) if there is an adverse impact on the integrity of its conservation objectives.

There is a material difference between a test that is to be applied which is addressed to the integrity of the conservation area objectives of the SAC rather than simply addressed to the integrity of the SAC. There is a greater degree of flexibility in the former than in the latter. The definition and description of the SAC's objectives thus becomes of critical importance; this is particularly so when one goes on to consider not only temporary adverse effects but also permanent so-called 'localised' adverse effects.

Temporary Adverse Effects

An application of Natural England's guidance coupled with that of the European Commission's Guidance: 'Managing Natura 2000' would suggest that an adverse effect on an SAC may nonetheless not amount to an adverse effect on the integrity of the SAC where the ecological functions of the SAC would recover within a period of time. If the population species can recover naturally then it might be said that the development has had no adverse affect upon the integrity of the conservation objectives of the SAC.

Thus, if the time taken for the habitat recovery was measured in days or even a couple of months one might see a powerful case for saying that there had been no adverse effect upon the integrity of the SAC's conservation objectives and its ecological system. Furthermore, it is to be noted that it is permissible to take into account mitigating features in assessing whether the proposal would have an adverse effect upon the integrity of the SAC (that is at the decision-making stage). Not all mitigation measures would be immediately effective. The wording of this guidance supports a suggestion that a degree of temporary adverse effect upon an SAC, may, nonetheless, not amount to an adverse effect upon the 'integrity' of an SAC.

Natural England on behalf of the UK, must report to the EU Commission on the conditions of SACs every three years. It has been suggested that a temporary disturbance might not affect the integrity of the site if it last less than three years (that is the period between reporting cycles). Whilst the reporting period may provide a convenient rule of thumb, there is no basis for saying that it should establish the time period for determining whether or not the effects are adverse since it has no particular ecological basis as far as one can see, nor could it, given the very different natures of different types of habitat.

It could be argued that adverse effects which lasted days (or perhaps as much as even a few months) were *de minimis* and represent no support for any wider proposition beyond a very narrow exception of *de minimis*. On the other hand, it could also be argued that the integrity of a site's conservation objectives is more than simply its medium- or long-term ability to recover from an adverse impact and that an adverse impact upon its integrity may also include the short-term impact upon the ecosystem. Indeed, if one were to take more lengthy periods of time before recovery, such as 20 to 30 years, or indeed, even 200 to 300 years, one sees that the proposition that there has been no adverse effect upon the *integrity* of the site to be inherently much more difficult to sustain.

In addition, as a matter of fact, the longer the 'recovery' period exists the more room exists for doubt as to whether it would actually take place. Furthermore, the longer the recovery period in question the longer the period when the SAC is adversely affected and the more difficult it would be credibly to maintain that the integrity of the site remains unaffected.

Permanent So-called 'Localised' Adverse Effects

A development might permanently adversely affect only part of an SAC, for example, an area used for feeding a protected species. Will that necessarily amount to an adverse affect upon the integrity of the conservation objectives of the SAC where it can be shown that the species in question will not be adversely affected by the small loss of habitats? Proceedings in the Republic of Ireland may lead to an answer to this question and address some of the issues which have been raised above.

Sweetman v An Bord Pleanála

Sweetman v An Bord Pleanála concerns a challenge to a decision dated the 20 November, 2008 by *An Bord Pleanála* ('The Planning Board') to grant permission for the Galway outer city bypass.[18] In brief, the Board found that the road would have a 'localised' severe impact on the Lough Corrib Special Area of Conservation, but would not adversely affect the *integrity* of the site.

Background Facts

Specifically, the decision which was the subject of the challenge, approved part of the proposed development, being that part between junction M (Garraun) and Junction A (Gortatleva) but refused to approve that part of the development, between Junction A (Gortaleva) and Junction W (An Baile Nua), including the western distributor connection. The latest estimate given to the high court for the cost of the scheme was €303.22 million with €12 million having already been spent. *The Irish Times* put the total costs at €317 million.[19] By partly approving the proposal, the Board departed from the recommendations of the inspector who

[18] http://fail.3cdn.net/99727f4b89a11a8717_szm6bdfr6.pdf.
[19] Mary Carolan, 'State urges referral of Galway bypass ruling to European court' *The Irish Times* 3 June 2010.

conducted a substantial oral hearing of 21 sitting days and had recommended that approval be refused.

The applicant, Mr Peter Sweetman, was described in his grounding affidavit as 'a photographer and a person having an interest in the environment and in promoting the protection of the environment'. Birmingham J commented that 'he is a veteran environmental activist, having lodged in excess of 500 submissions in relation to hundreds of different developments over the years'. A number of grounds were pursued in addition to that related to the application of the Habitats Directive.

In the Republic of Ireland where a complaint was made that there had been a failure on the part of the State to comply with its obligations and properly transpose into Irish law provisions of a directive, the Attorney General and the Minister must be named as respondents; similar provisions exist in Northern Ireland. The stance adopted by the Attorney General in respect of the Habitats Directive may prove significant because the Attorney General took the view that the approach of the Planning Board (the Board) was in breach of Article 6(3) of the Habitats Directive.

Birmingham J described the course of the road and its impact as follows

> the proposed road would pass through an area regarded by all as a candidate Special Area of Conservation ('cSAC'). If this happened, everyone was in agreement that there would be an impact on the area and indeed there was broad agreement on the physical scale of the impact, which, after certain mitigating measures identified were agreed, would see the loss of approximately 1.5 hectares of the Lough Corrib cSAC.

> The site as originally defined amounted to some 185 hectares and an extended area proposed for inclusion, which is the area most directly relevant to the proposal, amounted to 85 hectares. The dispute arose because, while the inspector and the Board were of the view that although the proposal would involve a significant effect on the site and would have a localised severe impact on the Lough Corrib cSAC, the effect would not be such as to adversely affect the integrity of the site. The applicant disagreed with the approach taken and complained that the Board's decision involves a serious mis-interpretation of European and domestic legislative provisions.

> The applicant supported by the Attorney General argued that if a conclusion is reached that a 'plan or programme' would have a significant effect on a site and that it is an adverse effect that such a finding equates with a conclusion that the project is one that will adversely affect the integrity of the site concerned and accordingly once there has been a conclusion that there will be a significant adverse effect it follows as a matter of law that the proposal must be refused approval at this stage and that if the PoP is to proceed resort must be had to an alternative procedure designed to deal specifically with projects that adversely effect the integrity of relevant sites.

The Opposing Arguments on the Wording of Article 6(3)

The applicant and the Attorney General stated that the scheme put in place by the legislation requires, in the first instance, that all PoPs, not directly connected with or necessary to the management of a site but likely to have a significant effect, should be the subject of an AA. Then, when the AA has concluded, the authorities must consider whether the impact which it has identified the PoP will have, is one that will adversely affect the integrity of the site, and then if, and only if, a conclusion is reached that the plan will not adversely affect the integrity of the site, can it be approved.

Staged Approach

The Board and interested parties[20] submitted that the scheme requires that once it is established that a PoP will have a significant effect, it is necessary to go on to a further stage which involves assessing whether the significant impact is one that either will or will not affect the integrity of the site having regard to its conservation objectives. This was referred to as a 'staged approach' and rejected by the applicant and the Attorney General. They submitted that once it is established that a project will have a significant and adverse impact, that this of itself means that the integrity of the site is affected. The Attorney General categorised the Board's drawing of a distinction between projects that will have a significant impact on a site but do not affect its integrity, and those which will affect the integrity of the site as a *de minimis* approach.

Added Protection

The applicant and the Attorney General argued that the reference to 'integrity' is designed to be, and is actually, an added protection for the site in question and that it was in no sense a derogation from the general level of protection provided. They suggested that it was designed to deal with the situation where an effect on the site, although not a direct one, might nevertheless undermine the integrity of the site. An example given was that it would deal with situations where 'upstream activity might impact on water quality, habitats or species downstream.'

Birmingham J rejected the arguments of the applicants and the Attorney General on the wording of Article 6(3). He first undertook a detailed common law style appraisal of the literal and ordinary understanding of the wording employed in the directive. He held that had the reference to integrity of the site been omitted entirely, then Article 6(3) of the Habitats Directive, would, it is absolutely clear, require any PoP to be assessed, and any PoP to be refused if it would have a significant adverse effect. However, absent any reference to the integrity of the site, the judge considered that

> there is absolutely nothing to confine the category of plans or projects requiring assessment to those where the impact is direct. On the contrary, the reference to the consideration of its impact either individually or in combination with other plans or projects would clearly seem to have in mind activity outside the boundaries of the site.

---

[20] Called 'notice parties' in the Republic of Ireland.

Birmingham J also stated that the simple exercise of re-reading Article 6(3), excluding the three words 'the integrity of' clearly demonstrated that the argument presented was erroneous. With those three words deleted, Article 6(3), so far as is material, provides any PoP likely to have a significant effect on a site, either on its own or in combination with other PoPs, should be subject to AA of its implications for the site, in view of the site's conservation objectives. Birmingham J considered that read with the three words in question deleted, the Article would offer protection that was comprehensive, unqualified and unconditional. He said that

> If there was any desire to extend the protection that the Directive would afford, and it is hard to see why there would be given that the protection is entirely comprehensive, that could be achieved with much greater clarity by inserting words such as 'whether direct or indirect' after the word 'thereon', so that the requirement for an appropriate assessment would be stated to apply to all plans or projects likely to have a significant effect on a site, whether directly or indirectly.

The Contextual and Purposive Arguments

The applicant placed a great of reliance upon the ECJ judgment in *Waddenzee*. This is not surprising given the EU environment law context of the case. Birmingham J analysed the approach as follows:

> 70 … Dealing with the relationship between Article 6(2) and Article 6(3) of the Habitats Directive, the ECJ had this to say at paras. 35 and 36 of the judgment:–
>
> 35. *The fact that a plan or project has been authorised according to the procedure laid down in Article 6(3) of the Habitats Directive renders superfluous, as regards the action to be taken on the protected site under the plan or project, a concomitant application of the rule of general protection laid down in Article 6(2).*
>
> 36. *Authorisation of a plan or project granted in accordance with Article 6(3) of the Habitats Directive necessarily assumes that it is considered not likely adversely to affect the integrity of the site concerned, and consequently, it is not likely to give rise to the deterioration or significant disturbances within the meaning of Article 6(2).* (emphasis added)
>
> 71. There is no doubt that the phrase that I have highlighted offers significant encouragement to the challengers. It appears to mean, without saying so expressly, that a conclusion that there will not be an adverse effect on the integrity of the site is equivalent to a conclusion that it is not likely to give rise to deterioration or significant disturbance. Put positively, this means that the words in question lead to a conclusion that a deterioration or significant disturbance is to be equated to an adverse impact on the integrity of the site.
>
> 72. It may be noted that Article 6(2) speaks of significant disturbance in the case of species, but that the reference to deterioration is unqualified. The applicant sees this as a matter of considerable importance.

Birmingham J however preferred to give greater weight to paragraph 38 in the *Waddenzee* judgment:

> The answer to the second question must therefore mean that Article 6(3) of the Habitats Directive establishes a procedure intended to ensure, by means of a preliminary examination, that a plan or project which is not directly connected with or necessary to the management of the site concerned but likely to have a significant effect on it is authorised only to the extent that it will not adversely affect the integrity of that site, while Article 6(2) of the Habitats Directive establishes an obligation of general protection consisting in avoiding deterioration and disturbances which could have significant effects in the light of the Directive's objectives, and cannot be applicable concomitantly with Article 6(3).

Birmingham J drew the conclusion from this passage that the ECJ acknowledged that the Habitats Directive 'clearly seems to envisage that there will be certain projects which will be permitted to proceed even though the proposal will have a significant effect on a site'. The judge accepted that irrespective of those areas where there is scope for disagreement:

> 74 ... anyone reading the judgment as a whole would have to accept that a high threshold must be crossed before a project can be approved as being one that will not adversely affect the integrity of the site. In this vein, para. 56 of the judgment, provides as follows:–

> 'It is therefore apparent that the plan or project in question may be granted authorisation only on the condition that the competent national authorities are convinced that it will not adversely affect the integrity of the site concerned.' (emphasis added)

The judge noted that paragraph 57 provides that where doubt remains as to the absence of adverse effects on the integrity of the site, the PoP would have to be refused.

> 75. The restrictive approach of paras. 56 and 57 of the judgment emerges with even greater clarity on para. 59 of the judgment which provides:–

> 'Therefore, pursuant to Article 6(3) of the Habitats Directive, the competent national authorities, taking account of the conclusions of the appropriate assessment of the implications of [the plan or project in question] for the site concerned, in the light of the site's conservation objectives, are to authorise such activity only if they have made certain that it will not adversely affect the integrity of that site. That is the case where no reasonable scientific doubt remains as to the absence of such effects.' (emphasis added)

The Court then referred to the case of *Monsanto Agricoltura Italia SpA and Others v Presidenza del Consiglio dei Ministri and Others*[21] in support of this view.

> 76. By any standards, it must be seen that this is indeed a formidable threshold to be crossed and it is this threshold which will have to be overcome, regardless of whether it is the interpretation of the challengers or of the defenders which is accepted.

---

[21] Case C-236/01 *Monsanto Agricoltura Italia SpA and Others v Presidenza del Consiglio dei Ministri and Others* [2003] ECR I-0000 paras 106 and 113.

77. Irrespective of how Article 6(3) of the Directive is to be interpreted, competent national authorities are, one way or another, significantly fettered when considering authorisation. Having regard to the objectives of the Directive, it is not at all surprising that it should be so. That the Directive sets such a high threshold, and does so irrespective of how the matters in dispute are resolved is a matter than can itself assist when it comes to interpretation.

78. The inspector in his report spoke of the provisions being in plain English. In that regard, in my view, he was perfectly correct. The language of the Habitats Directive and of the Regulations of 1997 is clear. If the language of each is read in its ordinary and natural meaning then it provides that the first stage involves an appropriate assessment of a plan or project with a view to the site's conservation objectives, and then, when that assessment has taken place and the conclusions of the assessment are available, the project will not be permitted to proceed unless competent national authorities ascertain that it will not adversely affect the integrity of the site concerned. Accordingly, once it is established that there will be a significant impact, there is what amounts to a presumption that the project will not be approved and that presumption is rebutted only if it is positively established that there will not in fact be an adverse impact on the integrity of the site. The language of the Habitats Directive and the Regulations of 1997 also make it clear that even if the integrity of the site is adversely affected, it is not necessarily the end of the matter and it is possible that some such projects may still proceed when the provisions of Article 6(4) are applicable. Article 6(4) is itself a two- tier structure, in that projects can be permitted to proceed for imperative reasons of overriding public interests, but there is a specific and very restrictive interpretation of the considerations which may be raised when the sites host a priority natural habitat and/or a priority species.

Birmingham J also relied upon the European Commission's guidance, 'Managing Natura 2000':

80. Paragraph 4.2 of the Natura 2000 document, headed 'Scope', states that Article 6(3) and (4) define a step-wise procedure for considering plans and projects:

(a) *The first part of this procedure consists of an assessment stage and is governed by Article 6(3), first sentence.*

(b) *The second part of the procedure, governed by Article 6(3), second sentence, relates to the decision of the competent national authorities.*

(c) *The third part of the procedure (governed by Article 6(4)) comes into play if, despite a negative assessment, it is proposed not to reject a plan or project but to give it further consideration.* (emphasis in the original)

The text of this section of the document refers to a simplified flow chart presented in Annex 3 at the end of the document. The flow chart, which also appears in a document entitled 'Methodological guidance on the provisions of Article 6(3) and (4) of the Habitats Directive 92/43/EEC', demonstrates by way of a diagram the 'step-wise procedure', to use the language of the Commission in the Natura 2000 document. Birmingham J held:

81. Paragraph 4.4.1. of the document addresses the question of significant effect. It says it is clear that what may be significant in relation to one site may not be significant in

relation to another. It offers the following example: loss of a hundred square metres of habitat may be significant in relation to an orchid site, while a similar loss in a large steppic site may be insignificant. Paragraph 4.6.3, headed 'The concept of the "integrity of the site"', might usefully be quoted in full:–

'It is clear from the context and from the purposes of the directive that the "integrity of the site" relates to the site's conservation objectives … For example, it is possible that a plan or project will adversely affect the integrity of a site only in a visual sense or only where habitat types or species other than those listed in Annex I or Annex II. In such cases, the effects do not amount to an adverse effect for the purposes of Article 6(3), provided that the coherence of the network is not affected.' (emphasis in original)

On the other hand, the expression 'integrity of the site' shows that focus is here on the specific site. Thus, it is not allowed to destroy a site or part of it on the basis that the conservation status of the habitat types and species it hosts will in any way remain favourable within the European territory of the Member State.

As regards the connotation or meaning of 'integrity', this can be considered as a quality or condition of being whole or complete. In a dynamic ecological context, it can also be considered as having the sense of resilience and ability to evolve in ways that are favourable to conservation.

The 'integrity of the site' has been usefully defined as 'the coherence of the site's ecological structures and function, across its whole area, or the habitats, complex of habitats and/or populations of species for which the site is or will be classified' (quotation from Planning Policy Guide 9, UK Department of the Environment, October 1994).

A site can be described as having a high degree of integrity where the inherent potential for meeting site conservation objectives is realised, the capacity for self-repair and self-renewal under dynamic conditions is maintained, and a minimum of external management support is required.

When looking at the 'integrity of the site', it is therefore important to take into account a range of factors, including the possibility of effects manifesting themselves in the short, medium and long-term.

The integrity of the site involves its ecological functions. The decision as to whether it is adversely affected should focus on and be limited to the site's conservation objectives.

Consequently, Birmingham J rejected the application. He said that he would have granted leave to bring the judicial review proceedings. He refused to make a reference to the CJEU.

Irish Supreme Court

Leave to appeal was granted in respect of the Habitats point only and the matter came before the Supreme Court. At the hearing before a five-judge Supreme Court counsel for the Attorney General was reported as saying that the State wanted the road to be built, but it was 'vital' that this was done in accordance with law and the requirements of EU law. Both the applicant and the Attorney General claimed that the Board's approval breached the Habitats Directive in that it allows for destruction of part of a protected limestone pavement area in the candidate Lough Corrib SAC to facilitate the scheme. The Attorney General submitted that as the project involved the destruction of some protected limestone paving that could not naturally renew itself, that this breached Article 6.3 of the Habitats Directive.

The Attorney General further argued that the Board's decision seemed to be based on an assumption that the integrity of the protected site was not breached because a portion only of it was affected. The Attorney General submitted that the Habitats Directive contains a prohibition on doing anything causing permanent deterioration to a protected habitat.

The Board contended that the destruction of 1.5 hectares of limestone paving within 85 hectares of a site containing limestone paving did not constitute a significant adverse impact on the 'integrity' of the site within the meaning of Article 6.3 of the Directive.

The Attorney General submitted that the CJEU should clarify the relevant provisions of the Directive. Both the Board and the Council argued there was no need to make the reference. It is generally unusual for national governments to seek to persuade their national courts to make references to the CJEU especially in matters of environmental law.

The Supreme Court agreed with the Attorney General and made its first ever reference to the CJEU on an environmental law matter. The Chief Justice, Mr Justice John Murray, referring to the Council's concern about incurring a further €2.8 million expenditure the next month through having to restart the compulsory purchase process because existing consents would lapse, remarked it was a matter for the legislature that compulsory purchase laws do not cater for such situations as had arisen before the court.

The questions to be submitted to the Court of Justice include the issue of what is meant under the Directive by 'adverse impact' on the 'integrity' of a protected site. For some reason which is not clear, it took the Supreme Court until 16 May 2011 to finalise and transmit the reference to the CJEU.[22] They are:

(i) What are the criteria in law top be applied by a competent authority to an assessment of the likelihood of a plan or project the subject of Article 6(3) of the Habitats Directive, having 'an adverse effect on the integrity of the site'?

(ii) Does the application of the precautionary principle have as its consequences that such a plan or project cannot be authorised if it would result in the permanent non-renewable loss of the whole or any part of the habitats in question?

---

[22] I am grateful to Dr Áine Ryall of University College, Cork and a member of the FTB Francis Taylor Building Academic Panel for providing me with a copy of the documentation accompanying the reference to the CJEU.

(iii)   What is the relationship, if any, between Article 6(4) and the making of a decision under Article 6(3) that a plan or project will not adversely affect the integrity of a site?

The case has been given the reference Case C-258/11 and judgment is awaited.

Conclusion

The 'integrity' of site must go beyond its medium and long term ability to recover with the aid of mitigation. A proposal which has an adverse effect by removing in the short term the habitat for certain communities is capable of having an adverse effect on the integrity of the SAC. On the other hand, there is plainly a reasonable argument in support of the view that there will be circumstances where a short period of disturbance whilst adverse to the SAC will not be such so as to amount to an adverse impact upon the integrity of the SAC. If that argument be right, how long is such a period? It would a matter of fact and degree having regard, in particular, to the length of cycles of the eco-systems of the particular SAC, as well as, the speed and nature of the recovery. However, I am inclined to the view that, in any event, even if this argument were to be accepted, such a period is likely to be regarded as being quite short.

The position which the European Commission may adopt in the *Sweetman* proceedings appears to have been foreshadowed with its informal meeting in the Commission headquarters on 17 November 2009 with representatives of the EU Commission and Irish politicians. The minutes have been made publicly available. Having noted the position adopted by the Planning Board and Galway County Council paragraph 8 the minutes reads:

> Without wishing to prejudge the Supreme Court ruling, the Commission officials considered that should the Supreme Court find in favour of the County Council, 'it was more likely than not' that the Commission would begin infringement proceedings against Ireland. This would be on foot of a complaint received or on the Commission's own initiative, as a positive judgment might raise issues relating to the fundamental interpretation of a point of EU law which could have an impact over all 27 EU Member States. Infringement proceedings would involve the intervention of the European Court of Justice.

Notwithstanding the carefully reasoned judgment of Birmingham J, where the harm is of a permanent nature it is difficult save in cases where the harm is *de minimis* to see that there will not be an adverse effect on the integrity of the SAC and its objectives. The reference to the CJEU by the Irish Supreme Court may answer this question. The fact that in that case the development involves some *permanent* damage to part of the SAC may prove significant to the CJEU. The CJEU may however avoid addressing the equally important question of whether damage to a SAC which may nonetheless be temporary and from which the ecosystem can recover over time can be said not to adversely affect the integrity of the SAC.

10

Are Imperative Reasons Imperiling the Habitats Directive? An Assessment of Article 6(4) and the IROPI Exception

REBECCA CLUTTEN AND ISABELLA TAFUR

Introduction

The Habitats Directive[1] is the European Union's flagship vehicle for ensuring the conservation of natural habitats, and aims to contribute towards ensuring biodiversity through the conservation of natural habitats and wild fauna and flora in the territory of its Member States. Such conservation was expressly recognised as one of the European Community's 'essential objective[s]', pursuant to Article 130r of the EC Treaty.[2] It seeks to achieve this conservation objective through the designation of particular sites for conservation, which are then subject to a variety of provisions which are intended to ensure that site's protection should a plan or project which might have a significant effect upon it be proposed. At Community level, such sites are listed by the Commission, and are known as Sites of Community Importance (SCIs). Member States are then under a duty to designate these SCIs as Special Areas of Conservation (SACs).[3] These SACs, together with Special Protection Areas (SPAs) designated under Directive 79/409 (the Birds Directive) form a 'coherent European ecological network of sites' (Natura 2000 sites).[4]

---

[1] Adopted on 21 May 1992 by the Council of the European Communities, Directive 92/43/EEC on the conservation of natural habitats and of wild fauna and flora (the Habitats Directive) has been subsequently amended by Council Directive 97/62/EC, Regulation (EC) No 1882/2003 of the European Parliament and of the Council of 29 September 2003, and Council Directive 2006/105/EC.

[2] See the first recital to the Habitats Directive; the recital is regarded as an essential tool to the interpretation of the wording and scope any European Directive.

[3] See Habitats Directive, Arts 3–5 for comprehensive details of the designation procedure. For an examination of the protection afforded during the designation process see Jones and Westaway, ch 4 in this volume.

[4] Habitats Directive, Art 3(1).

The Protective Provisions and Article 6

The provisions relating to the protection of the Natura 2000 sites and the habitats and species making up or found on them, are contained in Articles 6 to 16 of the Directive. Of these, Article 6 is of central importance. Article 6 places on Member States a number of positive obligations, including the obligations to 'establish the necessary conservation measures' for the sites (Art 6(1)); and to 'take appropriate steps to avoid, in the [SACs], the deterioration of natural habitats and the habitats of species as well as disturbance of the species for which the areas have been designated' (Article 6(2)).

> Article 6 contains a third requirement, which is for an 'Appropriate Assessment' of 'any plan or project not directly connected with or necessary to the management of the site but likely to have a significant effect thereon, either individually or in combination with other plans or projects' (Article 6(3)).[5]

Article 6(3) goes on to state that

> In the light of the conclusions of the assessment of the implications for the site and subject to the provisions of paragraph 4, *the competent national authorities shall agree to the plan or project only after having ascertained that it will not adversely affect the integrity of the site concerned* and if appropriate, after having obtained the opinion of the general public. (emphasis added).

It is therefore the case that, unless the competent national authority is satisfied that a plan or project (which will hereafter be referred to, somewhat imprecisely, as 'development'[6]) proposed will not adversely affect the integrity of a designated site, the Habitats Directive prevents that competent national authority from permitting that development.

Where given full effect, Article 6(3) provides for designated sites a very high degree of protection from the effects of adverse development. As is clear from the foregoing, this general prohibition on adverse development is, however, subject to the provisions of paragraph 4 of the Article. Article 6(4) provides that

> If, in spite of a negative assessment of the implications for the site and in the absence of alternative solutions, a plan or project must nevertheless be carried out for imperative reasons of overriding public interest, including those of a social or economic nature, the Member State shall take all compensatory measures necessary to ensure that the overall coherence of Natura 2000 is protected. It shall inform the Commission of the compensatory measures adopted.

---

[5] On the meaning of 'plan or project' see, Tromans, ch 5 in this volume. In the context of Environmental Impact Assessment (EIA Directive 85/337 EEC as amended by 97/11/EC and 2003/35/EC) the high court (of England and Wales) has held that significant effects need not be negative ones: *BT Plc v Gloucester City Council* [2001] EWHC Admin 1001; [2002] 2 P & CR 33[64–70]; [2002] JPL 993; and *R (Prophet) v York City Council* [2002] EWHC 588; [2002] JPL 1317.

[6] Noting that not all types of 'development', as understood by English planning lawyers, will be a 'plan or project' for the purposes of the Directive.

Where the site concerned hosts a priority natural habitat type and/or a priority species, the only considerations which may be raised are those relating to human health or public safety, to beneficial consequences of primary importance for the environment or, further to an opinion from the Commission, to other imperative reasons of overriding public interest.

The consequence of Article 6(4) is that a negative assessment will not always preclude a Member State from granting permission for the development proposed. In deciding whether or not to permit the development, the competent national authority must first satisfy itself that there are no alternative solutions. This includes consideration of all feasible alternatives, including the possibility of thoroughly revising or withdrawing the plan, of not implementing any plan or project, and of considering alternative locations or routes, different scales or designs of development or alternative processes.[7] Only once it is satisfied that no alternative solutions exist should the authority go on to consider whether there are imperative reasons of overriding public interest (IROPI) which justify the development proceeding.[8] However, a Member State cannot rely upon IROPI if it has failed to carry out an Appropriate Assessment.[9]

As is also clear from the text of Article 6(4), the nature of the IROPI that may be taken into account will initially depend on whether or not the development proposed will threaten a priority habitat or species, as listed in Annex IV of the Directive. If no such priority habitat or species will be threatened, the IROPI to which the competent national authority may have regard will include those broader considerations of a social or economic nature.

If there is such a threat to a priority habitat or species, it is said that the development may only be permitted where considerations of human health or public safety, or beneficial consequences of primary importance for the environment, justify the grant of permission. That restriction is, however, itself subject to further modification; the paragraph goes on to provide that, pursuant to an opinion from the Commission, there may be other IROPI justifying permission.[10]

In either case, if the presence of IROPI can be established, and development is permitted notwithstanding its negative impact on a designated site, that negative impact will have to be offset by the implementation of measures which ensure

[7] Guidance document on Article 6(4) of the 'Habitats Directive' 92/43/EEC, European Commission, para 1.3.1.

[8] In England, IROPI cases must be approved by the relevant Secretary of State, currently the Secretary of State for Communities and Local Government.

[9] Case C-404/09 *Commission v Spain*, judgment, 24 November 2011.

[10] The *rationale* behind such a tiered system is plain: where development would threaten those habitats or species that the Community considers to be a priority, a more robust approach ought to be taken to them, and if development adversely affecting those habitats or species is to be permitted, it is desirable for a Community institution to be involved, so as to ensure that IROPI not within the primary competence of the Member State (as human health and public safety would be said to be), or with an overall beneficial effect, genuinely are sufficiently imperative and overriding in the Community context to justify the derogation from the general principle of Article 6(3). Although this does not appear to work in practice—see the authors' comments below in this chapter under the sub-heading 'Opinions Issued by the European Commission'.

that compensation is provided corresponding precisely to the negative effects on the species or habitat concerned.[11]

One might then wonder, at this point, what it is that generates the concern expressed in the title of this article. Taken at face value, the exception in Article 6(4) appears narrow in scope, with plans or projects likely to have adverse effects on protected sites only being permitted where there are, at worst, imperative reasons of overriding public importance justifying the grant of that permission: a seemingly high threshold to satisfy.

Even a brief exploration of the history of the provision, however, shows us that—far from improving the position relating to adverse development in protected areas—the Habitats Directive in fact considerably broadened the extent to which adverse development could be permitted in protected areas from the position that prevailed immediately prior to its adoption. Further, in including but not defining the IROPI provision, the draftsmen gave Member States, and the ECJ, an escape route from the prohibition in Article 6(3) which is capable of being used in a broad and flexible way.[12] Whilst understandable for an institution which does not wish to appear to be usurping the sovereignty of its Member States, the consequence of this is, in the authors' view, that it risks compromising the achievement of the Directive's stated aims, and provides a lower standard of protection for designated sites than might otherwise have been possible.

Background to Article 6(4)

On 28 February 1991, during the deliberations into the Commission's proposals for a Habitats Directive, the ECJ handed down judgment in Case C-57/89 *Commission v Germany*[13] (the *Leybucht Dykes* case). In that case, Germany had proposed allowing the construction of a dyke in an area designated as a birds habitat under the Birds Directive. Article 2 of the Birds Directive required Member States to take measures to maintain the population of the species referred to in Article 1 of the same at a level corresponding to ecological, scientific and cultural requirements, whilst taking account of economic and recreational requirements. Article 4 of the Directive required Member States to take appropriate steps to avoid the significant pollution or deterioration of habitats or any disturbances affecting the birds.

---

[11] See fn 7, para 1.4.1.

[12] Birdlife International, in their 2010 position paper on the approach to alternative solutions and IROPI under the Habitats Directive, noted that there is currently 'considerable variation' in the application of the IROPI between Member States, with different sectors complaining that the test is applied either too strictly or too loosely. The paper is available at: http://www.birdlife.org.

[13] Case C-57/89 *Commission v Germany* [1991] ECR I-883.

Germany had argued that the construction of the dyke was necessary for the protection of the human population against flooding. The question for the court was whether Member States were able to impair an SPA under Article 4, and in its judgment, the court concluded that

> the power of the Member State to reduce the extent of a special protection area can be justified only on exceptional grounds. The grounds must correspond to a general interest which is superior to the general interest represented by the ecological objective of the directive. In that context the interests referred to in Article 2 of the directive, namely economic and recreational requirements, do not enter into consideration … the danger of flooding and the protection of the coast constitute sufficiently serious reasons to justify the dyke works [...] as long as those measures are confined to a strict minimum and involve only the smallest possible reduction of the special protection area.

In its analysis of Article 4 in *Leybucht Dykes*, the European Court of Justice (ECJ) further found that taking into account the economic interests of fishermen in deciding whether to allow the dyke was 'in principle incompatible with the requirements of the provision'.[14] That position was subsequently endorsed in Case C-355/90 *Commission v Spain*[15] (the *Santona Marshes* case) which applied the same 'exceptional grounds' tests in determining whether Member States should be allowed to permit pollution or other works which would lead to the deterioration of special protection areas under the Birds Directive. According to this strict analysis, neither economic nor recreational reasons (the latter of which the authors consider plainly could be included within a definition of 'social' reasons) could justify pollution, deterioration or disturbances to SPAs.

Member States were, however, nervous of and hostile towards a provision which tied them so firmly to prioritising the protection of designated areas over considerations of economic exigency.[16] Article 6(4) was drawn up to soften the blow delivered by the *Leybucht Dykes* and *Santona Marshes* decisions, specifically providing that both economic and social considerations could justify the adverse interference with both SACs and SPAs under the Birds Directive (indeed, it replaced the obligations previously arising under Article 4(4) of the Birds Directive).

In fact, Article 6(4) went one step further than simply mitigating the impact of the ECJ's earlier decisions on the Birds Directives by applying the exception to Article 6(3) to cases in which economic or social considerations militated in favour of development, and instead created a broader exception to cover *any* imperative reasons of overriding public interest. The result is that today, and since

---

[14] Paragraph 24, ie the requirement to take appropriate steps to avoid the significant pollution or deterioration of habitats or any disturbances affecting the birds.

[15] [1993] ECR I-4221.

[16] Reid also says that: 'Member States were unhappy at this almost absolute priority given to the conservation and the Directive was amended by the application of the provisions of the Habitats and Species Directive, which do permit conservation concerns to be sacrificed in limited circumstances where there are reasons of overriding public interest' C Reid, *Nature Conservation Law* (3rd edn) (W Green, 2009) 5.2.7.

the introduction of the Habitats Directive, there is in fact more scope for Member States to derogate from the requirements to protect SPAs and, in the authors' view, potentially a correspondingly lower degree of protection for those sites in that narrow respect.

Defining IROPI

While the history of Article 6(4) demonstrates that the IROPI exception is intended to be broader than was previously the case under the Birds Directive, it does not provide any further assistance in determining the scope of the provision. While Nollkaemper's description of the provision's 'unintelligible language' perhaps overstates the problem,[17] it is true that the Council's adoption of an exception based on IROPI without defining the concept or its parameters (other than the two, non-exhaustive, factors specifically included), means

(a)   that the task of interpreting this provision has effectively been delegated to other bodies; and

(b)   that the scope of the exception (and, correspondingly, the extent to which it compromises the conservations aims of the provision in Article 6(3)) is made dependent upon the way in which those bodies exercise that task.

Interpretation by the ECJ

In seeking to determine the extent of Article 6(4) the jurisprudence of the ECJ should, as always when considering Community law, be the primary source of guidance. Rather unexpectedly, however, the ECJ does not appear, in the near-two decades since the Directive was adopted, to have had directly to express a view on the question of what is meant by IROPI under Article 6(4).

The ECJ has considered, on several occasions, the interpretation of the 'imperative requirement' in other fields of Community law. In relation to the concept as an exception to the principle of free movement of goods, for example, Article 30 of the EC Treaty provides that prohibitions or restrictions on the free movement of goods can be justified on grounds of public morality, public policy or public security, the protection of the health and life of humans, animals and plants, the protection of national treasures and the protection of industrial and commercial property. In addition to the justifications in Article 30, the ECJ has also recognised that imperative requirements justifying national measures restricting freedom of

---

[17]   A Nollkaemper, 'Habitat Protection in European Community Law: Evolving Conceptions of a Balance of Interests' [1997] 9(2) *Journal of Environmental Law* 271–86.

movement include consumer protection, the effectiveness of fiscal supervision and the protection of the environment.[18]

The closest the ECJ appears to have come to directly considering the question in the context of the Habitats Directive was in Case C-304/05 *Commission v Italian Republic*.[19] There, it was acknowledged that in light of the judgment in Case C-239/04 *Castro Verde*,[20] Article 6(4), as a derogation from the criterion for authorisation laid down in Article 6(3), must be interpreted strictly.

The facts of *Commission v Italian Republic* were that the Italian Republic had decided to improve a skiing area and to provide associated facilities with a view to holding the 2005 World Alpine Ski Championships. The plans would have had adverse effects on the Santa Caterina Valfruva SPA. Italy had justified the decision to proceed with the development on the basis that a failure to carry out such plans would result in 'slow but unavoidable economic decline' and sought to justify the plans on the basis of their socio-economic value, including benefits to the tourist industry. Giving judgment, the court did not come to a conclusion as to whether such considerations would amount to IROPI justifying the plans, as it had already found that an appropriate assessment of sufficient scope as required by Article 6(3) had not been carried out. On that basis, it was considered that the Italian Republic could not have adequately weighed up the damage to the site against any imperative reasons of overriding public interest as it was required to do, and a breach of Article 6(4) could be found without the need to consider whether the reasons advanced actually constituted IROPI.

Beyond the trite position that Article 6(4) and, consequently, IROPI, are to be interpreted strictly, little guidance can in fact be gleaned from the decisions of the ECJ as to the interpretation of the phrase imperative reasons of overriding public interest in the context of the Habitats Directive.

Guidance from the Community Institutions

Another source of assistance on the interpretation of IROPI is that provided by the European Commission in its various publications. In 2000 the Commission published a guidance document entitled 'Managing Natura 2000 Sites', the section on Article 6(4) of which was subsequently 'replaced' (by almost identical text) by the 2007 publication 'Guidance document on Article 6(4) of the 'Habitats Directive' 92/43/EEC'. This guidance noted, in common with the above, that the

---

[18] See Case C-8/74 *Procureur du Roi v Dassonville* [1974] ECR 837; [1974] 2 CMLR; Case 120/78 *Rewe-Zentral AG v Bundesmonopolverwaltung für Branntwein* [1979] ECR 649 (*Cassis de Dijon*); Case C-302/86 *Commission v Denmark* [1988] ECR 4607.

[19] Case C-304/05 *Commission v Italian Republic* [2007] ECR I-7495.

[20] Case C-239/04 *Castro Verde* [2006] ECR I-10183. A case which concerned not IROPI, but the requirement to take into account whether any alternatives exist before invoking the derogation under Article 6(4).

ECJ had not given any clear indications as to the interpretation of the phrase 'imperative reasons of overriding public interest'.[21]

The guidance also notes, somewhat obviously, that the reference in Article 6(4) to reasons of overriding public interest indicates that only public interests (whether promoted by public or private bodies) could be balanced against the conservation aims of the Directive, so that projects lying entirely in the interest of companies or individuals could not be permitted as an exception to Article 6(3). This is likely to be of particular concern to developers, but is something that in practice many will be able to circumvent through suitable 'window dressing' of a development's benefits.

In determining to allow a plan or project to proceed in spite of likely adverse effects on a protected site, the guidance states that the competent national authorities must be satisfied that the balance of interests between the conservation objectives of the site and the imperative reasons weighs in favour of the latter.[22] In ascertaining whether this is the case, the authorities should bear in mind (again, perhaps somewhat obviously) that the public interest must be overriding: it must outweigh the public interest in conserving the site. More usefully, the guidance also suggests that the public interest is only likely to be overriding if it is a long-term interest: short-term economic interests or other interests yielding short-term benefits would not appear to be sufficient to outweigh the long-term conservation interests protected by the Directive.

On the question of IROPI in particular, the guidance concludes:

> It is reasonable to consider that the 'imperative reasons of overriding public interest, including those of a social and economic nature' refer to situations where plans or projects envisaged prove to be indispensable:
>
> — within the framework of actions or policies aiming to protect fundamental values for citizens' lives (health, safety, environment);
> — within the framework of fundamental policies for the State and society;
> — within the framework of carrying out activities of an economic or social nature, fulfilling specific obligations of public service.[23]

The guidance also notes that human health, public safety and primary beneficial consequences for the environment (as basis for derogation even for priority sites) constitute the most important reasons of overriding public interest.[24] There is, however, little advice in the Commission's guidance as to when plans or projects will be justified on these grounds: it states that it will be for the national authorities to check whether such a situation occurs, but that the Commission would be likely to examine any such situation in order to establish that Community law was being correctly applied. On the question of what the correct application of

---

[21] See fn 7 at 1.3.2.

[22] This weighing exercise reflects that advocated in the judgment in *Commission v Italian Republic* as we discussed above.

[23] See fn 7, 8.

[24] See fn 7 para 1.8.2.

the exception is, the guidance is silent, other than to mention that in the *Leybucht Dykes* case the ECJ confirmed that the danger of flooding and the protection of the coast did constitute imperative reasons of overriding public interest.

One thing that is clear is that the approach advocated by the Commission in its guidance in relation to Article 6(4) is generally restrictive in scope. Plans or projects which are likely to adversely affect protected sites should only be permitted where they are 'indispensable'. If this approach were to be followed by the Commission and the courts in practice, the authors consider it would still enable relatively robust protection to be provided to designated sites, in common with the conservation aims of such designation.

Opinions Issued by the European Commission

Should a Member State seek to justify plans or projects with an adverse impact on priority sites on the basis of IROPI other than human health or public safety, it will be recalled that it is permitted to do so under Article 6(4) providing that it first seeks the opinion of the Commission. The approach taken by the Commission may thus be illustrative of the Community's policy in relation to the conservation of designated sites and indicative of the scope of the exception under Article 6(4).

Before turning to consider the content of some of the opinions, it is noted that Member States, whilst required to seek an opinion from the Commission in the context of priority habitats and species, are not legally bound by the Commission's opinion. It is open to Member States to reject the assessment of the Commission and proceed with the development on the basis of IROPI if it so desires.

The Commission guidance states, however, that should a Member State decide to proceed with a plan or project in spite of a negative opinion from the Commission

> one can reasonably expect that the decision [of the Member State] will address the Commission's arguments and explain why its opinion has not been followed. In any case the Commission can assess whether the implementation of the plan or project is in conformity with the requirements of Community law and, if necessary, initiate appropriate legal action.[25]

It is noted that, where it is not satisfied that IROPI exist, the Commission is entitled to initiate proceedings against a Member State regardless of whether the relevant plan or project will affect a site hosting priority species, and so in that regard, it is difficult to see how the second part of Article 6(4) in fact offers any additional protection to such sites. The authors consider, and would note, that whilst the practice of non-binding decisions is entirely understandable from a constitutional perspective, the second part of Article 6(4) would have had greater scope

---

[25] See fn 7, para 1.8.3.

for ensuring the furtherance of the conservation aims contained in Article 6(3) had the opinions of the Commission been made binding in this context.

In his 2009 article 'Commission's Opinions under Article 6(4)',[26] Ludwig Krämer considered 11 opinions given by the Commission under Article 6(4), several of which are also mentioned in the Commission's 2007 guidance.[27] Consideration of the opinions set out in Krämer's article leads to the conclusion that the Commission is prepared to accept that Article 6(4) offers a much broader exception to the general rule in Article 6(3) than is suggested by the Commission's published guidance or by the wording of the Article itself.

Two applications for the construction of the A20 motorway in Germany were confirmed by the Commission to be justified, in spite of the significant effects they would have on protected bird habitats on the basis of IROPI.[28] Those reasons were that both the regions of Mecklenburg-Vorprommern and the Peene Valley, where parts of the motorway were to be built, suffered from high unemployment and a lower than average gross national product. Both regions were supported by the EC Structural Funds and the proposed motorway was part of the trans-European network, the construction of which had been accorded high priority by the German government and Parliament. Perhaps not surprisingly, a similar approach was taken a few years later in the Commission's Opinion 'concerning the construction of the new section 3 of the motorway A 20 B 206 West of Wittenborn to B 206 West of Weede south of Bad Segeberg in Schleswig-Holstein (Germany)'.[29]

The difficulty inherent in this reasoning is that infrastructure projects of this kind are almost always likely to create jobs and have a positive effect on the economic development of the area. To cite these as IROPI therefore very much broadens the exception under Article 6(4): one can conceive that almost any large scale development would then be capable of satisfying the criteria.

In another German case,[30] this time concerning a project to enlarge an existing industrial plant in order to complete the production of a jumbo passenger airline, on a SPA and Ramsar site, the Commission opined that there were IROPI in that the project was of outstanding importance for Hamburg and northern Germany and for the European aerospace industry: it would contribute to technological advances, generate highly-qualified new jobs and have a positive impact on the competitiveness of the European aeronautical industry. Economic considerations were again considered by the Commission to override the conservation interest in refusing to allow the project to proceed.

Interestingly, when the International Fund for Animal Welfare sought the disclosure of documents relating to this decision, the Commission initially refused.

---

[26] [2009] 21(1) *Journal of Environmental Law* 59–85.
[27] It is noted by Krämer that not all opinions to Member States are published; again, this does not assist those looking to understand the positions that the Commission adopts.
[28] Commission Opinions [1996] OJ L6/14 and [1995] OJ C178/3.
[29] Commission Opinion C (2010) 3674 dated 11 June 2010.
[30] Commission Opinion C (2000) 1079.

Following legal action it eventually agreed to disclose all material except a letter written to the President of the Commission by the German Chancellor in relation to the proposals on the site. The ECJ found that the Commission was entitled to withhold this document.[31] Whilst no issue is taken with the withholding of certain documents for legitimate public interest reasons, the fact that legal action had to be taken to force the hand of the Commission to release the majority of the documents again raises a question about the transparency of Commission views in respect of IROPI. There should, in the authors' view, be no real secrecy around the documentation upon which the Commission bases its decisions. Indeed, Birdlife International has suggested that in order to increase transparency in decision making, not only should the EC publish all opinions in relation to Article 6(4), but the competent national authority should also publish an explanation of how it has taken the opinion into account in reaching its decisions and, where relevant, its reasons for deviating from that opinion.[32] It is to everyone's advantage to understand what the Commission considers to be IROPI, and to have transparency as to the extent to which the conservation aims of Article 6(3) are being compromised.

In the case of a German proposal to extend a coal mine at Haniel, the Commission acknowledged that coal mining was not competitive in Germany and that it was inevitable that the mine would eventually close and the miners would lose their jobs, and considered that in the circumstances it was arguably better to use the money saved by closing the mine to relocate and retrain the workers. The Commission went on, however, to accept that the negative 'short-term' social and economic effects associated with a refusal to extend the mine (as the Commission itself described them) constituted IROPI. This decision is apparently in direct conflict with the Commission's own guidance, referred to above, which suggests that short-term benefits are not sufficient to override the long-term conservation interests protected by the Directive.

Sweden applied to the Commission for an opinion regarding its proposal to construct a railway between Nordmaling and Umeaa, which would affect several habitats, and one priority habitat. The Commission accepted that there were no viable alternatives because the two other possible options (each of which would either affect the Natura 2000 to a very limited degree or not at all) would result in a lower profit, because they would prolong the journey time by 10 to 20 per cent, make the transport operations more complicated and result in Umeaa remaining a dead-end station rather than becoming a through route. As Krämer argues, it is difficult to see how reduced profitability for a state-owned railway line, a longer journey time and the city of Umeaa not becoming a through route station can be regarded as imperative reasons of overriding public interest justifying the railway

---

[31] Case C-362/08 *Internationaler Hilfonds v Commission*. Judgment handed down on 18 January 2011.
[32] Birdlife International position paper of the Birds and Habitats Directives Task Force on the approach to alternative solutions and imperative reasons of overriding public interest under Art 6(4) of the EU Habitats Directive, adopted on 12 April 2010.

on that particular route, against what are supposed to be conservation aims of great importance contained in Article 6(3).[33] Whilst recognising that the railway was a state one and so in that context involved public finances and the general public interest, this decision is still, it seems to the authors, worryingly close to an acceptance of an imperative reason of overriding *private* interest.

The overwhelming impression from the opinions issued by the Commission is that Member States are able, with relative ease, to invoke economic arguments to overcome the presumption against development in protected areas under Article 6(3) of the Directive. Nollkaemper describes the Commission taking only a 'soft glance' at whether the reasons justifying the plan or project really are imperative.[34] That is a view with which the authors concur. In light of the Commission's approach, the exception in Article 6(4) begins to look increasingly wide.

The Approach in the United Kingdom

The Habitats Directive was transposed into UK domestic law by the Conservation (Natural Habitats, & c) Regulations 1994. These were subsequently repealed and replaced by the Conservation of Habitats and Species Regulations (2010/490), Regulation 62 of which transposes Article 6(4) of the Directive.

In 1998 the Department for the Environment, Food and Rural Affairs (Defra) issued a document entitled 'The Birds and Habitats Directives: Outline Government Position' in which it explained that the government expected there to be few cases where it would be judged that IROPI would allow development to proceed which would have adverse effects on the integrity of internationally important SPA or SAC designations. Similar predictions are set out in Government Circular 06/2005.[35]

In spite of such predictions, however, the 1998 publication went on to set out some guiding principles which were said to be relevant in deciding whether such reasons existed. They appear to be extremely broad, and relate in large part to the loose guidance given by the Commission. They are:

(a)   a need to address a serious risk to human health and public safety;
(b)   the interests of national security and defence;

---

[33] L Krämer, 'Commission's Opinions under Article 6(4)' (2009) 21(1) *Journal of Environmental Law* 59–85.

[34] A Nollkaemper, 'Habitat Protection in European Community Law: Evolving Conceptions of a Balance of Interests' (1997) 9(2) *Journal of Environmental Law* 271–86.

[35] See further, B Munro of the National Environmental Assessment Service, Environment Agency, 'IROPI: National Politics v environmental decisions' a paper delivered to the IAIA10 Conference Proceedings The Role of Impact Assessment in *Transitioning to the Green Economy* 30th Annual Meeting of the International Association for Impact Assessment 6–11 April 2010, International Conference Centre Geneva—Switzerland, available at: http://www.iaia.org. The paper sets out the IROPI approach adopted by the EA in promoting the costal flood alleviation scheme for Redcar.

(c) the provision of a clear and demonstrable direct environmental benefit on a national or international scale;

(d) a vital contribution to strategic economic development or regeneration; and

(e) where failure to proceed would have unacceptable social and/or economic consequences.

In respect of (e) above, we repeat that it would be very easy for any large project to claim that a failure to proceed would result in a loss of investment in an area and an absence of job creation which it could seek to classify as unacceptable economic consequences, particularly in the current economic climate. From the guidance in the 1998 publication, it seems that the national authorities would be happy to accept such justifications: indeed, the guidance states that projects of national importance were likely to be judged as giving rise to IROPI, and that important regional projects were also likely to be so judged, while projects of more local significance, although not ruled out, would be less likely to override the nature conservation value of the sites.

In April 2011, the Infrastructure Planning Commission (IPC) produced an advice note, 'Habitat Regulations Assessment relevant to nationally significant infrastructure projects'. Although addressing IROPI and what the IPC will require from applicants by way of documentation, the advice offered does not indicate the approach that the IPC is likely to take to such applications.[36] The decisions that have been reached by the national authorities (both the Courts and the Secretary of State) confirm the view that it appears relatively easy for developers to establish the existence of IROPI.

In the application for a Harbour Revision Order in the Port of Bristol[37] the Secretary of State acknowledged that the proposal was likely to have significant effects on the Severn Estuary SPA and Ramsar site, but concluded that there were IROPI which justified the project proceeding. These were the national interest in market competition, and economic resilience in having alternative locations for container handling outside the Greater South East that were not reliant on the national road and rail networks which were vulnerable to disruption and to general congestion. It was considered that the project would enhance the regional economic and social interests of South West England, enable the port to meet changes in international shipping trade and contribute to additional job opportunities. As previously noted, any large development project is likely to create jobs and enhance the economic interests of at least the region in which it is to

---

[36] Advice Note 10 available at: http://infrastructure.independent.gov.uk/wp-content/uploads/2011/04/Advice-note-10-HRA-web.pdf. For the approach in respect of offshore developments see, Caddell, ch 11 in this volume, 'The Designation of Marine Sacs', and 'Guidance on imperative reasons of overriding public interest under the Habitats Directive' published by the Maritime Management Organisation available at: http://www.marinemanagement.org.uk/licensing/supporting/documents/iropi.pdf.

[37] Secretary of State's decision letter, 25 March 2010, available at: http://www.dft.gov.uk.

be situated. If such considerations alone are to be so readily accepted as imperative reasons of overriding public interest, the Habitats Directive offers scant protection indeed to what are ostensibly our most significant and previous natural environments.

Furthermore, in that case the Secretary of State accepted the applicant's argument that there were imperative reasons for the project on that particular site because, although alternative solutions were available, there were no cheaper alternatives to containerisation, and a container terminal capable of serving deep sea vessels was a more efficient and effective means of promoting trade in goods than another type of terminal with lower draught clearance. The imperative reason justifying the adverse effects on the protected site appears, at least in part, to have been the applicant's desire to generate for itself the greatest possible profit. This justification was accepted by the Secretary of State without any indication of doubt.

In *Humber Sea Terminal Ltd v Secretary of State for Transport*[38] the need for a port to accommodate larger vessels on the Immingham Outer Harbour was found by the Secretary of State for Transport (in the absence of a public inquiry) to constitute an IROPI. While the Secretary of State's decision was challenged by way of judicial review, the finding of imperative reasons was not questioned. This was perhaps because the challenge was brought by a rival operator who sought a separate Harbour Revision Order in order to extend its own facilities, which would have sought to rely on the same or similar imperative reasons to justify any grant of permission. The High Court therefore accepted without question—such a question being beyond its remit in that case—the finding of the Secretary of State that the need for a port constituted an imperative reason which outweighed the importance of conserving a SPA.

In the Bathside Bay planning appeal[39] there was no dispute that the proposed container terminal would adversely affect the integrity of a European Site. The Secretary of State found, however, that the need for a container terminal to help meet the national need for container terminal capacity, as part of the development of a modern competitive ports industry, constituted an IROPI. The Secretary of State noted, in his consideration of the IROPI requirement, his agreement with the Inspector that such a terminal would also significantly assist in enhancing the socio-economic and economic interests of the sub-region, although he said that such a consideration alone would not suffice to constitute IROPI.

In another port case, the Secretary of State considered proposals for a London Gateway Port Harbour Empowerment Order,[40] concluding that the port should be permitted and the Order granted. While it was accepted that the proposed port was likely to have

---

[38] *Humber Sea Terminal Ltd v Secretary of State for Transport* [2005] EWHC 1289 (Admin); [2006] Env LR 4.

[39] Minded view letter from the First Secretary of State to DLA Piper, 21 December 2005.

[40] Minded view letter from the Secretary of State for Transport to Bircham Dyson Bell, 20 July 2005.

significant adverse effect upon the Thames Estuary and Marshes SPA, the need for container port terminals was found to outweigh those adverse effects. In fact, on the subject of IROPI the Secretary of State agreed with the Inspector that 'there was no reason to dissent from the Applicant's evidence on the topic of public interest and that the requirements of the Habitats Directive had been met in this respect.' (paragraph 98)

Such an approach suggests that both the Inspector and the Secretary of State were willing to simply accept at face value the applicant's assurances that the IROPI requirement had been met, without conducting a thorough investigation to ensure that was in fact the case. Clearly an applicant is likely to have a vested interest in establishing that IROPI exist, and competent authorities ought at least to take steps to independently assess and verify such claims, rather than simply accepting any justification put forward by the developer.

It is true that prior to the Bathside and London Gatweway proposals the Secretary of State had found in the Dibden Bay case[41] that a short-term (temporary) predicted shortfall in handling capacity should not be determinative in assessing imperative reasons of overriding public interest. However, in that case there were also a number of reasons militating against the proposed port. The Inspector had already ruled, for example, that no reliance could be placed on the Appropriate Assessment undertaken by the applicant, and furthermore, that there was no assurance that the works would go ahead even if consent were granted. In light of the uncertainty surrounding that proposal it would have been very difficult to justify the adverse effects it would inevitably cause on a European Site on the basis of IROPI. With alternative port proposals also being promoted at the time, it is unsurprising that the IROPI test was found not to have been met.

Notwithstanding, the selected domestic decisions tend to confirm the authors' concerns that IROPI is being given a broad interpretation, and that this is likely only to be to the detriment of the SPA and SAC scheme.

It should be said that, in relation to all of the cases in which IROPI has been justified, the authors do recognise that compensatory measures will be put in place. If, however, compensatory measures were in truth a sufficient and wholly satisfactory response to development in designated areas, it is our view that there would be no real need for Article 6(3) in the first place. Indeed, there is nothing in Article 6(4), or in the Commission guidance of 2007 which requires the Commission to ensure that compensatory measures are actually taken. The Commission does not take action against Member States if they fail to implement the compensatory measures to which they have committed, even if a favourable opinion is given by the Commission on the basis of those measures being implemented.[42]

---

[41] Decision letter of 20 April 2004, Reference P89/24/59.

[42] An interesting but apparently as yet undetermined question, beyond the scope of this chapter, is what happens if it is simply not possible (physically or, for example, economically) for such compensatory measures to be taken.

Conclusion

In spite of the rhetoric of conserving the EU's natural heritage at the centre of the Habitats Directive, the ease with which conservation interests can be overridden casts serious doubt on its effectiveness as a conservation tool. Neither the ECJ—now the Court of Justice of the European Union—nor the European Commission, with responsibility for ensuring compliance with European law, are taking measures to counteract the broadening of the exception under Article 6(4). Member States appear similarly at ease with a wide interpretation of IROPI. In answer to the question posed in the title of this paper, it seems that the purpose of the Habitats Directive really is imperilled by the interpretation being accorded in practice to the phrase 'imperative reasons of overriding public interest'.

11

The Maritime Dimensions of the Habitats Directive: Past Challenges and Future Opportunities

RICHARD CADDELL

Introduction

As is well known, the Habitats Directive[1] is the leading legal provision addressing nature conservation concerns within the EU Member States. Despite the unquestioned regulatory value of the directive, however, it has historically exerted a limited influence within the marine environment in comparison to terrestrial sites and species. In recent years, this position has begun to change markedly, with the EU demonstrating a considerable interest in marine environmental affairs. As a notable aspect of this general trend, an increasing emphasis has been placed on advancing the Natura 2000 network within inshore and offshore areas. This chapter accordingly seeks to examine the key challenges that are becoming apparent in the purported implementation of the directive in a maritime context.

This chapter suggests that, while the Habitats Directive offers the promise of the protection of aquatic species and habitats, considerable difficulties have been experienced in applying its provisions effectively within the marine environment. To this end, this chapter will first outline the move towards a greater degree of EU engagement with marine biodiversity concerns, before examining a number of the key challenges experienced with the Habitats Directive to date. These challenges range from an historical lack of guidance for marine biodiversity policy to the current practical difficulties experienced in gathering the requisite data to develop Special Areas of Conservation (SACs). The coexistence of major development projects at sea and the conservation of marine species and habitats will also be analysed. Likewise, as by-catch mitigation will constitute a significant component in the protection of major aquatic species, problems in reconciling sectoral

---

[1] Council Directive 92/43/EEC of 21 May 1992 on the conservation of natural habitats and of wild fauna and flora [1992] OJ L206/7.

competences will also be discussed. Finally some observations regarding future areas of priority activity are advanced.

The Conservation of Marine Species Under the Habitats Directive

A series of policy developments have emerged within the last decade to provide a greater impetus to marine biodiversity concerns under EU law. Nevertheless, in keeping with the practice of the Habitats Directive, such developments have been slow to emerge in comparison with terrestrial considerations. Indeed, when in 1998 the EC Biodiversity Strategy (ECBS) was elaborated to facilitate further management and conservation measures to address biodiversity loss throughout the Community,[2] it contained 'no reference in its text to the marine or aquatic environment'.[3] This position was rectified to an extent in 2001 with the adoption of four Biodiversity Action Plans (BAPs),[4] with the BAP on Natural Resources targeting the full transposition of the Habitats and Wild Birds Directives by 2002.[5] However, as noted below, this has proved somewhat overambitious in practice, especially in the context of marine species and habitats. Indeed, targets were set for the completion of the marine network by 2008, with management objectives to be agreed and instigated by 2010.[6] Furthermore, it was established that by 2010 'technical measures, including marine protected areas, [should be] effectively implemented to help ensure favourable conservation status of marine habitats and species not commercially exploited'.[7] This was reinforced in 2006 by a Communication on the further implementation of the relevant biodiversity provisions,[8] with the restoration of 'biodiversity and ecosystem services in the wider EU marine environment' considered a priority activity.[9]

Perhaps more significantly, the Sixth Environmental Action Programme (EAP) sought to further promote the protection of marine areas, especially under the Habitats Directive, as well as 'by other feasible Community means'. The EAP

---

[2] COM (1998) 42.

[3] C Lasén Diaz, 'The EC Habitats Directive Approaches its Tenth Anniversary: An Overview' (2001) 10 *Review of European Community and International Environmental Law* 287, 294.

[4] Communication from the Commission to the Council and the European Parliament, Biodiversity Action Plans in the areas of Conservation of Natural Resources, Agriculture, Fisheries, and Development and Economic Co-operation, COM (2001) 0162. The BAPs were introduced in conjunction with a pledge by the EU Heads of State and Government in June 2001 at the EU Spring Summit in Goteborg to 'halt the decline of biodiversity by 2010'.

[5] Para 1.

[6] 'Message from Malahide', objective 1.1, available at: http://www.ec.europa.eu/environment/nature/biodiversity/policy/pdf/malahide_message_final.pdf.

[7] Objective 7.3.

[8] COM (2006) 216.

[9] Objective 3.

has thereby provided a further impetus to develop the marine application of the directive. Indeed, a mid-term review of the EAP considered that the Habitats Directive presented a strong overall framework to achieve the stated goal of halting biodiversity loss, identifying 'the full and effective implementation of existing legislation' as the priority action in this respect.[10]

A further development of great importance was the adoption of the Marine Strategy Framework Directive (MSFD). Initial Commission proposals for a thematic marine strategy were unveiled in October 2005,[11] which identified a series of deficiencies within the pre-existing regulatory framework. Particular concerns were raised by institutional limitations and a deficient knowledge base, identifying a need to proceed with a dual EU-regional approach, based on ecosystem consideration and Member State interaction in framing future marine policy. Following lengthy consultations,[12] the MSFD was adopted in June 2008. The MSFD is intended to operate as an 'environmental pillar' to a further Maritime Policy,[13] for which a Green Paper was adopted in June 2006.[14]

The overall objective of the MSFD is to provide a legal framework 'to achieve or maintain good environmental status within the marine environment by the year 2020 at the latest'.[15] A 'good environmental status' involves the provision of 'ecologically diverse and dynamic oceans and seas which are clean, healthy and productive within their intrinsic conditions, and the use of the marine environment is at a level that is sustainable, thus safeguarding the potential for uses and activities by current and future generations'.[16] This objective is addressed through the development of individual and regional marine strategies by the Member States encompassing a clear assessment of their current environmental status and a targeted programme of measures to be introduced by 2016 at the latest.[17] The specific policies pursued under the Habitats Directive in respect of marine species and habitats will therefore be complemented by a series of overarching policies to improve environmental quality generally. Ultimately, however, these policies are largely facilitative, providing guidance for the future direction of marine environmental policies or, in the case of the MSFD, conferring a greater degree of impetus towards the development of national and regional initiatives. To date, however, the primary legislative provision that directly impacts upon the practical conservation of threatened marine species remains the Habitats Directive.

The Habitats Directive remains the best-known provision of EU environmental law and is certainly the most pertinent in prescribing clear obligations to advance

---

[10] COM (2007) 225, 7.

[11] COM (2005) 504.

[12] For a full account of the development of the Marine Strategy see L Juda, 'The European Union and Ocean Use Management: The Marine Strategy and the Maritime Policy' (2007) 38 *Ocean Development and International Law* 259.

[13] Preamble to the MSFD, Third Recital.

[14] SEC (2006) 689.

[15] Art 1(1).

[16] Art 3(5).

[17] Art 5(1).

the conservation of marine biodiversity. The primary aims and objectives of the Habitats Directive are stated in Article 2(1) as being to 'contribute towards ensuring bio-diversity through the conservation of natural habitats and of wild fauna and flora in the European territory of the Member States'. Measures taken under the Directive are accordingly designed to maintain or restore natural habitats and species of 'Community interest' at favourable conservation status.[18]

In the pursuit of these objectives, the Habitats Directive advances a two-pronged approach to the conservation of European fauna and flora. Firstly, the directive provides for the creation of a network of SACs, known collectively as 'Natura 2000'. The Natura 2000 network consists of sites identified by the Member States as comprising particular habitat types (listed in Annex I of the directive), as well as the habitats of particular species (listed in Annex II). To date, a host of marine habitats and species have been so listed. Secondly, Member States are required to establish a system for the strict protection, within their natural range, of animal species that are listed in Annex IV(a) of the directive. All Member States are required to ensure that the distinct conservation and management requirements established for such species are observed throughout their territory.[19]

Despite the fundamental importance of this legislation to European biodiversity generally, the Habitats Directive itself has, until relatively recently, encountered a number of obstacles in seeking to address marine species. Two primary inhibiting factors may be identified as having posed particular difficulties for the advancement of conservation efforts for marine biodiversity under the directive. First, the tone and wording of the Habitats Directive has, since its inception, exhibited a strong emphasis on terrestrial species and habitats. Although a marine remit is clearly established within the directive,[20] there are nevertheless copious references throughout this instrument to 'land-use planning' and 'landscape'[21] with no corresponding identification of marine spatial planning or seascapes. Likewise, the various Annexes of the directive have long been dominated by terrestrial species and habitats, while the designation of offshore areas—which comprise the main areas of critical habitat for many species—as SACs remains embryonic at present. Moreover, as discussed below, the EU authorities have been relatively slow to develop clear guidelines for the marine application of the directive, which has

---

[18] Art 2(2). A favourable conservation status in respect of natural habitat is defined in Art 1(e) as being where its natural range and areas covered within that range are stable or increasing; the specific structure and functions which are necessary for its long-term maintenance exist and are likely to continue to exist for the foreseeable future; and the conservation status of its typical species is also 'favourable'. A favourable conservation status in respect of species is defined in Art 1(i) as being where population dynamics data on the species concerned indicate that it is maintaining itself on a long-term basis as a viable component of its natural habitats; that its natural range is neither being reduced nor likely to become reduced for the foreseeable future; and there is, and will probably continue to be, a sufficiently large habitat to maintain its populations on a long-term basis.

[19] Art 2(1).

[20] Art 1(b) of the Habitats Directive states that 'natural habitats means terrestrial *or aquatic* areas' (emphasis added).

[21] See, eg the preamble to the directive, as well as Art 3(3).

further served to hinder the development of SACs in comparison with terrestrial protected areas.

Secondly, and perhaps most significantly, the precise jurisdictional reach of the Habitats Directive in marine terms initially lacked clarity. Under Article 2(1), the directive is merely stated to apply within the 'European territory' of the Member States. Since the inception of the directive it has been questionable whether the concept of 'territory' is essentially analogous to the 'territorial sea', or whether it applies to the full range of jurisdictional waters claimed by the Member States. Initial drafts of the directive originally defined 'territory' as 'including maritime areas under the sovereignty or jurisdiction of the Member States', a clarification that was ultimately omitted from the final version of the text. Consequently, an initial interpretation that the directive applied solely to coastal waters might not be considered entirely misguided. From an ecological standpoint, however, such a narrow view of the directive is essentially self-defeating in the context of species with an extended range, as opposed to those exhibiting more coastal tendencies.[22] Accordingly, the EU institutions have broadly considered the Habitats Directive to apply to national Exclusive Economic Zones (EEZs),[23] even if this viewpoint may not have been consistently endorsed within the practice of the Member States.[24]

Perhaps surprisingly, the first judicial consideration of this issue was only advanced in 2000. Here an application for judicial review was raised in the UK,[25] in response to the adoption by the UK government of a series of Regulations[26] to license future oil and gas exploration on the continental shelf, which had expressly confined the application of the Habitats Directive to the territorial sea.[27] The applicants considered that the restrictive approach taken by the UK authorities constituted a failure to correctly transpose obligations under the Habitats Directive into national law, given that a host of species—especially

---

[22] Similar sentiments have been expressed in relation to the maritime application of the Wild Birds Directive: D Owen, 'The Application of the Wild Birds Directive beyond the Territorial Sea of European Community Member States' (2001) 13 *Journal of Environmental Law* 38.

[23] In 2001, for instance, the Council Conclusions on the Strategy for the Integration of Environmental Concerns and Sustainable Development into the Common Fisheries Policy encouraged the Member States, in cooperation with the Commission, to 'continue their work towards the full implementation of these directives in their exclusive economic zones': Point 15, available at: http://ue.eu.int/ueDocs/cms_Data/docs/pressData/en/agricult/ACF20DE.html.

[24] For instance, the German *Bundesnaturschutzgesetz* (Federal Nature Conservation Act) initially stipulated that the Habitats Directive was to be applied solely within the territorial sea. In 2002 this provision was amended to specifically extend the application of the Natura 2000 programme to the EEZ: Art 38.

[25] *R v Secretary of State for Trade and Industry, ex p Greenpeace Ltd (No 2)* (2000) 2 CMLR 94 (QBD).

[26] Conservation (Natural Habitats etc) Regulations 1994.

[27] Regulation 2(1). Somewhat curiously, however, the UK government had previously officially considered that the Habitats Directive operates in a manner so as to preclude commercial whaling activities within the EEZ: PGG Davies, 'The Legality of Norwegian Commercial Whaling under the Whaling Convention and its Compatibility with European Community Law' (1994) 43 *International and Comparative Law Quarterly* 270, 281. It is, therefore, difficult to reconcile the distinction between the operation of the directive in these waters concerning the directed hunting of a protected species, with a non-application to other potentially harmful activities.

marine mammals—could be adversely affected by such activities. In granting the application, it was duly observed by the trial judge that a directive that seeks to protect such species 'will only achieve those aims, on a purposive construction, if it extends beyond territorial waters'.[28]

Echoing this rationale, the European Court of Justice (ECJ) subsequently confirmed in a later case, *Commission v UK*,[29] that an unduly narrow view of the jurisdictional purview of the Habitats Directive would essentially defeat the key aspirations of the legislation.[30] Indeed, in the prior Opinion of Advocate-General Kokott: 'While the Habitats Directive admittedly contains no express rule concerning its territorial scope, it is consonant with its objectives to apply it beyond coastal waters ... the directive protects habitats such as reefs and species such as sea mammals which are frequently, in part even predominantly, to be found outside territorial waters'.[31] Accordingly, it has become settled law that the Habitats Directive applies to and must be enforced within the EEZs and non-extended continental shelves claimed by the Member States.

In order to evaluate the application of the Habitats Directive to marine species, it is necessary to examine both aspects of the conservation regime prescribed by the directive, namely the scope and operation of Special Areas of Conservation for Annex II species and the strict protection measures particular listed species.

Special Areas of Conservation

As noted above, although the Habitats Directive is considered to be the cornerstone of EU nature conservation law, the various biodiversity Communications have consistently lamented the slow rate of progress towards advancing the Natura 2000 network. This has proved to be particularly challenging within the marine environment, where the establishment of SACs has long lagged behind terrestrial designations. Accordingly, rectifying the sparse coverage of the Habitats Directive, especially in the offshore environment, should be considered a significant area of activity for the Member States if the directive is to realise its full conservation potential in a marine context.

In the light of these concerns, and in line with the sentiments of the Sixth EAP, a series of initiatives has been launched in recent years to address the various shortcomings in the marine application of the Habitats Directive. In October 2002, at a meeting of Nature Directors of the Member States, it was agreed that further work was necessary in order to designate and manage sea-based Natura 2000 sites. In March 2003, a Marine Expert Group was established to outline a common

---

[28] (2000) 2 CMLR 94, 114 (*per* Maurice Kay J).
[29] Case C-6/04 *Commission v UK* [2005] ECR I-9017.
[30] At para 117.
[31] At para 132 of the Opinion of the Advocate General.

understanding of the provisions of Natura 2000 within the marine environment, which culminated in the adoption by the Commission in May 2007 of a series of indicative, yet non-binding, Guidelines for the designation and operation of marine SACs.[32] Such a development must be considered especially timely, given the Commission's observation that 'to date there have been relatively few Natura 2000 sites identified for the offshore marine environment and this represents the most significant gap in the Natura network'.[33] Nevertheless, as observed below, the Natura 2000 programme can be seen to be subject to particular difficulties in the marine environment—both in the designation of SACs in the first instance and in the subsequent management of such areas by the Member States.

The Designation of Marine SACs

As a preliminary point, it should be observed that the designation process for marine SACs is no different to that of their terrestrial counterparts, with the identification of the Natura 2000 network predicated solely on relevant scientific criteria.[34] Accordingly, it is incumbent upon the Member States to propose a list of appropriate native sites, containing the natural habitat types listed in Annex I, as well as those that host species listed in Annex II.[35] Criteria for the designation of SACs are provided in Annex III of the directive. For Annex II species, Annex III lays down the following considerations as site assessment criteria:

— size and density of the population of the species present on the site in relation to the populations present within national territory;
— the degree of conservation of the features of the habitat which are important for the species concerned and restoration possibilities;
— the degree of isolation of the population present on the site in relation to the natural range of the species; and
— the global assessment of the value of the site for the conservation of the species concerned.

On the basis of this information, the indicative list of such areas produced by the Member State is subsequently transmitted to the Commission, together with documentation concerning the name, location and extent of the site, a map of

---

[32] *Guidelines for the Establishment of the Natura 2000 Network in the Marine Environment: Application of the Habitats and Birds Directives*, available at: http://ec.europa.eu/environment/nature/natura2000/marine/docs/marine_guidelines.pdf (hereafter 'Marine Guidelines').
[33] Ibid, 6.
[34] Case C-166/97 *Commission v France* [1999] ECR I-1719; this point is reinforced in the Marine Guidelines. ibid, Section 2.10. As to the protection afforded during the designation stage see Jones and Westaway, ch 4 in this volume.
[35] Art 4(1).

the area, as well as data generated in the application of the Annex III criteria.[36] Thereafter, the Commission is responsible for producing a draft list of Sites of Community Importance (SCIs) in consultation with the Member State, which will then be formally adopted.[37] The Member State is then required to officially designate any such site within its jurisdiction as an SAC 'as soon as possible and within six years at most'.[38]

Despite the operation of an administrative system that—on the surface, at least—appears relatively uncomplicated, the establishment of the Natura 2000 network has ultimately proved to be a protracted process in practice, both in relation to terrestrial and marine SACs. That the demanding deadlines[39] for the completion of the network have not been met may be explained by the fact the relatively straightforward wording of the directive masks what is often a complex, expensive and labour-intensive series of research activities on the part of national nature conservation agencies. Moreover, the data required under Annex III to identify SCIs is often highly challenging to swiftly obtain in a marine context—especially in offshore waters—given the practical and financial difficulties posed in conducting concerted studies on these species and areas in the wild. Large-scale survey projects, conducted over large maritime areas, are often cost- and time-intensive, given that the areas are generally less accessible than those on land. In addition to funding considerations, studies may also be adversely affected by weather conditions, especially in unpredictable offshore areas, which may further inhibit the ability of researchers to access such species and gather the necessary data.[40] Moreover, some species eligible for SAC protection are rather more difficult to monitor than others. Natural camouflage and an extended and unpredictable range have impacted upon the ability of researchers to gather data effectively for particular populations, with coastal species generally easier to track—and accordingly identify crucial habitats—than more pelagic species.[41]

Secondly, the seemingly innocuous evidential threshold advanced within the Habitats Directive for the creation of SACs for marine species is, in reality, deceptively high. Article 4(1) provides that: 'For aquatic species which range over wide areas, such sites will be proposed only where there is a clearly identifiable

---

[36] Art 4(2).

[37] Under Art 20 this will be evaluated by a specialist Committee, which will then submit its recommendations to the Commission under Art 21 for adoption.

[38] Art 4(4).

[39] The Member States that were under the EU umbrella at the time of the conclusion of the Habitats Directive were originally scheduled to have furnished the European Commission with the requisite national lists by June 1995, with a list of Sites of Community Importance due to have been finalised by June 1998.

[40] Such considerations have impacted on the progress of studies by German researchers, for instance, given that '[g]ood survey conditions are rare for the German Exclusive Economic Zones in the Baltic and North Sea': U Siebert et al, 'A Decade of Harbour Porpoise Occurrence in German Waters—Analyses of Aerial Surveys, Incidental Sightings and Strandings' (2006) 56 *Journal of Sea Research* 65, 78.

[41] CB Embling et al, 'Using Habitat Models to Identify Suitable Sites for Marine Protected Areas for Harbour Porpoises' (2010) 143 *Biological Conservation* 267, at 267.

area representing the physical and biological factors essential to their life and reproduction.' It may be considered that the legislative intent of this provision is to prevent the designation of excessive expanses of the sea as protected areas and thereby permit the coexistence of vital economic activities with nature conservation. There is nonetheless some suggestion from current practice that this formulation is rather counter-productive. Indeed, the stringency of these requirements, and concomitant difficulties in demonstrating unequivocally that areas of high species density are also in fact 'essential to life and reproduction', is cited as a primary reason for truncating the parameters of a key SAC for harbour porpoises within the German EEZ.[42] A similarly staccato approach to the identification of marine SACs has also been experienced in Dutch waters.[43]

Some uniform principles were tentatively developed in respect of marine-based Natura 2000 sites by an ad hoc working group of the EC Habitats Committee in December 2000.[44] The working group considered potential designation criteria for protected areas for migratory marine species, using harbour porpoises as a benchmarking exercise. Areas representing the crucial factors for the life-cycle of the species were deemed identifiable, especially where

— there is a continuous or regular presence of the species, subject to seasonal variations;
— there is a good population density in relation to other areas; and
— there is a high ratio of young to adults during certain periods of the year.

Such considerations are not considered to be exhaustive and 'other biological elements are characteristic of these areas, such as very developed social and sexual life'[45] may also prove informative.

The practice in respect of harbour porpoise designations reveals that states have tended to adopt a broader approach in identifying potential Natura 2000 sites. Recent Danish practice has considered site fidelity in a reproductive context as the key aspect in ascertaining potential SACs.[46] Likewise, although there is little definitive practice informing the 'other biological elements' referred to by the Marine Guidelines, a 'high proportion of sensitive behaviour, i.e. resting' was deemed to be of additional significance in establishing German SACs for harbour porpoises.[47]

---

[42] SA Pedersen et al, 'Natura 2000 Sites and Fisheries in German Offshore Waters' (2009) 66 *ICES Journal of Marine Science* 155, 160.

[43] See H Dotinga and A Trouwborst, 'The Netherlands and the Designation of Marine Protected Areas in the North Sea: Implementing International and European Law' (2009) 5 *Utrecht Law Review* 21, 35–38.

[44] EC (2001) Habitats Committee, Hab 01/05.

[45] Marine Guidelines 47.

[46] J Teilmann et al, *High Density Areas for Harbour Porpoises in Danish Waters: NERI Technical Report No 657* (Åarhus, National Environmental Research Institute, 2008) 9.

[47] JC Krause et al, 'Rationale Behind Site Selection for the NATURA 2000 Network in the German EEZ' in H von Nordheim, D Boedeker and JC Krause (eds), *Progress in Marine Conservation in Europe: Natura 2000 Sites in German Offshore Waters* (Heidelberg, Springer Verlag, 2006) 72.

While the guidelines were elaborated with the harbour porpoise specifically in mind, they have been also successfully applied to other species of marine mammals.[48] Likewise, recent practice has seen a tentative emergence of the Natura 2000 network into offshore waters, with designations for SCIs pending in a number of Member States. The first concerted programme of activity to establish SACs within the EEZ of a Member State was undertaken by Germany in the light of the amendment of the *Bundesnaturschutzgesetz* to confer formal powers upon the pertinent authorities to do so. Accordingly, in 2004 a list of 10 new SCIs—the first in offshore waters within the Community—were proposed to the Commission,[49] with the western area of the island of Sylt ultimately designated as a SAC for harbour porpoises.[50]

There is some scope for optimism that, in the mid-term future, an increasing number of critical areas of habitat for Annex II species may be identified and proposed as SCIs by the Member States, as the offshore and inshore coverage of the Natura 2000 programme continues to develop.[51] In this regard, an ambitious target has been set for the completion of the Natura 2000 network, both in a terrestrial and marine context, by 2012. However, notwithstanding the instructive corpus of practice that has begun to emerge in recent years on the establishment of marine SACs, the prospects of the Member States ultimately meeting this demanding deadline are slim. Not only is the designation process dependent primarily upon the ability of national authorities to allocate substantial funds to identify key areas for marine species, data collection on this magnitude remains very much a long-term project. Where there is a considerable body of pre-existing historical data on key species and their habitats in the waters of a particular Member States, such a task is somewhat easier. However, many such areas are still considered data deficient,[52] which suggests that acquiring the necessary information to develop a coherent network of marine SACs is likely to extend significantly beyond the confines of the current Commission targets.

The Management of Marine SACs

The designation of maritime SACs under the Habitats Directive, like that of any marine protected area, is essentially meaningless unless accompanied by a clear set of management targets and enforcement provisions. Indeed, the establishment of

---

[48] For instance, the UK has designated two SACs in inshore waters for bottlenose dolphins in the Moray Firth, Scotland and Bae Ceredigion, Wales, respectively.

[49] Krause et al, above n 47, 66–67.

[50] Pedersen et al, 'Natura 2000 Sites and Fisheries' 160.

[51] For instance, the UK submitted twelve separate offshore sites as candidate SACs in three tranches between August 2008 and August 2011: see www.jncc.defra.gov.uk.

[52] Indeed, data availability on the distribution of Annex II species generally is considered 'very sparse': Marine Guidelines, 47.

an SAC entails a long-term commitment to the maintenance of such sites, given that protected areas in a marine context 'require effective governance and well-functioning management institutions if they are to be ecologically and socially successful'.[53] Moreover, a leading review of best practice for protected areas for marine mammals considers that such sites, as a basic necessity, require *inter alia* an ecosystem-based and socio-economic management plan, legal recognition and a clear enforcement programme.[54] The Habitats Directive establishes obligations on the Member States in relation to SACs, most notably under Article 6, which provides the broad framework of protective measures to be taken[55] and the coexistence of conservation strategies and economic activities within these sites.[56] Nevertheless, some concerns may be raised as to how effective such commitments may be in practice for marine SACs.

Under Article 6(1), the national authorities 'shall establish the necessary conservation measures involving, *if need be*, appropriate management plans specifically designed for the sites or integrated into other development plans, and appropriate statutory, administrative or contractual measures which correspond to the ecological requirements' of the habitats or species in question.[57] There is no express obligation to ultimately develop a targeted management plan of the type identified by Hoyt as crucial to the basic success of a protected area for major marine species. In practice, however, national conservation agencies have elaborated management plans for the marine SACs established to date.[58] Likewise, the Marine Guidelines strongly recommend the establishment of conservation plans for marine SACs, citing the OSPAR model as a particular example of good practice.[59]

The second limb of Article 6(1), however, is clear and unequivocal: Member States must establish appropriate measures to safeguard the ecological requirements of the site. Given the extreme variability in the conservation needs of habitats and species addressed under Annexes I and II, the Commission has sought to avoid undue prescription in the discharge of this obligation. Nevertheless, it is clear that such measures must correspond to the particular needs of the species

---

[53] A Charles and L Wilson, 'Human Dimensions of Marine Protected Areas' (2009) 66 *ICES Journal of Marine Science* 6, 9.

[54] E Hoyt, *Marine Protected Areas for Whales, Dolphins and Porpoises* (London, Earthscan, 2005) 75.

[55] Art 6(1) and (2).

[56] Art 6(3) and (4).

[57] Emphasis added.

[58] For instance, species action plans have been adopted by the UK for its two bottlenose dolphin SACs, while national action plans are also considered to be a key aspect of present and future Danish conservation initiatives: Teilmann, 'High Density Areas', 8. As noted by Krause et al, 'sound site selection must be followed by effective management if the overall conservation intent of marine NATURA 2000 sites is to be achieved', hence this is a key aspect of the German porpoise strategy: see above n 47 at 94.

[59] Marine Guidelines, at Section 5.5. The OSPAR Guidelines are themselves modelled upon those advanced by the IUCN.

throughout its life cycle.[60] In the context of Annex II species, such measures might, for instance, be envisaged to take particular account of migratory behaviour and provide for enhanced protection during breeding and birthing seasons.[61]

Particular obligations apply to the habitats of Annex II species under Article 6(2), which become operational as soon as a site is designated as an SCI.[62] This provision prescribes a two-pronged approach to habitat protection, with Member States to 'take appropriate steps to avoid, in the special areas of conservation, the deterioration of natural habitats and the habitats of species as well as disturbance of the species for which the areas have been designated, *in so far as such disturbance could be significant in relation to the objectives of this Directive*'.[63] However, while the requirements pertaining to habitat deterioration are clear, interpretive difficulties are raised by the 'disturbance' of marine SACs. The point at which this obligation will be triggered is difficult to quantify objectively; the directive offers no definition of 'significant' disturbance. Likewise, whether a disturbance will affect the conservation status of a protected species is dependent upon multiple factors such as the nature of the disturbing activity; the point at which it occurs within the life cycle of the species; the projected adverse impact upon individual animals; as well as stock numbers and dynamics to ascertain whether unsustainable material losses are likely to occur.

This lack of a generic 'tipping point' demonstrates the practical utility of a clear management plan where an SAC is created. Indeed, good practice would appear to involve the development of indicative guidelines within the management plan on proposed responses to disturbing activities likely to be faced within the SAC. Although the conditions within each SAC are highly individual in nature, the Marine Guidelines have cited oil and gas exploration[64] and ecotourism activities[65] as examples of typical sources of disturbance. Accordingly, the development of localised guidelines to address such activities may be considered an increasingly important aspect of SAC management on the part of the Member States. This is present on an ad hoc basis,[66] but while the development of national action plans appear to form a significant basis for the 'strict protection' of species under the directive, it is not yet clear whether localised initiatives are mandatory or merely desirable.

---

[60] *Managing NATURA 2000 Sites: The Provisions of Article 6 of the 'Habitats' Directive 92/43/EEC* (Brussels, European Commission, 2000) 18.

[61] On the specific issue of the conservation of migratory species under the Habitats Directive see R Caddell, 'Biodiversity Loss and the Prospects for International Cooperation: EU Law and the Conservation of Migratory Species of Wild Animals' (2008) 8 *Yearbook of European Environmental Law* 218, 238–40.

[62] Art 4(5). The same is true of Art 6(3) and (4), while the requirements of Art 6(1) do not apply until the site is formally established as an SAC.

[63] Emphasis added. The objectives of the directive in this regard are considered to be the maintenance of Annex II cetaceans at a favourable conservation status.

[64] Marine Guidelines, Section 5.9.3.

[65] The Marine Guidelines note that ecotourism 'needs to be carefully managed', Section 5.9.10.

[66] For example, ecotourism activities are regulated by localised codes of conduct in the Shannon Bay SAC: Hoyt, above n 54, 186–87.

As an emerging marine practice, it appears that buffer zones may be increasingly developed to address disturbances. The issue of disturbance is particularly acute for marine species, with the oceans known to be a highly effective propagator of sound, in a manner not generally replicated in a terrestrial context.[67] Consequently, marine species may be adversely affected by noise sources originating a considerable distance away from their key habitats, which has had a proven displacement effect upon a number of species, especially marine mammals.[68] As noted above, the directive requires designations to be based on scientific considerations. Given that standard scientific practices in Marine Protected Area (MPA) design consider the use of buffer zones seemingly as a matter of course,[69] there would appear to be little legal impediment to such a policy. The size and application of particular buffer zones will be essentially context-dependent, although the mitigation of shipping noise in areas of particular traffic concentration may require buffer zones of up to 10 kilometres in order to render habitat conditions in SACs tolerable for certain species.[70] The problems raised by the widespread use of low-frequency sonar[71] may require the establishment of even larger buffer zones,[72] which may have practical implications for future designation practices.

Where an SAC is ultimately designated under the directive, 'the inclusion of a site into the network Natura 2000 does not, a priori, exclude its future use'.[73] Accordingly, Article 6(3) and (4) establish the conditions under which such activities may be conducted within protected areas. These provisions are not uncontroversial, nor indeed may they always be considered especially clear. Moreover, they are likely to be invoked with increasing frequency given the major economic and social interests at stake in a number of areas of critical marine habitats.

Article 6(3) provides that: 'Any plan or project not directly connected with or necessary to the management of the site but likely to have a significant effect thereon, either individually or in combination with other plans or projects shall be subject to appropriate assessment of its implications for the site in view of the site's conservation objectives.' However, the directive is silent on what constitutes a 'plan or project' caught under the purview of this provision. The ECJ has clarified

---

[67] WJ Richardson, CR Greene, Jr, CI Malme and DH Thomson, *Marine Mammals and Noise* (San Diego, Academic Press, 1995) 159.

[68] For striking examples see P Tyack, 'Implications for Marine Mammals of Large-Scale Changes in the Marine Acoustic Environment' (2008) 89 *Journal of Mammalogy* 549 and DP Nowacek, LH Thorne, DW Johnson and PL Tyack, 'Responses of Cetaceans to Anthropogenic Noise' (2007) 37 *Mammal Review* 81.

[69] G Kelleher, *Guidelines for Marine Protected Areas* (Gland, IUCN, 1999).

[70] Embling, above n 41, 277.

[71] On this issue see ECM Parsons *et al*, 'Naval Sonar and Cetaceans: Just How Much Does the Gun Need to Smoke Before We Act?' (2008) 56 *Marine Pollution Bulletin* 1248. Sonar has been identified as a significant causal factor in whale strandings, and may have severe adverse impacts upon both protected species and their prey: see MP Simmonds and LF Lopez-Jurado, 'Whales and the Military' (1992) 351 *Nature* 448 and A Frantzis, 'Does Acoustic Testing Strand Whales?' (1998) 392 *Nature* 29.

[72] Embling, above n 41.

[73] Marine Guidelines, Section 5.9.3.

this issue,[74] viewing the definition as broadly following a related directive[75] and suggesting that 'the terms "plan" or "project" should be interpreted broadly, not restrictively'.[76] Likewise, the concept of a 'significant' effect is undefined and a substantial negative impact of such activities could be experienced within the SAC, without necessarily triggering a significant impact on the conservation status of the animals concerned. Much of the current litigation to date on this provision has concerned the need for an Environmental Impact Assessment (EIA) in individual circumstances,[77] for which there is a substantial array of specific EU legislation.

More significantly, Article 6(4) provides that

> If, in spite of a negative assessment of this implications for the site and in the absence of alternative solutions, a plan or project must nevertheless be carried out for imperative reasons of overriding public interest, including those of a social or economic nature, the Member State shall take all compensatory measures necessary to ensure that the overall coherence of Natura 2000 is protected.

Article 6(4) thereby seeks to reconcile the demands of economic and industrial activity of fundamental importance to the Member State with the practical demands of Community biodiversity commitments.

Nevertheless, Article 6(4) suffers from a marked lack of clarity concerning the threshold by which economic activities may be conducted within an SAC. Indeed, the notion of 'imperative reasons of overriding public interest' is among the most contentious—and certainly one of the most opaque—clauses of the Habitats Directive, for which the Commission readily admits that the ECJ 'has not given clear indications for the interpretation of this specific concept'.[78] De Sadeleer considers this phrase 'as referring to a general interest superior to the ecological objective of the Directive'.[79] A further interpretation of considerable influence mandates a balance of interests approach, whereby: 'A project that is of great public interest but involves only minor adverse effects to the protected area in question should be treated differently than a project with marginal economic

---

[74] Case C-127/02 *Landelijke Vereniging tot Behoud van de Waddenzee, Nederlandse Vereniging tot Bescherming van Vogels v Staatssecretaris van Landbouw, Natuurbeheer en Visserij* [2004] ECR I-7405.

[75] Council Directive 85/337/EEC of 27 June 1985 on the assessment of the effects of certain public and private projects on the environment [1985] OJ L175/40. This provision defines a 'project' (but not a 'plan') as 'the execution of construction works or of other installations or schemes' and 'other interventions in the natural surroundings and landscape including those involving the extraction of mineral resources', Art 1(2). The present case considered cockle fishing to constitute a project for the purposes of Directive 85/337/EEC and, by extension, the Habitats Directive.

[76] Opinion of Advocate-General Kokott, para 30, see Tromans, ch 5 in this volume.

[77] See, eg Case C-256/98 *Commission v France* [2000] ECR I-2487.

[78] *Guidance Document on Article 6(4) of the 'Habitats Directive' 92/43/EEC* (Brussels, European Commission, 2007) 7. On the notion of 'imperative reasons of overriding public interest' see Clutten and Tafur, ch 10 in this volume.

[79] N de Sadeleer, 'Habitats Conservation in EC Law—From Nature Sanctuaries to Ecological Networks' (2005) 5 *Yearbook of European Environmental Law* 215, 249.

public interest but important detrimental effects on ecological values.'[80] It is accordingly evident that the concept remains highly subjective and is dependent entirely on the particular conditions present within each individual SAC.

The obligations incumbent upon the Member States under Article 6(4) are also uncertain. There is little precise indication of the 'compensatory measures' required of the national authorities, aside from a vague intimation that nesting or resting sites should be moved to an appropriate safer point along migratory pathways or that so-called 'habitat banking' may be considered.[81] While this is more feasible for certain terrestrial or avian species or habitats, such policies represent a substantial challenge in a marine context. Instead, mitigation measures in marine SACs are likely to involve, for instance, temporal and spatial restrictions on fishing activities and the introduction of guidelines on seismic activities in areas of critical habitat.[82]

A Member State may only invoke this exemption on three broad grounds, namely considerations of human health or public safety, beneficial consequences of primary importance for the environment or 'further to an opinion from the Commission, to other reasons of overriding public interest'. Invocations of the first two criteria are likely to be relatively infrequent, although it should be observed that the current EU aspirations towards the further development of alternative energy sources[83] may involve an increasing volume of tidal barrages and offshore windfarms, which may raise concerns over the integrity of marine sites.[84] Subject to an appropriate EIA, the environment clause may be considered likely to override such concerns, while military activities may be justified under the 'public safety' exemption. The clearest area of conflict, however, is likely to occur in the context of the expansively worded sweep-up clause, 'other imperative reasons of overriding public interest'.

To date, a number of Opinions have been delivered by the Commission regarding Article 6(4) projects,[85] although they may not necessarily represent a precise template for the application of this provision in a marine context. Insofar as broad principles may be distilled from these Opinions, it appears that such a project will

---

[80] A Nollkaemper, 'Habitat Protection in European Community Law: Evolving Conceptions of a Balance of Interests' (1997) 9 *Journal of Environmental Law* 271, 280.

[81] *Guidance Document on Article 6(4)*, above n 78, 13. On the potential inter-relationship between habitat banking and the directive see C T Reid, 'The Privatisation of Biodiversity? Possible New Approaches to Nature Conservation Law in the UK' (2011) 23 *Journal of Environmental Law* 203, 214–19.

[82] On this issue generally, see R Compton et al, 'A Critical Examination of Worldwide Guidelines for Minimising Disturbance to Marine Mammals During Seismic Surveys' (2008) 32 *Marine Policy* 255.

[83] COM (2006) 848.

[84] Again, to use the harbour porpoise as an example, concerns have been raised about the implications of similar projects within SACs: A Kellermann, K Eskildsen and B Frank, 'The MINOS Project: Ecological Assessments of Possible Impacts of Offshore Wind Energy Projects' in von Nordheim, Boedeker and Krause, above n 47, 245–46.

[85] Available at: http://ec.europa.eu/environment/nature/natura2000/management/guidance_en.htm. On this issue generally, see L Krämer, 'The European Commission's Opinions under Article 6(4) of the Habitats Directive' (2009) 21 *Journal of Environmental Law* 59.

be permitted where the Member State demonstrates that it is essential to alleviate substantial unemployment or social hardship,[86] to secure the competitiveness of a Member State or Community industry on an international level,[87] to create vital infrastructure links[88] or to service fundamental human needs.[89]

Given the highly limited practice to date, the degree of toleration for development activities in marine SACs remains largely an exercise in conjecture. Nevertheless, certain key industrial activities have been identified within the Marine Guidelines for which supervision will be required when carried out in proximity to, or within SACs. In addition to ecotourism activities,[90] particular concern has been reserved for oil and gas exploitation, active sonar use, vessel-based noise and acoustic by-catch mitigation devices, all of which 'need to be regulated in accordance with the provisions of article 6(3) and (4) of the Habitats Directive if they are likely to have a significant effects [sic] on protected features at a Natura 2000 site'.[91] Likewise, fisheries activities may also require management measures within these areas, for which the Commission has produced concise outline guidance.[92] In this respect, additional complications are created by the demarcation of competence over fisheries management in particular areas, as noted below. Accordingly, with potential marine SACs encompassing locations of significant economic activity, it is likely that the parameters of Articles 6(3) and (4) in a marine context will become areas of considerable controversy and conflict in future years as the Natura 2000 network develops further in both inshore and offshore waters.

Strict Protection Measures

The second key conservation objective pursued by the Habitats Directive mandates that Member States 'shall take the requisite measures to establish a system of strict protection for the animal species listed in Annex IV(a) in their natural range'.[93] Article 12(1) prescribes, inter alia, the prohibition of all forms of

---

[86] *Prosper Haniel Colliery Development Plan*, Opinion of 24 April 2003.

[87] *Project Mainport Rotterdam Development Plan*, Opinion of 23 April 2003; *Mühlenberger Loch Development Plan*, Opinion of 19 April 2000.

[88] *Grenadilla Port Development Plan*; *Karlsruhe/Baden-Baden Airport Development Plan*, Opinion of 6 June 2005; *TGV Est Development Plan*, Opinion of 16 September 2004; *Peene Valley Development Plan*, Opinion of 18 December 1995.

[89] *La Breña II Dam Development Plan*, Opinion of 14 May 2004.

[90] As noted above, conditions have been imposed by the Irish authorities in respect of such activities in the Shannon Estuary SAC, which may represent an attractive model for other Member States to follow.

[91] Marine Guidelines, Section 5.9.2.

[92] *Fisheries Measures for Marine Natura 2000 Sites: A Consistent Approach to Requests for Fisheries Management Measures under the Common Fisheries Policy* (Brussels, European Commission, 2008).

[93] Art 12(1). As noted above, 'all species' of cetaceans are listed in Annex IV(a).

deliberate capture or killing of specimens[94] in the wild, of deliberate disturbance
of these species, particularly during the period of breeding, rearing, hibernation
and migration[95] and the deterioration or destruction of breeding sites or resting
places. A firm line has been taken on such activities, as demonstrated in the leading case of *Commission v Greece*,[96] in which multiple violations of Article 12 were
found to have arisen from the poor protection of turtles and their habitats in a
major area for tourism. Likewise, Article 12(2) prohibits the keeping, transport,
sale or exchange or offering for sale or exchange of such species. Furthermore,
Article 12(4) requires the Member States to establish a system to monitor the
incidental capture and killing of Annex IV(a) species, with by-catches considered a 'looming crisis' for stocks of many marine species protected under the
Directive.[97] As noted below, this has given rise to practical difficulties in the
context of fisheries regulation.

Likewise, Article 16(1)(c) permits derogations 'in the interests of public health
and public safety, or for other imperative reasons of overriding public interest,
including those of a social or economic nature and beneficial consequences of
primary importance to the environment'. As in the case of SACs, there is considerable elasticity in the wording of this provision to license important economic
and industrial activities within the marine environment, which may ultimately
result in a growing number of challenges to such derogations in future years.
There is limited decided authority in relation to these requirements specifically
addressing the 'strict protection' in a marine context. Nevertheless, the key case of
Commission v Ireland[98] suggests that the Court of Justice of the European Union
(CJEU) will not lightly tolerate a failure to facilitate such a system. In this respect,
subsequent complaints are likely to involve close scrutiny of the procedural
aspects of derogation practice, as well as the resources allocated to facilitating the
enforcement and monitoring obligations towards Annex IV(a) species.

In *Commission v Ireland*, infringement proceedings were brought for a series of
alleged breaches of the Habitats Directive concerning an eclectic group of species.
Particular concerns were raised regarding the impact of development projects
on marine mammals. First, it was alleged that the Irish authorities had failed
to establish a system of strict protection due to an absence of a national action
plan for cetaceans and a failure to fulfil surveillance and monitoring obligations.
Secondly, concerns were raised that a project to lay a gas pipeline in Broadhaven
Bay involved the use of explosives which, despite acknowledging that the sound

[94] 'Specimens' are defined in Art 1(m) as 'any animal or plan, whether alive or dead, of the species
listed in Annex IV and Annex V, any part or derivative thereof, as well as any other goods which appear,
from an accompanying document, the packaging or a mark or label, or from any other circumstances,
to be parts or derivatives of animals or plans of those species'.

[95] By virtue of Art 12(3), these two obligations 'shall apply to all stages of life of the animals', as
indeed does the obligation concerning sale and trade of the species in Art 12(2).

[96] Case C-103/00 *Commission v Greece* [2002] ECR I-1147.

[97] AJ Reid, 'The Looming Crisis: Interactions between Marine Mammals and Fisheries' (2008) 89
Journal of Mammalogy 541.

[98] Case C-183/05 *Commission v Ireland* [2007] ECR I-137.

created would have an adverse impact, was nonetheless authorised by the government without entering a derogation under Article 16. The Irish authorities responded that a species action plan was 'underway' and that monitoring projects were being conducted by conservation volunteers with more in-depth government studies in certain areas. Moreover, a national records database had since been established together with full adherence to the by-catch monitoring obligations prescribed under relevant fisheries legislation, while permission for seismic blasting had been granted in accordance with national rules.

The ECJ found Ireland to be in breach of its commitments on both counts. The failure to establish species action plans, considered 'an effective means of meeting the strict protection requirement under Article 12(1)',[99] could not be defended by demonstrating that initiatives to comply with this requirement were concluded after the expiry of the Reasoned Opinion issued by the Commission.[100] Particular criticism was reserved for surveillance activities, considered 'ad hoc and confined to certain geographical areas',[101] while resources for marine conservation were 'especially meagre' and wildlife rangers 'focussed on terrestrial duties and do not have any meaningful seagoing capacity'.[102] Accordingly, the Court ruled that a system of strict protection had not been demonstrated.[103] Furthermore, it was held that the national authorisation process for seismic blasting was too permissive, rendering breeding and resting sites 'subject to disturbances and threats which the Irish rules do not make it possible to prevent'.[104]

The Habitats Directive and the Marine Environment: Opportunities and Limitations

The Habitats Directive is clearly a vital instrument for the conservation of marine species, both through its provisions for the establishment of protected areas and its facilitative role in ensuring the strict protection of species and habitats throughout Community waters. Unlike many MPA-based approaches, the directive provides a strong prescriptive impetus for the creation of such areas, as well as a clear system for the review of decisions affecting the ecological integrity of SACs. While some reservations may be raised concerning the permissive nature of Article 6, the SAC regime demonstrates clear potential to transcend the 'paper sanctuaries' often associated with MPAs, which are commonly starved

---

[99] Opinion of Advocate-General Léger, para 39.
[100] At para 16 of the judgment. This position had been established in earlier (unrelated) litigation: Case C-282/02 *Commission v Ireland* ECR I-4653, para 40.
[101] Opinion of Advocate-General Léger, para 84.
[102] Ibid, 69.
[103] At para 31 of the judgment.
[104] Ibid, 36.

of resources and devoid of meaningful enforcement powers. Moreover, the ECJ has demonstrated a strong approach to deficiencies in the establishment of a Community-wide system of strict protection. The high political visibility of particular species, such as marine mammals, within the EU institutions will also ensure a proactive review of national policies that have the propensity to adversely affect their conservation status.

Nevertheless, these clear strengths obscure a series of underlying structural deficiencies within the Habitats Directive that undermine its overall effectiveness as a conservatory regime in a marine context. First, the designation of SACs is an obligation restricted to a relatively small list of species. As Hoyt observes, the reasons for this are contemporary to the drafting of the directive, with limited information available at the material time regarding the range, distribution and threats to such species.[105] Subsequently, a case may be made to expand the range species of species listed on Annex II, in line with an expanding knowledge base on the conservation needs of particular species.

Secondly, the designation criteria for SACs are not presently conducive to the swift establishment of an extensive marine network of protected areas. The stringency of Article 4(1) means that while a particular site may be identifiable as being high in species density, demonstrating definitively that it qualifies as representing physical and biological factors essential to life and reproduction is often rather more complicated. Moreover, existing data deficiencies are also 'understandably regarded as hindrances in the establishment of offshore NATURA 2000 sites'.[106] While the German experience demonstrates that such challenges are not insurmountable, practical difficulties may be experienced in other Member States. Indeed, the UK authorities consider that such sites take 'several years for an area to progress from being an Area of Search to being submitted as a cSAC',[107] while some of the more recent EU entrants may lack the research facilities to gather such information as swiftly and efficiently as Germany.[108]

Finally, concerns must also be raised by the often vague and permissive nature of the obligations imposed upon the Member States concerning SACs under Article 6, which is considered 'a poor piece of legislation that, unless strictly interpreted, contains big loopholes for major infrastructure projects in vulnerable areas'.[109] These loopholes are likely to be explored with increasing frequency given the major economic interests at stake in key areas of marine habitats throughout the Community. Given the practical difficulties associated in developing alternative habitat sites and lingering concerns over mitigation obligations for seismic

---

[105] Hoyt, above n 54, 183.

[106] Kraus et al, above n 47, 93.

[107] Cited by the JNCC at: http://jncc.defra.gov.uk/.

[108] The position within the post-2004 accession states is rather understudied. For a discussion of the experiences of one of the new Member States see R Caddell, 'Nature Conservation in Estonia: From Soviet Union to European Union' in DJ Galbreath (ed), *Contemporary Environmentalism in the Baltic States: From Phosphate Springs to 'Nordstream'* (Abingdon, Routledge, 2010) 28–53.

[109] Nollkaemper, above n 80, 286.

testing,[110] such areas will prove a considerable test to the Commission's ability to balance the interests of nature conservation and economic development.

Fisheries Concerns and the Habitats Directive

Finally, although the Habitats Directive will continue to frame nature conservation obligations in the marine environment, the role of the Common Fisheries Policy (CFP) should also be briefly observed. The implementation of the Natura 2000 network and securing the strict protection of particular species in EC waters have been clearly identified as ongoing priorities for Member States in addressing the conservation needs of marine biodiversity.[111] Despite this stated focus, an unintentional impediment to marine conservation efforts has become increasingly pronounced in recent years. It has become apparent that, in some areas, implementation difficulties will arise due to the division of competences between the EU institutions and the Member States in the field of fisheries.

Competence to address biodiversity concerns has developed incrementally under the constituent EU treaties.[112] The original 1957 EEC Treaty was not endowed with competence to regulate environmental concerns. This position was altered in the aftermath of the 1972 Stockholm Conference with the establishment in 1973 of the Environment and Consumer Protection Service and the first Programme of Action of the European Communities on the Environment.[113] From these preliminary initiatives, certain provisions of the EEC Treaty addressing the common market were used as a basis for legislative activity.[114] Subsequent reforms of the EC Treaty have established clear supervisory competence over ecological concerns. A key development in this regard was the adoption of the Single European Act in 1986, designed primarily to further develop the common market. The SEA elaborated a distinct 'Environmental Title',[115] which prescribed competence, inter alia, to 'protect, preserve and improve the quality of the environment'. These powers were subsequently consolidated within successive revisions of the EC Treaty.

Particular difficulties have arisen in the marine context due to conflicts between sectoral competences. This has been especially pronounced in the context of marine biodiversity, as opposed to terrestrial species, due to the need to address

---

[110] CR Weir and SJ Dolman, 'Comparative Review of the Regional Marine Mammal Mitigation Guidelines Implemented during Industrial Seismic Surveys, and Guidance towards a Worldwide Standard' (2007) 10 *Journal of International Wildlife Law and Policy* 1.

[111] 'Mid-Term Review of the Sixth EAP' 3.

[112] On the graduated emergence of competence of the EEC over biodiversity concerns see L Krämer, 'The Interdependency of Community and Member State Activity on Nature Protection within the European Community' (1993) 20 *Ecology Law Quarterly* 25.

[113] [1973] OJ C112/1.

[114] Namely ex-Art 100 (now Art 94) and ex-Art 235 (now Art 308).

[115] See also L Krämer, 'Thirty Years of European Environmental Law: Perspectives and Prospectives' (2002) 2 *Yearbook of European Environmental Law* 155.

fisheries interactions. By-catches are considered to pose a severe conservation threat to a number of key species, with the risks posed by European fisheries deemed especially acute.[116] There is accordingly an urgent need to address this issue as part of a wider policy to ensure the ecological integrity of SACs.

The specialist technical measures required to address by-catches would ordinarily be introduced and applied by a coastal state through its fisheries legislation. This has proved challenging in the EU context due to the nature of competences over fisheries concerns. The EC Treaty explicitly claimed competence over fisheries in 1992 by virtue of the Treaty on European Union.[117] Prior to this, fisheries measures were introduced as part of the Community's remit to regulate agricultural products, which included aspects of fisheries concerns.[118] In 1981 the ECJ confirmed that the EC exercised exclusive competence over fisheries.[119] Subject to powers delegated to the Member States, the European Council is therefore charged with establishing the conditions regulating fishing activities pursued by Community fleets. This includes the development of technical measures in respect of fishing and the conservation and exploitation of fisheries resources. In the context of the CFP, this is addressed by the Council through a 'Basic Regulation', with the current version adopted in 2002 following a root-and-branch reform of Community fisheries objectives.[120] However, these arrangements have created practical difficulties for Member States in pursuing individual policies to address incidental mortality within their jurisdictional waters.[121]

Chronologically, the first major legislative acknowledgement by the EU of the threat posed to marine wildlife from incidental capture came in 1992—through the Habitats Directive as opposed to specific fisheries legislation. In line with commitments towards individual protected species, incidental catches are addressed under Article 12(4) which establishes an obligation to address, inter alia, by-catches:

> Member States shall establish a system to monitor the incidental capture and killing of the animal species listed in Annex IV(a). In the light of the information gathered, Member States shall take further research or conservation measures as required to ensure that incidental capture and killing does not have a significant impact on the species concerned.

---

[116] RR Reeves, BD Smith, EA Crespo and G Notarbartolo di Sciara, *Dolphins, Whales and Porpoises: 2002–2010 Conservation Action Plan for the World's Cetaceans* (Gland, IUCN, 2003) 14–15.

[117] Art 3.

[118] For a comprehensive appraisal of the early operation of the CFP, see R Churchill and D Owen, *The EC Common Fisheries Policy* (Oxford, Oxford University Press, 2010).

[119] Case C-804/79 *Commission v United Kingdom* [1981] ECR 1045.

[120] Council Regulation (EC) No 2371/2002 of 20 December 2002 on the conservation and sustainable development of fisheries resources under the Common Fisheries Policy [2002] OJ L358/59.

[121] On the difficulties raised in this regard see A Proelss et al, 'Protection of Cetaceans in European Waters—A Case Study on Bottom-Set Gillnet Fisheries within Marine Protected Areas' (2011) 26 *International Journal of Marine and Coastal Law* 5.

This requirement is further bolstered in Article 15 of the directive, which requires Member States to prohibit 'the use of all indiscriminate means capable of causing local disappearance of, or serious disturbance to, populations of such species'.

For terrestrial species, there is little obvious legal impediment to the development of policies by the individual Member States to implement this obligation. However, for marine species, discharging commitments under Article 12(4) will inevitably require the introduction of restrictions on fishing activities. So, while Article 12(4) may technically mandate further by-catch mitigation measures, in practice Member States are not freely able to swiftly adopt such policies in the manner envisaged by this provision.

Instead, having transferred legislative competence over fisheries to the EC, a Member State wishing to introduce protection measures in the context of by-catches must instead rely on powers delegated by the Council. In this respect, the Basic Regulation prescribes a highly limited scope for the unilateral imposition of emergency environmental measures. Where a particularly pressing situation arises, a Member State must, in the first instance, request that the Commission introduces temporary emergency measures.[122] Member States retain a power under Article 8 to introduce measures for a period of up to three months in duration, but the development of mitigation strategies on a more sustained basis remains the responsibility of the EU. This position offers considerably less flexibility to Member States to mitigate individualised by-catch concerns in national waters that may not be replicated on a Community-wide basis and may be therefore less likely to command EU attention.

Indeed, this has been strikingly illustrated in the attempts by the UK to significant marine mammal by-catches from pair-trawling within its territorial sea, eventually leading to a judicial review of national policies.[123] With the UK having previously registered concerns over cetacean by-catches in this fishery in 2003,[124] the Commission rejected an application under Article 7 of Regulation 2371 for emergency measures.[125] The UK authorities responded with temporary emergency measures under Article 8,[126] but have since been restricted in attempts to develop a more permanent national solution in this particular location, despite the demands of Article 12(4) of the Habitats Directive. The dichotomy between environmental and fisheries competences therefore has clear and negative implications for the development of effective by-catch policies and the ability

---

[122] Art 7 of Regulation 2371/2002. A refusal may be overruled by the Council by a qualified majority vote.

[123] *Greenpeace Ltd v Secretary of State for the Environment, Food and Rural Affairs* [2005] EWHC 2144 (High Court judgment); [2005] EWCA Civ 1656 (Court of Appeal judgment).

[124] Written Question E-0482/03 [2003] OJ 243E/135. In response, remedial measures were 'not considered a high priority'.

[125] [2005] EWHC 2144, para 22.

[126] South-West Territorial Waters (Prohibition of Pair Trawling) Order 2004 (SI 2004/3397), amended by South-West Territorial Waters (Prohibition of Pair Trawling) (Amendment) Order 2005 (SI 2005/49).

of individual Member States to respond swiftly to emerging threats to protected marine species from fisheries interactions.

Conclusion

In many respects, the EU has an important role to play in the protection of the marine environment. It is endowed with legislative powers, structural funding and enforcement mechanisms that are largely absent from many other marine regulators. Despite the initially slow rate of progress, the Habitats Directive regime is seemingly better placed to deliver a network of MPAs with clear powers of designation, monitoring and review that are not generally replicated in other major marine regions. Likewise, the strong emphasis on marine concerns within the various political organs of the EU also present opportunities for the development of further regional legislation to protect such species, underpinned by a clear system of judicial enforcement. Moreover, there is considerable scope for financial assistance for research activities through schemes such as EU LIFE to contribute towards addressing the deficient knowledge base on species by funding long-term projects.

Despite these clear advantages, the legal framework pertaining to marine species is subject to certain key shortcomings that will require further supervision by the EU institutions in order to ensure that the legislation is properly and effectively transposed. While the Habitats Directive presents strong conservation possibilities in an aquatic context, the Commission must nonetheless continue to apply pressure on the Member States to designate further SACs for marine species. Moreover, considerable assistance may be required within the new Member States in order to ensure a relatively swift establishment of a network of SACs in the Baltic and Black Sea regions. Ultimately, however, conservation efforts under the Habitats Directive are to an extent undermined by the very high scientific thresholds for the identification of potential Natura 2000 sites in the first instance and, more importantly, by the permissive nature of Article 6 that allows considerable leeway for the continuation of major industrial activities within SACs. As Verschuuren notes: 'So far, many of the SPAs and SACs are small islands where large-scale economic activities are dominant'.[127] Given the major industrial importance of key areas of marine habitats, it is likely that this fate will be replicated in many emerging SACs.

As far as the further development of marine species policy is concerned, it may be considered that future regulatory initiatives are likely to be increasingly based around one key issue: anthropogenic ocean noise. More specifically, such policies

---

[127] J Verschuuren, 'Effectiveness of Nature Protection Legislation in the EU and the US: The Birds and Habitats Directive and the Endangered Species Act' (2003) 3 *Yearbook of European Environmental Law* 303, 328.

are likely to address the impacts of seismic testing and oil exploration activities, as well as vessel-source noise, which have not as yet been substantively tested in the context of the Habitats Directive. Tensions are also raised over the use of military sonar in European waters. Indeed, given that the EU is currently precluded from developing binding standards in relation to the use of military sonar,[128] consideration of this issue is likely to remain confined to the realms of ad hoc pronouncements and political lamentation concerning the effect of this equipment upon the marine environment.[129] Instead, initiatives through NATO will, in practice, be instrumental in developing safer standards for military sonar, which may then be incorporated into national legislation on a voluntary basis by the Member States. In the meantime, the Commission considers—somewhat optimistically, perhaps—that 'Article 6(3) and (4) of the Habitats Directive provides a balanced framework to solve possible conflicts of interest between military activities and nature protection issues'.[130]

Indeed, as far as civilian sources of noise and disturbance are concerned, Article 6 of the Habitats Directive will continue to play a primary—and not uncontroversial—role. Some concerns may be expressed that this provision, on its current construction, will offer a less than optimal degree of protection to marine species, while the balance of interests envisaged under Article 6 may be increasingly tipped in favour of economic interests. Given the importance of industrial and resource extraction activities in areas of critical habitats, it is likely that the public interest exemption will be increasingly invoked in a marine context. Moreover, there are a number of examples of national legislation within the Member States that, although in conformity with Article 6, nonetheless prescribe considerable preference to mineral extraction and the development of offshore windfarms over the conservation of protected areas.[131] Such legislation will continue to run the gauntlet of the permissive provisions of the Habitats Directive in this respect, for which there is a pressing need for clear guidance both from the Commission on operational requirements within and around marine SACs, as well as the CJEU in adjudicating what is likely to be an increasing volume of litigation on these issues.

Ultimately, and despite these deficiencies within the current framework, the EU offers significant regulatory opportunities to address the conservation needs of marine species and, moreover, has consistently exercised a strong political and legislative will to do so. The priority activities for the coming years should therefore be focused on nurturing and increasing the collective Natura 2000 capacity—

---

[128] Article 2(2) MSFD.

[129] European Parliament Resolution on the Environmental Effects of High-Intensity Active Naval Sonars [B6-0089/2004].

[130] Marine Guidelines, 101.

[131] A particular example is the current *Bundesnaturschutzgesetz* in Germany, in which '[t]he preference given to mining and wind power is rather astonishing': D Czybulka and T Bosecke, 'Marine Protected Areas in the EEZ in Light of International and European Community Law—Legal Basis and Aspects of Implementation' in von Nordheim, Boedeker and Krause, above n 47, 43.

possibly involving the amendment of Annex II of the Habitats Directive to include a greater number of species—as well as striking a more effective balance with oil and gas exploration and extraction in current and future SACs. Such activities should also be complemented by balancing fisheries and biodiversity competences and in continuing to advance influential conservation policies within key international fora.

12

Judicial Review, the Precautionary Principle and the Protection of Habitats: Do we have a System of Administrative Law yet?

DENIS EDWARDS

Introduction

In *Chevron USA v Natural Resources Defence Council*,[1] Justice Stevens writing for the US Supreme Court in its landmark decision on administrative law concluded his Opinion in this way:

> When a challenge to an agency construction of a statutory provision, fairly conceptualized, really centers on the wisdom of the agency's policy, rather than whether it is a reasonable choice within a gap left open by Congress, the challenge must fail. In such a case, federal judges—who have no constituency—have a duty to respect legitimate policy choices made by those who do. The responsibilities for assessing the wisdom of such policy choices and resolving the struggle between competing views of the public interest are not judicial ones: 'Our Constitution vests such responsibilities in the political branches': *TVA v Hill*, 437 US 153, 195 (1978).

It is notable that the Supreme Court signed-off its decision in *Chevron*, which mandates judicial deference to administrative decision-makers in many cases, by citing its leading environmental law decision in *TVA v Hill*[2] some six years previously. *TVA v Hill* is as much a high water mark of judicial intervention to restrain administrative decisions which have environmental impacts as *Chevron* is for deference. The quotation from *TVA v Hill* which Justice Stevens relies on in *Chevron* seems ironic given what the earlier decision actually decided.

In *TVA v Hill*, the Supreme Court ruled that, although 'the political branches' rather than the courts were responsible for resolving 'competing views of the

---

[1] *Chevron USA v Natural Resources Defence Council* 467 US 837 (1984) (*Chevron*).
[2] *TVA v Hill* 437 US 153 (1978).

public interest', section 7(a)(2) of the Endangered Species Act[3] meant that an almost completed dam on the Little Tennessee River could be stopped because it was 'likely … to jeopardize the continued existence' of snail darters. This rare species of small fish, only found in Tennessee, had been discovered shortly before completion of the dam. Having been listed as an endangered species by the relevant federal agency, the question for the Supreme Court was whether Congress intended the legislation to stop projects which, at considerable expense, were almost completed and which, moreover, had been begun before the legislation was enacted. The legislation was unclear on this point. Nevertheless, the Court's majority concluded that the legislation was to be understood as requiring the dam to be stopped. Neither the legislation's lack of clarity on its retrospective effects nor cost were relevant where the dam would jeopardise the continued existence of the snail darter.

In *Chevron*, the Supreme Court decided that judicial review of administrative (or agency) action involved two steps. First, where statutory language or intent is clear, judicial review is available to ensure that the decision-maker has complied with the law. The test of the lawfulness of the challenged decision in this case is 'correctness' and no deference is called for. It is for the court to say what the law means. But where the statute is silent on the particular matter, or the statutory language is ambiguous or has left a lacuna, judicial review is limited. Deference is the watchword: only if the decision-maker has come to what a British lawyer would essentially understand as a *Wednesbury*[4] unreasonable decision on the meaning or intendment of the statute, should the courts intervene. And the *Wednesbury*-like review entails no concept of 'anxious scrutiny'.[5]

Would *TVA v Hill* be decided differently in light of *Chevron*? The division of the Court in the earlier case concerned whether or not the statute was clear. The majority thought that it was while Justices Powell and Blackmun dissented, disagreeing that the statute intended to protect the snail darters where the dam was almost complete. The second step of *Chevron*, namely the test for judicial review where there was uncertainty about what the statute intended, was not reached. As to that, the *TVA v Hill* dissenters concurred in *Chevron* on the test for judicial review in such cases.

The interest which these two US Supreme Court decisions have for administrative law and environmental law in the UK lies in what they say about judicial review. When judicial review is used to challenge decisions affecting the

---

[3] 16 USC 1301–11.

[4] *Associated Provincial Picture Houses Ltd v Wednesbury Corporation* [1948] KB 223.

[5] A term unlikely to be recognised in US federal administrative law; but one which has something of a counterpart in the concept of 'strict scrutiny' which applies to laws or decisions infringing fundamental constitutional rights guaranteed by the US Bill of Rights. Strict scrutiny is the highest tier of scrutiny under the US Bill of Rights. The adoption of tiers of scrutiny itself resulted from criticism of *too much* judicial review at the time of the New Deal, mainly a result of the doctrine of substantive due process established by the well-known case of *Lochner v New York* 198 US 45 (1905), overruled by *West Coast Hotel v Parish* 300 US 379 (1937). The doctrine of tiers of scrutiny is most famously articulated in footnote 4 to Justice Stone's opinion in *Carolene Products* 304 US 144 (1938).

environment and in particular, where reliance is placed on the precautionary principle, on what basis do courts in this country decide whether the challenged decision is to be reviewed with deference to the decision-maker, or on a stricter, more intensive basis—whether it is termed 'hard edged' or correctness review, or 'anxious scrutiny'?

The UK Legal System

I suggest that in the UK legal systems we still do not have a clear answer to this question. This is largely because we still do not have an established doctrine on the intensity of judicial review, or rather the intensity with which the courts will review challenged decisions on the various grounds for judicial review which administrative law recognises. This suggestion may seem surprising to those who regularly teach and practise administrative law, who can fairly point out that the leading works on judicial review and numerous cases acknowledge that judicial review involves variable standards of review depending on the context. This is true. But my concern is that the courts' approach to the intensity of judicial review is unsystematic, lacks coherence and, importantly from litigants' and their advisors' point of view, is not predictable.

Before the Human Rights Act 1998 (HRA) gave rise to grounds for judicial review alleging breach of the Convention rights, the subject of the intensity of judicial review was either rolled-up with the question of justiciability or tied to the question of what one ground for judicial review, namely *Wednesbury* unreasonableness, meant for particular cases. Indeed, the latter question was usually posed in the context of whether review for *Wednesbury* unreasonableness in some cases required the court to consider the lawfulness of the substance of the challenged decision. These cases usually concerned decisions which were challenged by reference to the Convention rights.[6] Human rights considerations, therefore, provided the context of discussion of the intensity of judicial review. Since the introduction of the HRA, the subject of the variable intensity of judicial review has become more topical but it is far from clear how much of the discussion in that field carries over to the rest of judicial review, including where challenges are brought against decisions affecting the environment. This gives rise to a number of difficulties.

First, there is a danger of the 'bifurcation' of judicial review, a prospect much criticised by some leading commentators.[7] The risk is that there will develop one system of judicial review, burgeoning every year, comprising judicial review on human rights grounds, where, largely thanks to the novelty of 'proportionality', the courts vary the intensity of judicial review on the basis of a number of

---

[6] Before they were given effect in domestic law by the HRA.

[7] See Hunt, 'Against Bifurcation' in Dyzenhaus, Hunt and Huscroft, *A Simple Common Lawyer: Essays in Honour of Michael Taggart* (Hart Publishing, 2009).

considerations. In contrast, the other system—the rest of judicial review—continues to avoid the issue of the intensity of judicial review and adheres to the notion that the grounds for judicial review apply in the same way to all decisions. Outside human rights, there is no heightened scrutiny. This 'bifurcation' is at the very least unhelpful for administrative law. On the one hand it seems to accept that only one, albeit important, set of principles, human rights, merit a contextualised approach to judicial review which acknowledges that there are 'tiers of scrutiny' depending on the nature of the challenged decision and the grounds on which it is challenged. On the other, it hides the need for any *system* of administrative law to accept that judicial supervision of administrative decisions must always rest on grounds for judicial review the intensity of which differs from case to case.

Secondly, the notion that judicial review must always be exercised on the strictest or most anxious basis simply because human rights are raised will ultimately defeat the purpose which judicial review on human rights grounds serves. To say that anxious scrutiny of decisions is always required whenever a claimant argues that his human rights are infringed devalues human rights. There will be cases, unfortunately far too many, where the human rights arguments against the decision are so weak that to bring 'anxious scrutiny' to the decision makes judicial review look ridiculous.

Thirdly, the failure to acknowledge that judicial review beyond human rights must also have variable intensity means that judicial review in other cases, where fundamental human rights are not raised, may fail to bring more intense scrutiny to a challenged decision where the issues call for it. This may be true for at least some cases in which protection of the environment is one of the issues. The point is that an effective system of judicial review, whether or not on human rights grounds, must have not only its *Chevron*, acknowledging the need for deference; it must also have its *TVA v Hill*.

The UK Courts' Approach to the Habitats Directive

By considering some of the UK courts' decisions in judicial review claims based on the precautionary principle under the Habitats Directive,[8] I argue that the absence of a systematic approach to the intensity of judicial review is a defect in our administrative law. It explains why the UK experience of judicial review of decisions affecting the environment, in particular, where the issue has concerned the risk to habitats, has been mixed. Stookes describes the British courts as having trodden 'an uncertain habitats path'.[9] In her article, 'Is the Precautionary Principle

---

[8] Directive 92/43/EEC on the conservation of natural habitats (the Habitats Directive). The Habitats Directive was transposed into domestic law (for England and Wales and Scotland) by the Conservation (Natural Habitats, etc) Regulations 1994 (SI 1994/2716) (the Regulations). Separate Regulations implemented the Directive in Northern Ireland.
[9] See Stookes, ch 8 in this volume at p 143.

Justiciable',[10] Dr Elizabeth Fisher concluded that 'the precautionary principle ... requires a readjustment to how ... the court and executive interact' and that it is 'not just about the development of environmental law but administrative law more generally'.[11] Progress in both areas remains slow.

This is all the more troubling given that EU law has been central in the cases and that EU law has an established case law on the appropriate intensity of judicial review in different cases. Given that the EU Treaty enshrines the precautionary principle as one of the central principles of EU environmental law, in effect giving it a status akin to constitutional law in the EU and the Member States, it may be asked whether the lack of a coherent approach to the intensity of judicial review in the UK systems of administrative law means that judicial review in the UK is not always an effective remedy where the precautionary principle is relied on.

I explore some of these issues in the following way. First, what is the current state of the law on the intensity with which the courts review particular decisions which are challenged by way of judicial review? Secondly, by considering some recent UK cases, what is the appropriate test for judicial review relying on the precautionary principle under the Habitats Directive? Specifically, how have courts approached the question of the appropriate scrutiny that they should bring to decisions which are challenged in judicial review relying on the precautionary principle in this context? Finally, in light of my conclusion that there is no systematic approach to the intensity of judicial review, can it be said that domestic law satisfies the requirements of effectiveness under EU law?

The Variable Intensity of Judicial Review

In *R v Department for Education and Employment, ex p Begbie*,[12] Laws LJ stated that, 'it is now well established that the *Wednesbury* principle itself constitutes a sliding scale of review, more or less intrusive according to the nature and gravity of what is at stake'.[13] Yet it is still unclear, even in cases where judicial review relies on the Convention rights, how the court determines where on the 'scale' a particular decision falls to be reviewed.

At one extreme on the scale, considerations of justiciability will lead to there being no, or very minimal, judicial review. Some issues, for example, the state's decision to go to war,[14] are non-justiciable and in respect of those, the court is 'constitutionally

---

[10] (2001) 13 *Journal of Environmentl Law* 315.
[11] Ibid, 334.
[12] *R v Department for Education and Employment, ex p Begbie* [2000] 1 WLR 1115.
[13] Ibid, 1130.
[14] *Cf CND v The Prime Minister and others* [2002] EWHC 2777 (Admin). But at least the court was prepared to give CND the benefit of a protective costs order in order to establish that its claim was non-justiciable: *R v the Prime Minister (Costs)* [2002] EWHC 2712 (Admin).

disabled from entering on review'.[15] Beyond strictly non-justiciable issues, the political sensitivity of the issues raised by a claim can lead to concerns about the courts' capability to adjudicate on them. The problem here is either that the subject matter of the claim ultimately concerns high policy matters,[16] or the dispute between the parties raises 'polycentric' issues.[17] In such cases, there will either be no judicial review, or judicial review will be available on limited grounds,[18] or the court will exercise its supervisory jurisdiction with a 'light touch'.[19] Inevitably, the identification of non-justiciable matters remains controversial, as does the question of whether the court has no role at all over such matters.[20]

At the other extreme on Laws LJ's sliding scale, the court will bring the most intense scrutiny to the challenged decision. This has come to be termed 'anxious scrutiny'.[21] This developed before the HRA where decisions were claimed to breach fundamental human rights. In *R v Ministry of Defence, ex p Smith*,[22] Bingham MR explained that when deciding whether a decision was *Wednesbury* unreasonable, 'the test itself is sufficiently flexible to cover all situations'.[23] Where fundamental human rights were relied on, 'the human rights context is important': 'The more substantial the interference with human rights, the more the court will require by way of justification before it is satisfied that the decision is reasonable.'[24]

Since the HRA entered force in 2000, judicial review on human rights grounds has led to 'proportionality' being accepted as a ground for judicial review.[25] There is much support for the proposition that the courts should apply proportionality according

---

[15] De Smith, *Judicial Review of Administrative Action* (6th edn) (London, Sweet & Maxwell, 2007) para 11–097.

[16] Eg *R v Secretary of State for the Environment, ex p Notts CC* [1986] AC 240 (challenge to delegated legislation involving the implementation of national economic policy available on limited grounds for judicial review). For a recent discussion, see *R (Luton BC and others) v Secretary of State for Education* [2011] EWHC 217 (Admin).

[17] Eg *R v Cambridge District Health Authority, ex p B* [1995] 1 WLR 898 (courts cannot be arbiters in disputes about allocation of health service resources for particular patients where prospects of success of treatment limited or uncertain).

[18] As in *Notts CC* above n 16: judicial review to challenge the delegated legislation only available on grounds of illegality (including error of law, relevant and irrelevant considerations), procedural impropriety and irrationality so far as it alleges improper purposes or 'manifest absurdity'. See also *R v Secretary of State for the Environment, ex p Hammersmith and Fulham LBCs* [1991] 1 AC 521; and *R (Luton BC and others) v Secretary of State for Education*, above n 16.

[19] Eg *R v Chief Constable of Sussex, ex p International Trader's Ferry Ltd* [1999] 2 AC 418 (courts should defer to the decision-maker's specialist knowledge when judicially reviewing exercises of discretion to deploy limited resources).

[20] Cf *R (Bancoult) v Secretary of State for Foreign and Commonwealth Affairs* [2009] 1 AC 453.

[21] The term was first used in *R v Secretary of State for the Home Department, ex p Bugdaycay* [1987] AC 514, at 531 *per* Lord Bridge of Harwich. However, earlier cases indicate that *Wednesbury* unreasonableness can entail stricter requirements in some contexts: see, eg *Wheeler v Leicester CC* [1985] AC 1054.

[22] *R v Ministry of Defence, ex p Smith* [1996] 2 WLR 305.

[23] Ibid, 338.

[24] Ibid, 336 approving a submission of David Pannick QC.

[25] *R (Daly) v Secretary of State for the Home Department* [2001] 2 AC 532. Proportionality, as a general principle of EU law, is also a ground for judicial review when EU law is raised.

to a structured approach,[26] reflecting the fact that review for proportionality leads to more or less intense scrutiny of a decision depending on all the issues involved. There is sometimes an assumption that proportionality means heightened scrutiny,[27] even leading to merits review,[28] but this is not necessarily so. Proportionality is itself a variable standard, the rigour with which it is applied always depending on the relative importance which the court ascribes to the various interests which have to be balanced against each other. Similarly, whether measures are 'necessary' to achieve an important objective will often depend not on interest balancing as such, but on what the court thinks about how practicable alternative measures are to achieve the objective.

In any event, the acceptance of proportionality as a general ground for judicial review has led to a debate on what it means for *Wednesbury* unreasonableness.[29] In particular, how different is review for *Wednesbury* unreasonableness with anxious scrutiny from review for proportionality? Or, indeed, how different is review for proportionality, with deference to the decision-maker, from review for 'pure' *Wednesbury* unreasonableness?

For present purposes, the interest in these developments is that the courts have acknowledged the need for heightened scrutiny of challenged decisions in some contexts, mostly where human rights are relied on.[30] In the field of human rights, *Wednesbury* unreasonableness, whether with or without anxious scrutiny, has been superseded by proportionality—although even here, the picture is not completely clear that proportionality is always the test.[31] Beyond human rights, it is not clear whether 'anxious scrutiny' is ever called for, or if it is, when. Even limited to the ground for judicial review which is unreasonableness, it is also unclear what intermediates there are between 'anxious scrutiny' and 'pure' *Wednesbury*.

It has sometimes been decided that 'anxious scrutiny' can apply beyond human rights cases. For example, the Hong Kong courts have acknowledged that 'anxious scrutiny' can apply in cases where a decision affecting the environment is challenged on *Wednesbury* grounds.[32] In *Town Planning Board v Society for the Protection of the Harbour Ltd*, the Hong Kong Court of Final Appeal had to decide whether the government had properly conducted an environmental impact

---

[26] See *Daly*, ibid. The leading statement of what proportionality requires for judicial review is undoubtedly the landmark decision of the Supreme Court of Canada in *R v Oakes* [1986] 1 SCR 103 (albeit in the setting of constitutional judicial review). See further, Elliott, 'Proportionality and Deference: the importance of a structured approach', in Forsyth et al, *Effective Judicial Review: A Cornerstone of Good Government* (Oxford University Press, 2010).

[27] Eg *R v Shayler* [2003] 1 AC 247, para 33 *per* Lord Bingham ('much more rigorous review' than once thought permissible).

[28] Eg *R v Secretary of State for the Home Department, ex p Nasseri* [2010] 1 AC 1 paras 13, 14.

[29] See, eg Le Sueur, 'The Rise and Ruin of Unreasonableness' (2005) *Judicial Review* 32.

[30] *Huang v Secretary of State for the Home Department* [2007] 2 AC 167.

[31] Cf *Pro-Life Alliance v BBC* [2004] 1 AC 185 (decision banning political broadcast only to be interfered with if 'arbitrary'; Lord Scott dissenting, that proportionality analysis is appropriate).

[32] See *Town Planning Board v Society for the Protection of the Harbour Ltd* [2004] 1 HKRLD 396 (Court of Final Appeal); *Society for Protection of the Harbour Ltd v Chief Executive in Council (No 2)* [2004] 2 HKLD 902 (Court of First Instance).

assessment of a large transport development project which involved reclaiming part of Victoria Harbour. This harbour, a unique urban space, had been encroached many times in the past and the concern was that any further land reclamation would destroy the waterway. As to the appropriate level of scrutiny which the Court was required to bring to the challenged decision, the Court of Final Appeal observed:

> With the dynamic development of the common law, whilst the courts' jurisdiction on judicial review remains a supervisory one, a real question exists as to whether there is a sliding scale of review, with the intensity of review depending on the subject matter of the decision. On this approach, the standard of review would be most intensive where a fundamental human right is in question ... That question does not arise in the present case ... [where] the Ordinance does not give rise to any fundamental or constitutional right ... [but should] the standard ... only be the traditional standard for irrationality or ... having regard to the unique legal status of the harbour ... a more intensive one.[33]

When the matter was remitted back to the Court of First Instance, Hartmann J ruled that 'something more rigorous than the standard *Wednesbury* test is required' because of the need to preserve the unique legal status of the harbour.[34] However, the level of 'anxious scrutiny' called for in fundamental human rights cases 'set the test too high'.[35]

Significant as these Hong Kong cases are in showing that environmental interests can merit anxious scrutiny from the courts, they also serve to underline the difficulties of determining the appropriate level of scrutiny which the courts should bring to particular cases. In the first place, the practical implications of 'anxious scrutiny' continue to cause the courts considerable difficulties.[36] For example, does it allow the court *itself*, contrary to the usual practice in judicial review, to assess the weight which the decision-maker has given to relevant considerations? If so, does 'anxious scrutiny' mean merits review? The courts continue to stress that the judicial task is one of *review*. But if that is so, what is really different about 'anxious' scrutiny?

Secondly, in so far as more rigorous review, whether for proportionality or with anxious *Wednesbury*, requires more of the decision-maker by way of justification for the decision, including fuller reasons, more detailed evidence, better processes and clearer explanations about the weight placed on particular matters, the issue of any need for deference to the decision-maker's judgment remains controversial. Prompted again by the HRA and judicial review for proportionality which has

---

[33] *Town Planning Board v Society for the Protection of the Harbour Ltd* [2004] 1 HKRLD 396, paras 67–68.

[34] [2004] 2 HKRLD 902, para 79.

[35] Ibid.

[36] Most of the cases are in the field of immigration law. In one recent case, Maurice Kay LJ observed that the pace of the case law on what 'anxious scrutiny' meant in practice was 'frenetic' and appeared unmethodical: *MN (Tanzania)* [2011] EWCA Civ 193. Other cases exploring the meaning of 'anxious scrutiny' include: *QY (China)* [2009] EWCA Civ 680 and *AS (Sri Lanka)* [2009] EWHC 1763 (Admin) (judgment of Carnwath LJ).

grown in its wake, a rich commentary has grown up in English public law about deference and when it is and is not called for.[37] So far, the courts have declined to engage with this issue on a higher plane concerning their constitutional role,[38] preferring to deal with issues of deference only where the subject matter of the challenged decision, or the specialist nature of the decision-maker, calls for it.[39]

Thirdly, between the extremes of 'anxious' and pure *Wednesbury*, the intensity of judicial review and the role of judicial deference (if any) are also not clear. The cases which have been decided on the powers of regulators have tended to involve light touch review, with much deference and *Wednesbury* unreasonableness cast in its purest form of perversity.[40] In particular, in the few cases which there have been where the precautionary principle has been relied on to challenge a decision, considerations of non-justiciability have often been to the fore.[41]

Fourthly, discussion of the variable intensity of judicial review has focused on *Wednesbury* unreasonableness and proportionality. Some attention has been paid to it where *substantive* legitimate expectations are sought to be protected,[42] which permits the observation that consideration of the intensity of judicial review and the role of deference is only thought necessary where judicial review might touch on the substance or merits of a decision. But the appropriate intensity with which the court should exercise its inherent, supervisory jurisdiction, viz whether it should be on a more rigorous or 'anxious' basis, or start from paying deference to the decision-maker, is relevant for all of the grounds for judicial review. It is certainly not limited to *Wednesbury* unreasonableness.

Much of the problem in English law continues to be with the concept of 'jurisdiction'. It is often thought that *Anisminic* put an end to the complexity of this matter, taken as it eventually was, to abolish the distinction between errors of law which go to jurisdiction and those within it.[43] But this solution simply

---

[37] Eg Clayton, 'Judicial deference and "democratic dialogue": the legitimacy of judicial interven-tion under the Human Rights Act 1998' (2004) *Public Law* 33; and Allan, 'Human Rights and Judicial Review: A Critique of Due Deference' (2006) *Cambridge Law Journal* 671.

[38] *Cf Huang v Secretary of State for the Home Department* [2007] 2 AC 167, drawing the ire of at least one distinguished scholar: see Taggart, 'Proportionality, Deference, *Wednesbury*' (2008) *New Zealand Law Review* 423.

[39] *Cf AH (Sudan) v Secretary of State for the Home Department* [2008] 1 AC 678, para 30, *per* Baroness Hale of Richmond. See also *R (Cart) v Upper Tribunal* [2011] QB 120 and compare the different answer to the same issue by the Court of Session in *Eba v Advocate General for Scotland* [2010] CSIH 78. The Supreme Court has now decided both these cases: see *Cart* [2011] 3 WLR 107 and *Eba* [2011] 3 WLR 149, discussed further below.

[40] Eg *R (ABS Financial Planning Ltd) v Financial Services Compensation Scheme Ltd* [2010] EWHC 18 (Admin), para 62 *per* Beatson J.

[41] Eg *R v Secretary of State for Trade and Industry, ex p Duddridge* (1995) *J Env L* 224 (Div Ct), [1996] *Env LR* 325 (CA).

[42] This was the context for the discussion in *Begbie*, above n 12.

[43] *Anisminic v Foreign Compensation Commission* [1969] 2 AC 147, as glossed by *Pearlman v Harrow School* [1979] QB 56 and *Re Racal Communications* [1981] AC 374. But *cf R v Monopolies and Mergers Commission, ex p South Yorkshire Transport* [1993] 1 WLR 23, especially *per* Lord Mustill at 32. More recently, some judges have questioned whether the *Anisminic* settlement, that all errors of law are jurisdictional, is the last word on the matter: see, eg *R (Lumba) v Secretary of State for the Home Department* [2011] 2 WLR 671, *per* Lord Walker JSC at paras 192 and 193.

hides, or rather, avoids the real issues which are central to judicial review.[44] In short, a 'correctness' standard cannot always be the test for judicial review. There must be a systematic approach to the appropriate intensity of judicial review for all the grounds for judicial review, one which incorporates the need for deference, as appropriate, and also more rigorous scrutiny by the court on the basis of identifiable factors, including the particular grounds on which the decision is challenged. Only then can deference have its proper place and the court have the institutional confidence to bring the most rigorous scrutiny to decisions which call for it.

The growth of judicial review on Convention rights grounds and the doctrine of proportionality have eclipsed any meaningful analysis of the variable intensity of judicial review when human rights are not in issue. Too often, the matter is approached either by reference to non-justiciability or the need for deference, for example, because of the specialised nature of the decision-maker. There seems to be no middle way between this approach and 'anxious scrutiny', with the latter only being thought appropriate where human rights are raised. In turn, the courts have not settled on any test for deciding how intense judicial review should be for different types of cases. Difficult as the task is, it cannot be avoided for ever. The problem is how to decide in advance if the issues deserve more or less intense judicial review: correctness review, a more deferential, lighter touch, or something in between. Tuning judicial review to the context in which it is exercised is necessary if judicial review is to be effective.

Other Systems of Administrative Law

In other systems of administrative law, courts have attempted to grapple with these issues in a systematic way.[45] In the US, *Chevron* adopts a rule of deference save where the legislature has clearly provided for or envisaged the situation at hand, in which case the court can itself decide what the law requires. This is one approach.

---

[44] For example, it says nothing about the intensity of review for different types of error of law, or where deference is called for, eg of factual findings by specialist tribunals. Indeed, error as to those must meet a high threshold of 'unreasonableness': *Edwards v Bairstow* [1956] AC 14, especially at 36 *per* Lord Radcliffe (factual errors, at least by judicial tribunals, give rise to errors of law only if 'no person acting judicially' could have come to the decision).

[45] I am bound to acknowledge that in many other systems, including in the US and Canada, the term 'judicial review' encompasses judicial review of administrative action and judicial review on *constitutional* grounds (eg where legislative competence or constitutionally guaranteed human rights are raised). Under the UK arrangements, the absence of guaranteed constitutional norms means that judicial review covers both cases which have significant constitutional significance and those which do not. But the existence or not of constitutional review is not a reason to avoid debate on the intensity of judicial review for different categories of case. Indeed, it may be said that where fundamental EU law rules are raised in judicial review, the UK courts are engaged in constitutional review.

In Canada, a more nuanced, but recognisably *Chevron* approach, has recently been explained. The Supreme Court of Canada has made great efforts to establish a systematic approach to the appropriate intensity of judicial review in administrative law, trying and testing a number of formulae over the years. Most recently, in *Dunsmuir v New Brunswick*,[46] the Supreme Court decided that there were only two standards for judicial review: correctness or unreasonableness. In deciding which standard applied to the case at hand, and what the appropriate intensity of judicial review or deference should be, an adapted 'standard of review analysis' governed. In essence, correctness is the standard where constitutional issues (including Charter rights and, through them, fairness) are raised, or the question concerns the (threshold) jurisdiction of the decision-maker to decide the matter. It will also be the standard for questions of 'general law', including those which are 'of central importance to the legal system'. However, deference may be called for where questions of law are within 'the adjudicator's special area of expertise'. Deference is certainly required where the decision is protected by a privative (or ouster) clause.

Unreasonableless, applied more or less intensively depending on context and whether deference is called for, is the appropriate standard for reviewing issues of fact, discretion or policy and interpretations of the authority's 'own statute or statutes closely connected to its function, with which it will have particular familiarity'.

The result in *Dunsmuir* (and equally, the approach in *Chevron*) may not be universally welcomed or to everyone's taste. The point is that its important contribution is in acknowledging the need for a systematic approach to 'standard of review analysis', one which rationalises the grounds for judicial review according to standards for review and accepts both the need for deference in appropriate cases and a more rigorous, including correctness standard in others.

On one view, the British courts have begun to move in this direction in one narrow field, namely, where decisions of the Upper Tribunal refusing permission for a further appeal to the Court of Appeal or the Court of Session are challenged by way of judicial review. In the landmark decisions of *R (Cart) v Upper Tribunal*[47] and *Eba v Advocate General for Scotland*,[48] the Supreme Court held that unappealable decisions of the Upper Tribunal are only subject to judicial review if they raise an important point of principle or practice or some other compelling reason why the case should be heard. It follows that a court which is deciding whether to hear a judicial review claim against the Upper Tribunal must engage in a form of standard of review analysis before deciding even whether the claim can be heard. This being so, it is not a great jump to expect courts to engage in a standard of review analysis in all judicial review cases and not simply exceptional

---

[46] *Dunsmuir v New Brunswick* [2008] 1 SCR 190. For a discussion of this decision and its background, see Walters, 'Jurisdiction, Functionalism and Constitutionalism in Canadian Administrative Law', in Forsyth et al, *Effective Judicial Review: A Cornerstone of Good Governance* (Oxford University Press, 2010).

[47] *R (Cart) v Upper Tribunal* [2011] 3 WLR 107.

[48] *Eba v Advocate General for Scotland* [2011] 3 WLR 149.

ones. Indeed, the fact that something akin to it has to be done in some cases suggests that there are good reasons for doing it in all cases, as part of a systematic approach to judicial review.

European Union Law

The Court of Justice of the European Union (CJEU) has established an elaborate jurisprudence on the variable intensity of judicial review of EU acts and decisions. As Professor Craig has written:

> There is, in EU law, no case equivalent to *Chevron* in the USA, in which the CJEU has articulated a general approach to problems of [the variable intensity of judicial review]. A reading of the case law makes it clear none the less that the CJEU has in fact adopted a variable test for review when dealing with cases of this kind.[49]

The centrality of proportionality in EU law makes it inevitable that the CJEU varies the intensity of judicial review, whether of EU law or domestic measures, which are challenged before it. For example, in the well-known case of *R v MAFF, ex p Fedesa*,[50] the Court decided that where measures adopted under the Common Agricultural Policy are challenged, the test for judicial review is whether the measure is 'manifestly inappropriate having regard to the objective which the competent institution is seeking to pursue'.[51] In this field, the authorities had a 'margin of discretion' and judicial deference was called for.

In cases where complex scientific evidence is challenged, the CJEU has said that the test for 'manifest error' is a high one. In *Commission v Cambridge Healthcare Supplies Ltd*,[52] concerning a challenge to the licence for a medicine, the Court said (at paragraph 96 of its judgment)

> According to the Court's case-law, where a Community authority is called upon, in the performance of its duties, to make complex assessments, it enjoys a wide measure of discretion, the exercise of which is subject to a limited judicial review in the course of which the Community judicature may not substitute its assessment of the facts for the assessment made by the authority concerned. Thus, in such cases, the Community judicature must restrict itself to examining the accuracy of the findings of fact and law made by the authority concerned and to verifying, in particular, that the action taken by that authority is not vitiated by a manifest error or a misuse of powers and that it did not clearly exceed the bounds of its discretion.[53]

---

[49] Craig, 'Judicial Review, Intensity and Deference in EU Law', in Dyzenhaus: *The Unity of Public Law* (Hart Publishing, 2004) 339.

[50] Case C-331/88 *R v MAFF, ex p Fedesa* [1990] ECR 4023.

[51] Ibid, para 14.

[52] *Commission v Cambridge Healthcare Supplies Ltd* Case C-471/00.

[53] This dictum was relied on by the Court of Appeal in *Secretary of State for Environment, Food and Rural Affairs v Downs* [2009] Env LR 7, where (at para 43) Sullivan LJ considered it unnecessary on the facts of the case to identify where 'manifest error' ends and *Wednesbury* unreasonableness begins.

Clearly, deference has its place when the CJEU is exercising its powers of judicial review. That said, although the EU Treaties have excluded some matters from the EU courts' jurisdiction,[54] the CJEU does not have a doctrine of non-justiciability. The Court has not as a matter of principle bound itself not to review certain subjects on the grounds that they raise 'political questions' or concern policy which does not lend itself to judicial decision-making.

Where fundamental rules or principles of EU law are limited by national measures, the CJEU will bring more intense scrutiny to bear on the justification for the limitation. The case law is replete with instances of the CJEU deciding that although national measures limiting EU rights are in principle justifiable, on the evidence they were not proportionate. The anvil on which national measures often break is that they were not the least restrictive which could have been adopted to achieve the desired objective.[55] Alternatively, the severity of the impact which national measures have on free movement rules cannot be justified by the importance of the objectives which they are said to serve.[56]

The CJEU is the ultimate authority on what EU law means. While it is often said that there is a 'dialogue' between the CJEU and national courts, this does not mean that national courts can freely give their own meaning to EU law, or subject its requirements to the same approach which they take to judicial review in domestic law. The overriding principle is that EU law requires national law to ensure the full effectiveness of EU law and all national rules, substantive or procedural, must comply with this principle. Where EU law is raised in a case, the intensity of judicial review under domestic law must correspond to the requirements of EU law.

The Precautionary Principle and Judicial Review

In the few domestic judicial review cases which have considered the precautionary principle, the standard of review has been, at most, deferential to the decision-maker. In England, the leading case is still *R v Secretary of State for Trade and Industry, ex parte Duddridge*.[57] In the Divisional Court, the prevailing view was that the precautionary principle would normally give rise to non-justiciable matters. Smith J concluded that the principle gave rise to a balancing process requiring weighing up competing policy matters. In so far as the claim was justiciable, the decision of the Secretary of State was not *Wednesbury* unreasonable.

---

[54] Eg Arts 275 and 276 TFEU.
[55] Eg Case 30/77 *R v Bouchereau* [1977] ECR 1999.
[56] Eg Case 33/74 *Van Binsbergen* [1974] ECR 1999.
[57] *R v Secretary of State for Trade and Industry, ex p Duddridge* (1995) J Env L 224 (Div Ct), [1996] Env LR 325 (CA). The Divisional Court's judgment is discussed at length by Fisher, 'Is the Precautionary Principle Justiciable' (2001) *Journal of Environmental Law* 315, 323–24.

The standard for that was high, in line with the usual approach to challenges to regulatory decisions based on policy choices.

Dr Fisher's article, published in 2001 considered the way in which other common law courts have applied the precautionary principle in judicial review cases. Suffice to say that the principle has been relied on more frequently and with more varied results in other systems, though some part of the reason for this may be the availability of merits review by specialised courts and tribunals.

In the EU, the precautionary principle has been introduced into legislation in several areas and the principle has come before the EU courts a number of times. The results have been somewhat mixed. However, it does appear that the EU courts have adopted their standard practice of varying the intensity of their judicial review function according to the interests raised by the case. Sometimes, deference has been in the ascendant,[58] but at other times, more heightened scrutiny of the decision-maker's decision, including a greater judicial disposition to evaluate the evidence, has been apparent.[59] One commentator has said that in EU law 'the precautionary principle adapts proportionality to conditions of scientific uncertainty.'[60] Others are less complimentary and even doubt whether the precautionary principle is an appropriate tool for judicial review at all.[61]

In the field of environmental protection, the precautionary principle has been raised to a constitutional principle by Article 191(2) of the Treaty on the Functioning of the EU (TFEU). In this field, the CJEU has emphasised the importance of the principle as a measure of the legality of Member State measures, in particular where EU legislation has expressly given effect to the principle. One of the leading decisions of the CJEU is *Waddenzee*,[62] interpreting Article 6 of the Habitats Directive, which leads on to the next part of this paper.

Judicial Review and the Habitats Directive

The essential purpose of the Habitats Directive is the conservation of certain natural habitats and of wild fauna and flora. The Directive provides for special

---

[58] Eg Case T-13/99 *Pfizer* [2002] ECR II-3305 (banning animal foodstuffs containing antibiotics justified on the precautionary principle so as to avoid greater human immunity to antibiotics).

[59] Eg Case T-74/00 *Artegodan* [2002] ECR II-49 (precautionary principle did not justify banning medicinal products with amphetamine-like agents).

[60] Corkin, 'Science, Legitimacy and the Law: Regulating Risk Regulation Judiciously in the EC', (2008) 33 *European Law Review* 359, 374.

[61] See Ian Forrester, 'The Dangers of Too Much Precaution' in Hoskins and Robinson: *A True European: Essays for Judge David Edward* (Hart Publishing, 2003). Interestingly, Ian Forrester was counsel for Pfizer in case T-13/99 above.

[62] Case C-127/02 *Landelijke Vereniging tot Behoud van de Waddenzee, Nederlandse Vereniging tot Bescherming van Vogels v Staatssecretaris van Landbouw, Natuurbeheer en Visserij (Waddenzee)* [2004] ECR I-7405.

areas of conservation to be established in order to protect sites comprising natural habitats listed in Annex I to the Directive and sites comprising the habitats of species listed in Annex II. Along with Special Protection Areas (SPAs) designated under the Birds Directive,[63] Special Areas of Conservation (SACs) make up a scheme of protected areas, termed 'Natura 2000'.

The conservation objectives of the Directive are secured in a number of ways, most notably by the precautionary principle. For present purposes, it is necessary to consider Articles 6 and 12 of the Directive. Article 6(3) of the Directive provides:

> Any plan or project not directly connected with or necessary to the management of the site but likely to have a significant effect thereon, either individually or in combination with other plans or projects, shall be subject to appropriate assessments of its implications for the site in view of the site's conservation objectives. In the light of the conclusions of the assessment of the implications for the site and subject to the provisions of paragraph 4, the competent national authorities shall agree to the plan or project only after having ascertained that it will not adversely affect the integrity of the site and if appropriate after having obtained the opinion of the general public.

Accordingly, national authorities must perform assessments of the impact of plans or projects which are 'likely to have significant effects' on the site before the plan or project is approved. Normally, only plans or projects which will not adversely affect the integrity of the site can be authorised.

Article 12(1) provides:

> Member States shall take the requisite measures to establish a system of strict protection for the animal species listed in Annex IV(a) in their natural range, prohibiting –

> (a) all forms of deliberate capture or killing of specimens of these species in the wild;
> (b) deliberate disturbance of these species, particularly during the period of breeding, rearing, hibernation and migration;
> (c) deliberate destruction or taking of eggs from the wild;
> (d) deterioration or destruction of breeding sites or resting places.

When applying these provisions of the Habitats Directive, it is necessary to recall the EU Treaty background against which they must be understood. Article 191(2) of the TFEU requires that EU environmental policy is based on the need for a 'high level of protection' of the environment. It must be 'based on the precautionary principle and on the principles that preventive action should be taken' to protect the environment.

Although Article 191(2) probably does not have direct effect,[64] it is a prescriptive provision of the TFEU and, as such, is one which binds all domestic courts. This follows from Article 4(3) of the Treaty on European Union (TEU) (ex Article 10 of the EC Treaty). Further, the new provision in Article 19(1) of the TEU,

---

[63] Directive 79/409/EEC.

[64] *Cf* Fisher, above n 57, 323, citing *R v Secretary of State for Trade and Industry, ex p Duddridge* [1996] Env LR 325 (CA).

requiring Member States to provide 'remedies sufficient to ensure effective legal protection in the fields covered by Union law', arguably bolsters the established case law under Article 4(3) TEU concerning the duties of domestic courts to ensure the full effectiveness of EU law even where EU law rules do not have direct effect.[65]

Now it might reasonably be thought that Articles 6(3) and 12(1) of the Habitats Directive, where they are relied on in judicial review, give rise to a combination of pure questions of law, questions of mixed fact and law which are, of course, questions of law and questions, or issues, which require evaluation; in other words, of matters of fact and degree. Questions of law include what is a 'plan or project', what is 'likely' to have a 'significant effect', and what is 'deliberate disturbance or destruction'. Questions for evaluation, upon evidence, include whether national measures establish a system of 'strict' protection and whether a plan or project will *adversely* 'affect the integrity' of a site. At the very least, the court is as well placed to decide the questions of law which arise as are the appropriate authorities. Questions which depend solely on evaluation of the evidence may require some deference, though how much will ultimately be a matter for EU law. In both cases, however, the court ought to decide what approach to take to the test for judicial review, again in light of what the CJEU has decided.

Since all these terms raise questions of EU law, the CJEU ultimately decides what they mean, not least in the light of the precautionary principle enshrined in Article 191 TFEU. How should domestic courts approach judicial review claims which rely on Articles 6(3) and 12(1) of the Habitats Directive? Should authorities' decisions always be reviewed on a 'correctness' standard? Or only in respect of some issues? At the other extreme of the sliding scale, when is deference to the authority called for, how much and in respect of what issues?

The European Court of Justice's (ECJ) leading judgment on Article 6 of the Habitats Directive suggests that, what I will term heightened scrutiny, is called for over some questions arising under the Directive. For example, in *Waddenzee*[66] the ECJ decided that for the purposes of Article 6(3) of the Directive, the word 'likely' meant 'probable'. As Scott notes, the ECJ employed a teleological and precautionary approach in its judgment.[67] When authorities approve a plan or project affecting a protected site, an appropriate assessment is called for when there is 'a mere probability' that there will be a significant effect on the site concerned.[68] Further, 'a risk exists if it cannot be excluded on the basis of *objective* information that the plan or project will have significant effects on the site concerned'.[69] The threshold of 'probability' and the need for 'objective' information points in the direction of correctness as the standard for judicial review.[70]

---

[65] The line of cases begins with Case 14/83 *Von Colson* [1984] ECR 1891.

[66] *Waddenzee*, above n 62, [2004] ECR I-7405.

[67] See Scott, ch 6 in this volume at pp 103–07.

[68] *Waddenzee*, above n 62, para 41.

[69] Ibid, para 44 (emphasis added).

[70] See, Scott ch 6 in this volume at pp 106–07.

Moreover, the Habitats Directive 'must be interpreted' in accordance with the precautionary principle in Article 191(2). Accordingly

> in case of doubt as to the absence of significant effects … an assessment must be carried out, [which] makes it possible to ensure effectively that plans or projects which adversely affect the integrity of the site concerned are not authorised, and thereby contributes to achieving … the Habitats Directive … main aim, namely, ensuring biodiversity through the conservation of natural habitats and of wild fauna and flora.[71]

Where a plan or project is likely to undermine a site's conservation objectives, that is, probably will do so, 'it must be considered likely to have a significant effect on that site'.[72] Again, this points to a more rigorous role for judicial review, if not actually review for correctness.

Finally, an 'appropriate assessment', must identify, in the light of the 'best scientific knowledge in the field … all the aspects of the plan or project which can … affect' the objectives of the Directive.[73] Once more, the need for 'the best' scientific knowledge and the clear pointer to what should be decided where this does not exist, or has not been obtained, point to heightened scrutiny in judicial review.

At the very least, there are some aspects of Article 6(3) of the Directive, and also of Article 12(1), which call for heightened judicial scrutiny of decisions which are challenged under these provisions. *Waddenzee* confirms that judicial review has a key role in ensuring the full effectiveness of the Directive's requirements and defines important terms of the Directive in a way which calls for judicial review on rigorous grounds.

In practice, what this means is that authorities seeking to justify their decisions are required to present transparent reasons, supported by the best evidence available, explaining why they have approved (or not approved) a plan or project.

Space does not permit consideration of every case in which UK courts have considered the Habitats Directive. However, three recent cases, one from Scotland,[74] one from Northern Ireland[75] and the Supreme Court's decision in *R (Morge) v Hampshire CC*[76] allow three case studies of how the domestic courts approach the standard for judicial review under the Habitats Directive. It will be seen that the absence of any 'standard of review analysis' is problematic in all three cases.

(i) Skye Windfarm

Highland Council's decision to grant planning permission for a wind farm on Skye was challenged on a number of grounds, including by reference to Article 6(3) of

---

[71] *Waddenzee*, above n 62, para 44.

[72] Ibid, para 49.

[73] Ibid, para 54.

[74] *Skye Windfarm Action Group Ltd v Highland Council* [2008] CSOH 19 (*Skye Windfarm*).

[75] *Re Sandale Developments Ltd* [2010] NIQB 43 (*Sandale*).

[76] *R (Morge) v Hampshire CC* [2011] UKSC 2; [2011] 1 WLR 268 (*Morge*). For a detailed critical examination of *Morge* see George and Graham, ch 3 in this volume.

the Habitats Directive. The wind farm was to be on land nearby the Cuillins SPA, designated under Article 4(1) of the Birds Directive. The SPA had been designated because it regularly supported a breeding population of golden eagles. The petitioners claimed that the Council had failed to conduct an appropriate assessment of the effects of the wind farm on the population of golden eagles.

A number of issues were raised by the petitioners. One concerned whether the Council had uncritically accepted evidence, including that from Scottish Natural Heritage (SNH), as to the low risk posed by the wind farm to the birds. It was claimed that the Council had failed to apply the precautionary principle and had proceeded on the most optimistic assessments. The petitioners relied on *Waddenzee* while the Council countered that there had been no 'error' in their decision-making.

The court dismissed the challenge under the Habitats Directive. Despite finding that the evidence demonstrated 'considerable uncertainty as to the future trends of the population of golden eagles in Skye', the court held that the Council had relied on evidence which had applied the *Waddenzee* approach as to 'no reasonable scientific doubt'. This evidence had concluded that the risk posed by the wind farm to the eagles' habitat was minimal. The Council had 'applied the correct legal test'. The court was not 'persuaded that there was no basis for [the] conclusion on the integrity test [in Article 6(3) of the Directive] or that the Council acted illegally in not carrying out further appraisals' for itself.

It emerges from the court's judgment that the court was troubled by the question of what the appropriate standard for judicial review should be. At the outset of the court's judgment, it is pure *Wednesbury*. The judge, Lord Hodge, reminded himself that judicial review did not entail review of the merits of a decision: 'it is not competent for the Court to review the act or decision on its merits, nor may it substitute its own opinion for that of the person or body to whom the matter has been delegated or entrusted'.[77] By the end, however, it is clear that he was far from sure about the test for judicial review. The following passage of the judgment is illuminating:

> During the debate I expressed concern as to how the court could be satisfied that SNH, in giving their final advice, had had regard to the 'no reasonable scientific doubt' test set out in *Waddenzee*. On the final day of the hearing [counsel for the Council] lodged in process a letter from SNH which clarified [their] approach. It confirmed that SNH had incorporated the interpretation of Articles 6(3) and 6(4) of the Habitats Directive into their staff guidance shortly after the *Waddenzee* judgment and that they had used the 'no reasonable scientific doubt' test in their appraisal[s] (paragraph 135).

Although the court was swamped with detailed evidence from both parties, it does appear to have realised that *Waddenzee* requires more from judicial review than the ordinary standard of *Wednesbury* unreasonableness. Arguably, however, the court fell back from the task of deciding whether the Council had reached the correct legal decision on Article 6(3) of the Directive, not least in not deciding

---

[77] *Skye Windfarm*, para 29, quoting Lord Nimmo Smith in *World Wildlife Fund v The Scottish Ministers* [1999] 1 CMLR 1021, para 6.

whether the Directive required the Council *itself* to do the required assessments. There is an apparent tension in the judgment between engaging in more intense scrutiny of the Council's decisions, as the judge perceives may be required by *Waddenzee,* and the reluctance to perform anything that might be criticised as review of the merits of the challenged decision.

Be that as it may, *Skye Windfarm* highlights the court's realisation that judicial review according to the pure standards of *Wednesbury* unreasonableness may not be enough. If not approving correctness review, or even anxious scrutiny, the decision reveals a judicial questioning about what the court's 'standard of review analysis' should be. The very fact that the proper approach is not clear, let alone that the question about it only occurs to the judge at the end of the trial—and apparently not at all to counsel—suggests that more work needs to be done on this subject.

(ii) Sandale

The applicant challenged a decision of the Northern Ireland Department of the Environment granting outline planning permission for the construction of a secondary school on a site bounded by a stream which eventually flows into the River Foyle. The site was not within the River Foyle SAC, established under Article 3(1) of the Habitats Directive, among the Annex II species protected by which are salmon. Nevertheless, the applicant argued that the Department's decision breached the Habitats Directive because the Department had failed to carry out an assessment of the environmental effects of the development on the SAC. The Department defended its decision on the ground that, when it granted outline planning permission, it had no information or reasonable expectation as to the presence of any of the species or the existence of any potential hazard to salmon as the applicant claimed.

Weatherup J upheld the challenge, relying principally on *Waddenzee* and the precautionary principle. As to when an appropriate assessment is called for, the judge said:

> The triggering of the environmental protection mechanism follows from the mere probability that such an effect attaches to the plan or project, a probability or a risk that the plan or project will have significant effects on the site concerned. In the light, in particular, of the precautionary principle, such a risk exists if it cannot be excluded on the basis of the objective information that the plan or project will have significant effects on the site concerned. In case of doubt as to the absence of significant effects such an assessment must be carried out. Thus any plan or project not directly connected with or necessary to the management of the site is to be subject to an appropriate assessment of its implications for the site in view of the site's conservation objectives if it cannot be excluded on the basis of objective information that it will have a significant effect on that site.[78]

---

[78] *Sandale,* above n 75, para 19.

A clearer statement of the law is not possible. Having first identified the applicable law, Weatherup J then assessed what the Department had done and the evidence upon which it relied so as to justify the challenged decision. He concluded that 'the essence of environmental assessment concerns the *potential* impact of development'.[79] What was required was 'objective information about the … potential impact'. He continued:

> The concept of 'screening' implies some attempt to become sufficiently informed. One known feature was the presence of the watercourse. Such a feature should alert Planning Service to consideration of environmental issues concerning that feature. It is an example of what the Department described as a 'spacially relevant hazard'. It is an example in the EA Determination Sheet of a feature that might be important or sensitive for reasons of ecology. It demands examination of the impact of the development on that feature …

> Given the particulars furnished on behalf of the applicant … and the presence of domestic and European protected species, the absence of any reference to ecology, habitats or Zwildlife is striking. More particularly, the information that has now emerged does indicate that the risk exists that the proposed development will have significant effects on the SAC, in that the salmon may be affected by discharges into the watercourse. The precautionary principle dictates that the risk exists because it cannot be excluded on the present state of knowledge …

> The Department concluded that the principle of the development was acceptable and detailed proposals could be dealt with through the normal development control process. That approach did not address the ecology, habitats and wildlife matters. If the reference to the normal development control process was a reference to the imposition of conditions to the grant of outline planning permission and the later consideration of reserved matters, this could not in any event have been a legitimate means of dealing with the habitats, species and EIA obligations.[80]

On any view, this is review for correctness. Weatherup J's approach faithfully adhered to the requirements of *Waddenzee* as to the correct legal test for when an assessment was called for. The Department sought to justify its decision and failure to perform an appropriate assessment, relying on its discretionary powers but these were reviewed, not on the usual standards of *Wednesbury* unreasonableness but on a heightened standard which was justified by reference to EU law.

Interestingly, unlike in *Skye Windfarm*, Weatherup J did not feel the need to remind himself of the traditional limits in domestic law of the court's supervisory jurisdiction. Even in so far as evaluative judgments of the Department were before the court, the test applied to the decision reached by the Department was

---

[79] Ibid, para 38 (emphasis added).
[80] Ibid, paras 40, 42 and 49.

one of correctness. They had not done what the Habitats Directive, as construed in *Waddenzee*, required.[81]

It might be countered that, unlike in *Skye Windfarm* and *Morge*, Weatherup J was dealing with a threshold failure to perform an appropriate assessment, rather than reviewing the conclusions reached following one. I accept that one approach to judicial review could be that more intense scrutiny, or correctness review, is required on the threshold issue of whether to perform an assessment in the first place, and another, more deferential approach is required when the challenge is to decisions made following an appropriate assessment.

However, it is far from clear that this is in line with what *Waddenzee* requires. Certainly, the domestic courts must be rigorous in ensuring that domestic authorities perform assessments of plans or projects which call for them. But it also requires effective judicial review of whether the assessments are appropriate and have led to conclusions, including in light of the precautionary principle, which are justified by the evidence and lawful.

In any event, in domestic law, the law is that *all* errors of law are jurisdictional. So it is not the case that domestic law approves of a distinction between a different 'standard of judicial review analysis' for threshold legality, or jurisdictional, questions and other (non-jurisdictional) errors of law. Further, in the light of *Morge*, it is arguable that as much deference is payable to authorities on threshold *legal* questions, in this case on the meaning of Article 12(1)(b) of the Habitats Directive, as to other questions which arise under the Directive.

(iii) Morge

The Claimant challenged the Council's decision granting planning permission for a bus route on the grounds that it would lead to a 'deliberate disturbance' of the habitat of protected bats, contrary to Article 12(1)(b) of the Habitats Directive. Before the Supreme Court, two issues fell to be determined. First, what level of 'disturbance' qualified under Article 12(1)(b) of the Directive; and secondly, what did the Directive (or the implementing regulations) require of the local authority?

On the first issue, the Supreme Court unanimously held that, for disturbance to qualify under Article 12(1)(b), it did not have to be 'significant'. But the focus of Article 12(1)(b), in contrast to 12(1)(a), was on 'species' rather than specimens of species.

Lord Brown held that 'certain broad considerations ... govern the approach to article 12(1)(b)'. Among these was an 'assessment of the nature and extent

---

[81] It is also interesting that Weatherup J, relying expressly on the precautionary principle, stresses the importance of the potential impact of development. The contrast with *Skye Windfarm*, where the court notes the 'considerable uncertainty' surrounding the golden eagle population in Skye but then seems to overlook it, is striking.

of the negative impact of the [challenged] activity ... upon the species and
... a judgment as to whether that is sufficient to constitute a "disturbance".[82]
However, beyond approving the EU Commission's own guidance on the matter,
it was 'difficult to take the question of the proper interpretation and application
of article 12(1)(b) much further'.[83]

On the second issue, the Court decided that where Natural England had concluded that development was lawful for the purposes of the Directive, a planning
authority was entitled to rely on that conclusion. However, the Court was divided
on the question of what a planning committee had to have regard to in order to
comply with the requirements of the Habitats Directive. The majority concluded
that the planning committee only had to consider the Directive's requirements so
far as they might be affected by its decision. This was the limit of the obligation
imposed by regulation 3(4) of the Regulations.

Lord Kerr dissented on this issue, concluding that the planning committee did
not have before it the evidence which it was obliged to have before making its
decision. Unlike the majority, he could not say what they *would* have decided, if
they had had the information. Significantly, Lord Kerr reached this conclusion
having first said this:

> It is, of course, tempting to reach one's own conclusion as to whether the undoubted
> impact on the various species of bats that will be occasioned by this development is
> sufficient—or not—to meet the requirement of disturbance within the meaning of
> article 12. But this is not the function of a reviewing court. Unless satisfied that, on the
> material evidence, the deciding authority could have reached no conclusion other than
> that there would not be such a disturbance, it is no part of a court's duty to speculate
> on what the regulatory committee would have decided if it had received the necessary
> information about the requirements of the Habitats Directive, much less to reach its own
> view as to whether those requirements had been met.[84]

Lord Kerr's judgment is the only one to engage with the standard of review
appropriate to the case, albeit only on the second issue concerning the powers
of the planning committee. Although he does not adopt a correctness standard,
his approach is informed by the closeness of the committee's vote granting planning permission without the committee having had the information which it
should have had. It may be said that this is, in effect, a heightened standard for
judicial review, inspired by ensuring that the elected decision-makers make lawful
decisions in light of the information which the law requires them to have.[85]

The other Justices in *Morge* do not address the appropriate standard of review
of decisions challenged under the Habitats Directive. Part of the problem is

---

[82] *Morge*, above n 76, para 19.
[83] Ibid, para 20.
[84] Ibid, para 84.
[85] This approach touches on the subject of whether judicial review should be more intense when
it is necessary to protect the democratic process. Cf Ely, *Democracy and Distrust* (Harvard University
Press, 1980).

that the precautionary principle goes completely unmentioned. While the case concerned Article 12 of the Directive and not Article 6(3), unavoidably the case raises the precautionary principle. In any event, even on the strictly legal questions which were discussed by the Justices, it is unclear whether those questions are ultimately for the Court or the decision-makers, subject to judicial review for *Wednesbury* unreasonableness, presumably according to the normal standard.

The striking feature of the majority judgments in *Morge* is the deftness with which the Court first avoids the central *legal* question which arose—the meaning of 'disturbance'—and then leaves the issues to administrative decision-makers in light of their expertise. Leaving aside the absence of guidance from the Supreme Court on the law, what inevitably follows from the judgment is that decisions on disturbance of habitats which are challenged in judicial review will be reviewed principally on pure *Wednesbury* grounds. There is no suggestion that a correctness review, let alone heightened scrutiny by reference to the precautionary principle will be called for. On the contrary, the Court's decision merely gives decision-makers some considerations which should be 'borne in mind'.

Finally, as for whether the legal issues raised in the case deserved to be referred to the CJEU under Article 267 TFEU, it was 'unrealistic to suppose that the CJEU would *feel able* to provide any greater or different assistance' than the Supreme Court itself was able to give.[86] George and Graham[87] say with some force that 'this reasoning ignored the purpose of the preliminary ruling procedure, which is to ensure that there is uniform interpretation of law across the EU'. It certainly confirms again the ingenuity with which the English courts can refine the test for cases which should be subject to the preliminary ruling procedure.[88]

Judicial Review and Effectiveness

Given the predominance of EU law in the field of protection of the environment, it is legitimate to ask whether judicial review is an effective remedy for the purposes of EU law in this area. Does the principle of effectiveness in EU law require domestic courts to give more attention to 'standard of review analysis', so that judicial review has the appropriate intensity when the context and issues call for it?

On the one hand, the systems and traditions of administrative law are different in the Member States across the EU. For example, German administrative law has far less of a 'hang-up' about merits review than administrative law in the UK. EU law has been particularly influenced by German administrative law, notably the doctrine of proportionality, though it has also been influenced by English

---

[86] Ibid, para 25 (emphasis added).
[87] See George and Graham, ch 3 in this volume at p 60.
[88] Cf *Office of Fair Trading v Abbey National* [2009] UKSC 6, paras 48–50 (even if EU law not *acte clair*, delay in obtaining CJEU's ruling a reason not to refer).

administrative law.[89] It would be difficult to argue that EU law prefers one system of judicial review rather than another as a model for judicial review when EU law is relied on before domestic courts.

On the other hand, EU law does not require national judicial procedures to conform to any particular standard, as long as the principles of equivalence and effectiveness are respected by the domestic legal order. EU law does not purport to establish a system of remedies which the domestic legal orders should ensure are available.

However, it would be wrong to conclude that EU law has nothing to say about the standard of remedies which national law must provide.[90] The principle of effectiveness not only governs national procedural rules it is also a standard which all domestic law must satisfy if it is to be compatible with EU law.[91] One important way in which the effectiveness principle is satisfied is by requiring more extensive justification for decisions which are challenged by reference to EU law rules. In the field of environmental law, consultation, transparent reasons based on detailed evidence and proper procedures achieve the objectives of effectiveness in EU law where decisions are challenged because of their impact on the environment.

However, open decision-making following proper procedures still requires adequate judicial supervision. Since EU law itself recognises the need for the variable intensity of judicial review, a failure of domestic law to have, or at least attempt, a systematic approach to the standards of judicial review which are called for by different types of cases is open to the challenge that it does not satisfy the need to ensure the full effectiveness of EU law.

Conclusion

A properly functioning system of administrative law requires judicial review by independent judges of decision-makers exercising statutory or other public law powers. So much is uncontroversial for any legal system committed to the rule of law and the separation of powers. More difficult is the task of identifying how much judicial control there should be in different types of cases.

Most systems of administrative law have had difficulty with the appropriate intensity of judicial review which a particular administrative decision calls for. The question has been answered in different ways at different times, with the answer usually depending on the nature of the decision being challenged, the grounds on which it is challenged, the expertise of the decision-maker and the competence

---

[89]   Eg Case 17/74 *Transocean Marine v Commission* [1974] ECR 1063.

[90]   See Ward, 'National and EC Remedies under the EU Treaty: Limits and the Role of the ECHR', in Barnard and Odudu, *The Outer Limits of EU Law* (Hart Publishing, 2009) especially 331–32.

[91]   *Cf Fleming v HMRC* [2008] 1 WLR 195 (EU law obligation on domestic courts, following from principle of effectiveness, to make domestic law compatible with EU law).

which the court considers it has, or lacks, to decide the matters brought before it. No system of administrative law can function effectively if the test for legality of a challenged decision is always one of correctness. Equally, a system which always adhered to a test of rationality—whether the decision was one which fell within an ample band of decisions which the decision-maker could properly reach—would not be an effective one. Too much deference is as bad as too little.

I suggest three provisional conclusions:

(i) The experience of courts in the UK with the precautionary principle under the Habitats Directive reveals much of wider interest for administrative law in this country. There is a continuing absence of a systematic approach to the appropriate intensity of judicial review which cases call for.

(ii) The absence of a systematic approach to the appropriate intensity of judicial review causes courts particular difficulties when they are required to decide cases raising the precautionary principle. It is not clear what the standard of review should be, either for questions of law or the assessment of complex evidence relied on by decision-makers.

(iii) It is arguable, given the importance which EU law sets on the precautionary principle, in particular under the Habitats Directive, that the lack of coherence and predictability surrounding the appropriate intensity of judicial review interferes with the full effectiveness of EU law.

13

The Principle of Equilibrium in Environmental Law: The Example of the Habitats Directive

ANDREW WAITE

Introduction

The thesis of this chapter is that the whole *corpus* of environmental law should be sufficient to satisfy the needs of the environment. However, it should not go further. Over-regulation should be avoided. The law should be proportionate to its goals. The principle of equilibrium is both a guide for legislators and regulators and a tool of interpretation for judicial decision makers. It also describes the process whereby those affected by law including enforcement authorities and those governed by it, seek to avoid a regulatory deficit on the one hand and excessive control on the other.[1] The Habitats Directive represents a particular challenge for the application of this principle, particularly if Stookes is correct in his observation that: 'There is inherent conflict within the Directive between habitat and species conservation and improvement and the pursuit of plans and projects.'[2] How is this conflict to be resolved?

Equilibrium

This principle of equilibrium complements other established principles such as the 'precautionary principle', 'the polluter pays', 'sustainable development' and the principle of 'non-regression',[3] but seeks to set a limit to their field of operation.

---

[1] The principle is further explained in A Waite, 'The Quest for Environmental Law Equilibrium' (2005) 7 *Environmental Law Review* 34–62 from which parts of this chapter are derived.

[2] See, Stookes, ch 8 in this volume at pp 140–41.

[3] See M Prieur, 'De L'Urgente Nécessité de Reconnaître le Principe de "Non Regréssion" en Droit del'Environnement' 2010 (2) *Revista Romana de Dreptul mediului (Romanian Journal of Environmental Law)* 9.

Any attempt to frame a principle in this way immediately begs the fundamental question: what is meant by the terms 'environment' and 'environmental law'. They can have different meanings which may be more or less appropriate in different circumstances, matters on which there is unlikely to be a consensus. 'Environment' may include the man-made as well as the natural environment. The latter term may shade into the former considering that much of our 'natural environment' is the result of centuries or even millennia of human activity. The man-made environment may include not only significant archaeological monuments but also more modern structures of dubious aesthetic value.[4]

The scope of environmental law may cover only the fields of pollution control and nature conservation at one end of the spectrum or at the other all aspects of the law which affect the environment, whether positively or detrimentally. At another level, environmental law may be considered as the black letter stuff of statutes and principles enunciated by judges or as the more complex structure comprising not only the black letter law but also the underlying principles, the procedural rules and the way the law works in practice.[5]

The principle of environmental equilibrium can be used to evaluate environmental law in any of these senses and both individual environmental laws or the whole body of environmental law. However, it works best when the environment is considered holistically as an interdependent and connected series of media, habitats and living beings and environmental law is taken to be the whole structure and apparatus of law affecting the environment.

Environmental Law

Environmental law must respond to and satisfy the demands of the laws of nature in order to be effective. However, as explained above, in its wider form it is more complex than a set of legal rules arising directly from an appreciation of the laws of nature. Those laws give rise to a series of 'environmental imperatives', which if disobeyed lead to a greater or lesser degree of adverse environmental impacts. Environmental imperatives lead to the development of environmental principles, such as 'polluter pays', the precautionary principle and sustainable development. Environmental principles in turn underlie the framework of black letter legal rules.

Beyond the black letter law lie the rules on enforcement and public participation and beyond them again the practical working of the law through those who enforce it and those who operate within its framework.

Environmental law can be compared to the layers of an onion. The core A represents the environmental imperatives. The next layer B represents environmental

---

[4] Waite, above n 1, 56–57.
[5] Ibid, 57–62.

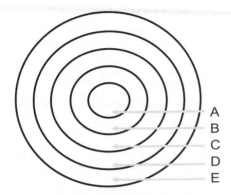

A = ENVIRONMENTAL IMPERATIVES
B = ENVIRONMENTAL PRINCIPLES/POLICY DRIVERS
C = SUBSTANTIVE ENVIRONMENTAL LAW
D = ACCESS TO JUSTICE – DUTIES/POWERS OF ENFORCEMENT
E = BEHAVIOUR OF ENVIRONMENTAL ACTORS

principles, followed by layer C: the substantive environmental law. Beyond that, layer D denotes the rules on access to justice, public participation and rights to environmental information, as well as duties and powers to enforce the law, all of which are essential to the proper functioning of the substantive legal rules. The outermost later E represents the behaviour of the 'actors' in the arena of environmental law: litigants, enforcing authorities, non-governmental organisations, lawyers, judges, legal aid authorities, industrial operators, property owners and other citizens. The practical operation of the law depends on the existence of each of these different types of 'actor', their training, awareness of environmental issues and commitment to taking appropriate action.

The 'onion rings' interact in complex ways which affect the practical operation of the law including compliance by industry and the quality and extent of enforcement by the regulatory authorities. For example, the content of the substantive environmental law may affect the behaviour of the environmental actors. Uncertainty as to the meaning of a law or onerous requirements to bring a case before the courts are likely to discourage the authorities from enforcing it. Courts sometimes adopt a more interventionist approach if the law and/or its enforcement are perceived to be weak. Occasionally, compliance and enforcement may lapse because the law is perceived to be too stringent. On the other hand, the behaviour of the environmental actors and the administrative and judicial infrastructure which underpins it may affect the development of the substantive rules of environmental law.[6]

---

[6] A Waite, 'A New Garden of Eden? Stimuli to Enforcement and Compliance in Environmental Law' (2007) 24 *Pace Environmental Law Review* 343, 344–46.

The principle of equilibrium can best be explained by reference to the three equations below in which the letters have the same connotation as in the text above.[7]

$B \times C \times D \times E = A$	-	Environmental Law Equilibrium
$B \times C \times D \times E > A$	-	Excessive Environmental Controls
$B \times C \times D \times E < A$	-	Environmental Law Deficit

In the first equation, the ideal position is achieved if each letter has the numerical value of 1. That denotes that each element of environmental law (B, C, D and E) is functioning at the optimum level. However, if one aspect, for example, C (the substantive rules of environmental law), is excessive, with a numerical value of say 2, that may be compensated if other factors such as D (access to justice), or E (behaviour of environmental actors) are less effective, having a lower numerical value of say 1/2. It is rare for compensatory factors to achieve the exact optimum balance represented by the value one.

In the second equation, representing excessive environmental controls, the apparatus of environmental law (B × C × D × E) is greater than that which is required to meet the environmental imperatives. In that case, at least one of the letters B, C, D or E must have a numerical value greater than one. The third equation represents the environmental law deficit. In that case, the apparatus of environmental law (B × C × D × E) is less than that which is required to meet the environmental imperatives. At least one of the letters, B, C, D or E must have a numerical value of less than one.

In general, it appears that the environmental law deficit is the major problem to confront, as is evidenced by the deteriorating position on a number of environmental fronts, such as storm and flood damage consequent on climate change and plummeting fish stocks due to over-fishing. However, in some instances, excessive environmental control occurs which is likely to be not only detrimental to legitimate economic growth but also to the needs of environmental protection. An example of this is the application of former waste management controls[8] to the remediation of contaminated land[9] which resulted in the abandonment of many beneficial attempts to clean up or reuse contaminated soil because the degree of

---

[7] However, it must be emphasised that the equations are only illustrative. The numerical value assigned to each letter is indicative of a value judgement which is necessary in each case. Attempts at precise numerical evaluation are likely to prove unrewarding in practice. See Waite, above n 1, 37.

[8] Part II of the Environmental Protection Act 1990; Waste Management Licensing Regulations 1994, SI 1994, No 1056 (as amended); EC Framework Waste Directive (91/156/EC); Waite, above n 1, 38.

[9] Environment Agency's Guidance on the Application of Waste Management Licensing to Remediation, Version 2.0, January 2001.

regulation involved made the project uneconomic. A report[10] concluded that the then current system:

— led to unjustified management costs for those who wanted to remediate land;
— discouraged redevelopment of brownfield land; and
— did not provide enough incentive for the use of alternative technologies.

Interestingly, the report set out a formula for the achievement of any environmental law equilibrium

an ideal system should deliver:

— proportionate, but precautionary, control of risk to the environment;
— 'better regulation';
— long-term environmental, economic and social objectives.[11]

The report explained the concept of 'better regulation':

The system also needs to work with the market in providing better solutions to environmental problems in the UK. This means it must be efficient, clear for the regulated parties and provide certainty and confidence in the market place. It must also be enforceable, so that the public have confidence in it. It should also have a transparent appraisal process and outputs.

It is also clear that the system must be fair and workable, both in theory and in practice, so that it begins to become something routine rather than a major obstacle.[12]

The legal framework has subsequently been adjusted by means of a more flexible approach to environmental permitting[13] and a reinterpretation of the meaning of waste by the courts[14] and the Environment Agency[15] under which contaminated soil which is fit for purpose can be used on land in some situations without the need to categorise it as waste material.

A further example of the application of this principle, this time by the legislators, is the sidelining of the decision of the European Court of Justice (ECJ) in *Van de Walle*,[16] in which the court decided that petrol, which had leaked from

---

[10] 'The Remediation Permit—Towards a Single Regeneration Licence', produced by the Remediation Permit Working Group, chaired by Phil Kirby OBE (2002).

[11] Ibid, 4.

[12] Ibid, 25, paras 3.16 and 3.17. A Better Regulation Executive (BRE) is now part of the Department of Business, Innovation and Skills in the UK and leads the regulatory reform agenda across the government. The BRE lists five principles of good regulation: any regulation should be transparent, accountable, proportionate, consistent and targeted only at cases where action is needed. See also the UK Government's Red Tape Challenge designed to deal with unnecessary and onerous regulation available at: http://www.redtapechallenge.cabinetoffice.gov.uk/environment.

[13] Environmental Permitting (England and Wales) Regulations 2010, SI 2010/675 as amended.

[14] See, eg *EA v Thorn International UK Ltd* [2008] EWHC 2595 (Admin) and *EA v Inglenorth Ltd* [2009] All ER (D) 167.

[15] Definition of Waste: Developing Greenfield and Brownfield Sites (2006) and Position Statement—Definition of Waste: Development Industry Code of Practice.

[16] Case C-1/03 *Van de Walle v Texaco Belgium SA* [2004] ECR I-7613.

a tank at a petrol filling station and the soil contaminated by it should both be treated as waste. That decision was interpreted by many to mean that all contaminated soil was waste and that remedial action was therefore required to dispose of or recover it.[17] The colossal potential impact of that interpretation on industrialised countries led governments and regulatory authorities to ignore the *Van de Walle* decision in practice. In the light of objections from all sides, the new Waste Framework Directive excludes unexcavated contaminated soil from the scope of the Directive altogether.[18]

The Operation of the Principle

The principle of environmental law equilibrium cannot yield a precise answer to the question of whether the law protects the environment without causing injustice by going too far. That question involves many variables. Scientific knowledge is incomplete and changes over time, so perceptions of what is necessary to protect the environment, and indeed what is the environment we must protect, will also change. In turn, there will be different views as to the appropriate policies and legal frameworks required to achieve the necessary protection. Different interest groups may advance alternative perspectives on what constitutes an environmental law deficit and what is excessive environmental control.

The answer will turn on a series of value judgments, which will differ from person to person. It will be apparent, therefore, that although any person may have a view on whether environmental law equilibrium has been achieved, in general, only the state or an organ of the state can make the necessary evaluation if it is to have any binding effect. What the principle does provide is a framework for analysing the effect of environmental law and making decisions on how it should be interpreted, amended or applied. In the case of the Habitats Directive, this issue is directly in play when considering the approach as to what is meant by 'likely' in Article 6(3). In the approach adopted by Advocate General Kokott and the ECJ in *Landelijke Vereniging tot Behoud van de Waddenzee v Staatssecretaris van Landbouw Natuurbehher en Visserij*[19] (*Waddenzee*) the equilibrium was tipped towards the precautionary rather than the pragmatic principle. That approach was welcomed by many,[20] but had it struck the correct balance?

---

[17] See A Waite, 'A New Garden of Eden? Stimuli to Enforcement and Compliance in Environmental Law' (2007) 24 *Pace Environmental Law Review* 343, 347, fn 13 for the view that that interpretation is incorrect.

[18] Waste Framework Directive 2008/98/EC, Art 2.1(b).

[19] *Landelijke Vereniging tot Behoud van de Waddenzee v Staatssecretaris van Landbouw Natuurbehher en Visserij* [2005] All ER (EC) 353; [2004] ECR I-7405; [2005] 2 CMLR 31; [2005] Env LR 14.

[20] See eg Scott, ch 6 in this volume.

There is nothing new in the environmental law equilibrium principle. It applies in the law-making process where the balance is struck in the cut and thrust of political debate and in legislative reviews designed to ensure that legislation is both effective and not unduly oppressive. Some such reviews are mandated by the legislation itself, others by executive decree. There are many examples in the environmental sphere.

President Obama's Executive Order, No 13563[21] required federal agencies to carry out a 'retrospective analysis of rules that may be outmoded, ineffective, insufficient or excessively burdensome and to modify, streamline, expand, repeal them in accordance with what has been learned'. The US Environmental Protection Agency (EPA) published a notice in the Federal Register to comply with that Order requesting comments to facilitate the EPA's review of its regulations.[22] The EPA's 'non-exhaustive list of issues or impacts' to consider include the following:

— Which regulations could achieve the intended environmental results using less costly methods, technology or innovative techniques? How could the regulations be changed?
— Which regulations could be improved by harmonising requirements across programmes or agencies to better meet the regulatory objectives?
— Which regulations have requirements that are overlapping and could be streamlined or eliminated?
— Which regulations have proven to be excessively burdensome?
— Which regulations have high costs and low benefits?
— Which regulations have large impacts on small businesses?
— Which regulations have complicated or time-consuming requirements?

This thorough approach to regulatory review and reform has been paralleled by the comprehensive review process in the UK[23] which resulted in several important changes in UK environmental law such as the inclusion of waste management licensing and several other regimes within the environmental permitting system[24] and the introduction of civil penalties.[25]

The UK Government's publication of the Red Tape Challenge Environment Theme proposals in March 2012 following an extensive consultation represents a further thrust in this direction. The government proposes to scrap 53 pieces of

---

[21] Executive Order 13563 'Improving Regulations and Regulatory Reviews' 18 January 2011.

[22] Federal Register, 23 February 2011.

[23] The Legislative and Regulatory Reform Act 2006 gives ministers certain powers to make 'legislative reform orders' that remove or reduce burdens resulting directly or indirectly from legislation. See Standing Order 141 approved on 4 July 2007 which sets out the criteria for draft legislative reform orders taken into account by the Regulatory Reform Committee in reporting to the House of Commons.

[24] Environmental Permitting (England and Wales) Regulations 2010, SI 2010/675, particularly reg 8.

[25] See the Regulatory Enforcement and Sanctions Act 2008; the Environmental Sanctions (England) Order 2010, SI 2010/1157 and the Macrory Review, Regulatory Justice: Making Sanctions Effective available at: http://www.berr.gov.uk/files/file44593.pdf.

legislation which are obsolete and improve 132 mainly through simplification or consolidation.

A number of EU environmental directives have inbuilt mandatory review provisions[26] and the EU Commission reviews environmental legislation on a systematic basis.[27] The underlying premise for these reviews is the need for equilibrium in the law as suggested above.

The notion of equilibrium also pervades a number of legislative schemes. The tension between a 'taking' of property which is compensatable under Article 5 of the US Constitution and the lawful exercise of the police power which is not has produced a plethora of litigation.[28] There is a similar tension evident in environmental human rights cases, where the qualified rights most applicable[29] allow derogations where that is necessary for the legitimate benefit of others and the community as a whole.[30]

EU legislation sets the bar at an elevated level, seeking a high level of environmental protection, relying frequently on the precautionary principle and the 'polluter pays' principle. The Habitats Directive is a classic example of this approach in which a 'strict' level of protection is demanded. On the other hand, the principle of proportionality in EU law recognises that legislation must be suitable for achieving its purpose and should not stray beyond what is required to achieve that purpose.[31] The need for a balance is also implicit in the sustainable development principle which recognises the creative tension between the right to develop[32] and the limitation on that right, that is it must be sustainable.

Specific legislation also has inbuilt limitations reflecting attempts to strike the appropriate balance between economic progress and environmental protection. Only high levels of environmental damage will trigger the operator's duty to take preventive and remedial measures under the Environmental Liability Directive[33] in cases of damage to protected species and natural habitats and water damage.[34]

---

[26] Eg The EU Environmental Liability Directive (2004/35/CE), Art 18. For an example in UK law, see Regulation 110 of the Environmental Permitting (England and Wales) Regulations 2010, SI 2010/675, inserted by reg 11 of the Environmental Permitting (England and Wales) (Amendment) Regulations 2012, SI 2012/630. A review requirement is now standard practice for new regulations in the UK. See HM Government: Sunsetting Regulations: Guidance, December 2011 – http://www.bis. gov.uk/policies/bre/effectiveness-of-regulations/sunsetting-regulations.

[27] The European Commission analyses the effectiveness of environmental legislation, often relying on external studies by bodies such as the Institute for European Environmental Policy.

[28] David K Brooks, 'Regulatory Takings—Where Environmental Protection and Private Property Collide' (2002) 17 *Natural Resources and Environment*, 10–13, 57–63.

[29] Art 8 of the European Convention on Human Rights 1950 (Right to respect for private and family life and home) and Art 1 of the First Protocol (Protection of Property).

[30] See particularly, *Hatton v UK* (2003) 37 EHRR 28.

[31] See A Arnull et al, *Wyatt & Dashwood's European Union Law*, (6th edn) (Hart Publishing, 2011) 122–24. It should be noted that the principle of proportionality has not, so far, been an effective judicial review mechanism in the CJEU.

[32] A right to development is recognised by Principle 3 of the Rio Declaration 1992.

[33] 2004/35/CE.

[34] Art 2.1 On the other hand, the threshold for land damage is surprisingly low: 'any damage that creates a significant risk of human health being adversely affected': Art 2.1(c) Contrast the

It is also notable that in dealing with remedial options the Directive requires that these should be evaluated using the best available technology based on the following criteria (inter alia):

— the effect on public health and safety;
— cost;
— the likelihood of success; and
— taking account of relevant social, economic and cultural concerns and other relevant concerns specific to the locality.[35]

Other examples of the legislators' aim to achieve equilibrium in environmental law are the concepts of best practicable means (BPM), best available techniques not entailing excessive cost (BATNEEC), and best available techniques (BAT) which have long been a central feature of pollution control law. Each of these concepts balances cost against the aim of controlling emissions.

Governments frequently give guidance to their agencies and officials as to how to apply the law in order to achieve equilibrium. Examples in the UK include the Statutory Guidance[36] issued under the contaminated land legislation (Part IIA of the Environmental Protection Act 1990) and the Environment Agency's prosecution policy[37] which sets out the considerations to be taken into account by Agency officers in deciding whether to prosecute environmental offences.

Judicial Application of the Equilibrium Principle

It is easy to assert that the equilibrium principle exists and that it ought to be applied by judges. It is more difficult to decide exactly how the balance should be struck in individual cases. A notable example of the difficulty can be found in the case of *R (Greenpeace Ltd) v Secretary of State for the Environment Food and Rural Affairs*[38] which involved rival interpretations of the Convention on the International Trade in Endangered Species of Wild Fauna and Flora (CITES) and the EU Regulation[39] which implements it. The majority of the Court of Appeal pointed out that CITES operates through a system of formal documentary checks. Business certainty required that if the documents were valid

threshold for significant harm to human health under Part IIA of the Environmental Protection Act 1990.

[35] Annex II of the Directive.

[36] Contaminated Land Statutory Guidance (April 2012) which gives guidance designated to achieve the practicability, effectiveness and durability of remediation and a fair allocation of liabilities between those responsible for the contamination.

[37] Enforcement and Sanctions Guidance, issued 4 January 2011.

[38] *R (Greenpeace Ltd) v Secretary of State for the Environment Food and Rural Affairs* [2003] Env LR 9; [2002] I WLR 3304. For a fuller discussion of this case see Waite, above n 1, 54–55.

[39] Council Reg 338/97 on the protection of species of wild flora and fauna by regulatory trade therein.

on their face, they should not be open to challenge. However, Laws LJ (dissenting) held that where an export permit had been issued which was not in accordance with the substantive (as opposed to merely documentary) requirements of CITES, it should be considered invalid. The judge's reasoning deserves to be quoted:

> The interpretation of statutes is hardly ever entirely value-free. It is neither surprising nor regrettable that in confronting their task of interpretation, the judges have to a greater or lesser degree been moved by the aspirations of their time. Such a process does no more than bring to life the plain fact that the law—perhaps especially the common law—will reflect contemporary influences, even though it is not a creature of them; it must do so, or it would ossify. In the century before last, the sanctity of contract, with all that it said for trade across the British Empire and beyond, was a powerful engine of statutory construction. Now, the world is a more fragile place. Considerations of ecology and the protection of the environment are interests of high importance. The delicate balances of the natural order are continuously liable to be disturbed by human activity which in particular threatens the survival of many flora and fauna. These concerns are today well known and well accepted. Within the proper limits of the courts' role, and in appropriate contexts, I think we should be ready to give them special weight.

> The Convention, through certainly it seeks to support viable international trade, is first and foremost intended as a legal antidote to some of the damage done by man's exploitation of nature's resources. That purpose must, in my judgement, serve as the most influential factor in the interpretation of the Regulation.[40]

Another area where the courts have laboured to find equilibrium is in the difficult and sometimes opaque case law on the meaning of waste. The Waste Framework Directive (WFD) has enunciated two broad objectives: first, ensuring the responsible disposal and recovery of waste and second, restricting the production of waste under the overarching aim of achieving a high level of environmental protection.[41] The pronouncements of the CJEU have often favoured the former at the expense of the latter objective. For example, in the *ARCO/Epon* case,[42] the CJEU stated that 'the concept of waste cannot be interpreted restrictively'. However, that approach tends to cast the regulatory net around many items which may have a continued useful existence. The added regulatory burden may render such a useful life uneconomic to the holder and thereby increase the waste stream. That runs counter to the waste prevention objective of the Directive.[43] It fell to Carnwath LJ to grapple with this issue in *R (OSS Group Ltd) v Environment*

---

[40] [2003] Env LR 9, paras 33–34.

[41] 2006/12/EC, sixth recital; 2008/98/EC, sixth and ninth recitals.

[42] *ARCO Chemie Nederland Ltd v Minister van Volkshuisvesting, Ruimtelijke Ordening en Milieubeheer* (C-418/97; sub nom. Epon, Re (C-419/97); *Vereniging Dorps belang Hees v Directeur van de dienst Milieu en Water van de provincie Gelderland* (C-419-97) [2000] ECR I-4475, para 40.

[43] E Scotford, 'Trash or Treasure: Policy Tensions in EC Waste Regulation' (2007) 19 *Journal of Environmental Law* 367; A Waite, 'The Definition of Waste: The Riddle of the Sands' in Fischer-Lescano, Gasser, Marauhn and Ronzitti (eds), *Peace in Liberty, Festschrift fur Michael Bothe zūm 70 Geburtstag* (Nomos/Dike, 2008 787, 789. The new Waste Framework Directive 2008/98/EC tilts the balance further in favour of waste prevention. Art 4 requires EU Member States to apply the waste hierarchy (which prioritises waste prevention) in waste legislation and policy.

Agency,[44] in relation to the question of when material ceases to be waste. The case concerned the collection of waste lubricating and fuel oil from garages and workshops and its conversion into marketable fuel oil. The question was when the material ceases to be waste for the purposes of the WFD: at the completion of the process of its preparation for use as fuel or when it is actually burnt? Carnwath LJ (with whose judgment the other members of the Court agreed) after an exhaustive examination of the CJEU cases held that for the materials to cease to be waste

> It should be enough that the holder has converted the waste material into a distinct, marketable product, which can be used in exactly the same way as an ordinary fuel, with no worse environmental effects. It cannot be said that such a material is being 'discarded' in any ordinary sense of the term, and there is nothing in the objectives of the Directive which requires any fictitious assumption to that effect.[45]

In reaching that conclusion, he followed the approach of the Administrative Law Division of the Dutch Council of State in *Icopower BV v Secretary of State*,[46] which he considered to be

> a practical and common sense approach to the issue, which is consistent with the letter and spirit of the Directive and with the case-law. *It is also consistent with the objective of encouraging the recovery of waste materials for uses which replace new materials* (emphasis added).

The same might be said about the solution which emerged in connection with the Thames Basin Heaths Special Protection Area. An overly legalistic application of the Habitats Directive might have lead to the sterilisation of land around the SPA in an area where housing development was greatly needed. The development of the Suitable Alternative Natural Greenspace (SANG) mechanism at a regional level to standardise the mitigation to be provided by local authorities and developers in connection with development in the vicinity of the Thames Basin Heaths SPA was a proportionate and precautionary reaction which enabled the achievement of long-term environmental, economic and social objectives.[47] In the subsequent unsuccessful legal challenge to the SANG approach *Hart District Council v Secretary of State for Communities and Local Government, Luckmore Ltd and Barratt Homes Ltd*[48] Sullivan J (as he then was) opined that the underlying principle was that the Habitats Directive was intended to be 'an aid to effective environmental decision-making, not a legal obstacle course'.

In these cases, the courts have interpreted the law to provide what they conceive to be the appropriate balance between the needs of environmental protection and other requirements.

The Indian courts have used judicial review to confront a perceived failure by the regulatory authorities to enforce the law. 'Where there is a perceived vacuum

---

[44] *R (OSS Group Ltd) v Environment Agency* [2007] EWCA Civ 611; [2007] 3 CMLR 30.
[45] Para 63.
[46] ABRvS 14 May 2003, *LJN: AF8611*.
[47] See Ricketts and Bischoff, ch 7 in this volume.
[48] *Hart District Council v Secretary of State for Communities and Local Government, Luckmore Limited and Barratt Homes Ltd* [2008] EWHC 1204.

in governance, the court rushes to fill it'.[49] In the rising tide of public interest litigation the courts have:

— ordered municipalities to enforce public nuisance laws against polluters;
— ordered local governments to obtaining funds to construct drains and sewers;
— enforced Pollution Control Board Standards; and
— supervised the administration of legislation on forests and mines.

In doing so, the courts have developed procedural innovations which Anderson describes as a revolution in constitutional jurisprudence.[50] In particular:

— rules of standing were broadened to allow representative or public interest actions;
— letters from aggrieved citizens have been formulated as writ petitions;
— some judges have adopted *Suo Motu* jurisdiction without any request by a litigant;
— special commissions/committees have been appointed to establish factual issues, such as monitoring air quality and traffic congestion; and
— courts have retained jurisdiction after orders were made in order to monitor enforcement.

Suo Motu jurisdiction has also been adopted by some judges in Pakistan.[51] In the mid-1990s Justice Saleem Akhtar, after reading about the issue in a local newspaper persuaded his judicial colleagues to issues an injunction forbidding the disposal of chemical waste off the coast of Balochistan. Similarly in *Lahore Conservation Society v Government of Punjab*,[52] Chaudhry CJ after reading letters in a newspaper, issued an order preventing the continuance of a road expansion project. The order prohibited the felling of trees and asked the government to investigate alternative solutions.

Nardi notes that environmental lawyers have sought guidelines for the use of the *Suo Motu* jurisdiction. The long-term effectiveness of judicial policy making has also been questioned. It has been observed that courts lack the technical capacity to formulate long-term environmental policy.[53] This approach could also discourage action by the appointed regulatory bodies. For example, it appears that when the *Suo Motu* jurisdiction is exercised, some local environmental protection agencies are reluctant to take action for fear of being held in contempt of court.

---

[49] L Rajamani, 'Public Interest Environmental Litigation in India: Exploring Issues of Access, Participation, Equity, Effectiveness and Sustainability', (2007) *Journal of Environmental Law* 293–321; MR Anderson, 'Environmental Protection in India' in A Boyle and M Anderson (eds) *Human Rights Approaches to Environmental Protection* (Oxford University Press, 1998) ch 10, 210–11.

[50] Ibid, 210–11.

[51] Dominic Nardi, 'Pakistan's Judiciary: Suo Motu Tango' available at: http://www.comparativeconstitutions.org/2010/05/dominic-nardi-on-pakistans-judiciary.html.

[52] *Lahore Conservation Society v Government of Punjab* CP No 16/2006.

[53] This has not prevented the Indian Courts from appointing expert committees to assist them.

Applying the Equilibrium Principle

As demonstrated above, the equilibrium principle is not new. It pervades environmental law and its practice. However, its pervasiveness may mean that it is not always fully understood or applied systematically. In order for that to happen transparent guidelines need to be incorporated into the corpus of environmental law to facilitate the application of the principle. At this point, as indicated above, clarification is needed on what constitutes environmental law: environmental law in the narrow sense of the rules designed to protect the environment or environmental law in the broad sense of rules which impact the environment whether positively or negatively. The equilibrium principle will only operate to its optimum extent if all such laws are generated, interpreted, applied and reviewed under its searching lens. Whatever criticisms may be levelled against environmental protection laws, laws which accidentally or by design damage the environment will inevitably have a greater adverse impact.

What is needed is an overarching 'green' law with the following components:

— All new laws should be checked before they are passed to ensure that:
(a) in the case of environmental protection laws they are sufficient for their purpose without being unduly oppressive; and (b) in the case of other laws they have no (unacceptable) adverse impacts on the environment.

— Regulatory authorities should be required to exercise their functions so as to achieve environmental law equilibrium.

— Judges should interpret legislation in a manner which achieves environmental law equilibrium wherever that is consistent with the words of the legislation.[54] In cases where such an interpretation is not possible, judges should issue a declaration to that effect.[55] A stronger version of this principle would enable courts to declare statutes invalid if they contravene the principle.[56] Two examples can be considered: (1) a statute which requires all wetlands to be drained or infilled; and (2) a statute which requires all wetlands to be drained or infilled unless protected under nature conservation laws. Option (1) would be invalid in EU Member States as it would contravene the Habitats Directive. Option (2) might

---

[54] See, eg Human Rights Act 1998 s 3.

[55] See, eg Human Rights Act 1998 s 4.

[56] Such a proposal is likely to be extremely controversial but might be justified on the basis that due to its importance environmental law is a type of 'higher law' in the sense of Stammler's concept of 'natural law with changing content'. It may then be possible to deal with environmentally damaging laws in the manner that Radbruch's formula treated as non-law any legislation which offended the principle of justice to an intolerable degree. There may be little consensus as to which laws offend the equilibrium principle sufficiently to fall foul of the Radbruch approach. However, if compatibility with the principle of environmental equilibrium is elevated to a constitutional requirement, judges would have the task of making the appropriate value-judgement as they do in other constitutional cases. See also, S Coyle and K Morrow, *Philosophical Foundations of Environmental Law* (Hart Publishing, 2004).

be considered depending on its purpose. For example, if the purpose was to displace human populations or to eradicate a resident species without good reason, the statute would be considered invalid. The case of displacing human populations would infringe Article 8 (right to respect for private and family life and home) and Article 1 of the First Protocol (Protection of Property) of the European Convention on Human Rights 1950. On the other hand, if the purpose were to protect the human population from disease or to provide land for much needed housing, a different conclusion might be reached. A similar approach could be applied to other laws, such as those providing for financial grants or tax advantages to those who undertake agricultural improvements which have material adverse impacts on the environment.[57]

— Legislation should be reviewed periodically to check its compatibility with the equilibrium principle.

— Whether these precepts are incorporated into an overarching constitutional law (dark green) or embodied in individual statutes (mid green) or applied as official/unofficial guidelines (light green), the equilibrium principle should ensure that due consideration is given to the task of ensuring that environmental protection laws are effective but not oppressive and that other laws are not unduly detrimental to the environment.

Applying the Equilibrium Principle to the Habitats Directive

The Habitats Directive[58] is nearly 20 years old but it is probably too early to be sure how effective it is. However, the signs are encouraging that it is on track to meet its stated objectives.[59] Article 6(3) and 6(4) provide a strict but carefully balanced regime requiring an 'appropriate assessment' of any 'plan or project'

---

[57] It is notable that Radbruch's formula resulted in the invalidation of a notorious Nazi law on citizenship by the German Federal Constitutional Court in 1968. In the UK, three Law Lords in *R (Jackson) v Attorney General* [2005] 1 AC 262, envisaged the possibility that judges might invalidate a statute which violated the rule of law to an unacceptable degree by attempting to abolish judicial review or the ordinary role of the courts: see Lord Steyn, para 102; Lord Hope of Craighead, paras 104–109, Baroness Hale of Richmond, para 159. However, that approach is controversial: see Tom Bingham, *The Rule of Law* (Penguin, 2011) 166–68. Nevertheless, if such an approach is accepted in the field of human rights, it is but a short step to extend to the environment those rights which protect human beings: see C Stone, 'Should Trees have Standing—Towards Legal Rights for Natural Objects', (1972) 45 *Southern Californian Law Review* 450. See also the dissenting Opinion of Justice Douglas in *Sierra Club v Morton* [1972] 405 US 727.

[58] 92/43/EEC.

[59] Art 2 states:

1. The aim of this Directive shall be to contribute towards ensuring bio-diversity through the conservation of natural habitats and of wild fauna and flora in the European territory of the Member States to which the Treaty applies.

'likely to have a significant effect' on a 'European' site. Competent authorities may 'agree to the plan or project only after having ascertained that it will not adversely affect the integrity of the site concerned'. Significantly, 'if appropriate' the authorities are to obtain the opinion of the general public in taking their decision. In the event of a negative assessment (and where there are no alternative solutions) a plan or project may nevertheless be carried out 'for reasons of overriding public interest, including those of a social or economic nature' subject to taking 'all compensatory measures necessary to ensure that the overall coherence of Natura 2000 is protected'.

Needless to say, the various elements in this scheme of protection have been analysed and fine tuned by the courts including the ECJ in a series of cases which are explored elsewhere in this volume.[60]

In addition to habitats protection, the Habitats Directive also contains a code for the protection of species. This includes a requirement for the prohibition of the 'deliberate disturbance' of certain species.[61] That phase has been subject to a recent decision by the UK Supreme Court[62] in which it was held that whether or not there is a 'disturbance' depends on the merits of each case. The position could differ even for a particular species according to the season or different periods of its life cycle. The threshold for a disturbance, however, was not as high as that suggested by the Court of Appeal that it must have 'a detrimental impact so as to affect the conservation status of the species at population level' or that it must affect the survival chances of a protected species.[63]

The task of assessing whether the right balance has been struck by the Habitats Directive, the courts' interpretation of it, and its implementation by the competent authorities is facilitated by the requirement in Article 17 for Member States to produce a report on the implementation measures taken every six years. The Commission must then produce a composite report based on the national reports submitted.

The UK's Second Report[64] and the Commission's composite report[65] for the period 2001–2006 indicate that although many sites have not yet achieved 'good conservation status' this is not surprising given that many sites were chosen because

---

2. Measures taken pursuant to this Directive shall be designed to maintain or restore, at favourable conservation status, natural habitats and species of wild fauna and flora, of Community interest.
3. Measures taken pursuant to this Directive shall take account of economic, social and cultural requirements and regional and local characteristics.

[60] See, eg *R (Akester) v Defra and Wightlink Ltd* [2010] EWHC 232(Admin) on what is a 'plan or project'. See Tromans, ch 5 in this volume.

[61] Art 12.1.

[62] *R (Morge) v Hampshire County Council* [2011] UKSC 2. See George and Graham, ch 3 in this volume.

[63] Ibid, para 21.

[64] Available at: http//www.jncc.gov.uk/article17.

[65] Available at: http://ec.europa.eu/environment/nature/knowledge/rep_habitats/index_en.htm; http://bd.eionet.europa.eu/article17.

they were threatened. The reports provide a valuable resource for measuring future trends. They reveal that, although grasslands, wetlands and coastal habitats face continuing threats, there are positive signs that some threatened species are beginning to recolonise parts of their range. Andrew Dodd argues that the Habitats Directive is moving in the right direction but that there is still some way to go. He concludes that[66]

> The nature directives have been a positive force in helping safeguard the best of Europe's wildlife. Their protective role—preventing damage and promoting the recovery of rare or threatened species—has been particularly successful. Less successful has been securing the positive management of protected areas and sustaining populations of more widespread species in the countryside. The fate of Europe's farmland birds is testament to this failure. The reasons are simple: lack of sufficient political will and the commensurate funding. If the political will exists alongside adequate funding and creative and positive implementation, the directives contain the necessary tools for Member States to deliver their goals.

This demonstrates that it is not only the legal rules but also their implementation which is critical to ensuring appropriate environmental protection.

Concerns that the Habitats Directive impedes vital development were raised in the report by the Department for Environment, Food and Rural Affairs: Habitats and Wild Birds Directives Implementation Review published in March 2012. The Report concluded that in most cases the implementation of the Directives works well, permitting key infrastructure developments, while maintaining protection of the environment. The Directives are seen as only one contributing factor where delays occur. The Report considers that the 'green economy' can only thrive if the requirements of EU legislation are not 'gold plated' and are implemented and communicated in a manner which is congenial to business. Four areas are identified where implementation could be improved for the benefit of the economy and the environment:

— facilitating nationally significant infrastructure projects;
— improving implementation processes and streamlining guidance;
— improving the quality, quantity and sharing of data; and
— improving the developer's experience as a customer of the regulatory and planning bodies involved.

Conclusion

Environmental protection law will only succeed if it can accommodate proportionate economic growth. That is what the phrase 'sustainable development'

---

[66] A Dodd, 'EU Nature Directives: Rights, responsibilities and results, UKELA, (2008) 20 *Environment Law and Management* 237, 244–45.

is meant to encapsulate but its practical definition has provided elusive. The equilibrium principle might provide an answer that is flexible and workable. In short, it requires that:

— Environmental law (including the legal rules, environmental principles, procedural rules relating to enforcement and access to justice and the way in which the law is applied in practice) should be sufficient to protect the environment but should avoid going further.
— Any environmental laws which do not achieve equilibrium should be changed to ensure that equilibrium is achieved. Investigations should be made to ascertain whether change is required to the substantive legal rules, the underlying legal principles, the procedural rules or the way in which the law is applied in practice.
— Laws which have a negative impact on the environment should be amended to ensure that, so far as reasonably practicable, the negative impacts are removed or at least minimised.

This document is meant purely as a documentation tool and the institutions do not assume any liability for its contents

►**B**

COUNCIL DIRECTIVE 92/43/EEC

of 21 May 1992

on the conservation of natural habitats and of wild fauna and flora

(OJ L 206, 22.7.1992, p. 7)

Amended by:

		Official Journal		
		No	page	date
►**M1**	Council Directive 97/62/EC of 27 October 1997	L 305	42	8.11.1997
►**M2**	Regulation (EC) No 1882/2003 of the European Parliament and of the Council of 29 September 2003	L 284	1	31.10.2003
►**M3**	Council Directive 2006/105/EC of 20 November 2006	L 363	368	20.12.2006

Amended by:

►**A1**	Act of Accession of Austria, Sweden and Finland	C 241	21	29.8.1994
	(adapted by Council Decision 95/1/EC, Euratom, ECSC)	L 1	1	1.1.1995
►**A2**	Act concerning the conditions of accession of the Czech Republic, the Republic of Estonia, the Republic of Cyprus, the Republic of Latvia, the Republic of Lithuania, the Republic of Hungary, the Republic of Malta, the Republic of Poland, the Republic of Slovenia and the Slovak Republic and the adjustments to the Treaties on which the European Union is founded	L 236	33	23.9.2003

*

Corrected by:

►**C1**   Corrigendum, OJ L 176, 20.7.1993, p. 29 (92/43)

COUNCIL DIRECTIVE 92/43/EEC

of 21 May 1992

on the conservation of natural habitats and of wild fauna and flora

THE COUNCIL OF THE EUROPEAN COMMUNITIES,

Having regard to the Treaty establishing the European Economic Community, and in particular Article 130s thereof,

Having regard to the proposal from the Commission ([1]),

Having regard to the opinion of the European Parliament ([2]),

Having regard to the opinion of the Economic and Social Committee ([3]),

Whereas the preservation, protection and improvement of the quality of the environment, including the conservation of natural habitats and of wild fauna and flora, are an essential objective of general interest pursued by the Community, as stated in Article 130r of the Treaty;

Whereas the European Community policy and action programme on the environment (1987 to 1992) ([4]) makes provision for measures regarding the conservation of nature and natural resources;

Whereas, the main aim of this Directive being to promote the maintenance of biodiversity, taking account of economic, social, cultural and regional requirements, this Directive makes a contribution to the general objective of sustainable development; whereas the maintenance of such biodiversity may in certain cases require the maintenance, or indeed the encouragement, of human activities;

Whereas, in the European territory of the Member States, natural habitats are continuing to deteriorate and an increasing number of wild species are seriously threatened; whereas given that the threatened habitats and species form part of the Community's natural heritage and the threats to them are often of a transboundary nature, it is necessary to take measures at Community level in order to conserve them;

Whereas, in view of the threats to certain types of natural habitat and certain species, it is necessary to define them as having priority in order to favour the early implementation of measures to conserve them;

Whereas, in order to ensure the restoration or maintenance of natural habitats and species of Community interest at a favourable conservation status, it is necessary to designate special areas of conservation in order to create a coherent European ecological network according to a specified timetable;

Whereas all the areas designated, including those classified now or in the future as special protection areas pursuant to Council Directive 79/409/EEC of 2 April 1979 on the conservation of wild birds ([5]), will have to be incorporated into the coherent European ecological network;

Whereas it is appropriate, in each area designated, to implement the necessary measures having regard to the conservation objectives pursued;

([1]) OJ No C 247, 21. 9. 1988, p. 3 and
   OJ No C 195, 3. 8. 1990, p. 1.
([2]) OJ No C 75, 20. 3. 1991, p. 12.
([3]) OJ No C 31, 6. 2. 1991, p. 25.
([4]) OJ No C 328, 7. 12. 1987, p. 1.
([5]) OJ No L 103, 25. 4. 1979, p. 1. Directive as last amended by Directive 91/244/ECC (OJ No L 115, 8. 5. 1991, p. 41).

▼**B**

Whereas sites eligible for designation as special areas of conservation are proposed by the Member States but whereas a procedure must nevertheless be laid down to allow the designation in exceptional cases of a site which has not been proposed by a Member State but which the Community considers essential for either the maintenance or the survival of a priority natural habitat type or a priority species;

Whereas an appropriate assessment must be made of any plan or programme likely to have a significant effect on the conservation objectives of a site which has been designated or is designated in future;

Whereas it is recognized that the adoption of measures intended to promote the conservation of priority natural habitats and priority species of Community interest is a common responsibility of all Member States; whereas this may, however, impose an excessive financial burden on certain Member States given, on the one hand, the uneven distribution of such habitats and species throughout the Community and, on the other hand, the fact that the 'polluter pays' principle can have only limited application in the special case of nature conservation;

Whereas it is therefore agreed that, in this exceptional case, a contribution by means of Community co-financing should be provided for within the limits of the resources made available under the Community's decisions;

Whereas land-use planning and development policies should encourage the management of features of the landscape which are of major importance for wild fauna and flora;

Whereas a system should be set up for surveillance of the conservation status of the natural habitats and species covered by this Directive;

Whereas a general system of protection is required for certain species of flora and fauna to complement Directive 79/409/EEC; whereas provision should be made for management measures for certain species, if their conservation status so warrants, including the prohibition of certain means of capture or killing, whilst providing for the possibility of derogations on certain conditions;

Whereas, with the aim of ensuring that the implementation of this Directive is monitored, the Commission will periodically prepare a composite report based, *inter alia,* on the information sent to it by the Member States regarding the application of national provisions adopted under this Directive;

Whereas the improvement of scientific and technical knowledge is essential for the implementation of this Directive; whereas it is consequently appropriate to encourage the necessary research and scientific work;

Whereas technical and scientific progress mean that it must be possible to adapt the Annexes; whereas a procedure should be established whereby the Council can amend the Annexes;

Whereas a regulatory committee should be set up to assist the Commission in the implementation of this Directive and in particular when decisions on Community co-financing are taken;

Whereas provision should be made for supplementary measures governing the reintroduction of certain native species of fauna and flora and the possible introduction of non-native species;

Whereas education and general information relating to the objectives of this Directive are essential for ensuring its effective implementation,

▼**B**

HAS ADOPTED THIS DIRECTIVE:

Definitions

Article 1

For the purpose of this Directive:

(a) *conservation* means a series of measures required to maintain or restore the natural habitats and the populations of species of wild fauna and flora at a favourable status as defined in (e) and (i);

(b) *natural habitats* means terrestrial or aquatic areas distinguished by geographic, abiotic and biotic features, whether entirely natural or semi-natural;

(c) *natural habitat types of Community interest* means those which, within the territory referred to in Article 2:

  (i) are in danger of disappearance in their natural range;

    or

  (ii) have a small natural range following their regression or by reason of their intrinsically restricted area;

    or

▼**M3**

  (iii) present outstanding examples of typical characteristics of one or more of the nine following biogeographical regions: Alpine, Atlantic, Black Sea, Boreal, Continental, Macaronesian, Mediterranean, Pannonian and Steppic.

▼**B**

Such habitat types are listed or may be listed in Annex I;

(d) *priority natural habitat types* means natural habitat types in danger of disappearence, which are present on the territory referred to in Article 2 and for the conservation of which the Community has particular responsibility in view of the proportion of their natural range which falls within the territory referred to in Article 2; these priority natural habitat types are indicated by an asterisk (*) in Annex I;

(e) *conservation status of a natural habitat* means the sum of the influences acting on a natural habitat and its typical species that may affect its long-term natural distribution, structure and functions as well as the long-term survival of its typical species within the territory referred to in Article 2.

  ►**C1** The conservation status ◄ of a natural habitat will be taken as 'favourable' when:

  — its natural range and areas it covers within that range are stable or increasing, and

  — the specific structure and functions which are necessary for its long-term maintenance exist and are likely to continue to exist for the foreseeable future, and

  — the conservation status of its typical species is favourable as defined in (i);

(f) *habitat of a species* means an environment defined by specific abiotic and biotic factors, in which the species lives at any stage of its biological cycle;

(g) *species of Community interest* means species which, within the territory referred to in Article 2, are:

▼**B**

(i) endangered, except those species whose natural range is marginal in that territory and which are not endangered or vulnerable in the western palearctic region; or

(ii) vulnerable, i.e. believed likely to move into the endangered category in the near future if the causal factors continue operating; or

(iii) rare, i.e. with small populations that are not at present endangered or vulnerable, but are at risk. The species are located within restricted geographical areas or are thinly scattered over a more extensive range; or

(iv) endemic and requiring particular attention by reason of the specific nature of their habitat and/or the potential impact of their exploitation on their habitat and/or the potential impact of their exploitation on their conservation status.

Such species are listed or may be listed in Annex II and/or Annex IV or V;

(h) *priority species* means species referred to in (g) (i) for the conservation of which the Community has particular responsibility in view of the proportion of their natural range which falls within the territory referred to in Article 2; these priority species are indicated by an asterisk (*) in Annex II;

(i) *conservation status of a species* means the sum of the influences acting on the species concerned that may affect the long-term distribution and abundance of its populations within the territory referred to in Article 2;

The *conservation status* will be taken as 'favourable' when:

— population dynamics data on the species concerned indicate that it is maintaining itself on a long-term basis as a viable component of its natural habitats, and

— the natural range of the species is neither being reduced nor is likely to be reduced for the foreseeable future, and

— there is, and will probably continue to be, a sufficiently large habitat to maintain its populations on a long-term basis;

(j) *site* means a geographically defined area whose extent is clearly delineated;

(k) *site of Community importance* means a site which, in the biogeographical region or regions to which ▶**C1** it belongs, ◀ contributes significantly to the maintenance or restoration of a favourable conservation status of a natural habitat type in Annex I or of a species in Annex II and may also contribute significantly to the coherence of Natura 2000 referred to in Article 3, and/or contributes significantly to the maintenance of biological diversity within the biogeographic region or regions concerned.

For animal species ranging over wide areas, sites of Community importance shall correspond to the places within the natural range of such species which present the physical or biological factors essential to their life and reproduction;

(l) *special area of conservation* means a site of Community importance designated by the Member States through a statutory, administrative and/or contractual act where the necessary conservation measures are applied for the maintenance or restoration, at a favourable conservation status, of the natural habitats and/or the populations of the species for which the site is designated;

(m) *specimen* means any animal or plant, whether alive or dead, of the species listed in Annex IV and Annex V, any part or derivative thereof, as well as any other goods which appear, from an accompanying document, the packaging or a mark or label, or from any other circumstances, to be parts or derivatives of animals or plants of those species;

(n) *the committee* means the committee set up pursuant to Article 20.

Article 2

1.   The aim of this Directive shall be to contribute towards ensuring bio-diversity through the conservation of natural habitats and of wild fauna and flora in the European territory of the Member States to which the Treaty applies.

2.   Measures taken pursuant to this Directive shall be designed to maintain or restore, at favourable conservation status, natural habitats and species of wild fauna and flora of Community interest.

3.   Measures taken pursuant to this Directive shall take account of economic, social and cultural requirements and regional and local characteristics.

Conservation of natural habitats and habitats of species

Article 3

1.   A coherent European ecological network of special areas of conservation shall be set up under the title Natura 2000. This network, composed of sites hosting the natural habitat types listed in Annex I and habitats of the species listed in Annex II, shall enable the natural habitat types and the species' habitats concerned to be maintained or, where appropriate, restored at a favourable conservation status in their natural range.

The Natura 2000 network shall include the special protection areas classified by the Member States pursuant to Directive 79/409/EEC.

2.   Each Member State shall contribute to the creation of Natura 2000 in proportion to the representation within its territory of the natural habitat types and the habitats of species referred to in paragraph 1. To that effect each Member State shall designate, in accordance with Article 4, sites as special areas of conservation taking account of the objectives set out in paragraph 1.

3.   Where they consider it necessary, Member States shall endeavour to improve the ecological coherence of Natura 2000 by maintaining, and where appropriate developing, features of the landscape which are of major importance for wild fauna and flora, as referred to in Article 10.

Article 4

1.   On the basis of the criteria set out in Annex III (Stage 1) and relevant scientific information, each Member State shall propose a list of sites indicating which natural habitat types in Annex I and which species in Annex II that are native to its territory the sites host. For animal species ranging over wide areas these sites shall correspond to the places within the natural range of such species which present the physical or biological factors essential to their life and reproduction. For aquatic species which range over wide areas, such sites will be proposed only where there is a clearly identifiable area representing the physical and biological factors essential to their life and reproduction. Where appropriate, Member States shall propose adaptation of the list in the light of the results of the surveillance referred to in Article 11.

The list shall be transmitted to the Commission, within three years of the notification of this Directive, together with information on each site. That information shall include a map of the site, its name, location, extent and the data resulting from application of the criteria specified in Annex III (Stage 1) provided in a format established by the Commission in accordance with the procedure laid down in Article 21.

2. On the basis of the criteria set out in Annex III (Stage 2) and in the framework both of each of the ►<u>M3</u> nine ◄ biogeographical regions referred to in Article 1 (c) (iii) and of the whole of the territory referred to in Article 2 (1), the Commission shall establish, in agreement with each Member State, a draft list of sites of Community importance drawn from the Member States' lists identifying ►<u>C1</u> those which host one ◄ or more priority natural habitat types or priority species.

Member States whose sites hosting one or more priority natural habitat types and priority species represent more than 5 % of their national territory may, in agreement with the Commission, request that the criteria listed in Annex III (Stage 2) be applied more flexibly in selecting all the sites of Community importance in their territory.

The list of sites selected as sites of Community importance, identifying those which host one or more priority natural habitat types or priority species, shall be adopted by the Commission in accordance with the procedure laid down in Article 21.

3. The list referred to in paragraph 2 shall be established within six years of the notification of this Directive.

4. Once a site of Community importance has been adopted in accordance with the procedure laid down in paragraph 2, the Member State concerned shall designate that site as a special area of conservation as soon as possible and within six years at most, establishing priorities in the light of the importance of the sites for the maintenance or restoration, at a favourable conservation status, of a natural habitat type in Annex I or a species in Annex II and for the coherence of Natura 2000, and in the light of the threats of degradation or destruction to which those sites are exposed.

5. As soon as a site is placed on the list referred to in the third subparagraph of paragraph 2 it shall be subject to Article 6 (2), (3) and (4).

Article 5

1. In exceptional cases where the Commission finds that a national list as referred to in Article 4 (1) fails to mention a site hosting a priority natural habitat type or priority species which, on the basis of relevant and reliable scientific information, it considers to be essential for the maintenance of that priority natural habitat type or for the survival of that priority species, a bilateral consultation procedure shall be initiated between that Member State and the Commission for the purpose of comparing the scientific data used by each.

2. If, on expiry of a consultation period not exceeding six months, the dispute remains unresolved, the Commission shall forward to the Council a proposal relating to the selection of the site as a site of Community importance.

3. The Council, acting unanimously, shall take a decision within three months of the date of referral.

4. During the consultation period and pending a Council decision, the site concerned shall be subject to Article 6 (2).

Article 6

1. For special areas of conservation, Member States shall establish the necessary conservation measures involving, if need be, appropriate management plans specifically designed for the sites or integrated into

▼**B**

other development plans, and appropriate statutory, administrative or contractual measures which correspond to the ecological requirements of the natural habitat types in Annex I and the species in Annex II present on the sites.

2.   Member States shall take appropriate steps to avoid, in the special areas of conservation, the deterioration of natural habitats and the habitats of species as well as disturbance of the species for which the areas have been designated, in so far as such disturbance could be significant in relation to the objectives of this Directive.

3.   Any plan or project not directly connected with or necessary to the management of the site but likely to have a significant effect thereon, either individually or in combination with other plans or projects, shall be subject to appropriate assessment of its implications for the site in view of the site's conservation objectives. In the light of the conclusions of the assessment of the implications for the site and subject to the provisions of paragraph 4, the competent national authorities shall agree to the plan or project only after having ascertained that it will not adversely affect the integrity of the site concerned and, if appropriate, after having obtained the opinion of the general public.

4.   If, in spite of a negative assessment of the implications for the site and in the absence of alternative solutions, a plan or project must nevertheless be carried out for imperative reasons of overriding public interest, including those of a social or economic nature, the Member State shall take all compensatory measures necessary to ensure that the overall coherence of Natura 2000 is protected. It shall inform the Commission of the compensatory measures adopted.

Where the site concerned hosts a priority natural habitat type and/or a priority species, the only considerations which may be raised are those relating to human health or public safety, to beneficial consequences of primary importance for the environment or, further to an opinion from the Commission, to other imperative reasons of overriding public interest.

Article 7

Obligations arising under Article 6 (2), (3) and (4) of this Directive shall replace any obligations arising under the first sentence of Article 4 (4) of Directive 79/409/EEC in respect of areas classified pursuant to Article 4 (1) or similarly recognized under Article 4 (2) thereof, as from the date of implementation of this Directive or the date of classification or recognition by a Member State under Directive 79/409/EEC, where the latter date is later.

Article 8

1.   In parallel with their proposals for sites eligible for designation as special areas of conservation, hosting priority natural habitat types and/or priority species, the Member States shall send, as appropriate, to the Commission their estimates relating to the Community co-financing which they consider necessary to allow them to meet their obligations pursuant to Article 6 (1).

2.   In agreement with each of the Member States concerned, the Commission shall identify, for sites of Community importance for which co-financing is sought, those measures essential for the maintenance or re-establishment at a favourable conservation status of the priority natural habitat types and priority species on the sites concerned, as well as the total costs arising from those measures.

3.   The Commission, in agreement with the Member States concerned, shall assess the financing, including co-financing, required for the operation of the measures referred to in paragraph 2, taking into

account, amongst other things, the concentration on the Member State's territory of priority natural habitat types and/or priority species and the relative burdens which the required measures entail.

4.   According to the assessment referred to in paragraphs 2 and 3, the Commission shall adopt, having regard to the available sources of funding under the relevant Community instruments and according to the procedure set out in Article 21, a prioritized action framework of measures involving co-financing to be taken when the site has been designated under Article 4 (4).

5.   The measures which have not been retained in the action framework for lack of sufficient resources, as well as those included in the abovementioned action framework which have not received the necessary co-financing or have only been partially co-financed, shall be reconsidered in accordance with the procedure set out in Article 21, in the context of the two-yearly review of the action framework and may, in the maintime, be postponed by the Member States pending such review. This review shall take into account, as appropriate, the new situation of the site concerned.

6.   In areas where the measures dependent on co-financing are postponed, Member States shall refrain from any new measures likely to result in deterioration of those areas.

Article 9

The Commission, acting in accordance with the procedure laid down in Article 21, shall periodically review the contribution of Natura 2000 towards achievement of the objectives set out in Article 2 and 3. In this context, a special area of conservation may be considered for declassification where this is warranted by natural developments noted as a result of the surveillance provided for in Article 11.

Article 10

Member States shall endeavour, where they consider it necessary, in their land-use planning and development policies and, in particular, with a view to improving the ecological ►**C1** coherence of the Natura ◄ 2000 network, to encourage the management of features of the landscape which are of major importance for wild fauna and flora.

Such features are those which, by virtue of their linear and continuous structure (such as rivers with their banks or the traditional systems for marking field boundaries) or their function as stepping stones (such as ponds or small woods), are essential for the migration, dispersal and genetic exchange of wild species.

Article 11

Member States shall undertake surveillance of the conservation status of the natural habitats and species referred to in Article 2 with particular regard to priority natural habitat types and priority species.

Protection of species

Article 12

1.   Member States shall take the requisite measures to establish a system of strict protection for the animal species listed in Annex IV (a) in their natural range, prohibiting:

(a) all forms of deliberate capture or killing of specimens of these species in the wild;

(b) deliberate disturbance of these species, particularly during the period of breeding, rearing, hibernation and migration;

(c) deliberate destruction or taking of eggs from the wild;

(d) deterioration or destruction of breeding sites or resting places.

2.   For these species, Member States shall prohibit the keeping, transport and sale or exchange, and offering for sale or exchange, of specimens taken from the wild, except for those taken legally before this Directive is implemented.

3.   The prohibition referred to in paragraph 1 (a) and (b) and paragraph 2 shall apply to all stages of life of the animals to which this Article applies.

4.   Member States shall establish a system to monitor the incidental capture and killing of the animal species listed in Annex IV (a). In the light of the information gathered, Member States shall take further research or conservation measures as required to ensure that incidental capture and killing does not have a significant negative impact on the species concerned.

Article 13

1.   Member States shall take the requisite measures to establish a system of strict protection for the plant species listed in Annex IV (b), prohibiting:

(a) the deliberate picking, collecting, cutting, uprooting or destruction of such plants in their natural range in the wild;

(b) the keeping, transport and sale or exchange and offering for sale or exchange of specimens of such species taken in the wild, except for those taken legally before this Directive is implemented.

2.   The prohibitions referred to in paragraph 1 (a) and (b) shall apply to all stages of the biological cycle of the plants to which this Article applies.

Article 14

1.   If, in the light of the surveillance provided for in Article 11, Member States deem it necessary, they shall take measures to ensure that the taking in the wild of specimens of species of wild fauna and flora listed in Annex V as well as their exploitation is compatible with their being maintained at a favourable conservation status.

2.   Where such measures are deemed necessary, they shall include continuation of the surveillance provided for in Article 11. Such measures may also include in particular:

— regulations regarding access to certain property,

— temporary or local prohibition of the taking of specimens in the wild and exploitation of certain populations,

— regulation of the periods and/or methods of taking specimens,

— application, when specimens are taken, of hunting and fishing rules which take account of the conservation of such populations,

— establishment of a system of licences for taking specimens or of quotas,

— regulation of the purchase, sale, offering for sale, keeping for sale or transport for sale of specimens,

— breeding in captivity of animal species as well as artificial propagation of plant species, under strictly controlled conditions, with a view to reducing the taking of specimens of the wild,

— assessment of the effect of the measures adopted.

Article 15

In respect of the capture or killing of species of wild fauna listed in Annex V (a) and in cases where, in accordance with Article 16, derogations are applied to the taking, capture or killing of species listed in Annex IV (a), Member States shall prohibit the use of all indiscriminate means capable of causing local disappearance of, or serious disturbance to, populations of such species, and in particular:

(a) use of the means of capture and killing listed in Annex VI (a);

(b) any form of capture and killing from the modes of transport referred to in Annex VI (b).

Article 16

1.   Provided that there is no satisfactory alternative and the derogation is not detrimental to the maintenance of the populations of the species concerned at a favourable conservation status in their natural range, Member States may derogate from the provisions of Articles 12, 13, 14 and 15 (a) and (b):

(a) in the interest of protecting wild fauna and flora and conserving natural habitats;

(b) to prevent serious damage, in particular to crops, livestock, forests, fisheries and water and other types of property;

(c) in the interests of public health and public safety, or for other imperative reasons of overriding public interest, including those of a social or economic nature and beneficial consequences of primary importance for the environment;

(d) for the purpose of research and education, of repopulating and re-introducing these species and for the breedings operations necessary for these purposes, including the artificial propagation of plants;

(e) to allow, under strictly supervised conditions, on a selective basis and to a limited extent, the taking or keeping of certain specimens of the species listed in Annex IV in limited numbers specified by the competent national authorities.

2.   Member States shall forward to the Commission every two years a report in accordance with the format established by the Committee on the derogations applied under paragraph 1. The Commission shall give its opinion on these derogations within a maximum time limit of 12 months following receipt of the report and shall give an account to the Committee.

3.   The reports shall specify:

(a) the species which are subject to the derogations and the reason for the derogation, including the nature of the risk, with, if appropriate, a reference to alternatives rejected and scientific data used;

(b) the means, devices or methods authorized for the capture or killing of animal species and the reasons for their use;

(c) the circumstances of when and where such derogations are granted;

(d) the authority empowered to declare and check that the required conditions obtain and to decide what means, devices or methods may be used, within what limits and by what agencies, and which persons ►**C1** are to carry out the ◄ task;

(e) the supervisory measures used and the results obtained.

Information

Article 17

1.   Every six years from the date of expiry of the period laid down in Article 23, Member States shall draw up a report on the implementation of the measures taken under this Directive. This report shall include in particular information concerning the conservation measures referred to in Article 6 (1) as well as evaluation of the impact of those measures on the conservation status of the natural habitat types of Annex I and the species in Annex II and the main results of the surveillance referred to in Article 11. The report, in accordance with the format established by the committee, shall be forwarded to the Commission and made accessible to the public.

2.   The Commission shall prepare a composite report based on the reports referred to in paragraph 1. This report shall include an appropriate evaluation of the progress achieved and, in particular, of the contribution of Natura 2000 to the achievement of the objectives set out in Article 3. A draft of the part of the report covering the information supplied by a Member State shall be forwarded to the Member State in question for verification. After submission to the committee, the final version of the report shall be published by the Commission, not later than two years after receipt of the reports referred to in paragraph 1, and shall be forwarded to the Member States, the European Parliament, the Council and the Economic and Social Committee.

3.   Member States may mark areas designated under this Directive by means of Community notices designed for that purpose by the committee.

Research

Article 18

1.   Member States and the Commission shall encourage the necessary research and scientific work having regard to the objectives set out in Article 2 and the obligation referred to in Article 11. They shall exchange information for the purposes of proper coordination of research carried out at Member State and at Community level.

2.   Particular attention shall be paid to scientific work necessary for the implementation of Articles 4 and 10, and transboundary cooperative research between Member States shall be encouraged.

Procedure for amending the Annexes

Article 19

Such amendments as are necessary for adapting Annexes I, II, III, V and VI to technical and scientific progress shall be adopted by the Council acting by qualified majority on a proposal from the Commission.

Such amendments as are necessary for adapting Annex IV to technical and scientific progress shall be adopted by the Council acting unanimously on a proposal from the Commission.

▼B

Committee

▼M2

Article 20

The Commission shall be assisted by a committee.

Article 21

1.   Where reference is made to this Article, Articles 5 and 7 of Decision 1999/468/EC (¹) shall apply, having regard to the provisions of Article 8 thereof.

The period laid down in Article 5(6) of Decision 1999/468/EC shall be set at three months.

2.   The Committee shall adopt its rules of procedure.

▼B

Supplementary provisions

Article 22

In implementing the provisions of this Directive, Member States shall:

(a) study the desirability of re-introducing species in Annex IV that are native to their territory where this might contribute to their conservation, provided that an investigation, also taking into account experience in other Member States or elsewhere, has established that such re-introduction contributes effectively to re-establishing these species at a favourable conservation status and that it takes place only after proper consultation of the public concerned;

(b) ensure that the deliberate introduction into the wild of any species which is not native to their territory is regulated so as not to prejudice natural habitats within their natural range or the wild native fauna and flora and, if they consider it necessary, prohibit such introduction. The results of the assessment undertaken shall be forwarded to the committee for information;

(c) promote education and general information on the need to protect species of wild fauna and flora and to conserve their habitats and natural habitats.

Final provisions

Article 23

1.   Member States shall bring into force the laws, regulations and administrative provisions necessary to comply with this Directive within two years of its notification. They shall forthwith inform the Commission thereof.

2.   When Member States adopt such measures, they shall contain a reference to this Directive or be accompanied by such reference on the occasion of their official publication. The methods of making such a reference shall be laid down by the Member States.

(¹) Council Decision 1999/468/EC of 28 June 1999 laying down the procedures for the exercise of implementing powers conferred on the Commission (OJ L 184, 17.7.1999, p. 23).

▼ __B__

3.   Member States shall communicate to the Commission the main provisions of national law which they adopt in the field covered by this Directive.

Article 24

This Directive is addressed to the Member States.

▼ <u>M3</u>

ANNEX I

NATURAL HABITAT TYPES OF COMMUNITY INTEREST WHOSE CONSERVATION REQUIRES THE DESIGNATION OF SPECIAL AREAS OF CONSERVATION

Interpretation

Guidance on the interpretation of habitat types is given in the 'Interpretation Manual of European Union Habitats' as approved by the committee set up under Article 20 ('Habitats Committee') and published by the European Commission ([1]).

The code corresponds to the NATURA 2000 code.

The sign '*' indicates priority habitat types.

1. COASTAL AND HALOPHYTIC HABITATS

11.	Open sea and tidal areas
1110	Sandbanks which are slightly covered by sea water all the time
1120	* *Posidonia* beds (*Posidonion oceanicae*)
1130	Estuaries
1140	Mudflats and sandflats not covered by seawater at low tide
1150	* Coastal lagoons
1160	Large shallow inlets and bays
1170	Reefs
1180	Submarine structures made by leaking gases
12.	**Sea cliffs and shingle or stony beaches**
1210	Annual vegetation of drift lines
1220	Perennial vegetation of stony banks
1230	Vegetated sea cliffs of the Atlantic and Baltic Coasts
1240	Vegetated sea cliffs of the Mediterranean coasts with endemic *Limonium* spp.
1250	Vegetated sea cliffs with endemic flora of the Macaronesian coasts
13.	**Atlantic and continental salt marshes and salt meadows**
1310	*Salicornia* and other annuals colonizing mud and sand
1320	*Spartina* swards (*Spartinion maritimae*)
1330	Atlantic salt meadows (*Glauco-Puccinellietalia maritimae*)
1340	* Inland salt meadows
14.	**Mediterranean and thermo-Atlantic salt marshes and salt meadows**
1410	Mediterranean salt meadows (*Juncetalia maritimi*)
1420	Mediterranean and thermo-Atlantic halophilous scrubs (*Sarcocornetea fruticosi*)
1430	Halo-nitrophilous scrubs (*Pegano-Salsoletea*)
15.	**Salt and gypsum inland steppes**
1510	* Mediterranean salt steppes (*Limonietalia*)
1520	* Iberian gypsum vegetation (*Gypsophiletalia*)
1530	* Pannonic salt steppes and salt marshes

([1]) 'Interpretation Manual of European Union Habitats', version EUR 15/2" adopted by the Habitats Committee on 4 October 1999 and 'Amendments to the "Interpretation Manual of European Union Habitats" with a view to EU enlargement' (Hab. 01/11b-rev. 1) adopted by the Habitats Committee on 24 April 2002 after written consultation, European Commission, Directorate General for Environment.

▼ **M3**

16. **Boreal Baltic archipelago, coastal and landupheaval areas**

1610   Baltic esker islands with sandy, rocky and shingle beach vegetation and sublittoral vegetation

1620   Boreal Baltic islets and small islands

1630   * Boreal Baltic coastal meadows

1640   Boreal Baltic sandy beaches with perennial vegetation

1650   Boreal Baltic narrow inlets

2. COASTAL SAND DUNES AND INLAND DUNES

21.   **Sea dunes of the Atlantic, North Sea and Baltic coasts**

2110   Embryonic shifting dunes

2120   Shifting dunes along the shoreline with *Ammophila arenaria* ('white dunes')

2130   * Fixed coastal dunes with herbaceous vegetation ("grey dunes')

2140   * Decalcified fixed dunes with *Empetrum nigrum*

2150   * Atlantic decalcified fixed dunes (*Calluno-Ulicetea*)

2160   Dunes with *Hippophaë rhamnoides*

2170   Dunes with *Salix repens* ssp. *argentea* (*Salicion arenariae*)

2180   Wooded dunes of the Atlantic, Continental and Boreal region

2190   Humid dune slacks

21A0   Machairs (* in Ireland)

22.   **Sea dunes of the Mediterranean coast**

2210   *Crucianellion maritimae* fixed beach dunes

2220   Dunes with *Euphorbia terracina*

2230   *Malcolmietalia* dune grasslands

2240   *Brachypodietalia* dune grasslands with annuals

2250   * Coastal dunes with *Juniperus* spp.

2260   *Cisto-Lavenduletalia* dune sclerophyllous scrubs

2270   * Wooded dunes with *Pinus pinea* and/or *Pinus pinaster*

23.   **Inland dunes, old and decalcified**

2310   Dry sand heaths with *Calluna* and *Genista*

2320   Dry sand heaths with *Calluna* and *Empetrum nigrum*

2330   Inland dunes with open *Corynephorus* and *Agrostis* grasslands

2340   * Pannonic inland dunes

3. FRESHWATER HABITATS

31.   **Standing water**

3110   Oligotrophic waters containing very few minerals of sandy plains (*Littorelletalia uniflorae*)

3120   Oligotrophic waters containing very few minerals generally on sandy soils of the West Mediterranean, with *Isoetes* spp.

3130   Oligotrophic to mesotrophic standing waters with vegetation of the *Littorelletea uniflorae* and/or of the *Isoëto-Nanojuncetea*

3140   Hard oligo-mesotrophic waters with benthic vegetation of *Chara* spp.

3150   Natural eutrophic lakes with *Magnopotamion* or *Hydrocharition* — type vegetation

3160   Natural dystrophic lakes and ponds

3170   * Mediterranean temporary ponds

3180   * Turloughs

▼ M3

3190   Lakes of gypsum karst

31A0   * Transylvanian hot-spring lotus beds

32.   **Running water — sections of water courses with natural or semi-natural dynamics (minor, average and major beds) where the water quality shows no significant deterioration**

3210   Fennoscandian natural rivers

3220   Alpine rivers and the herbaceous vegetation along their banks

3230   Alpine rivers and their ligneous vegetation with *Myricaria germanica*

3240   Alpine rivers and their ligneous vegetation with *Salix elaeagnos*

3250   Constantly flowing Mediterranean rivers with *Glaucium flavum*

3260   Water courses of plain to montane levels with the *Ranunculion fluitantis* and *Callitricho-Batrachion* vegetation

3270   Rivers with muddy banks with *Chenopodion rubri* p.p. and *Bidention* p.p. vegetation

3280   Constantly flowing Mediterranean rivers with *Paspalo-Agrostidion* species and hanging curtains of *Salix* and *Populus alba*

3290   Intermittently flowing Mediterranean rivers of the *Paspalo-Agrostidion*

4. TEMPERATE HEATH AND SCRUB

4010   **Northern Atlantic wet heaths with *Erica tetralix***

4020   * Temperate Atlantic wet heaths with *Erica ciliaris* and *Erica tetralix*

4030   European dry heaths

4040   * Dry Atlantic coastal heaths with *Erica vagans*

4050   * Endemic macaronesian heaths

4060   Alpine and Boreal heaths

4070   * Bushes with *Pinus mugo* and *Rhododendron hirsutum* (*Mugo-Rhododendretum hirsuti*)

4080   Sub-Arctic *Salix* spp. Scrub

4090   Endemic oro-Mediterranean heaths with gorse

40A0   * Subcontinental peri-Pannonic scrub

40B0   Rhodope *Potentilla fruticosa* thickets

40C0   * Ponto-Sarmatic deciduous thickets

5. SCLEROPHYLLOUS SCRUB (MATORRAL)

51.   **Sub-Mediterranean and temperate scrub**

5110   Stable xerothermophilous formations with *Buxus sempervirens* on rock slopes (*Berberidion* p.p.)

5120   Mountain *Cytisus purgans* formations

5130   *Juniperus communis* formations on heaths or calcareous grasslands

5140   * *Cistus palhinhae* formations on maritime wet heaths

52.   **Mediterranean arborescent matorral**

5210   Arborescent matorral with *Juniperus* spp.

5220   * Arborescent matorral with *Zyziphus*

5230   * Arborescent matorral with *Laurus nobilis*

53.   **Thermo-Mediterranean and pre-steppe brush**

5310   *Laurus nobilis* thickets

5320   Low formations of Euphorbia close to cliffs

5330   Thermo-Mediterranean and pre-desert scrub

54.	**Phrygana**
5410	West Mediterranean clifftop phryganas (*Astragalo-Plantaginetum subulatae*)
5420	Sarcopoterium spinosum phryganas
5430	Endemic phryganas of the *Euphorbio-Verbascion*

6. NATURAL AND SEMI-NATURAL GRASSLAND FORMATIONS

61.	**Natural grasslands**
6110	* Rupicolous calcareous or basophilic grasslands of the *Alysso-Sedion albi*
6120	* Xeric sand calcareous grasslands
6130	Calaminarian grasslands of the *Violetalia calaminariae*
6140	Siliceous Pyrenean *Festuca eskia* grasslands
6150	Siliceous alpine and boreal grasslands
6160	Oro-Iberian *Festuca indigesta* grasslands
6170	Alpine and subalpine calcareous grasslands
6180	Macaronesian mesophile grasslands
6190	Rupicolous pannonic grasslands (*Stipo-Festucetalia pallentis*)

62.	**Semi-natural dry grasslands and scrubland facies**
6210	Semi-natural dry grasslands and scrubland facies on calcareous substrates (*Festuco-Brometalia*) (* important orchid sites)
6220	* Pseudo-steppe with grasses and annuals of the *Thero-Brachypodietea*
6230	* Species-rich *Nardus* grasslands, on silicious substrates in mountain areas (and submountain areas in Continental Europe)
6240	* Sub-Pannonic steppic grasslands
6250	* Pannonic loess steppic grasslands
6260	* Pannonic sand steppes
6270	* Fennoscandian lowland species-rich dry to mesic grasslands
6280	* Nordic alvar and precambrian calcareous flatrocks
62A0	Eastern sub-Mediterranean dry grasslands (*Scorzoneratalia villosae*)
62B0	* Serpentinophilous grassland of Cyprus
62C0	* Ponto-Sarmatic steppes
62D0	Oro-Moesian acidophilous grasslands

63.	**Sclerophillous grazed forests (dehesas)**
6310	Dehesas with evergreen *Quercus* spp.

64.	**Semi-natural tall-herb humid meadows**
6410	*Molinia* meadows on calcareous, peaty or clayey-silt-laden soils (*Molinion caeruleae*)
6420	Mediterranean tall humid grasslands of the *Molinio-Holoschoenion*
6430	Hydrophilous tall herb fringe communities of plains and of the montane to alpine levels
6440	Alluvial meadows of river valleys of the *Cnidion dubii*
6450	Northern boreal alluvial meadows
6460	Peat grasslands of Troodos

65.	**Mesophile grasslands**
6510	Lowland hay meadows (*Alopecurus pratensis, Sanguisorba officinalis*)
6520	Mountain hay meadows
6530	* Fennoscandian wooded meadows

▼ **M3**

7. RAISED BOGS AND MIRES AND FENS

71.   **Sphagnum acid bogs**

7110   * Active raised bogs

7120   Degraded raised bogs still capable of natural regeneration

7130   Blanket bogs (* if active bog)

7140   Transition mires and quaking bogs

7150   Depressions on peat substrates of the *Rhynchosporion*

7160   Fennoscandian mineral-rich springs and springfens

72.   **Calcareous fens**

7210   * Calcareous fens with *Cladium mariscus* and species of the *Caricion davallianae*

7220   * Petrifying springs with tufa formation (*Cratoneurion*)

7230   Alkaline fens

7240   * Alpine pioneer formations of the *Caricion bicoloris-atrofuscae*

73.   **Boreal mires**

7310   * Aapa mires

7320   * Palsa mires

8. ROCKY HABITATS AND CAVES

81.   **Scree**

8110   Siliceous scree of the montane to snow levels (*Androsacetalia alpinae and Galeopsietalia ladani*)

8120   Calcareous and calcshist screes of the montane to alpine levels (*Thlaspietea rotundifolii*)

8130   Western Mediterranean and thermophilous scree

8140   Eastern Mediterranean screes

8150   Medio-European upland siliceous screes

8160   * Medio-European calcareous scree of hill and montane levels

82.   **Rocky slopes with chasmophytic vegetation**

8210   Calcareous rocky slopes with chasmophytic vegetation

8220   Siliceous rocky slopes with chasmophytic vegetation

8230   Siliceous rock with pioneer vegetation of the *Sedo-Scleranthion* or of the *Sedo albi-Veronicion dillenii*

8240   * Limestone pavements

83.   **Other rocky habitats**

8310   Caves not open to the public

8320   Fields of lava and natural excavations

8330   Submerged or partially submerged sea caves

8340   Permanent glaciers

9. FORESTS

(Sub)natural woodland vegetation comprising native species forming forests of tall trees, with typical undergrowth, and meeting the following criteria: rare or residual, and/or hosting species of Community interest

90.   **Forests of Boreal Europe**

9010   * Western Taïga

9020   * Fennoscandian hemiboreal natural old broad-leaved deciduous forests (*Quercus, Tilia, Acer, Fraxinus or Ulmus*) rich in epiphytes

Appendix

9030	* Natural forests of primary succession stages of landupheaval coast
9040	Nordic subalpine/subarctic forests with *Betula pubescens* ssp. *czerepanovii*
9050	Fennoscandian herb-rich forests with *Picea abies*
9060	Coniferous forests on, or connected to, glaciofluvial eskers
9070	Fennoscandian wooded pastures
9080	* Fennoscandian deciduous swamp woods
91.	**Forests of Temperate Europe**
9110	*Luzulo-Fagetum* beech forests
9120	Atlantic acidophilous beech forests with *Ilex* and sometimes also *Taxus* in the shrublayer (*Quercion robori-petraeae or Ilici-Fagenion*)
9130	*Asperulo-Fagetum* beech forests
9140	Medio-European subalpine beech woods with *Acer* and *Rumex arifolius*
9150	Medio-European limestone beech forests of the *Cephalanthero-Fagion*
9160	Sub-Atlantic and medio-European oak or oak-hornbeam forests of the *Carpinion betuli*
9170	*Galio-Carpinetum* oak-hornbeam forests
9180	* *Tilio-Acerion* forests of slopes, screes and ravines
9190	Old acidophilous oak woods with *Quercus robur* on sandy plains
91A0	Old sessile oak woods with *Ilex* and *Blechnum* in the British Isles
91B0	Thermophilous *Fraxinus angustifolia* woods
91C0	* Caledonian forest
91D0	* Bog woodland
91E0	* Alluvial forests with *Alnus glutinosa* and *Fraxinus excelsior* (*Alno-Padion, Alnion incanae, Salicion albae*)
91F0	Riparian mixed forests of *Quercus robur, Ulmus laevis* and *Ulmus minor, Fraxinus excelsior* or *Fraxinus angustifolia*, along the great rivers (*Ulmenion minoris*)
91G0	* Pannonic woods with *Quercus petraea* and *Carpinus betulus*
91H0	* Pannonian woods with *Quercus pubescens*
91I0	* Euro-Siberian steppic woods with *Quercus* spp.
91J0	* *Taxus baccata* woods of the British Isles
91K0	Illyrian *Fagus sylvatica* forests (*Aremonio-Fagion*)
91L0	Illyrian oak-hornbeam forests (*Erythronio-Carpinion*)
91M0	Pannonian-Balkanic turkey oak –sessile oak forests
91N0	* Pannonic inland sand dune thicket (*Junipero-Populetum albae*)
91P0	Holy Cross fir forest (*Abietetum polonicum*)
91Q0	Western Carpathian calcicolous *Pinus sylvestris* forests
91R0	Dinaric dolomite Scots pine forests (*Genisto januensis-Pinetum*)
91S0	* Western Pontic beech forests
91T0	Central European lichen Scots pine forests
91U0	Sarmatic steppe pine forest
91V0	Dacian Beech forests (*Symphyto-Fagion*)
91W0	Moesian beech forests
91X0	* Dobrogean beech forests
91Y0	Dacian oak & hornbeam forests
91Z0	Moesian silver lime woods

▼ **M3**

91AA   * Eastern white oak woods

91BA   Moesian silver fir forests

91CA   Rhodopide and Balkan Range Scots pine forests

92.   **Mediterranean deciduous forests**

9210   * Apeninne beech forests with *Taxus* and *Ilex*

9220   * Apennine beech forests with *Abies alba* and beech forests with *Abies nebrodensis*

9230   Galicio-Portuguese oak woods with *Quercus robur* and *Quercus pyrenaica*

9240   *Quercus faginea* and *Quercus canariensis* Iberian woods

9250   *Quercus trojana* woods

9260   *Castanea sativa* woods

9270   Hellenic beech forests with *Abies borisii-regis*

9280   *Quercus frainetto* woods

9290   *Cupressus* forests (*Acero-Cupression*)

92A0   *Salix alba* and *Populus alba* galleries

92B0   Riparian formations on intermittent Mediterranean water courses with *Rhododendron ponticum, Salix* and others

92C0   *Platanus orientalis* and *Liquidambar orientalis* woods (*Platanion orientalis*)

92D0   Southern riparian galleries and thickets (*Nerio-Tamaricetea* and *Securinegion tinctoriae*)

93.   **Mediterranean sclerophyllous forests**

9310   Aegean *Quercus brachyphylla* woods

9320   *Olea* and *Ceratonia* forests

9330   *Quercus suber* forests

9340   *Quercus ilex* and *Quercus rotundifolia* forests

9350   *Quercus macrolepis* forests

9360   * Macaronesian laurel forests (*Laurus, Ocotea*)

9370   * Palm groves of *Phoenix*

9380   Forests of *Ilex aquifolium*

9390   * Scrub and low forest vegetation with *Quercus alnifolia*

93A0   Woodlands with *Quercus infectoria* (*Anagyro foetidae-Quercetum infectoriae*)

94.   **Temperate mountainous coniferous forests**

9410   Acidophilous *Picea* forests of the montane to alpine levels (*Vaccinio-Piceetea*)

9420   Alpine *Larix decidua* and/or *Pinus cembra* forests

9430   Subalpine and montane *Pinus uncinata* forests (* if on gypsum or limestone)

95.   **Mediterranean and Macaronesian mountainous coniferous forests**

9510   * Southern Apennine *Abies alba* forests

9520   *Abies pinsapo* forests

9530   * (Sub-) Mediterranean pine forests with endemic black pines

9540   Mediterranean pine forests with endemic Mesogean pines

9550   Canarian endemic pine forests

9560   * Endemic forests with *Juniperus* spp.

▼ <u>M3</u>

9570	* *Tetraclinis articulata* forests
9580	* Mediterranean *Taxus baccata* woods
9590	* *Cedrus brevifolia* forests (*Cedrosetum brevifoliae*)
95A0	High oro-Mediterranean pine forests

▼ <u>M3</u>

ANIMAL AND PLANT SPECIES OF COMMUNITY INTEREST WHOSE CONSERVATION REQUIRES THE DESIGNATION OF SPECIAL AREAS OF CONSERVATION

Interpretation

(a) Annex II follows on from Annex I for the establishment of a consistent network of special areas of conservation.

(b) The species listed in this Annex are indicated:

— by the name of the species or subspecies, or

— by all the species belonging to a higher taxon or to a designated part of that taxon.

The abbreviation 'spp.' after the name of a family or genus designates all the species belonging to that family or genus.

(c) Symbols

An asterisk (*) before the name of a species indicates that it is a priority species.

Most species listed in this Annex are also listed in Annex IV. Where a species appears in this Annex but does not appear in either Annex IV or Annex V, the species name is followed by the symbol (o); where a species which appears in this Annex also appears in Annex V but does not appear in Annex IV, its name is followed by the symbol (V).

(a) *ANIMALS*

VERTEBRATES

MAMMALS

INSECTIVORA

Talpidae

> *Galemys pyrenaicus*

CHIROPTERA

Rhinolophidae

> *Rhinolophus blasii*
>
> *Rhinolophus euryale*
>
> *Rhinolophus ferrumequinum*
>
> *Rhinolophus hipposideros*
>
> *Rhinolophus mehelyi*

Vespertilionidae

> *Barbastella barbastellus*
>
> *Miniopterus schreibersii*
>
> *Myotis bechsteinii*
>
> *Myotis blythii*
>
> *Myotis capaccinii*
>
> *Myotis dasycneme*
>
> *Myotis emarginatus*
>
> *Myotis myotis*

Pteropodidae

> *Rousettus aegyptiacus*

RODENTIA

Gliridae

Myomimus roachi

Sciuridae

    * *Marmota marmota latirostris*

    * *Pteromys volans (Sciuropterus russicus)*

    Spermophilus citellus (Citellus citellus)

    * *Spermophilus suslicus (Citellus suslicus)*

Castoridae

    Castor fiber (except the Estonian, Latvian, Lithuanian, Finnish and Swedish populations)

Cricetidae

    Mesocricetus newtoni

Microtidae

    Microtus cabrerae

    * *Microtus oeconomus arenicola*

    * *Microtus oeconomus mehelyi*

    Microtus tatricus

Zapodidae

    Sicista subtilis

CARNIVORA

Canidae

    * *Alopex lagopus*

    * *Canis lupus* (except the Estonian population; Greek populations: only south of the 39th parallel; Spanish populations: only those south of the Duero; Latvian, Lithuanian and Finnish populations).

Ursidae

    * *Ursus arctos* (except the Estonian, Finnish, and Swedish populations)

Mustelidae

    * *Gulo gulo*

    Lutra lutra

    Mustela eversmanii

    * *Mustela lutreola*

    Vormela peregusna

Felidae

    Lynx lynx (except the Estonian, Latvian and Finnish populations)

    * *Lynx pardinus*

Phocidae

    Halichoerus grypus (V)

    * *Monachus monachus*

    Phoca hispida bottnica (V)

    * *Phoca hispida saimensis*

    Phoca vitulina (V)

ARTIODACTYLA

Cervidae

    * *Cervus elaphus corsicanus*

    Rangifer tarandus fennicus (o)

▼ M3

Bovidae

* *Bison bonasus*

Capra aegagrus (natural populations)

* *Capra pyrenaica pyrenaica*

Ovis gmelini musimon (Ovis ammon musimon) (natural populations — Corsica and Sardinia)

Ovis orientalis ophion (Ovis gmelini ophion)

* *Rupicapra pyrenaica ornata(Rupicapra rupicapra ornata)*

Rupicapra rupicapra balcanica

* *Rupicapra rupicapra tatrica*

CETACEA

Phocoena phocoena

Tursiops truncatus

REPTILES

CHELONIA (TESTUDINES)

Testudinidae

Testudo graeca

Testudo hermanni

Testudo marginata

Cheloniidae

* *Caretta caretta*

* *Chelonia mydas*

Emydidae

Emys orbicularis

Mauremys caspica

Mauremys leprosa

SAURIA

Lacertidae

Lacerta bonnali (Lacerta monticola)

Lacerta monticola

Lacerta schreiberi

Gallotia galloti insulanagae

* *Gallotia simonyi*

Podarcis lilfordi

Podarcis pityusensis

Scincidae

Chalcides simonyi (Chalcides occidentalis)

Gekkonidae

Phyllodactylus europaeus

OPHIDIA (SERPENTES)

Colubridae

* *Coluber cypriensis*

Elaphe quatuorlineata

Elaphe situla

* *Natrix natrix cypriaca*

▼ M3

Viperidae

* *Macrovipera schweizeri (Vipera lebetina schweizeri)*

Vipera ursinii (except *Vipera ursinii rakosiensis*)

* *Vipera ursinii rakosiensis*

AMPHIBIANS

CAUDATA

Salamandridae

Chioglossa lusitanica

Mertensiella luschani (Salamandra luschani)

* *Salamandra aurorae (Salamandra atra aurorae)*

Salamandrina terdigitata

Triturus carnifex (Triturus cristatus carnifex)

Triturus cristatus (Triturus cristatus cristatus)

Triturus dobrogicus (Triturus cristatus dobrogicus)

Triturus karelinii (Triturus cristatus karelinii)

Triturus montandoni

Triturus vulgaris ampelensis

Proteidae

* *Proteus anguinus*

Plethodontidae

Hydromantes (Speleomantes) ambrosii

Hydromantes (Speleomantes) flavus

Hydromantes (Speleomantes) genei

Hydromantes (Speleomantes) imperialis

Hydromantes (Speleomantes) strinatii

Hydromantes (Speleomantes) supramontis

ANURA

Discoglossidae

* *Alytes muletensis*

Bombina bombina

Bombina variegata

Discoglossus galganoi(including Discoglossus 'jeanneae')

Discoglossus montalentii

Discoglossus sardus

Ranidae

Rana latastei

Pelobatidae

* *Pelobates fuscus insubricus*

FISH

PETROMYZONIFORMES

Petromyzonidae

Eudontomyzon spp. (o)

Lampetra fluviatilis (V) (except the Finnish and Swedish populations)

Lampetra planeri (o) (except the Estonian, Finnish, and Swedish populations)

▼ <u>M3</u>

Lethenteron zanandreai (V)

Petromyzon marinus (o) (except the Swedish populations)

ACIPENSERIFORMES

Acipenseridae

* *Acipenser naccarii*

* *Acipenser sturio*

CLUPEIFORMES

Clupeidae

Alosaspp. (V)

SALMONIFORMES

Salmonidae

Hucho hucho (natural populations) (V)

Salmo macrostigma (o)

Salmo marmoratus (o)

Salmo salar (only in fresh water) (V) (except the Finnish populations)

Coregonidae

* *Coregonus oxyrhynchus* (anadromous populations in certain sectors of the North Sea)

Umbridae

Umbra krameri (o)

CYPRINIFORMES

Cyprinidae

Alburnus albidus (o) *(Alburnus vulturius)*

Anaecypris hispanica

Aspius aspius (V) (except the Finnish populations)

Barbus comiza (V)

Barbus meridionalis (V)

Barbus plebejus (V)

Chalcalburnus chalcoides (o)

Chondrostoma genei (o)

Chondrostoma lusitanicum (o)

Chondrostoma polylepis (o) *(including C. willkommi)*

Chondrostoma soetta (o)

Chondrostoma toxostoma (o)

Gobio albipinnatus (o)

Gobio kessleri (o)

Gobio uranoscopus (o)

Iberocypris palaciosi (o)

* *Ladigesocypris ghigii* (o)

Leuciscus lucumonis (o)

Leuciscus souffia (o)

Pelecus cultratus (V)

Phoxinellus spp. (o)

* *Phoxinus percnurus*

Rhodeus sericeus amarus (o)

▼ M3

      Rutilus pigus (V)

      Rutilus rubilio (o)

      Rutilus arcasii (o)

      Rutilus macrolepidotus (o)

      Rutilus lemmingii (o)

      Rutilus frisii meidingeri (V)

      Rutilus alburnoides (o)

      Scardinius graecus (o)

Cobitidae

      Cobitis elongata (o)

      Cobitis taenia (o) (except the Finnish populations)

      Cobitis trichonica (o)

      Misgurnus fossilis (o)

      Sabanejewia aurata (o)

      Sabanejewia larvata (o) *(Cobitis larvata* and *Cobitis conspersa)*

SILURIFORMES

Siluridae

      Silurus aristotelis (V)

ATHERINIFORMES

Cyprinodontidae

      Aphanius iberus (o)

      Aphanius fasciatus (o)

      * *Valencia hispanica*

      * *Valencia letourneuxi (Valencia hispanica)*

PERCIFORMES

Percidae

      Gymnocephalus baloni

      Gymnocephalus schraetzer (V)

      * *Romanichthys valsanicola*

      Zingel spp. ((o) except *Zingel asper* and *Zingel zingel* (V))

Gobiidae

      Knipowitschia (Padogobius) panizzae (o)

      Padogobius nigricans (o)

      Pomatoschistus canestrini (o)

SCORPAENIFORMES

Cottidae

      Cottus gobio (o) (except the Finnish populations)

      Cottus petiti (o)

INVERTEBRATES

ARTHROPODS

CRUSTACEA

Decapoda

      Austropotamobius pallipes (V)

      * *Austropotamobius torrentium* (V)

▼ <u>M3</u>

Isopoda

    * *Armadillidium ghardalamensis*

INSECTA

Coleoptera

    Agathidium pulchellum (o)

    Bolbelasmus unicornis

    Boros schneideri (o)

    Buprestis splendens

    Carabus hampei

    Carabus hungaricus

    * *Carabus menetriesi pacholei*

    * *Carabus olympiae*

    Carabus variolosus

    Carabus zawadszkii

    Cerambyx cerdo

    Corticaria planula (o)

    Cucujus cinnaberinus

    Dorcadion fulvum cervae

    Duvalius gebhardti

    Duvalius hungaricus

    Dytiscus latissimus

    Graphoderus bilineatus

    Leptodirus hochenwarti

    Limoniscus violaceus (o)

    Lucanus cervus (o)

    Macroplea pubipennis (o)

    Mesosa myops (o)

    Morimus funereus (o)

    * *Osmoderma eremita*

    Oxyporus mannerheimii (o)

    Pilemia tigrina

    * *Phryganophilus ruficollis*

    Probaticus subrugosus

    Propomacrus cypriacus

    * *Pseudogaurotina excellens*

    Pseudoseriscius cameroni

    Pytho kolwensis

    Rhysodes sulcatus (o)

    * *Rosalia alpina*

    Stephanopachys linearis (o)

    Stephanopachys substriatus (o)

    Xyletinus tremulicola (o)

Hemiptera

    Aradus angularis (o)

Appendix

▼ <u>M3</u>

Lepidoptera

Agriades glandon aquilo (o)

Arytrura musculus

* *Callimorpha (Euplagia, Panaxia) quadripunctaria* (o)

Catopta thrips

Chondrosoma fiduciarium

Clossiana improba (o)

Coenonympha oedippus

Colias myrmidone

Cucullia mixta

Dioszeghyana schmidtii

Erannis ankeraria

Erebia calcaria

Erebia christi

Erebia medusa polaris (o)

Eriogaster catax

Euphydryas (Eurodryas, Hypodryas) aurinia (o)

Glyphipterix loricatella

Gortyna borelii lunata

Graellsia isabellae (V)

Hesperia comma catena (o)

Hypodryas maturna

Leptidea morsei

Lignyoptera fumidaria

Lycaena dispar

Lycaena helle

Maculinea nausithous

Maculinea teleius

Melanargia arge

* *Nymphalis vaualbum*

Papilio hospiton

Phyllometra culminaria

Plebicula golgus

Polymixis rufocincta isolata

Polyommatus eroides

Pseudophilotes bavius

Xestia borealis (o)

Xestia brunneopicta (o)

* *Xylomoia strix*

Mantodea

Apteromantis aptera

Odonata

Coenagrion hylas (o)

Coenagrion mercuriale (o)

▼ <u>M3</u>

    Coenagrion ornatum (o)

    Cordulegaster heros

    Cordulegaster trinacriae

    Gomphus graslinii

    Leucorrhinia pectoralis

    Lindenia tetraphylla

    Macromia splendens

    Ophiogomphus cecilia

    Oxygastra curtisii

Orthoptera

    Baetica ustulata

    Brachytrupes megacephalus

    Isophya costata

    Isophya harzi

    Isophya stysi

    Myrmecophilus baronii

    Odontopodisma rubripes

    Paracaloptenus caloptenoides

    Pholidoptera transsylvanica

    Stenobothrus (Stenobothrodes) eurasius

ARACHNIDA

Pseudoscorpiones

    Anthrenochernes stellae (o)

MOLLUSCS

GASTROPODA

    Anisus vorticulus

    Caseolus calculus

    Caseolus commixta

    Caseolus sphaerula

    Chilostoma banaticum

    Discula leacockiana

    Discula tabellata

    Discus guerinianus

    Elona quimperiana

    Geomalacus maculosus

    Geomitra moniziana

    Gibbula nivosa

    * *Helicopsis striata austriaca* (o)

    Hygromia kovacsi

    Idiomela (Helix) subplicata

    Lampedusa imitatrix

    * *Lampedusa melitensis*

    Leiostyla abbreviata

    Leiostyla cassida

▼ <u>M3</u>

    Leiostyla corneocostata

    Leiostyla gibba

    Leiostyla lamellosa

    * *Paladilhia hungarica*

    Sadleriana pannonica

    Theodoxus transversalis

    Vertigo angustior (o)

    Vertigo genesii (o)

    Vertigo geyeri (o)

    Vertigo moulinsiana (o)

BIVALVIA

Unionoida

    Margaritifera durrovensis (Margaritifera margaritifera) (V)

    Margaritifera margaritifera (V)

    Unio crassus

Dreissenidae

    Congeria kusceri

(b) *PLANTS*

PTERIDOPHYTA

ASPLENIACEAE

    Asplenium jahandiezii (Litard.) Rouy

    Asplenium adulterinum Milde

BLECHNACEAE

    Woodwardia radicans (L.) Sm.

DICKSONIACEAE

    Culcita macrocarpa C. Presl

DRYOPTERIDACEAE

    Diplazium sibiricum (Turcz. ex Kunze) Kurata

    * *Dryopteris corleyi* Fraser-Jenk.

    Dryopteris fragans (L.) Schott

HYMENOPHYLLACEAE

    Trichomanes speciosum Willd.

ISOETACEAE

    Isoetes boryana Durieu

    Isoetes malinverniana Ces. & De Not.

MARSILEACEAE

    Marsilea batardae Launert

    Marsilea quadrifolia L.

    Marsilea strigosa Willd.

OPHIOGLOSSACEAE

    Botrychium simplex Hitchc.

    Ophioglossum polyphyllum A. Braun

GYMNOSPERMAE

PINACEAE

    * *Abies nebrodensis* (Lojac.) Mattei

ANGIOSPERMAE

ALISMATACEAE

    * *Alisma wahlenbergii* (Holmberg) Juz.

    Caldesia parnassifolia (L.) Parl.

    Luronium natans (L.) Raf.

AMARYLLIDACEAE

    Leucojum nicaeense Ard.

    Narcissus asturiensis (Jordan) Pugsley

    Narcissus calcicola Mendonça

    Narcissus cyclamineus DC.

    Narcissus fernandesii G. Pedro

    Narcissus humilis (Cav.) Traub

    * *Narcissus nevadensis* Pugsley

    Narcissus pseudonarcissus L. subsp. *nobilis* (Haw.) A. Fernandes

    Narcissus scaberulus Henriq.

    Narcissus triandrus L. subsp. *capax* (Salisb.) D. A. Webb.

    Narcissus viridiflorus Schousboe

ASCLEPIADACEAE

    Vincetoxicum pannonicum (Borhidi) Holub

BORAGINACEAE

    * *Anchusa crispa* Viv.

    Echium russicum J.F.Gemlin

    * *Lithodora nitida* (H. Ern) R. Fernandes

    Myosotis lusitanica Schuster

    Myosotis rehsteineri Wartm.

    Myosotis retusifolia R. Afonso

    Omphalodes kuzinskyanae Willk.

    * *Omphalodes littoralis* Lehm.

    * *Onosma tornensis* Javorka

    Solenanthus albanicus (Degen & al.) Degen & Baldacci

    * *Symphytum cycladense* Pawl.

CAMPANULACEAE

    Adenophora lilifolia (L.) Ledeb.

    Asyneuma giganteum (Boiss.) Bornm.

    * *Campanula bohemica* Hruby

    * *Campanula gelida* Kovanda

    Campanula romanica Săvul.

    * *Campanula sabatia* De Not.

    * *Campanula serrata* (Kit.) Hendrych

    Campanula zoysii Wulfen

    Jasione crispa (Pourret) Samp. subsp. *serpentinica* Pinto da Silva

    Jasione lusitanica A. DC.

CARYOPHYLLACEAE

Appendix

Arenaria ciliata L. subsp. *pseudofrigida* Ostenf. & O.C. Dahl

Arenaria humifusa Wahlenberg

* *Arenaria nevadensis* Boiss. & Reuter

Arenaria provincialis Chater & Halliday

* *Cerastium alsinifolium* Tausch *Cerastium dinaricum* G. Beck & Szysz.

Dianthus arenarius L. subsp. *arenarius*

* *Dianthus arenarius* subsp. *bohemicus* (Novak) O.Schwarz

Dianthus cintranus Boiss. & Reuter subsp. *cintranus* Boiss. & Reuter

* *Dianthus diutinus* Kit.

* *Dianthus lumnitzeri* Wiesb.

Dianthus marizii (Samp.) Samp.

* *Dianthus moravicus* Kovanda

* *Dianthus nitidus* Waldst. et Kit.

Dianthus plumarius subsp. *regis-stephani* (Rapcs.) Baksay

Dianthus rupicola Biv.

* *Gypsophila papillosa* P. Porta

Herniaria algarvica Chaudhri

* *Herniaria latifolia* Lapeyr. subsp. *litardierei* Gamis

Herniaria lusitanica (Chaudhri) subsp. *berlengiana* Chaudhri

Herniaria maritima Link

* *Minuartia smejkalii* Dvorakova

Moehringia jankae Griseb. ex Janka

Moehringia lateriflora (L.) Fenzl.

Moehringia tommasinii Marches.

Moehringia villosa (Wulfen) Fenzl

Petrocoptis grandiflora Rothm.

Petrocoptis montsicciana O. Bolos & Rivas Mart.

Petrocoptis pseudoviscosa Fernández Casas

Silene furcata Rafin. subsp. *angustiflora* (Rupr.) Walters

* *Silene hicesiae* Brullo & Signorello

Silene hifacensis Rouy ex Willk.

* *Silene holzmanii* Heldr. ex Boiss.

Silene longicilia (Brot.) Otth.

Silene mariana Pau

* *Silene orphanidis* Boiss

* *Silene rothmaleri* Pinto da Silva

* *Silene velutina* Pourret ex Loisel.

CHENOPODIACEAE

* *Bassia (Kochia) saxicola* (Guss.) A. J. Scott

* *Cremnophyton lanfrancoi* Brullo et Pavone

* *Salicornia veneta* Pignatti & Lausi

CISTACEAE

Cistus palhinhae Ingram

Halimium verticillatum (Brot.) Sennen

▼ <u>M3</u>

Helianthemum alypoides Losa & Rivas Goday

Helianthemum caput-felis Boiss.

* *Tuberaria major* (Willk.) Pinto da Silva & Rozeira

COMPOSITAE

* *Anthemis glaberrima* (Rech. f.) Greuter

Artemisia campestris L. subsp. *bottnica* A.N. Lundström ex Kindb.

* *Artemisia granatensis* Boiss.

* *Artemisia laciniata* Willd.

Artemisia oelandica (Besser) Komaror

* *Artemisia pancicii* (Janka) Ronn.

* *Aster pyrenaeus* Desf. ex DC

* *Aster sorrentinii* (Tod) Lojac.

Carlina onopordifolia Besser

* *Carduus myriacanthus* Salzm. ex DC.

* *Centaurea alba* L. subsp. *heldreichii* (Halacsy) Dostal

* *Centaurea alba* L. subsp. *princeps* (Boiss. & Heldr.) Gugler

* *Centaurea akamantis* T. Georgiadis & G. Chatzikyriakou

* *Centaurea attica* Nyman subsp. *megarensis* (Halacsy & Hayek) Dostal

* *Centaurea balearica* J. D. Rodriguez

* *Centaurea borjae* Valdes-Berm. & Rivas Goday

* *Centaurea citricolor* Font Quer

Centaurea corymbosa Pourret

Centaurea gadorensis G. Blanca

* *Centaurea horrida* Badaro

Centaurea immanuelis-loewii Degen

Centaurea jankae Brandza

* *Centaurea kalambakensis* Freyn & Sint.

Centaurea kartschiana Scop.

* *Centaurea lactiflora* Halacsy

Centaurea micrantha Hoffmanns. & Link subsp. *herminii* (Rouy) Dostál

* *Centaurea niederi* Heldr.

* *Centaurea peucedanifolia* Boiss. & Orph.

* *Centaurea pinnata* Pau

Centaurea pontica Prodan & E. I. Nyárády

Centaurea pulvinata (G. Blanca) G. Blanca

Centaurea rothmalerana (Arènes) Dostál

Centaurea vicentina Mariz

Cirsium brachycephalum Juratzka

* *Crepis crocifolia* Boiss. & Heldr.

Crepis granatensis (Willk.) B. Blanca & M. Cueto

Crepis pusilla (Sommier) Merxmüller

Crepis tectorum L. subsp. *nigrescens*

Erigeron frigidus Boiss. ex DC.

* *Helichrysum melitense* (Pignatti) Brullo et al

▼ <u>M3</u>

Hymenostemma pseudanthemis (Kunze) Willd.

Hyoseris frutescens Brullo et Pavone

* *Jurinea cyanoides* (L.) Reichenb.

* *Jurinea fontqueri* Cuatrec.

* *Lamyropsis microcephala* (Moris) Dittrich & Greuter

Leontodon microcephalus (Boiss. ex DC.) Boiss.

Leontodon boryi Boiss.

* *Leontodon siculus* (Guss.) Finch & Sell

Leuzea longifolia Hoffmanns. & Link

Ligularia sibirica (L.) Cass.

* *Palaeocyanus crassifolius* (Bertoloni) Dostal

Santolina impressa Hoffmanns. & Link

Santolina semidentata Hoffmanns. & Link

Saussurea alpina subsp. *esthonica* (Baer ex Rupr) Kupffer

* *Senecio elodes* Boiss. ex DC.

Senecio jacobea L. subsp. *gotlandicus* (Neuman) Sterner

Senecio nevadensis Boiss. & Reuter

* *Serratula lycopifolia* (Vill.) A.Kern

Tephroseris longifolia (Jacq.) Griseb et Schenk subsp. *moravica*

CONVOLVULACEAE

* *Convolvulus argyrothamnus* Greuter

* *Convolvulus fernandesii* Pinto da Silva & Teles

CRUCIFERAE

Alyssum pyrenaicum Lapeyr.

* *Arabis kennedyae* Meikle

Arabis sadina (Samp.) P. Cout.

Arabis scopoliana Boiss

* *Biscutella neustriaca* Bonnet

Biscutella vincentina (Samp.) Rothm.

Boleum asperum (Pers.) Desvaux

Brassica glabrescens Poldini

Brassica hilarionis Post

Brassica insularis Moris

* *Brassica macrocarpa* Guss.

Braya linearis Rouy

* *Cochlearia polonica* E. Fröhlich

* *Cochlearia tatrae* Borbas

* *Coincya rupestris* Rouy

* *Coronopus navasii* Pau

Crambe tataria Sebeok

Diplotaxis ibicensis (Pau) Gómez-Campo

* *Diplotaxis siettiana* Maire

Diplotaxis vicentina (P. Cout.) Rothm.

Draba cacuminum Elis Ekman

▼ M3

Draba cinerea Adams

Draba dorneri Heuffel.

Erucastrum palustre (Pirona) Vis.

* *Erysimum pieninicum* (Zapal.) Pawl.

* *Iberis arbuscula* Runemark

Iberis procumbens Lange subsp. *microcarpa* Franco & Pinto da Silva

* *Jonopsidium acaule* (Desf.) Reichenb.

Jonopsidium savianum (Caruel) Ball ex Arcang.

Rhynchosinapis erucastrum (L.) Dandy ex Clapham subsp. *cintrana* (Coutinho) Franco & P. Silva *(Coincya cintrana* (P. Cout.) Pinto da Silva)

Sisymbrium cavanillesianum Valdés & Castroviejo

Sisymbrium supinum L.

Thlaspi jankae A.Kern.

CYPERACEAE

Carex holostoma Drejer

* *Carex panormitana* Guss.

Eleocharis carniolica Koch

DIOSCOREACEAE

* *Borderea chouardii* (Gaussen) Heslot

DROSERACEAE

Aldrovanda vesiculosa L.

ELATINACEAE

Elatine gussonei (Sommier) Brullo et al

ERICACEAE

Rhododendron luteum Sweet

EUPHORBIACEAE

* *Euphorbia margalidiana* Kuhbier & Lewejohann

Euphorbia transtagana Boiss.

GENTIANACEAE

* *Centaurium rigualii* Esteve

* *Centaurium somedanum* Lainz

Gentiana ligustica R. de Vilm. & Chopinet

Gentianella anglica (Pugsley) E. F. Warburg

* *Gentianella bohemica* Skalicky

GERANIACEAE

* *Erodium astragaloides* Boiss. & Reuter

Erodium paularense Fernández-González & Izco

* *Erodium rupicola* Boiss.

GLOBULARIACEAE

* *Globularia stygia* Orph. ex Boiss.

GRAMINEAE

Arctagrostis latifolia (R. Br.) Griseb.

Arctophila fulva (Trin.) N. J. Anderson

Avenula hackelii (Henriq.) Holub

Bromus grossus Desf. ex DC.

▼ <u>M3</u>

Calamagrostis chalybaea (Laest.) Fries

Cinna latifolia (Trev.) Griseb.

Coleanthus subtilis (Tratt.) Seidl

Festuca brigantina (Markgr.-Dannenb.) Markgr.-Dannenb.

Festuca duriotagana Franco & R. Afonso

Festuca elegans Boiss.

Festuca henriquesii Hack.

Festuca summilusitana Franco & R. Afonso

Gaudinia hispanica Stace & Tutin

Holcus setiglumis Boiss. & Reuter subsp. *duriensis Pinto da Silva*

Micropyropsis tuberosa Romero — Zarco & Cabezudo

Poa granitica Br.-Bl. subsp. *disparilis* (E. I. Nyárády) E. I. Nyárády

* *Poa riphaea* (Ascher et Graebner) Fritsch

Pseudarrhenatherum pallens (Link) J. Holub

Puccinellia phryganodes (Trin.) Scribner + Merr.

Puccinellia pungens (Pau) Paunero

* *Stipa austroitalica* Martinovsky

* *Stipa bavarica* Martinovsky & H. Scholz

Stipa danubialis Dihoru & Roman

* *Stipa styriaca* Martinovsky

* *Stipa veneta* Moraldo

* *Stipa zalesskii* Wilensky

Trisetum subalpestre (Hartman) Neuman

GROSSULARIACEAE

* *Ribes sardoum* Martelli

HIPPURIDACEAE

Hippuris tetraphylla L. Fil.

HYPERICACEAE

* *Hypericum aciferum* (Greuter) N.K.B. Robson

IRIDACEAE

Crocus cyprius Boiss. et Kotschy

Crocus hartmannianus Holmboe

Gladiolus palustris Gaud.

Iris aphylla L. subsp. *hungarica* Hegi

Iris humilis Georgi subsp. *arenaria* (Waldst. et Kit.) A. et D.Löve

JUNCACEAE

Juncus valvatus Link

Luzula arctica Blytt

LABIATAE

Dracocephalum austriacum L.

* *Micromeria taygetea* P. H. Davis

Nepeta dirphya (Boiss.) Heldr. ex Halacsy

* *Nepeta sphaciotica* P. H. Davis

Origanum dictamnus L.

▼ **M3**

Phlomis brevibracteata Turril

Phlomis cypria Post

Salvia veneris Hedge

Sideritis cypria Post

Sideritis incana subsp. *glauca* (Cav.) Malagarriga

Sideritis javalambrensis Pau

Sideritis serrata Cav. ex Lag.

Teucrium lepicephalum Pau

Teucrium turredanum Losa & Rivas Goday

* *Thymus camphoratus* Hoffmanns. & Link

Thymus carnosus Boiss.

* *Thymus lotocephalus* G. López & R. Morales *(Thymus cephalotos* L.)

LEGUMINOSAE

Anthyllis hystrix Cardona, Contandr. & E. Sierra

* *Astragalus algarbiensis* Coss. ex Bunge

* *Astragalus aquilanus* Anzalone

Astragalus centralpinus Braun-Blanquet

* *Astragalus macrocarpus* DC. subsp. *lefkarensis*

* *Astragalus maritimus* Moris

Astragalus peterfii Jáv.

Astragalus tremolsianus Pau

* *Astragalus verrucosus* Moris

* *Cytisus aeolicus* Guss. ex Lindl.

Genista dorycnifolia Font Quer

Genista holopetala (Fleischm. ex Koch) Baldacci

Melilotus segetalis (Brot.) Ser. subsp. *fallax Franco*

* *Ononis hackelii* Lange

Trifolium saxatile All.

* *Vicia bifoliolata* J.D. Rodríguez

LENTIBULARIACEAE

* *Pinguicula crystallina* Sm.

Pinguicula nevadensis (Lindb.) Casper

LILIACEAE

Allium grosii Font Quer

* *Androcymbium rechingeri* Greuter

* *Asphodelus bento-rainhae* P. Silva

* *Chionodoxa lochiae* Meikle in Kew Bull.

Colchicum arenarium Waldst. et Kit.

Hyacinthoides vicentina (Hoffmans. & Link) Rothm.

* *Muscari gussonei* (Parl.) Tod.

Scilla litardierei Breist.

* *Scilla morrisii* Meikle

Tulipa cypria Stapf

Tulipa hungarica Borbas

Appendix

▼ **M3**

LINACEAE

    * *Linum dolomiticum* Borbas

    * *Linum muelleri* Moris *(Linum maritimum muelleri)*

LYTHRACEAE

    * *Lythrum flexuosum* Lag.

MALVACEAE

    Kosteletzkya pentacarpos (L.) Ledeb.

NAJADACEAE

    Najas flexilis (Willd.) Rostk. & W.L. Schmidt

    Najas tenuissima (A. Braun) Magnus

OLEACEAE

    Syringa josikaea Jacq. Fil. ex Reichenb.

ORCHIDACEAE

    Anacamptis urvilleana Sommier et Caruana Gatto

    Calypso bulbosa L.

    * *Cephalanthera cucullata* Boiss. & Heldr.

    Cypripedium calceolus L.

    Dactylorhiza kalopissii E.Nelson

    Gymnigritella runei Teppner & Klein

    Himantoglossum adriaticum Baumann

    Himantoglossum caprinum (Bieb.) V.Koch

    Liparis loeselii (L.) Rich.

    * *Ophrys kotschyi* H.Fleischm. et Soo

    * *Ophrys lunulata* Parl.

    Ophrys melitensis (Salkowski) J et P Devillers-Terschuren

    Platanthera obtusata (Pursh) subsp. *oligantha* (Turez.) Hulten

OROBANCHACEAE

    Orobanche densiflora Salzm. ex Reut.

PAEONIACEAE

    Paeonia cambessedesii (Willk.) Willk.

    Paeonia clusii F.C. Stern subsp. *rhodia* (Stearn) Tzanoudakis

    Paeonia officinalis L. subsp. *banatica* (Rachel) Soo

    Paeonia parnassica Tzanoudakis

PALMAE

    Phoenix theophrasti Greuter

PAPAVERACEAE

    Corydalis gotlandica Lidén

    Papaver laestadianum (Nordh.) Nordh.

    Papaver radicatum Rottb. subsp. *hyperboreum* Nordh.

PLANTAGINACEAE

    Plantago algarbiensis Sampaio *(Plantago bracteosa* (Willk.) G. Sampaio)

    Plantago almogravensis Franco

PLUMBAGINACEAE

    Armeria berlengensis Daveau

* *Armeria helodes* Martini & Pold

Armeria neglecta Girard

Armeria pseudarmeria (Murray) Mansfeld

* *Armeria rouyana* Daveau

Armeria soleirolii (Duby) Godron

Armeria velutina Welw. ex Boiss. & Reuter

Limonium dodartii (Girard) O. Kuntze subsp. *lusitanicum* (Daveau) Franco

* *Limonium insulare* (Beg. & Landi) Arrig. & Diana

Limonium lanceolatum (Hoffmans. & Link) Franco

Limonium multiflorum Erben

* *Limonium pseudolaetum* Arrig. & Diana

* *Limonium strictissimum* (Salzmann) Arrig.

POLYGONACEAE

Persicaria foliosa (H. Lindb.) Kitag.

Polygonum praelongum Coode & Cullen

Rumex rupestris Le Gall

PRIMULACEAE

Androsace mathildae Levier

Androsace pyrenaica Lam.

* *Cyclamen fatrense* Halda et Sojak

* *Primula apennina* Widmer

Primula carniolica Jacq.

Primula nutans Georgi

Primula palinuri Petagna

Primula scandinavica Bruun

Soldanella villosa Darracq.

RANUNCULACEAE

* *Aconitum corsicum* Gayer *(Aconitum napellus* subsp. *corsicum)*

Aconitum firmum (Reichenb.) Neilr subsp. *moravicum* Skalicky

Adonis distorta Ten.

Aquilegia bertolonii Schott

Aquilegia kitaibelii Schott

* *Aquilegia pyrenaica* D.C. subsp. *cazorlensis* (Heywood) Galiano

* *Consolida samia* P.H. Davis

* *Delphinium caseyi* B.L.Burtt

Pulsatilla grandis Wenderoth *Pulsatilla patens* (L.) Miller

* *Pulsatilla pratensis* (L.) Miller subsp. *hungarica* Soo

* *Pulsatilla slavica* G.Reuss.

* *Pulsatilla subslavica* Futak ex Goliasova

Pulsatilla vulgaris Hill. subsp. *gotlandica* (Johanss.) Zaemelis & Paegle

Ranunculus kykkoensis Meikle

Ranunculus lapponicus L.

* *Ranunculus weyleri* Mares

RESEDACEAE

▼ M3

Reseda decursiva Forssk.

ROSACEAE

Agrimonia pilosa Ledebour

Potentilla delphinensis Gren. & Godron

Potentilla emilii-popii Nyárády

* *Pyrus magyarica* Terpo

Sorbus teodorii Liljefors

RUBIACEAE

Galium cracoviense Ehrend.

* *Galium litorale* Guss.

Galium moldavicum (Dobrescu) Franco

* *Galium sudeticum* Tausch

* *Galium viridiflorum* Boiss. & Reuter

SALICACEAE

Salix salvifolia Brot. subsp. *australis* Franco

SANTALACEAE

Thesium ebracteatum Hayne

SAXIFRAGACEAE

Saxifraga berica (Beguinot) D.A. Webb

Saxifraga florulenta Moretti

Saxifraga hirculus L.

Saxifraga osloënsis Knaben

Saxifraga tombeanensis Boiss. ex Engl.

SCROPHULARIACEAE

Antirrhinum charidemi Lange

Chaenorrhinum serpyllifolium (Lange) Lange subsp. *lusitanicum* R. Fernandes

* *Euphrasia genargentea* (Feoli) Diana

Euphrasia marchesettii Wettst. ex Marches.

Linaria algarviana Chav.

Linaria coutinhoi Valdés

Linaria loeselii Schweigger

* *Linaria ficalhoana* Rouy

Linaria flava (Poiret) Desf.

* *Linaria hellenica* Turrill

Linaria pseudolaxiflora Lojacono

* *Linaria ricardoi* Cout.

Linaria tonzigii Lona

* *Linaria tursica* B. Valdés & Cabezudo

Odontites granatensis Boiss.

* *Pedicularis sudetica* Willd.

Rhinanthus oesilensis (Ronniger & Saarsoo) Vassilcz

Tozzia carpathica Wol.

Verbascum litigiosum Samp.

Veronica micrantha Hoffmanns. & Link

▼M3

    * *Veronica oetaea* L.-A. Gustavsson

SOLANACEAE

    *Atropa baetica Willk.

THYMELAEACEAE

    * *Daphne arbuscula* Celak

    Daphne petraea Leybold

    * *Daphne rodriguezii* Texidor

ULMACEAE

    Zelkova abelicea (Lam.) Boiss.

UMBELLIFERAE

    * *Angelica heterocarpa* Lloyd

    Angelica palustris (Besser) Hoffm.

    * *Apium bermejoi* Llorens

    Apium repens (Jacq.) Lag.

    Athamanta cortiana Ferrarini

    * *Bupleurum capillare* Boiss. & Heldr.

    * *Bupleurum kakiskalae* Greuter

    Eryngium alpinum L.

    * *Eryngium viviparum* Gay

    * *Ferula sadleriana* Lebed.

    Hladnikia pastinacifolia Reichenb.

    * *Laserpitium longiradium* Boiss.

    * *Naufraga balearica* Constans & Cannon

    * *Oenanthe conioides* Lange

    Petagnia saniculifolia Guss.

    Rouya polygama (Desf.) Coincy

    * *Seseli intricatum* Boiss.

    Seseli leucospermum Waldst. et Kit

    Thorella verticillatinundata (Thore) Briq.

VALERIANACEAE

    Centranthus trinervis (Viv.) Beguinot

VIOLACEAE

    Viola delphinantha Boiss.

    * *Viola hispida* Lam.

    Viola jaubertiana Mares & Vigineix

    Viola rupestris F.W. Schmidt subsp. *relicta* Jalas

LOWER PLANTS

BRYOPHYTA

    Bruchia vogesiaca Schwaegr. (o)

    Bryhnia novae-angliae (Sull & Lesq.) Grout (o)

    * *Bryoerythrophyllum campylocarpum* (C. Müll.) Crum. *(Bryoerythrophyllum machadoanum* (Sergio) M. O. Hill) (o)

    Buxbaumia viridis (Moug.) Moug. & Nestl. (o)

    Cephalozia macounii (Aust.) Aust. (o)

    Cynodontium suecicum (H. Arn. & C. Jens.) I. Hag. (o)

▼ M3

Dichelyma capillaceum (Dicks) Myr. (o)

Dicranum viride (Sull. & Lesq.) Lindb. (o)

Distichophyllum carinatum Dix. & Nich. (o)

Drepanocladus (Hamatocaulis) vernicosus (Mitt.) Warnst. (o)

Encalypta mutica (I. Hagen) (o)

Hamatocaulis lapponicus (Norrl.) Hedenäs (o)

Herzogiella turfacea (Lindb.) I. Wats. (o)

Hygrohypnum montanum (Lindb.) Broth. (o)

Jungermannia handelii (Schiffn.) Amak. (o)

Mannia triandra (Scop.) Grolle (o)

* *Marsupella profunda* Lindb. (o)

Meesia longiseta Hedw. (o)

Nothothylas orbicularis (Schwein.) Sull. (o)

Ochyraea tatrensis Vana (o)

Orthothecium lapponicum (Schimp.) C. Hartm. (o)

Orthotrichum rogeri Brid. (o)

Petalophyllum ralfsii (Wils.) Nees & Gott. (o)

Plagiomnium drummondii (Bruch & Schimp.) T. Kop. (o)

Riccia breidleri Jur. (o)

Riella helicophylla (Bory & Mont.) Mont. (o)

Scapania massolongi (K. Müll.) K. Müll. (o)

Sphagnum pylaisii Brid. (o)

Tayloria rudolphiana (Garov) B. & S. (o)

Tortella rigens (N. Alberts) (o)

SPECIES FOR MACARONESIA

PTERIDOPHYTA

HYMENOPHYLLACEAE

Hymenophyllum maderensis Gibby & Lovis

DRYOPTERIDACEAE

* *Polystichum drepanum* (Sw.) C. Presl.

ISOETACEAE

Isoetes azorica Durieu & Paiva ex Milde

MARSILEACEAE

* *Marsilea azorica* Launert & Paiva

ANGIOSPERMAE

ASCLEPIADACEAE

Caralluma burchardii N. E. Brown

* *Ceropegia chrysantha* Svent.

BORAGINACEAE

Echium candicans L. fil.

* *Echium gentianoides* Webb & Coincy

Myosotis azorica H. C. Watson

Myosotis maritima Hochst. in Seub.

CAMPANULACEAE

▼ M3

* *Azorina vidalii* (H. C. Watson) Feer

Musschia aurea (L. f.) DC.

* *Musschia wollastonii* Lowe

CAPRIFOLIACEAE

* *Sambucus palmensis* Link

CARYOPHYLLACEAE

Spergularia azorica (Kindb.) Lebel

CELASTRACEAE

Maytenus umbellata (R. Br.) Mabb.

CHENOPODIACEAE

Beta patula Ait.

CISTACEAE

Cistus chinamadensis Banares & Romero

* *Helianthemum bystropogophyllum* Svent.

COMPOSITAE

Andryala crithmifolia Ait.

* *Argyranthemum lidii* Humphries

Argyranthemum thalassophylum (Svent.) Hump.

Argyranthemum winterii (Svent.) Humphries

* *Atractylis arbuscula* Svent. & Michaelis

Atractylis preauxiana Schultz.

Calendula maderensis DC.

Cheirolophus duranii (Burchard) Holub

Cheirolophus ghomerytus (Svent.) Holub

Cheirolophus junonianus (Svent.) Holub

Cheirolophus massonianus (Lowe) Hansen & Sund.

Cirsium latifolium Lowe

Helichrysum gossypinum Webb

Helichrysum monogynum Burtt & Sund.

Hypochoeris oligocephala (Svent. & Bramw.) Lack

* *Lactuca watsoniana* Trel.

* *Onopordum nogalesii* Svent.

* *Onorpordum carduelinum* Bolle

* *Pericallis hadrosoma* (Svent.) B. Nord.

Phagnalon benettii Lowe

Stemmacantha cynaroides (Chr. Son. in Buch) Ditt

Sventenia bupleuroides Font Quer

* *Tanacetum ptarmiciflorum* Webb & Berth

CONVOLVULACEAE

* *Convolvulus caput-medusae* Lowe

* *Convolvulus lopez-socasii* Svent.

* *Convolvulus massonii* A. Dietr.

CRASSULACEAE

Aeonium gomeraense Praeger

Appendix

Aeonium saundersii Bolle

Aichryson dumosum (Lowe) Praeg.

Monanthes wildpretii Banares & Scholz

Sedum brissemoretii Raymond-Hamet

CRUCIFERAE

* *Crambe arborea* Webb ex Christ

Crambe laevigata DC. ex Christ

* *Crambe sventenii* R. Petters ex Bramwell & Sund.

* *Parolinia schizogynoides* Svent.

Sinapidendron rupestre (Ait.) Lowe

CYPERACEAE

Carex malato-belizii Raymond

DIPSACACEAE

Scabiosa nitens Roemer & J. A. Schultes

ERICACEAE

Erica scoparia L. subsp. *azorica* (Hochst.) D. A. Webb

EUPHORBIACEAE

* *Euphorbia handiensis* Burchard

Euphorbia lambii Svent.

Euphorbia stygiana H. C. Watson

GERANIACEAE

* *Geranium maderense* P. F. Yeo

GRAMINEAE

Deschampsia maderensis (Haeck. & Born.) Buschm.

Phalaris maderensis (Menezes) Menezes

GLOBULARIACEAE

* *Globularia ascanii* D. Bramwell & Kunkel

* *Globularia sarcophylla* Svent.

LABIATAE

* *Sideritis cystosiphon* Svent.

* *Sideritis discolor* (Webb ex de Noe) Bolle

Sideritis infernalis Bolle

Sideritis marmorea Bolle

Teucrium abutiloides L'Hér.

Teucrium betonicum L'Hér.

LEGUMINOSAE

* *Anagyris latifolia* Brouss. ex. Willd.

Anthyllis lemanniana Lowe

* *Dorycnium spectabile* Webb & Berthel

* *Lotus azoricus* P. W. Ball

Lotus callis-viridis D. Bramwell & D. H. Davis

* *Lotus kunkelii* (E. Chueca) D. Bramwell & al.

* *Teline rosmarinifolia* Webb & Berthel.

* *Teline salsoloides* Arco & Acebes.

▼ M3

    Vicia dennesiana H. C. Watson

LILIACEAE

    * *Androcymbium psammophilum* Svent.

    Scilla maderensis Menezes

    Semele maderensis Costa

LORANTHACEAE

    Arceuthobium azoricum Wiens & Hawksw.

MYRICACEAE

    * *Myrica rivas-martinezii* Santos.

OLEACEAE

    Jasminum azoricum L.

    Picconia azorica (Tutin) Knobl.

ORCHIDACEAE

    Goodyera macrophylla Lowe

PITTOSPORACEAE

    * *Pittosporum coriaceum* Dryand. ex. Ait.

PLANTAGINACEAE

    Plantago malato-belizii Lawalree

PLUMBAGINACEAE

    * *Limonium arborescens* (Brouss.) Kuntze

    Limonium dendroides Svent.

    **Limonium spectabile* (Svent.) Kunkel & Sunding

    **Limonium sventenii* Santos & Fernández Galván

POLYGONACEAE

    Rumex azoricus Rech. fil.

RHAMNACEAE

    Frangula azorica Tutin

ROSACEAE

    * *Bencomia brachystachya* Svent.

    Bencomia sphaerocarpa Svent.

    * *Chamaemeles coriacea* Lindl.

    Dendriopoterium pulidoi Svent.

    Marcetella maderensis (Born.) Svent.

    Prunus lusitanica L. subsp. *azorica* (Mouillef.) Franco

    Sorbus maderensis (Lowe) Dode

SANTALACEAE

    Kunkeliella subsucculenta Kammer

SCROPHULARIACEAE

    * *Euphrasia azorica* H.C. Watson

    Euphrasia grandiflora Hochst. in Seub.

    * *Isoplexis chalcantha* Svent. & O'Shanahan

    Isoplexis isabelliana (Webb & Berthel.) Masferrer

    Odontites holliana (Lowe) Benth.

    Sibthorpia peregrina L.

Appendix

SOLANACEAE

* *Solanum lidii* Sunding

UMBELLIFERAE

Ammi trifoliatum (H. C. Watson) Trelease

Bupleurum handiense (Bolle) Kunkel

Chaerophyllum azoricum Trelease

Ferula latipinna Santos

Melanoselinum decipiens (Schrader & Wendl.) Hoffm.

Monizia edulis Lowe

Oenanthe divaricata (R. Br.) Mabb.

Sanicula azorica Guthnick ex Seub.

VIOLACEAE

Viola paradoxa Lowe

LOWER PLANTS

BRYOPHYTA

* *Echinodium spinosum* (Mitt.) Jur. (o)

* *Thamnobryum fernandesii* Sergio (o).

ANNEX III

CRITERIA FOR SELECTING SITES ELIGIBLE FOR IDENTIFICATION AS SITES OF COMMUNITY IMPORTANCE AND DESIGNATION AS SPECIAL AREAS OF CONSERVATION

STAGE 1: **Assessment at national level of the relative importance of sites for each natural habitat type in Annex I and each species in Annex II (including priority natural habitat types and priority species)**

A. *Site assessment criteria for a given natural habitat type in Annex I*

    (a) Degree of representativity of the natural habitat ►**C1** type on the site. ◄

    (b) Area of the site covered by the natural habitat type in relation to the total area covered by that natural habitat type within national territory.

    (c) Degree of conservation of the structure and functions of the natural habitat type concerned and restoration possibilities.

    (d) Global assessment of the value of the site for conservation of the natural habitat type concerned.

B. *Site assessment criteria for a given species in Annex II*

    (a) Size and density of the population of the species present on the site in relation to the populations present within national territory.

    (b) Degree of conservation of the features of the habitat which are important for the species concerned and restoration possibilities.

    (c) Degree of isolation of the population present on the site in relation to the natural range of the species.

    (d) Global assessment of the value of the site for conservation of the species concerned.

C. On the basis of these criteria, Member States will classify the sites which they propose on the national list as sites eligible for identification as sites of Community importance according to their relative value for the conservation of each natural habitat type in Annex I or each species in Annex II.

D. That list will show the sites containing the priority natural habitat types and priority species selected by the Member States on the basis of the criteria in A and B above.

STAGE 2: **Assessment of the Community importance of the sites included on the national lists**

1. All the sites identified by the Member States in Stage 1 which contain priority natural habitat types and/or species will be considered as sites of Community importance.

2. The assessment of the Community importance of other sites on Member States' lists, i.e. their contribution to maintaining or re-establishing, at a favourable conservation status, a natural habitat in Annex I or a species in Annex II and/or to the coherence of Natura 2000 will take account of the following criteria:

    (a) relative value of the site at national level;

    (b) geographical situation of the site in relation to migration routes of species in Annex II and whether it belongs to a continuous ecosystem situated on both sides of one or more internal Community frontiers;

    (c) total area of the site;

    (d) number of natural habitat types in Annex I and species in Annex II present on the site;

    (e) global ecological value of the site for the biogeographical regions concerned and/or for the whole of the territory referred to in Article 2, as regards both ►**C1** the characteristic or unique ◄ aspect of its features and the way they are combined.

Appendix

ANIMAL AND PLANT SPECIES OF COMMUNITY INTEREST IN NEED OF STRICT PROTECTION

The species listed in this Annex are indicated:

— by the name of species or subspecies, or

— by the body of species belonging to a higher taxon or to a designated part of that taxon.

The abbreviation 'spp.' after the name of a family or genus designates all the species belonging to that family or genus.

(a) *ANIMALS*

VERTEBRATES

MAMMALS

INSECTIVORA

Erinaceidae

> *Erinaceus algirus*

Soricidae

> *Crocidura canariensis*

> *Crocidura sicula*

Talpidae

> *Galemys pyrenaicus*

MICROCHIROPTERA

> All species

MEGACHIROPTERA

Pteropodidae

> *Rousettus aegyptiacus*

RODENTIA

Gliridae

> All species except *Glis glis* and *Eliomys quercinus*

Sciuridae

> *Marmota marmota latirostris*

> *Pteromys volans (Sciuropterus russicus)*

> *Spermophilus citellus (Citellus citellus)*

> *Spermophilus suslicus (Citellus suslicus)*

> *Sciurus anomalus*

Castoridae

> *Castor fiber* (except the Estonian, Latvian, Lithuanian, Polish, Finnish and Swedish, populations)

Cricetidae

> *Cricetus cricetus* (except the Hungarian populations)

> *Mesocricetus newtoni*

Microtidae

> *Microtus cabrerae*

> *Microtus oeconomus arenicola*

> *Microtus oeconomus mehelyi*

> *Microtus tatricus*

▼ **M3**

Zapodidae

> *Sicista betulina*
>
> *Sicista subtilis*

Hystricidae

> *Hystrix cristata*

CARNIVORA

Canidae

> *Alopex lagopus*
>
> *Canis lupus (*except the Greek populations north of the 39th parallel; Estonian populations, Spanish populations north of the Duero; Bulgarian, Latvian, Lithuanian, Polish, Slovak populations and Finnish populations within the reindeer management area as defined in paragraph 2 of the Finnish Act No 848/90 of 14 September 1990 on reindeer management)

Ursidae

> *Ursus arctos*

Mustelidae

> *Lutra lutra*
>
> *Mustela eversmanii*
>
> *Mustela lutreola*
>
> *Vormela peregusna*

Felidae

> *Felis silvestris*
>
> *Lynx lynx* (except the Estonian population)
>
> *Lynx pardinus*

Phocidae

> *Monachus monachus*
>
> *Phoca hispida saimensis*

ARTIODACTYLA

Cervidae

> *Cervus elaphus corsicanus*

Bovidae

> *Bison bonasus*
>
> *Capra aegagrus* (natural populations)
>
> *Capra pyrenaica pyrenaica*
>
> *Ovis gmelini musimon (Ovis ammon musimon)* (natural populations — Corsica and Sardinia)
>
> *Ovis orientalis ophion (Ovis gmelini ophion)*
>
> *Rupicapra pyrenaica ornata (Rupicapra rupicapra ornata)*
>
> *Rupicapra rupicapra balcanica*
>
> *Rupicapra rupicapra tatrica*

CETACEA

> All species

REPTILES

TESTUDINATA

Testudinidae

> *Testudo graeca*

▼ <u>M3</u>

    Testudo hermanni

    Testudo marginata

Cheloniidae

    Caretta caretta

    Chelonia mydas

    Lepidochelys kempii

    Eretmochelys imbricata

Dermochelyidae

    Dermochelys coriacea

Emydidae

    Emys orbicularis

    Mauremys caspica

    Mauremys leprosa

SAURIA

Lacertidae

    Algyroides fitzingeri

    Algyroides marchi

    Algyroides moreoticus

    Algyroides nigropunctatus

    Gallotia atlantica

    Gallotia galloti

    Gallotia galloti insulanagae

    Gallotia simonyi

    Gallotia stehlini

    Lacerta agilis

    Lacerta bedriagae

    Lacerta bonnali (Lacerta monticola)

    Lacerta monticola

    Lacerta danfordi

    Lacerta dugesi

    Lacerta graeca

    Lacerta horvathi

    Lacerta schreiberi

    Lacerta trilineata

    Lacerta viridis

    Lacerta vivipara pannonica

    Ophisops elegans

    Podarcis erhardii

    Podarcis filfolensis

    Podarcis hispanica atrata

    Podarcis lilfordi

    Podarcis melisellensis

    Podarcis milensis

    Podarcis muralis

▼ M3

      Podarcis peloponnesiaca

      Podarcis pityusensis

      Podarcis sicula

      Podarcis taurica

      Podarcis tiliguerta

      Podarcis wagleriana

Scincidae

      Ablepharus kitaibelii

      Chalcides bedriagai

      Chalcides ocellatus

      Chalcides sexlineatus

      Chalcides simonyi (Chalcides occidentalis)

      Chalcides viridianus

      Ophiomorus punctatissimus

Gekkonidae

      Cyrtopodion kotschyi

      Phyllodactylus europaeus

      Tarentola angustimentalis

      Tarentola boettgeri

      Tarentola delalandii

      Tarentola gomerensis

Agamidae

      Stellio stellio

Chamaeleontidae

      Chamaeleo chamaeleon

Anguidae

      Ophisaurus apodus

OPHIDIA

Colubridae

      Coluber caspius

      Coluber cypriensis

      Coluber hippocrepis

      Coluber jugularis

      Coluber laurenti

      Coluber najadum

      Coluber nummifer

      Coluber viridiflavus

      Coronella austriaca

      Eirenis modesta

      Elaphe longissima

      Elaphe quatuorlineata

      Elaphe situla

      Natrix natrix cetti

      Natrix natrix corsa

Appendix

Natrix natrix cypriaca

Natrix tessellata

Telescopus falax

Viperidae

Vipera ammodytes

Macrovipera schweizeri (Vipera lebetina schweizeri)

Vipera seoanni (except Spanish populations)

Vipera ursinii

Vipera xanthina

Boidae

Eryx jaculus

AMPHIBIANS

CAUDATA

Salamandridae

Chioglossa lusitanica

Euproctus asper

Euproctus montanus

Euproctus platycephalus

Mertensiella luschani (Salamandra luschani)

Salamandra atra

Salamandra aurorae

Salamandra lanzai

Salamandrina terdigitata

Triturus carnifex (Triturus cristatus carnifex)

Triturus cristatus (Triturus cristatus cristatus)

Triturus italicus

Triturus karelinii (Triturus cristatus karelinii)

Triturus marmoratus

Triturus montandoni

Triturus vulgaris ampelensis

Proteidae

Proteus anguinus

Plethodontidae

Hydromantes (Speleomantes) ambrosii

Hydromantes (Speleomantes) flavus

Hydromantes (Speleomantes) genei

Hydromantes (Speleomantes) imperialis

Hydromantes (Speleomantes) strinatii (Hydromantes (Speleomantes) italicus)

Hydromantes (Speleomantes) supramontis

ANURA

Discoglossidae

Alytes cisternasii

Alytes muletensis

Alytes obstetricans

▼ __M3__

    Bombina bombina

    Bombina variegata

    Discoglossus galganoi (including *Discoglossus 'jeanneae'*)

    Discoglossus montalentii

    Discoglossus pictus

    Discoglossus sardus

Ranidae

    Rana arvalis

    Rana dalmatina

    Rana graeca

    Rana iberica

    Rana italica

    Rana latastei

    Rana lessonae

Pelobatidae

    Pelobates cultripes

    Pelobates fuscus

    Pelobates syriacus

Bufonidae

    Bufo calamita

    Bufo viridis

Hylidae

    Hyla arborea

    Hyla meridionalis

    Hyla sarda

FISH

ACIPENSERIFORMES

Acipenseridae

    Acipenser naccarii

    Acipenser sturio

SALMONIFORMES

Coregonidae

    Coregonus oxyrhynchus (anadromous populations in certain sectors of the North Sea, except the Finnish populations)

CYPRINIFORMES

Cyprinidae

    Anaecypris hispanica

    Phoxinus percnurus

ATHERINIFORMES

Cyprinodontidae

    Valencia hispanica

PERCIFORMES

Percidae

    Gymnocephalus baloni

    Romanichthys valsanicola

▼ <u>M3</u>

Zingel asper

INVERTEBRATES

ARTHROPODS

CRUSTACEA

Isopoda

Armadillidium ghardalamensis

INSECTA

Coleoptera

Bolbelasmus unicornis

Buprestis splendens

Carabus hampei

Carabus hungaricus

Carabus olympiae

Carabus variolosus

Carabus zawadszkii

Cerambyx cerdo

Cucujus cinnaberinus

Dorcadion fulvum cervae

Duvalius gebhardti

Duvalius hungaricus

Dytiscus latissimus

Graphoderus bilineatus

Leptodirus hochenwarti

Pilemia tigrina

Osmoderma eremita

Phryganophilus ruficollis

Probaticus subrugosus

Propomacrus cypriacus

Pseudogaurotina excellens

Pseudoseriscius cameroni

Pytho kolwensis

Rosalia alpina

Lepidoptera

Apatura metis

Arytrura musculus

Catopta thrips

Chondrosoma fiduciarium

Coenonympha hero

Coenonympha oedippus

Colias myrmidone

Cucullia mixta

Dioszeghyana schmidtii

Erannis ankeraria

Erebia calcaria

▼ <u>M3</u>

  Erebia christi

  Erebia sudetica

  Eriogaster catax

  Fabriciana elisa

  Glyphipterix loricatella

  Gortyna borelii lunata

  Hypodryas maturna

  Hyles hippophaes

  Leptidea morsei

  Lignyoptera fumidaria

  Lopinga achine

  Lycaena dispar

  Lycaena helle

  Maculinea arion

  Maculinea nausithous

  Maculinea teleius

  Melanargia arge

  Nymphalis vaualbum

  Papilio alexanor

  Papilio hospiton

  Parnassius apollo

  Parnassius mnemosyne

  Phyllometra culminaria

  Plebicula golgus

  Polymixis rufocincta isolata

  Polyommatus eroides

  Proserpinus proserpina

  Pseudophilotes bavius

  Xylomoia strix

  Zerynthia polyxena

Mantodea

  Apteromantis aptera

Odonata

  Aeshna viridis

  Cordulegaster heros

  Cordulegaster trinacriae

  Gomphus graslinii

  Leucorrhinia albifrons

  Leucorrhinia caudalis

  Leucorrhinia pectoralis

  Lindenia tetraphylla

  Macromia splendens

  Ophiogomphus cecilia

  Oxygastra curtisii

▼ <u>**M3**</u>

Stylurus flavipes

Sympecma braueri

Orthoptera

Baetica ustulata

Brachytrupes megacephalus

Isophya costata

Isophya harzi

Isophya stysi

Myrmecophilus baronii

Odontopodisma rubripes

Paracaloptenus caloptenoides

Pholidoptera transsylvanica

Saga pedo

Stenobothrus (Stenobothrodes) eurasius

ARACHNIDA

Araneae

Macrothele calpeiana

MOLLUSCS

GASTROPODA

Anisus vorticulus

Caseolus calculus

Caseolus commixta

Caseolus sphaerula

Chilostoma banaticum

Discula leacockiana

Discula tabellata

Discula testudinalis

Discula turricula

Discus defloratus

Discus guerinianus

Elona quimperiana

Geomalacus maculosus

Geomitra moniziana

Gibbula nivosa

Hygromia kovacsi

Idiomela (Helix) subplicata

Lampedusa imitatrix

Lampedusa melitensis

Leiostyla abbreviata

Leiostyla cassida

Leiostyla corneocostata

Leiostyla gibba

Leiostyla lamellosa

Paladilhia hungarica

▼ <u>M3</u>

  Patella ferruginea

  Sadleriana pannonica

  Theodoxus prevostianus

  Theodoxus transversalis

BIVALVIA

Anisomyaria

  Lithophaga lithophaga

  Pinna nobilis

Unionoida

  Margaritifera auricularia

  Unio crassus

Dreissenidae

  Congeria kusceri

ECHINODERMATA

Echinoidea

  Centrostephanus longispinus

(b) **PLANTS**

Annex IV (b) contains all the plant species listed in Annex II (b) ([1]) plus those mentioned below:

PTERIDOPHYTA

ASPLENIACEAE

  Asplenium hemionitis L.

ANGIOSPERMAE

AGAVACEAE

  Dracaena draco (L.) L.

AMARYLLIDACEAE

  Narcissus longispathus Pugsley

  Narcissus triandrus L.

BERBERIDACEAE

  Berberis maderensis Lowe

CAMPANULACEAE

  Campanula morettiana Reichenb.

  Physoplexis comosa (L.) Schur.

CARYOPHYLLACEAE

  Moehringia fontqueri Pau

COMPOSITAE

  Argyranthemum pinnatifidum (L.f.) Lowe subsp. *succulentum* (Lowe) C. J. Humphries

  Helichrysum sibthorpii Rouy

  Picris willkommii (Schultz Bip.) Nyman

  Santolina elegans Boiss. ex DC.

  Senecio caespitosus Brot.

  Senecio lagascanus DC. subsp. *lusitanicus* (P. Cout.) Pinto da Silva

  Wagenitzia lancifolia (Sieber ex Sprengel) Dostal

([1]) Except bryophytes in Annex II (b).

▼ **M3**

CRUCIFERAE

Murbeckiella sousae Rothm.

EUPHORBIACEAE

Euphorbia nevadensis Boiss. & Reuter

GESNERIACEAE

Jankaea heldreichii (Boiss.) Boiss.

Ramonda serbica Pancic

IRIDACEAE

Crocus etruscus Parl.

Iris boissieri Henriq.

Iris marisca Ricci & Colasante

LABIATAE

Rosmarinus tomentosus Huber-Morath & Maire

Teucrium charidemi Sandwith

Thymus capitellatus Hoffmanns. & Link

Thymus villosus L. subsp. *villosus* L.

LILIACEAE

Androcymbium europaeum (Lange) K. Richter

Bellevalia hackelli Freyn

Colchicum corsicum Baker

Colchicum cousturieri Greuter

Fritillaria conica Rix

Fritillaria drenovskii Degen & Stoy.

Fritillaria gussichiae (Degen & Doerfler) Rix

Fritillaria obliqua Ker-Gawl.

Fritillaria rhodocanakis Orph. ex Baker

Ornithogalum reverchonii Degen & Herv.-Bass.

Scilla beirana Samp.

Scilla odorata Link

ORCHIDACEAE

Ophrys argolica Fleischm.

Orchis scopulorum Simsmerh.

Spiranthes aestivalis (Poiret) L. C. M. Richard

PRIMULACEAE

Androsace cylindrica DC.

Primula glaucescens Moretti

Primula spectabilis Tratt.

RANUNCULACEAE

Aquilegia alpina L.

SAPOTACEAE

Sideroxylon marmulano Banks ex Lowe

SAXIFRAGACEAE

Saxifraga cintrana Kuzinsky ex Willk.

Saxifraga portosanctana Boiss.

▼ <u>M3</u>

    Saxifraga presolanensis Engl.

    Saxifraga valdensis DC.

    Saxifraga vayredana Luizet

SCROPHULARIACEAE

    Antirrhinum lopesianum Rothm.

    Lindernia procumbens (Krocker) Philcox

SOLANACEAE

    Mandragora officinarum L.

THYMELAEACEAE

    Thymelaea broterana P. Cout.

UMBELLIFERAE

    Bunium brevifolium Lowe

VIOLACEAE

    Viola athois W. Becker

    Viola cazorlensis Gandoger

Appendix

ANNEX V

ANIMAL AND PLANT SPECIES OF COMMUNITY INTEREST WHOSE TAKING IN THE WILD AND EXPLOITATION MAY BE SUBJECT TO MANAGEMENT MEASURES

The species listed in this Annex are indicated:

— by the name of the species or subspecies, or

— by the body of species belonging to a higher taxon or to a designated part of that taxon.

The abbreviation 'spp.' after the name of a family or genus designates all the species belonging to that family or genus.

(a) *ANIMALS*

VERTEBRATES

MAMMALS

RODENTIA

Castoridae

> *Castor fiber (Finnish, Swedish, Latvian, Lithuanian, Estonian and Polish populations)*

Cricetidae

> *Cricetus cricetus (Hungarian populations)*

CARNIVORA

Canidae

> *Canis aureus*

> *Canis lupus (Spanish populations north of the Duero, Greek populations north of the 39th parallel, Finnish populations within the reindeer management area as defined in paragraph 2 of the Finnish Act No 848/90 of 14 September 1990 on reindeer management, Bulgarian, Latvian, Lithuanian, Estonian, Polish and Slovak populations)*

Mustelidae

> *Martes martes*

> *Mustela putorius*

Felidae

> *Lynx lynx (Estonian population)*

Phocidae

> *All species not mentioned in Annex IV*

Viverridae

> *Genetta genetta*

> *Herpestes ichneumon*

DUPLICIDENTATA

Leporidae

> *Lepus timidus*

ARTIODACTYLA

Bovidae

> *Capra ibex*

> *Capra pyrenaica (exceptCapra pyrenaica pyrenaica)*

> *Rupicapra rupicapra (exceptRupicapra rupicapra balcanica,Rupicapra rupicapra ornata andRupicapra rupicapra tatrica)*

AMPHIBIANS

ANURA

Ranidae

> *Rana esculenta*
>
> *Rana perezi*
>
> *Rana ridibunda*
>
> *Rana temporaria*

FISH

PETROMYZONIFORMES

Petromyzonidae

> *Lampetra fluviatilis*
>
> *Lethenteron zanandrai*

ACIPENSERIFORMES

Acipenseridae

> *All species not mentioned in Annex IV*

CLUPEIFORMES

Clupeidae

> *Alosa spp.*

SALMONIFORMES

Salmonidae

> *Thymallus thymallus*
>
> *Coregonus spp. (exceptCoregonus oxyrhynchus — anadromous populations in certain sectors of the North Sea)*
>
> *Hucho hucho*
>
> *Salmo salar (only in fresh water)*

CYPRINIFORMES

Cyprinidae

> *Aspius aspius*
>
> *Barbus spp.*
>
> *Pelecus cultratus*
>
> *Rutilus friesii meidingeri*
>
> *Rutilus pigus*

SILURIFORMES

Siluridae

> *Silurus aristotelis*

PERCIFORMES

Percidae

> *Gymnocephalus schraetzer*
>
> *Zingel zingel*

INVERTEBRATES

COELENTERATA

CNIDARIA

> *Corallium rubrum*

▼ <u>M3</u>

MOLLUSCA

GASTROPODA — STYLOMMATOPHORA

　　Helix pomatia

BIVALVIA — UNIONOIDA

Margaritiferidae

　　Margaritifera margaritifera

Unionidae

　　Microcondylaea compressa

　　Unio elongatulus

ANNELIDA

HIRUDINOIDEA — ARHYNCHOBDELLAE

Hirudinidae

　　Hirudo medicinalis

ARTHROPODA

CRUSTACEA — DECAPODA

Astacidae

　　Astacus astacus

　　Austropotamobius pallipes

　　Austropotamobius torrentium

Scyllaridae

　　Scyllarides latus

INSECTA — LEPIDOPTERA

Saturniidae

　　Graellsia isabellae

(b) *PLANTS*

ALGAE

RHODOPHYTA

CORALLINACEAE

　　Lithothamnium coralloides Crouan frat.

　　Phymatholithon calcareum (Poll.) Adey & McKibbin

LICHENES

CLADONIACEAE

　　Cladonia L. subgenus *Cladina* (Nyl.) Vain.

BRYOPHYTA

MUSCI

LEUCOBRYACEAE

　　Leucobryum glaucum (Hedw.) AAngstr.

SPHAGNACEAE

　　Sphagnum L. spp. (except *Sphagnum pylaisii* Brid.)

PTERIDOPHYTA

　　Lycopodium spp.

ANGIOSPERMAE

AMARYLLIDACEAE

　　Galanthus nivalis L.

▼ M3

Narcissus bulbocodium L.

Narcissus juncifolius Lagasca

COMPOSITAE

Arnica montana L.

Artemisia eriantha Tern

Artemisia genipi Weber

Doronicum plantagineum L. subsp. *tournefortii* (Rouy) P. Cout.

Leuzea rhaponticoides Graells

CRUCIFERAE

Alyssum pintadasilvae Dudley.

Malcolmia lacera (L.) DC. subsp. *graccilima* (Samp.) Franco

Murbeckiella pinnatifida (Lam.) Rothm. subsp. *herminii* (Rivas-Martinez) Greuter & Burdet

GENTIANACEAE

Gentiana lutea L.

IRIDACEAE

Iris lusitanica Ker-Gawler

LABIATAE

Teucrium salviastrum Schreber subsp. *salviastrum* Schreber

LEGUMINOSAE

Anthyllis lusitanica Cullen & Pinto da Silva

Dorycnium pentaphyllum Scop. subsp. *transmontana* Franco

Ulex densus Welw. ex Webb.

LILIACEAE

Lilium rubrum Lmk

Ruscus aculeatus L.

PLUMBAGINACEAE

Armeria sampaio (Bernis) Nieto Feliner

ROSACEAE

Rubus genevieri Boreau subsp. *herminii* (Samp.) P. Cout.

SCROPHULARIACEAE

Anarrhinum longipedicelatum R. Fernandes

Euphrasia mendonçae Samp.

Scrophularia grandiflora DC. subsp. *grandiflora* DC.

Scrophularia herminii Hoffmanns & Link

Scrophularia sublyrata Brot.

Appendix

ANNEX VI

**PROHIBITED METHODS AND MEANS OF CAPTURE AND KILLING
AND MODES OF TRANSPORT**

(a) **Non-selective means**

MAMMALS

— Blind or mutilated animals used as live decoys

— Tape recorders

— Electrical and electronic devices capable of killing or stunning

— Artificial light sources

— Mirrors and other dazzling devices

— Devices for illuminating targets

— Sighting devices for night shooting comprising an electronic image magnifier or image converter

— Explosives

— Nets which are non-selective according to their principle or their conditions of use

— Traps which are non-selective according to their principle or their conditions of use

— Crossbows

— Poisons and poisoned or anaesthetic bait

— Gassing or smoking out

— Semi-automatic or automatic weapons with a magazine capable of holding more than two rounds of ammunition

FISH

— Poison

— Explosives

(b) **Modes of transport**

— Aircraft

— Moving motor vehicles

INDEX